Cast of Characters

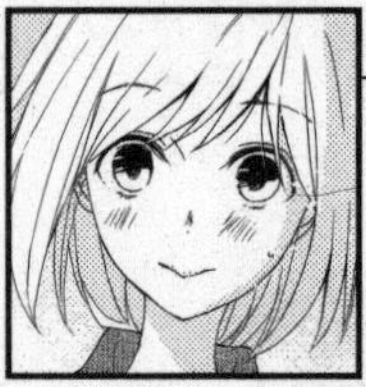

Fumi Nishioka

An apprentice Sweeper with the powers of a Queen, this second-year high school student dreams of finding her very own Prince Charming.

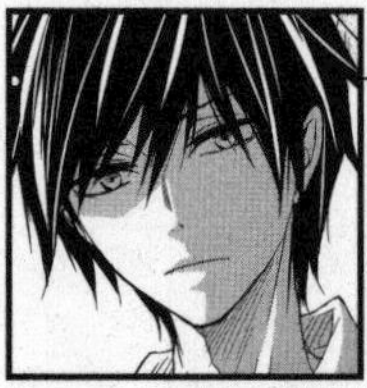

Kyutaro Horikita

A mind Sweeper who cleanses people's minds of dangerous impurities. He's incredibly awkward with people, but he has feelings for Fumi.

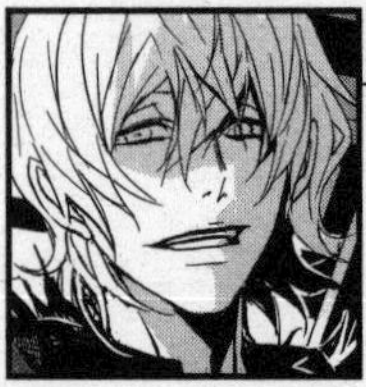

Ataru Shikata

A bug handler who uses bugs to manipulate people. He wants to ensure that Fumi awakens as a Black Queen.

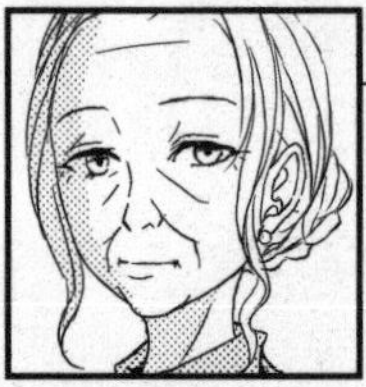

Miyako Horikita

The prior head of the Genbu Gate Sweepers. She can be both strict and kind, and she watches over and advises Fumi.

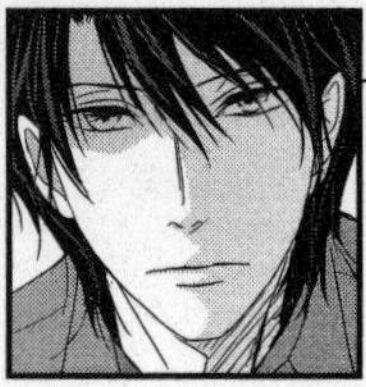

Koichi Kitagawa

The chairman of the school Fumi and Kyutaro attend. He's a Sweeper as well as being Kyutaro's brother-in-law.

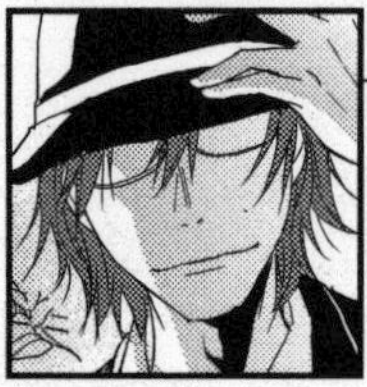

Takaya Kitahara

A psychiatrist who's related to the Genbu Gate Sweepers. He's an expert with suggestive therapy, and he counsels Fumi.

Story Thus Far

The Horikitas are a family of Sweepers—people who cleanse impurities from human hearts. After seeing Fumi's potential, they take her on as an assistant and trainee. However, Fumi has the untapped, immense power of a Queen, and she's awakened both the White Queen and the Black Queen inside of her.

Fumi and Kyutaro enter bug handler Ataru's mind vault, where Ataru has set a trap to turn Fumi into the Black Queen. Fumi comes to realize what she must do to kill the Black Queen within her...

MONTHLY BETSUCOMI SALE DATE NOTICE ON TWITTER

CHAPTER 21

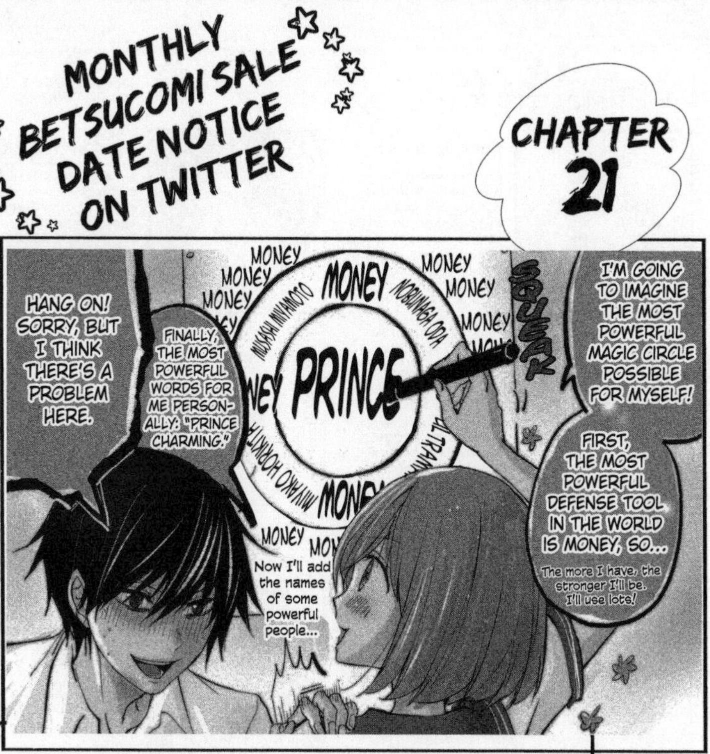
I'M GOING TO IMAGINE THE MOST POWERFUL MAGIC CIRCLE POSSIBLE FOR MYSELF!
FIRST, THE MOST POWERFUL DEFENSE TOOL IN THE WORLD IS MONEY, SO...
The more I have, the stronger I'll be. I'll use lots!
SQUEAK
MONEY
MONEY
MONEY
MONEY
MONEY
MONEY
MONEY
NOBUNAGA ODA
MUSASHI MIYAMOTO
PRINCE
FINALLY, THE MOST POWERFUL WORDS FOR ME PERSON-ALLY: "PRINCE CHARMING."
Now I'll add the names of some powerful people...
HANG ON! SORRY, BUT I THINK THERE'S A PROBLEM HERE.

LET'S SEE... WHAT'S UP IN *QUEEN'S QUALITY* THIS MONTH?

(1) A MAGIC CIRCLE IS CREATED BY THE PERSON WHO'LL USE IT. (THE STRONGER THE BETTER!)
(2) IN THE SCENE WITH THE MAGIC CIRCLE, KYUTARO IS ***NOT*** PICKING HIS NOSE.
(3) IS HE A NINJA?

THE ILLUSTRATION IN THIS NOTICE IS PRETTY SILLY, BUT CHAPTER 21 IS A VITAL ONE FOR THE BLACK QUEEN!

If you're curious, this is where he looked like he was picking his nose. →

I fixed it for this edition.

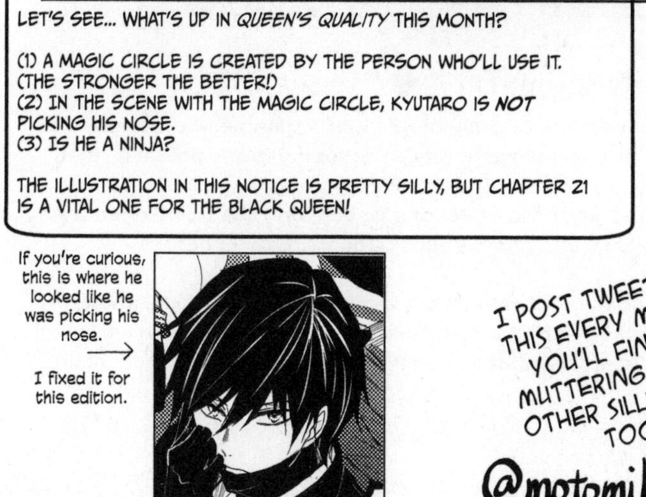

I POST TWEETS LIKE THIS EVERY MONTH. YOU'LL FIND ME MUTTERING ABOUT OTHER SILLY STUFF TOO.

@motomikyosuke

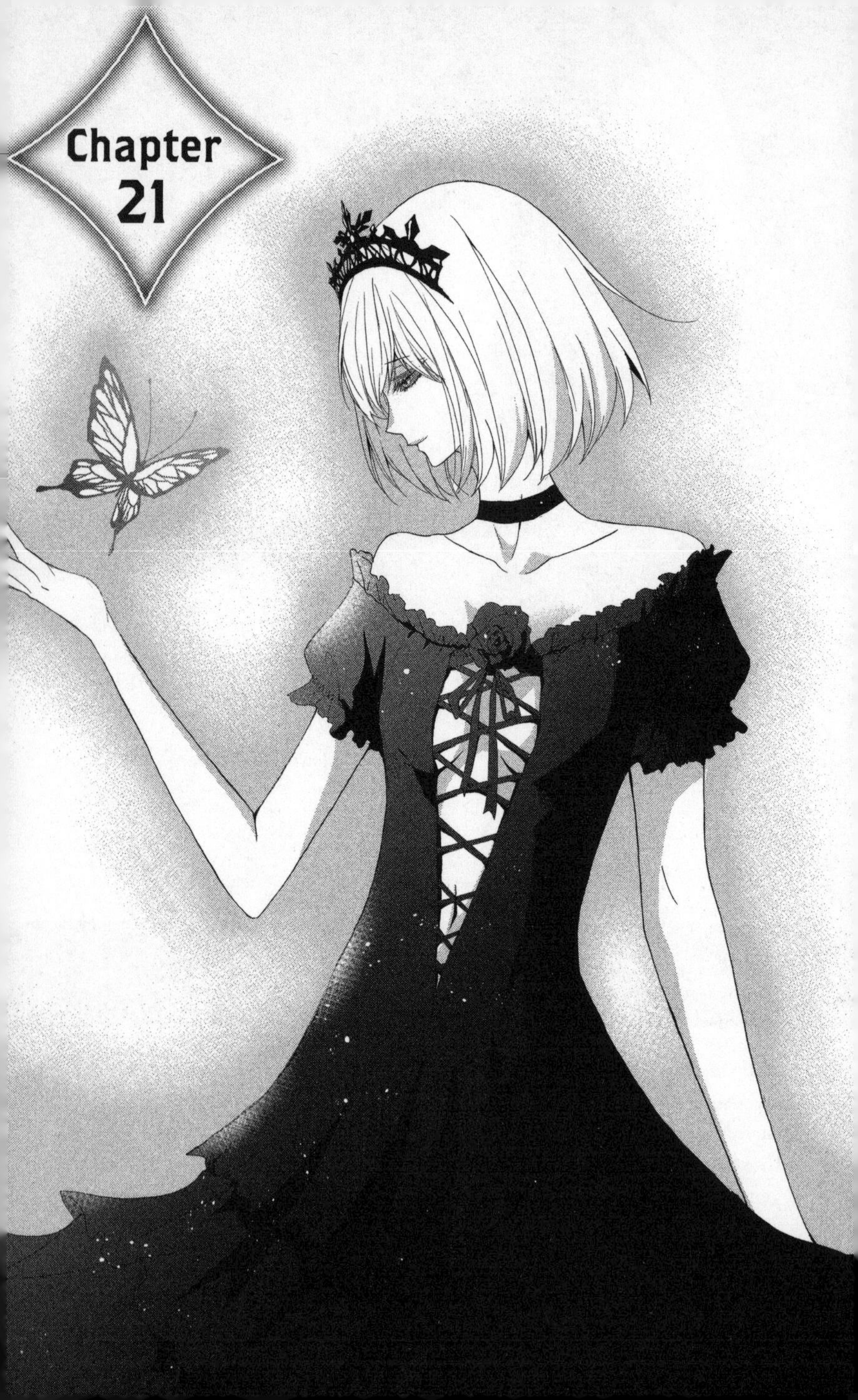
Chapter
21

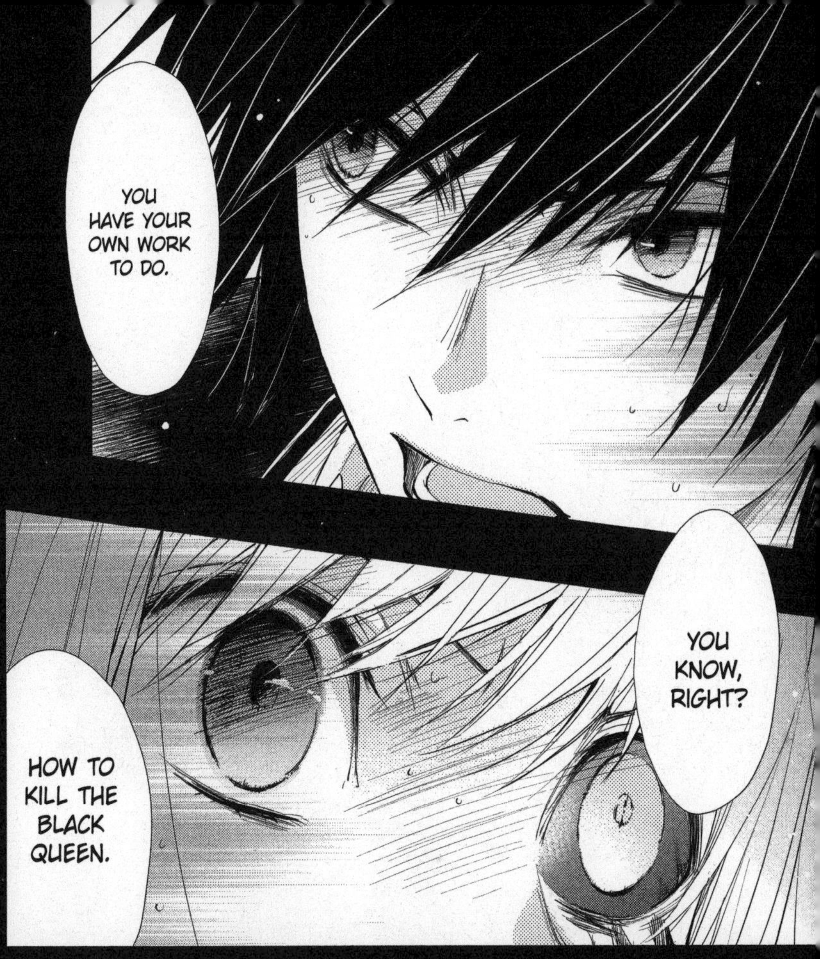
YOU HAVE YOUR OWN WORK TO DO.
YOU KNOW, RIGHT?
HOW TO KILL THE BLACK QUEEN.

Hello, everyone! This is Kyousuke Motomi. Welcome to volume 5 of *Queen's Quality* (or *Queequa*). I hope you enjoy this climactic volume! Thank you for spending this time with me.

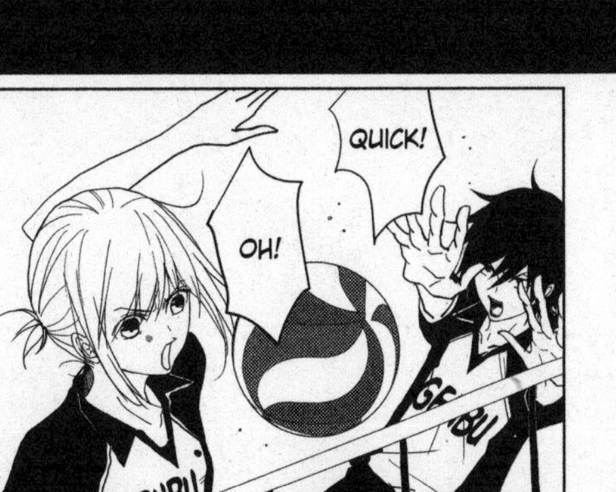
QUICK!
OH!
GENBU
GENBU

This manga isn't about volleyball, so I hope you have a better idea for me.

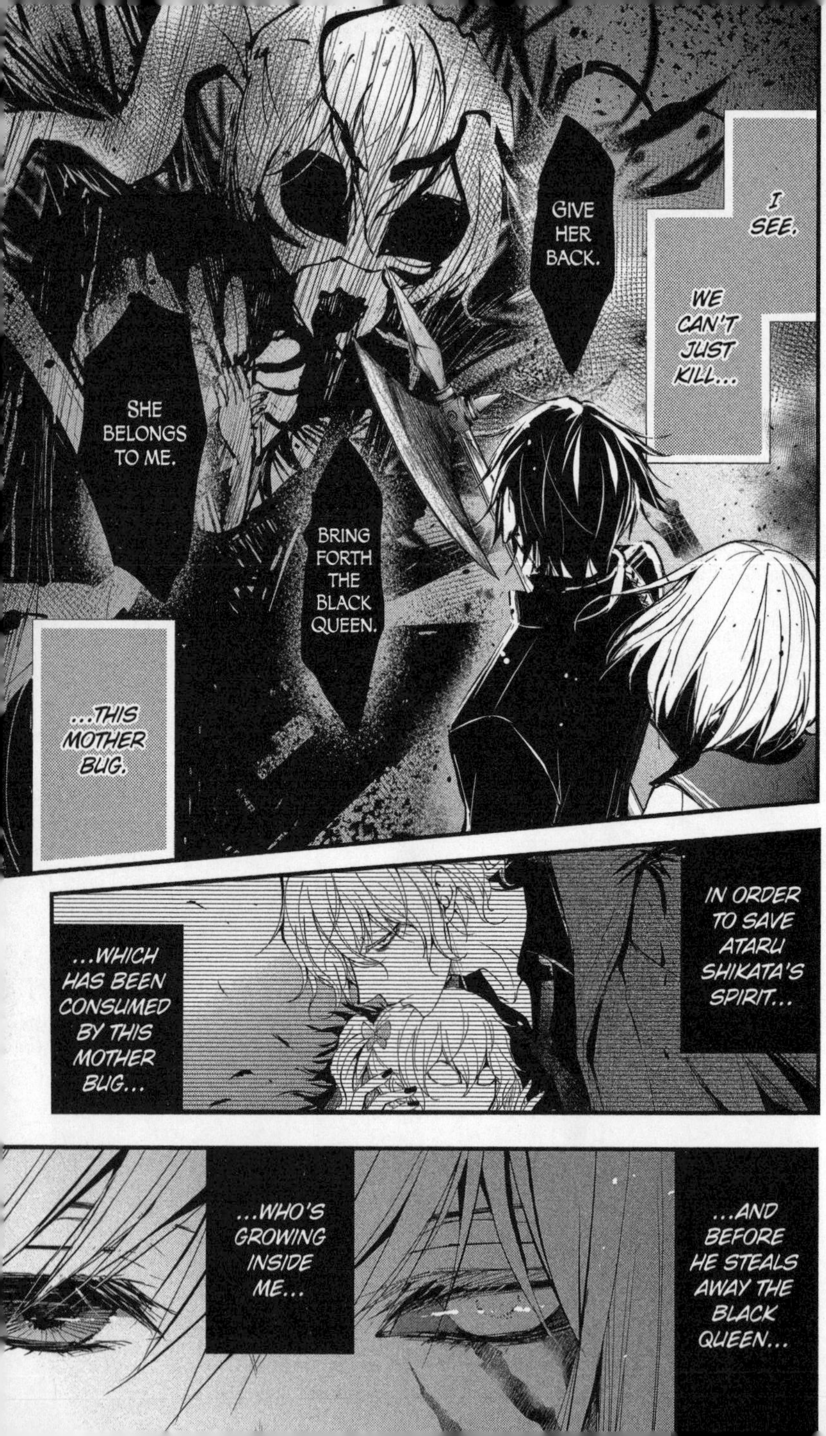
I SEE.
WE CAN'T JUST KILL...
GIVE HER BACK.
SHE BELONGS TO ME.
BRING FORTH THE BLACK QUEEN.
...THIS MOTHER BUG.
IN ORDER TO SAVE ATARU SHIKATA'S SPIRIT...
...WHICH HAS BEEN CONSUMED BY THIS MOTHER BUG...
...AND BEFORE HE STEALS AWAY THE BLACK QUEEN...
...WHO'S GROWING INSIDE ME...

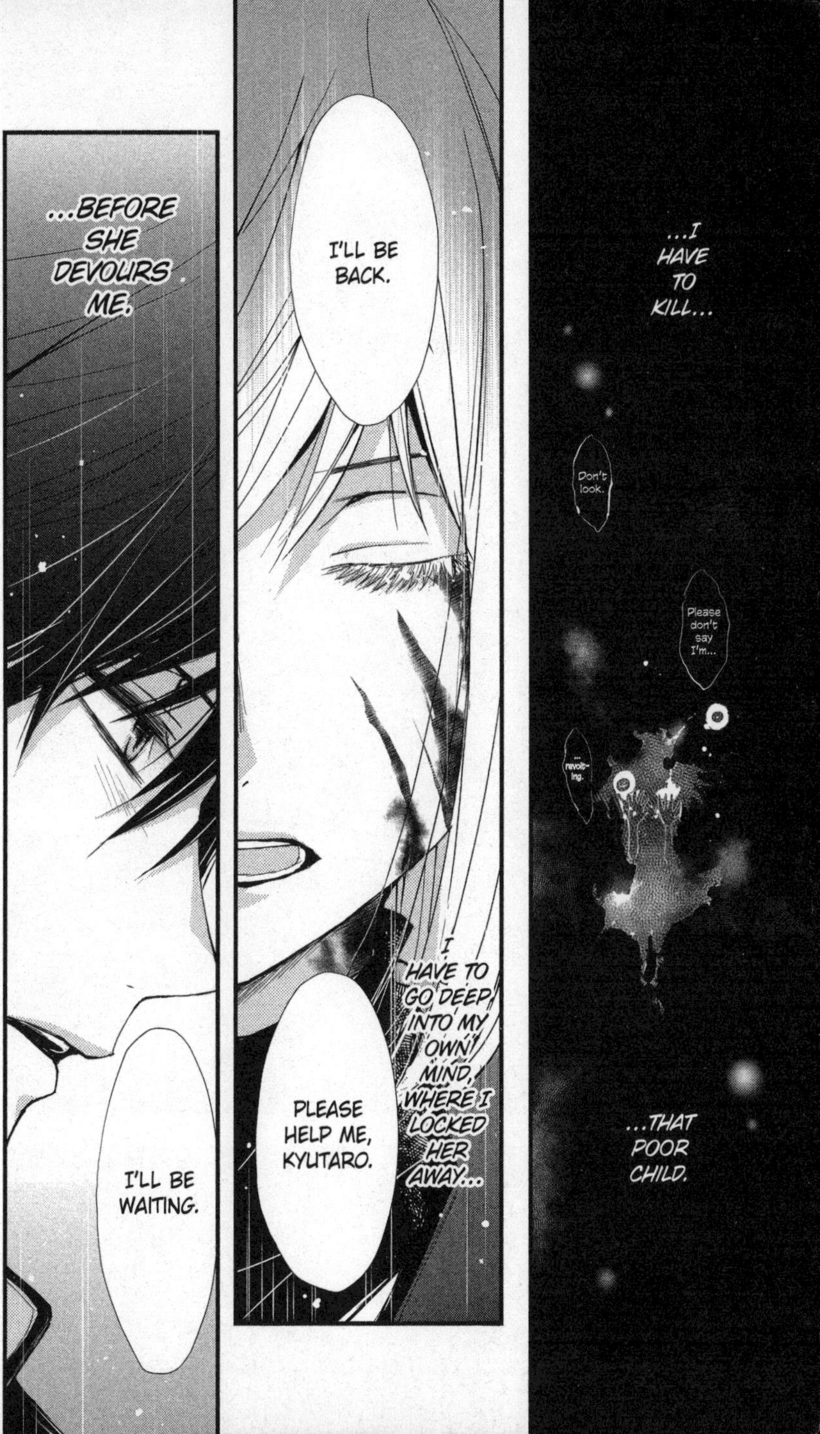
...I HAVE TO KILL...
Don't look.
Please don't say I'm...
...revolting.
...THAT POOR CHILD.
I'LL BE BACK.
I HAVE TO GO DEEP INTO MY OWN MIND, WHERE I LOCKED HER AWAY...
PLEASE HELP ME, KYUTARO.
...BEFORE SHE DEVOURS ME.
I'LL BE WAITING.

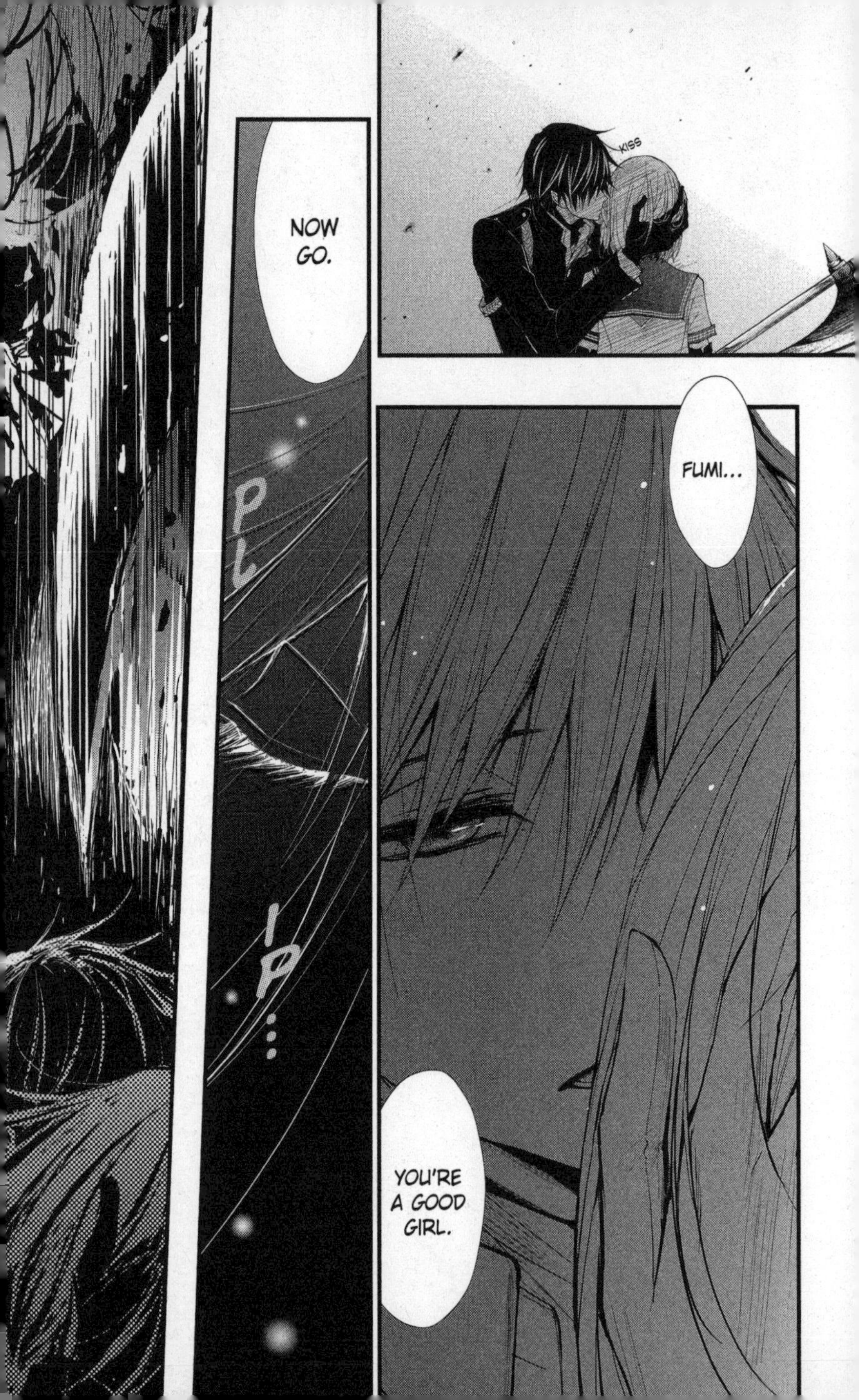
KISS
FUMI...
YOU'RE A GOOD GIRL.
NOW GO.
PLIP...

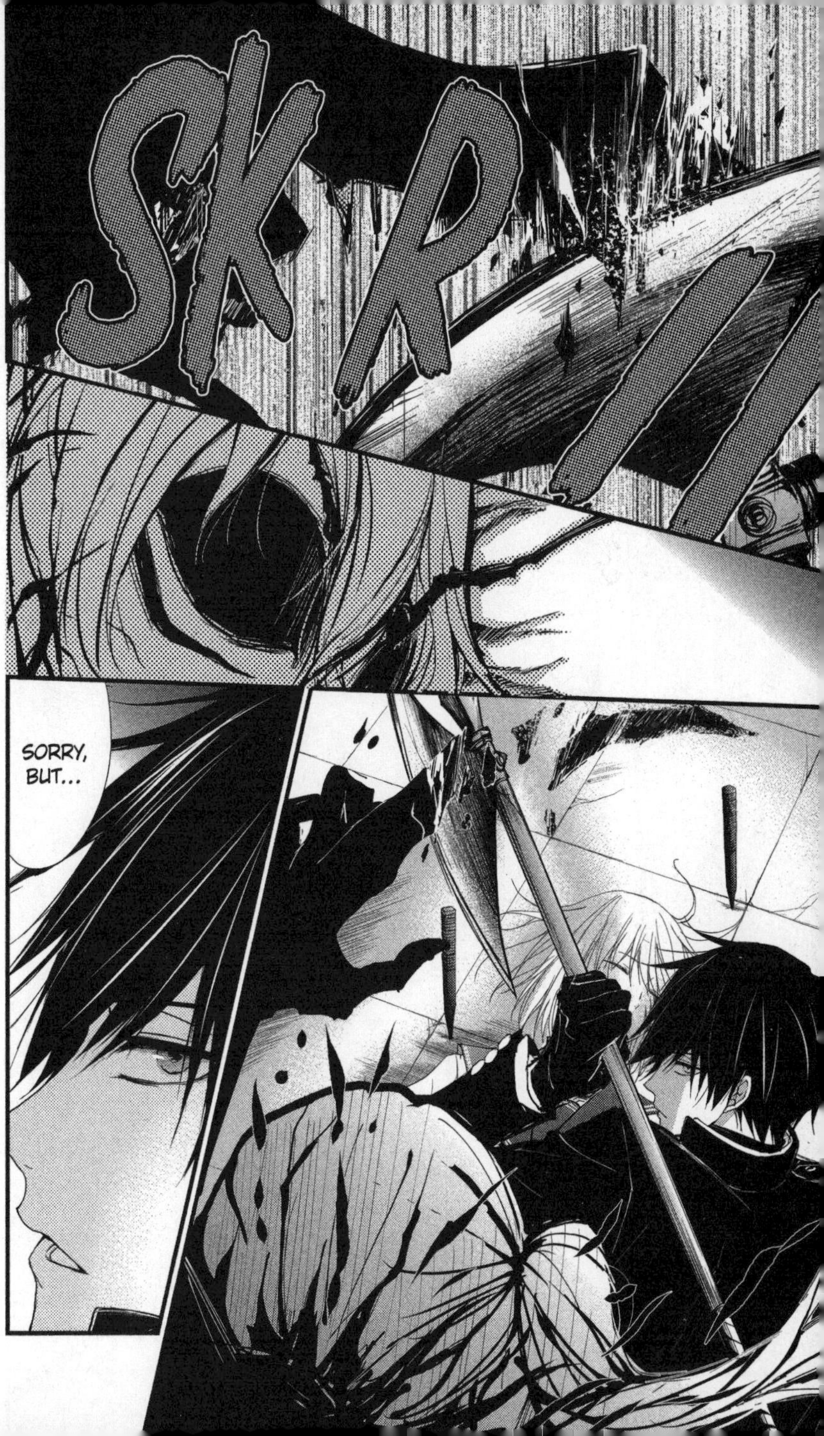
SKRIII
SORRY, BUT...

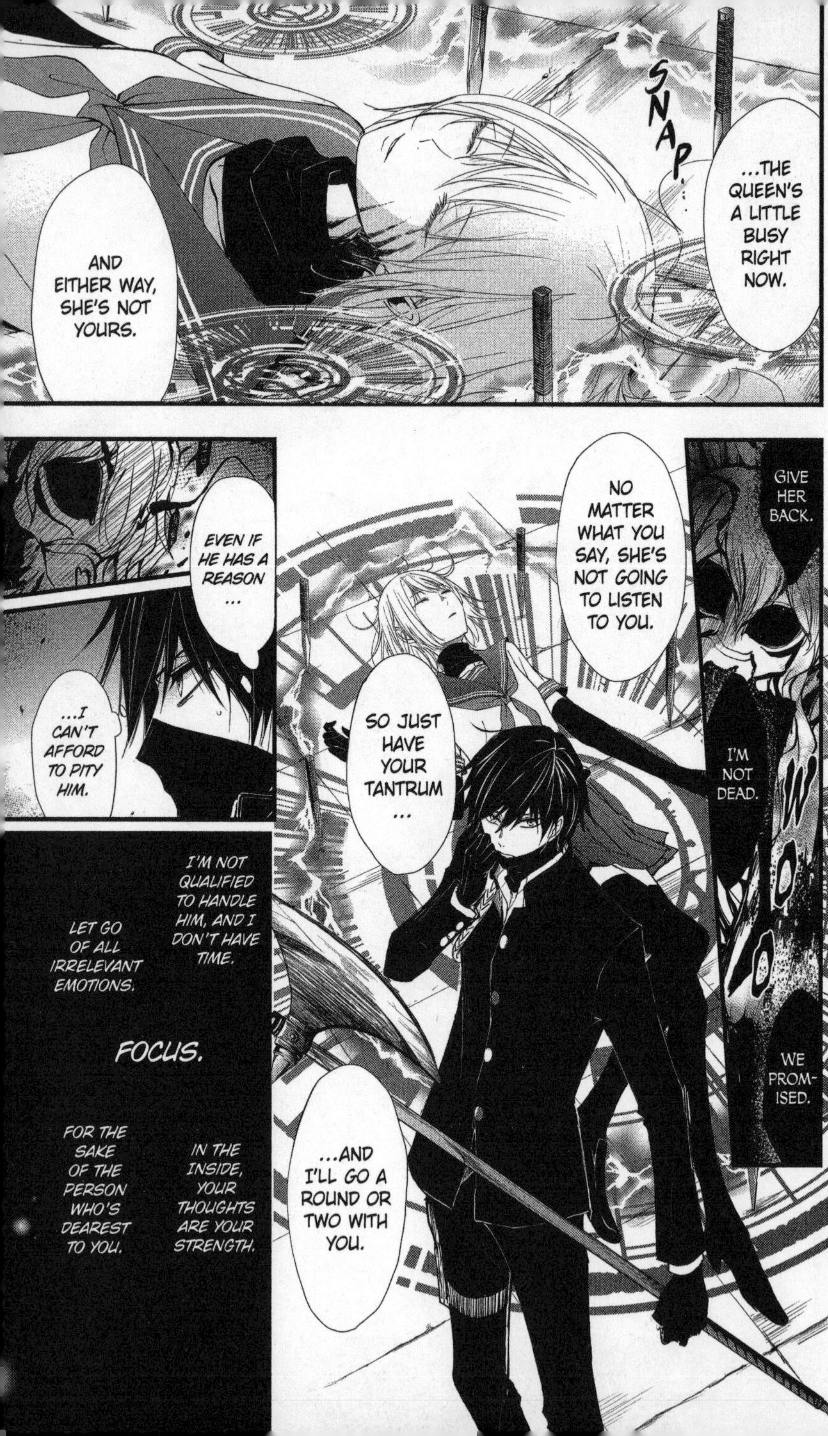
SNAP
...THE QUEEN'S A LITTLE BUSY RIGHT NOW.
AND EITHER WAY, SHE'S NOT YOURS.
GIVE HER BACK.
I'M NOT DEAD.
WOOO
WE PROMISED.
NO MATTER WHAT YOU SAY, SHE'S NOT GOING TO LISTEN TO YOU.
SO JUST HAVE YOUR TANTRUM...
...AND I'LL GO A ROUND OR TWO WITH YOU.
EVEN IF HE HAS A REASON...
...I CAN'T AFFORD TO PITY HIM.
I'M NOT QUALIFIED TO HANDLE HIM, AND I DON'T HAVE TIME.
LET GO OF ALL IRRELEVANT EMOTIONS.
FOCUS.
IN THE INSIDE, YOUR THOUGHTS ARE YOUR STRENGTH.
FOR THE SAKE OF THE PERSON WHO'S DEAREST TO YOU.

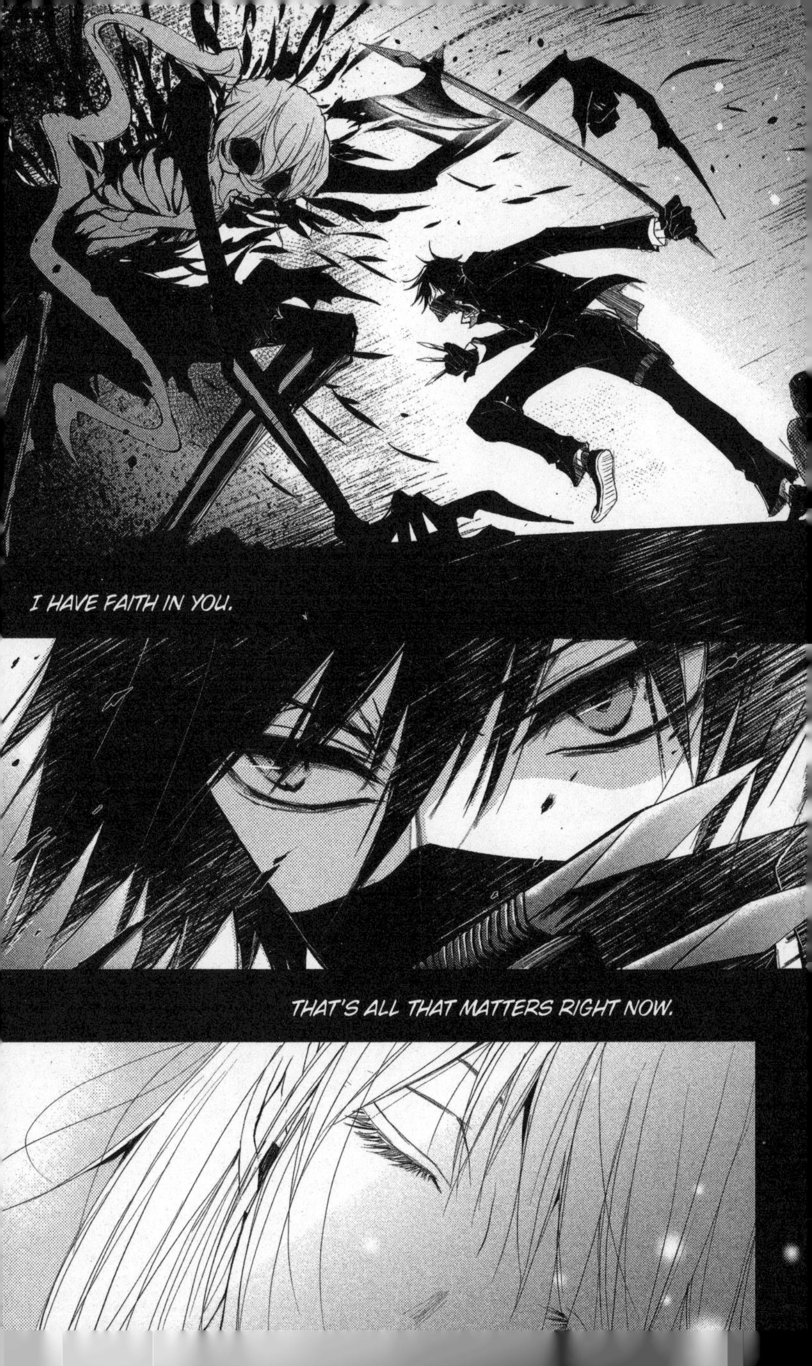
I HAVE FAITH IN YOU.
THAT'S ALL THAT MATTERS RIGHT NOW.

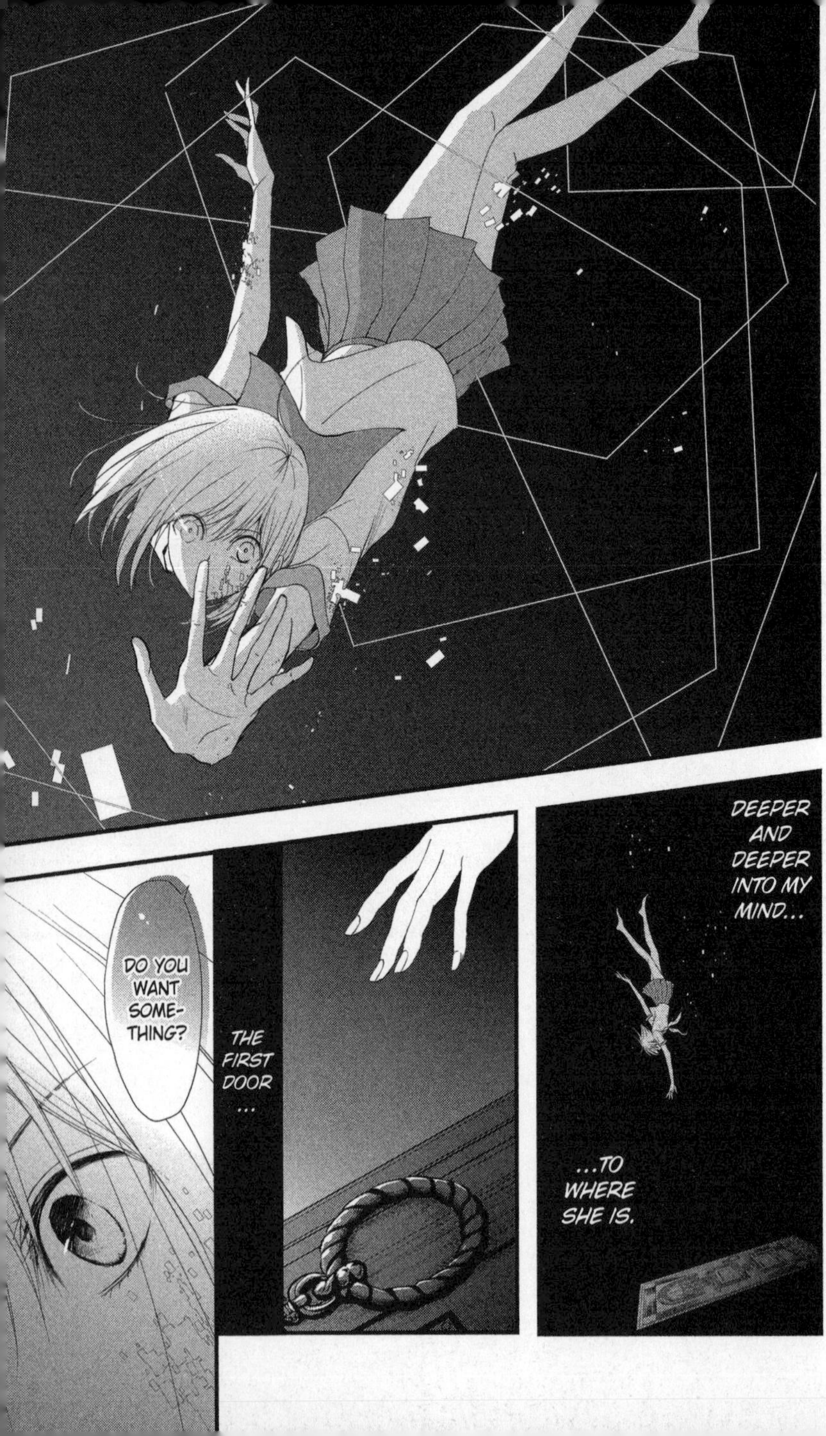
DEEPER AND DEEPER INTO MY MIND...
...TO WHERE SHE IS.
THE FIRST DOOR ...
DO YOU WANT SOME-THING?

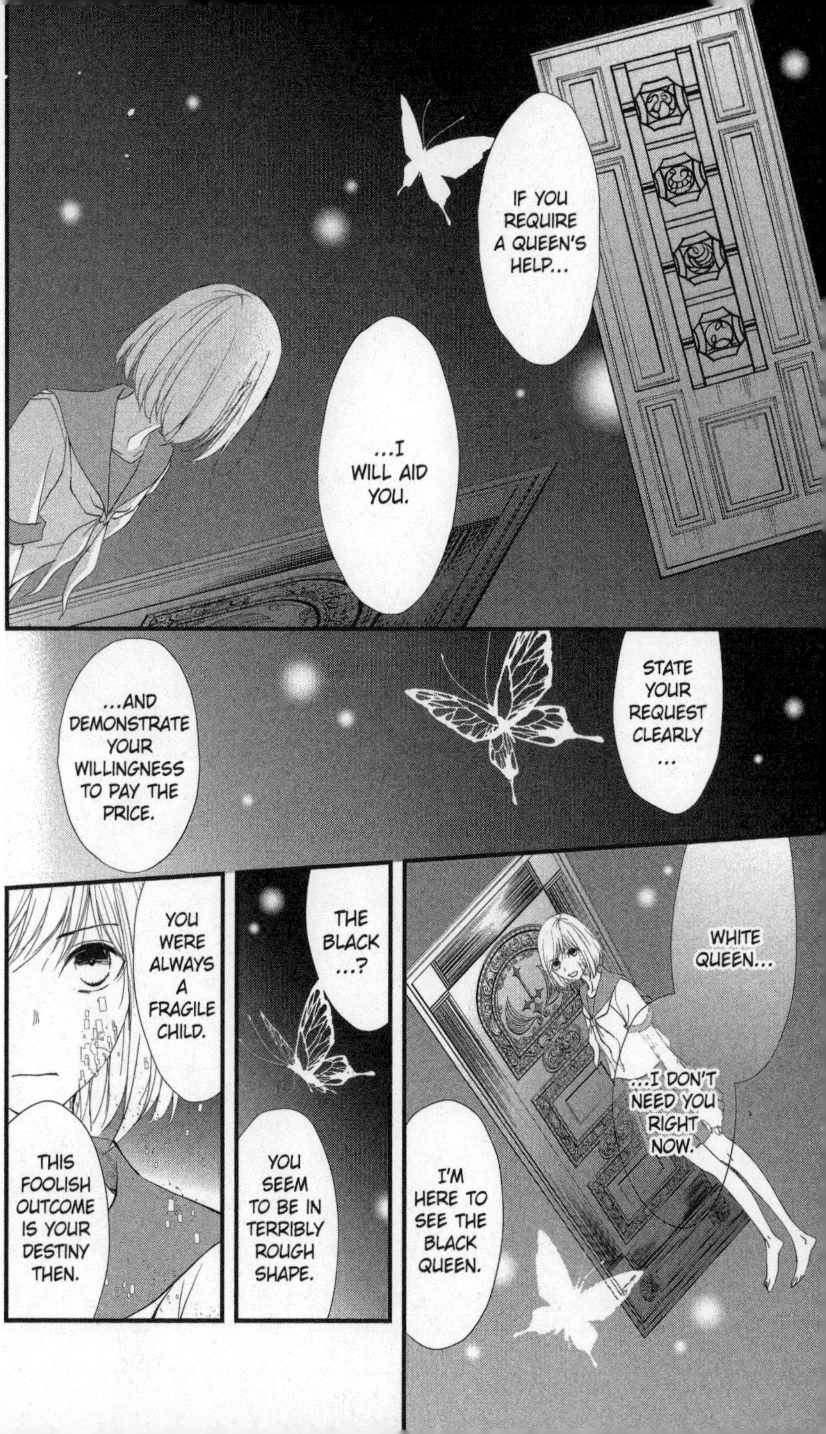
IF YOU REQUIRE A QUEEN'S HELP...
...I WILL AID YOU.
STATE YOUR REQUEST CLEARLY ...
...AND DEMONSTRATE YOUR WILLINGNESS TO PAY THE PRICE.
WHITE QUEEN...
...I DON'T NEED YOU RIGHT NOW.
I'M HERE TO SEE THE BLACK QUEEN.
THE BLACK ...?
YOU SEEM TO BE IN TERRIBLY ROUGH SHAPE.
YOU WERE ALWAYS A FRAGILE CHILD.
THIS FOOLISH OUTCOME IS YOUR DESTINY THEN.

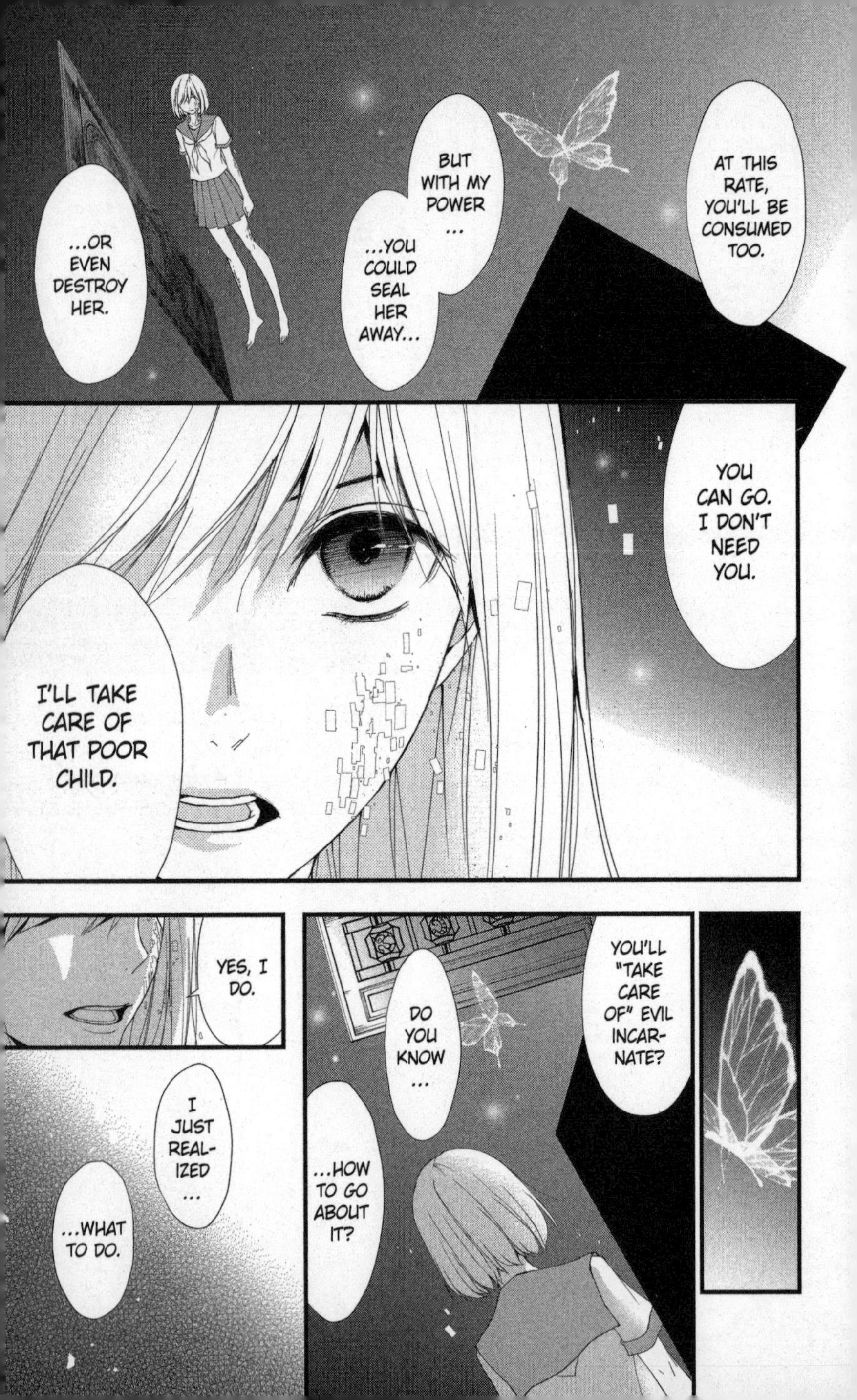
AT THIS RATE, YOU'LL BE CONSUMED TOO.
BUT WITH MY POWER...
...YOU COULD SEAL HER AWAY...
...OR EVEN DESTROY HER.
YOU CAN GO. I DON'T NEED YOU.
I'LL TAKE CARE OF THAT POOR CHILD.
YOU'LL "TAKE CARE OF" EVIL INCARNATE?
DO YOU KNOW...
...HOW TO GO ABOUT IT?
YES, I DO.
I JUST REALIZED...
...WHAT TO DO.

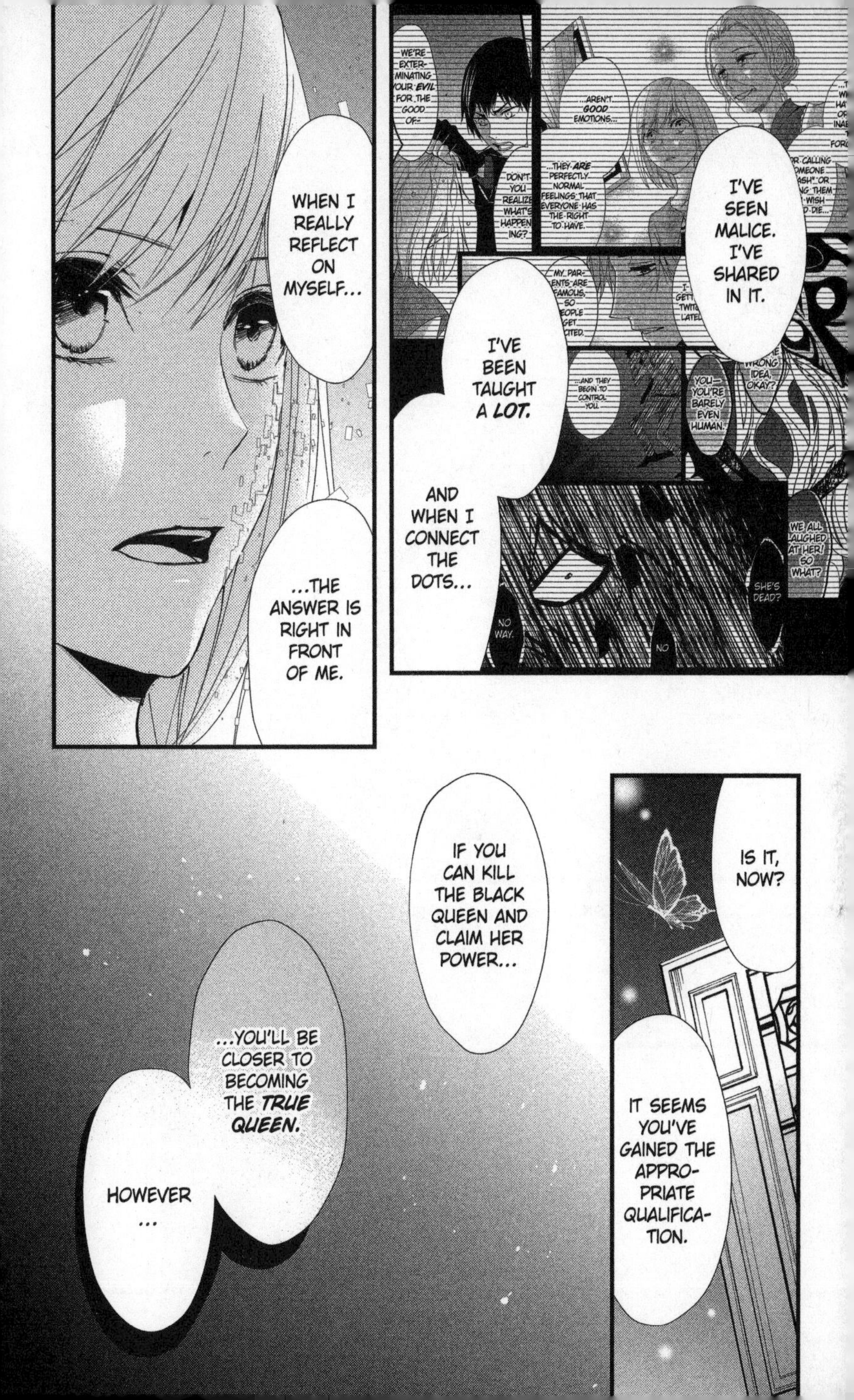
WE'RE EXTER-MINATING YOUR EVIL FOR THE GOOD OF-
...AREN'T GOOD EMOTIONS...
DON'T YOU REALIZE WHAT'S HAPPEN-ING?
...THEY ARE PERFECTLY NORMAL FEELINGS THAT EVERYONE HAS THE RIGHT TO HAVE.
I'VE SEEN MALICE. I'VE SHARED IN IT.
...AND THEY BEGIN TO CONTROL YOU.
WRONG IDEA, OKAY?
YOU— YOU'RE BARELY EVEN HUMAN.
I'VE BEEN TAUGHT A LOT.
WE ALL LAUGHED AT HER! SO WHAT?
SHE'S DEAD?
AND WHEN I CONNECT THE DOTS...
NO
NO WAY.
WHEN I REALLY REFLECT ON MYSELF...
...THE ANSWER IS RIGHT IN FRONT OF ME.
IS IT, NOW?
IT SEEMS YOU'VE GAINED THE APPRO-PRIATE QUALIFICA-TION.
IF YOU CAN KILL THE BLACK QUEEN AND CLAIM HER POWER...
...YOU'LL BE CLOSER TO BECOMING THE TRUE QUEEN.
HOWEVER ...

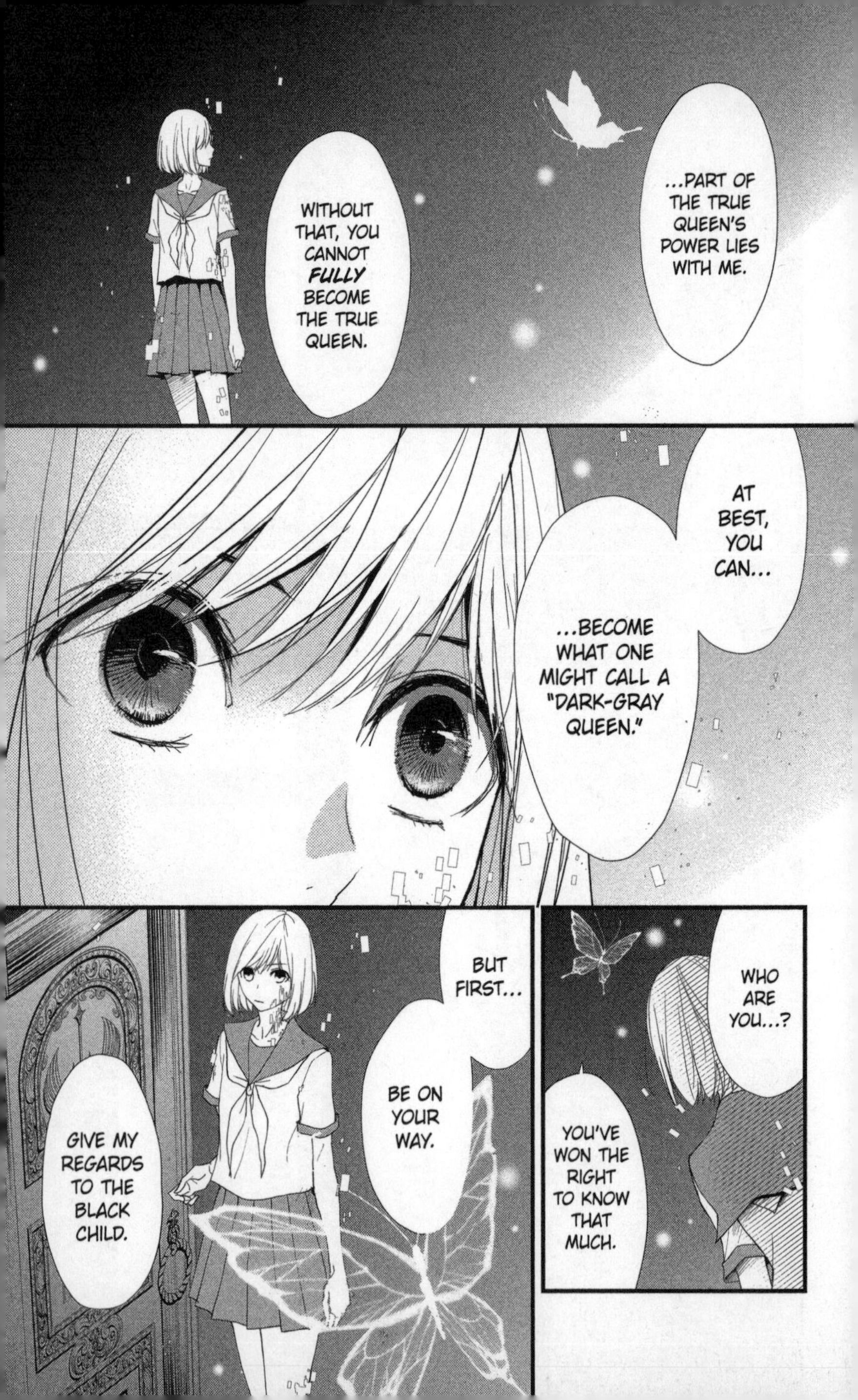
...PART OF THE TRUE QUEEN'S POWER LIES WITH ME.
WITHOUT THAT, YOU CANNOT *FULLY* BECOME THE TRUE QUEEN.
AT BEST, YOU CAN...
...BECOME WHAT ONE MIGHT CALL A "DARK-GRAY QUEEN."
WHO ARE YOU...?
YOU'VE WON THE RIGHT TO KNOW THAT MUCH.
BUT FIRST...
BE ON YOUR WAY.
GIVE MY REGARDS TO THE BLACK CHILD.

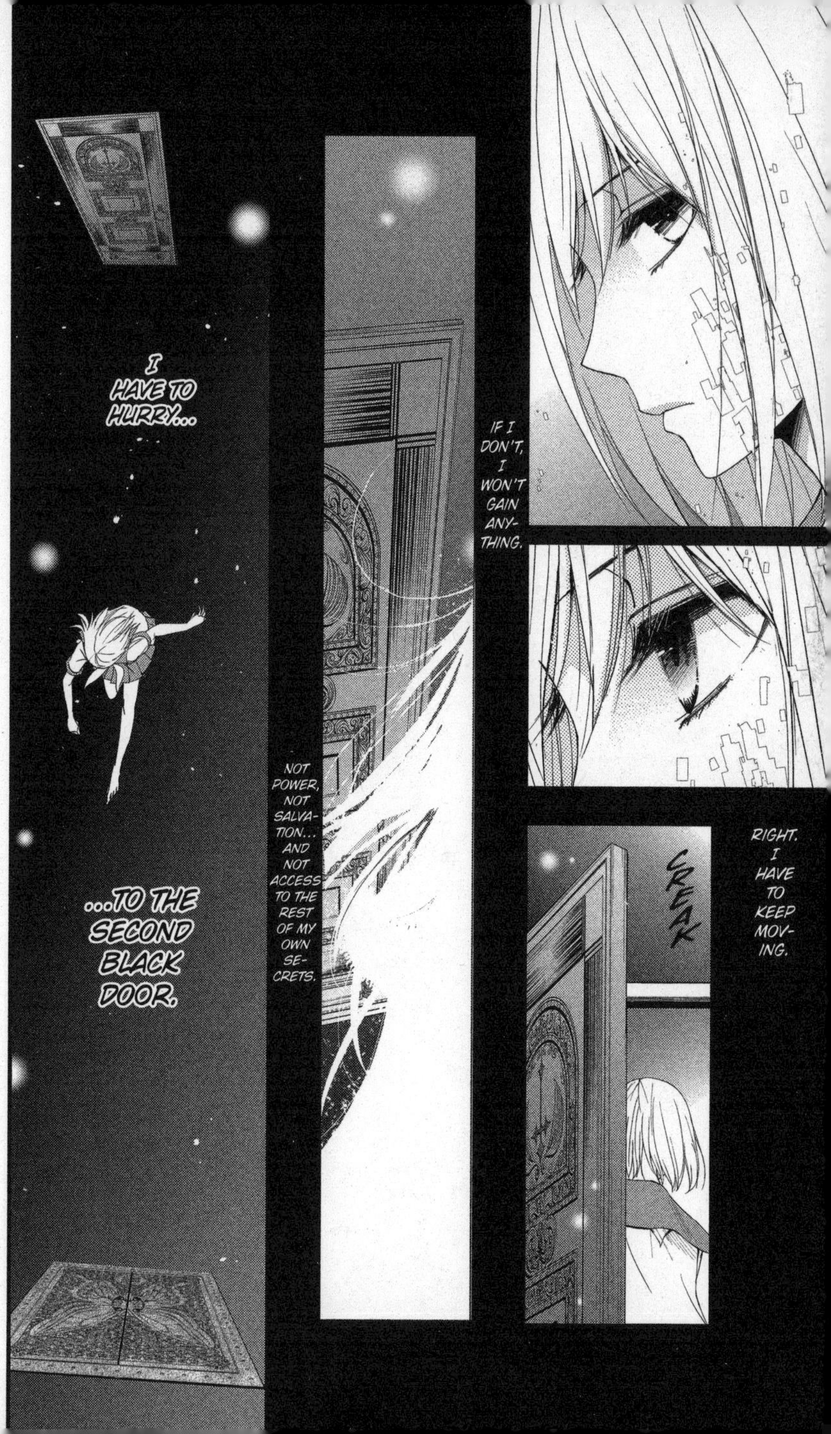
IF I DON'T, I WON'T GAIN ANYTHING.
RIGHT. I HAVE TO KEEP MOVING.
CREAK
NOT POWER, NOT SALVATION... AND NOT ACCESS TO THE REST OF MY OWN SECRETS.
I HAVE TO HURRY...
...TO THE SECOND BLACK DOOR.

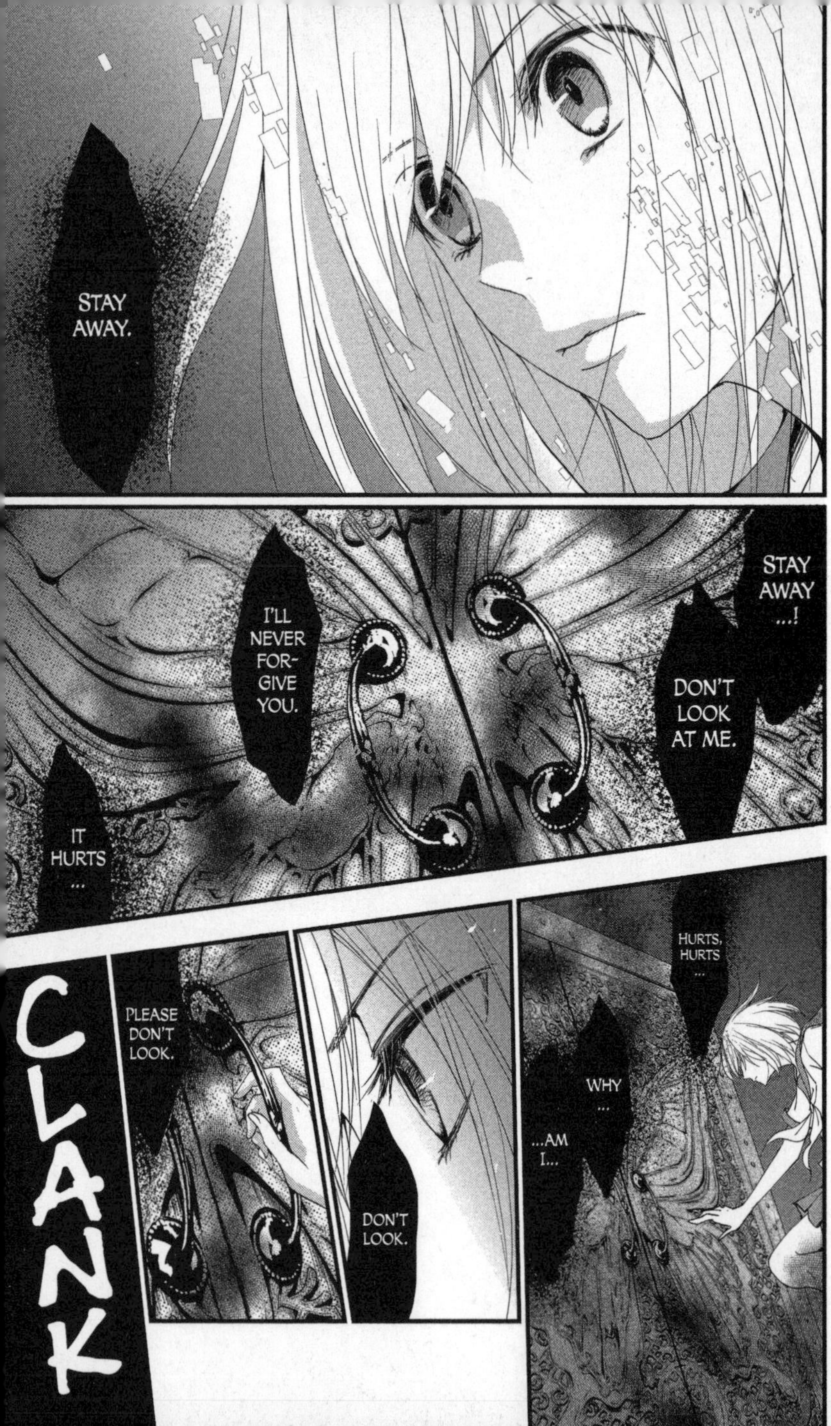
STAY AWAY.
STAY AWAY ...!
DON'T LOOK AT ME.
I'LL NEVER FOR-GIVE YOU.
IT HURTS ...
HURTS, HURTS ...
WHY ...
...AM I...
DON'T LOOK.
PLEASE DON'T LOOK.
CLANK

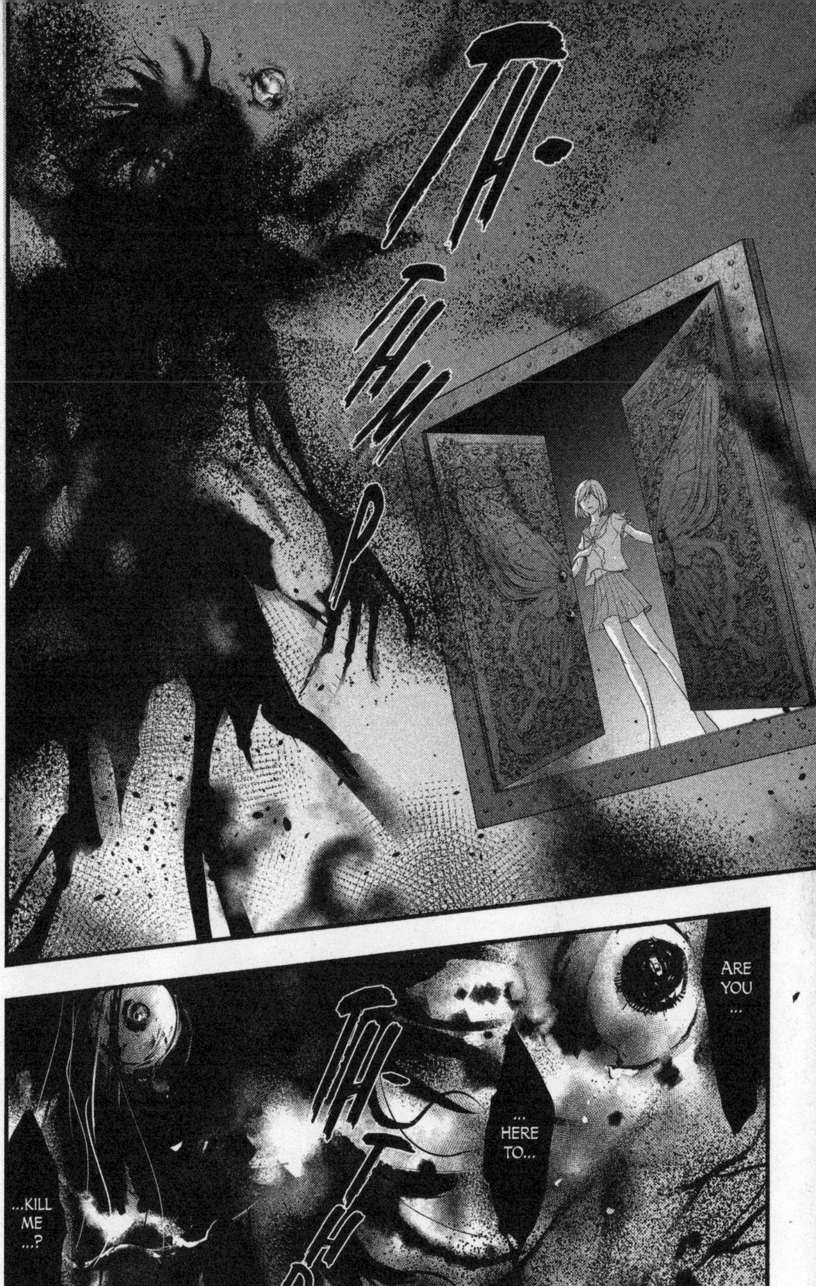
TH-THMP
ARE YOU ...
... HERE TO...
TH-THD
...KILL ME ...?

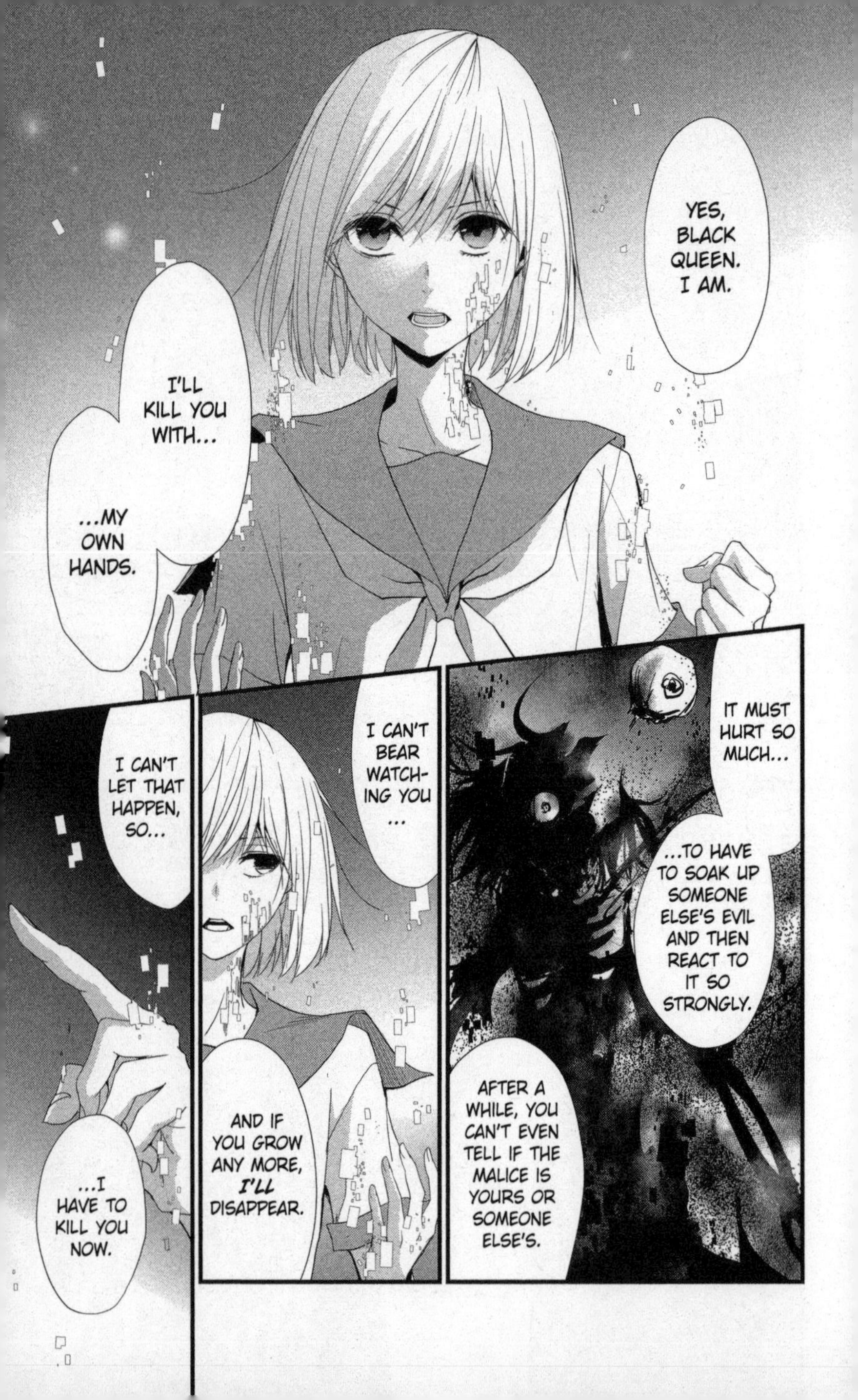
YES, BLACK QUEEN. I AM.
I'LL KILL YOU WITH...
...MY OWN HANDS.
IT MUST HURT SO MUCH...
...TO HAVE TO SOAK UP SOMEONE ELSE'S EVIL AND THEN REACT TO IT SO STRONGLY.
AFTER A WHILE, YOU CAN'T EVEN TELL IF THE MALICE IS YOURS OR SOMEONE ELSE'S.
I CAN'T BEAR WATCHING YOU ...
AND IF YOU GROW ANY MORE, *I'LL* DISAPPEAR.
I CAN'T LET THAT HAPPEN, SO...
...I HAVE TO KILL YOU NOW.

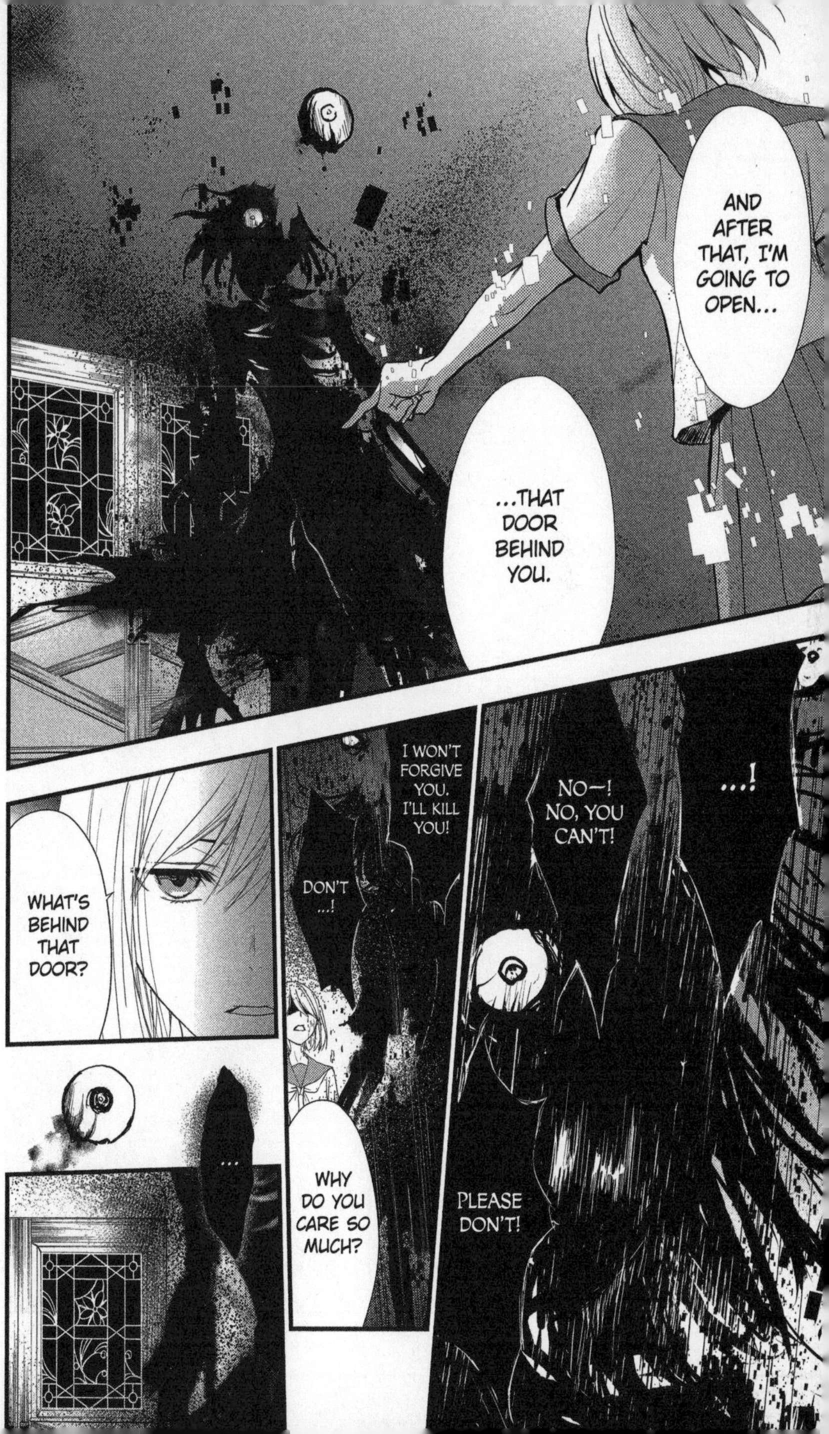
AND AFTER THAT, I'M GOING TO OPEN...
...THAT DOOR BEHIND YOU.
...!
NO—! NO, YOU CAN'T!
PLEASE DON'T!
I WON'T FORGIVE YOU. I'LL KILL YOU!
DON'T ...!
WHY DO YOU CARE SO MUCH?
WHAT'S BEHIND THAT DOOR?
...

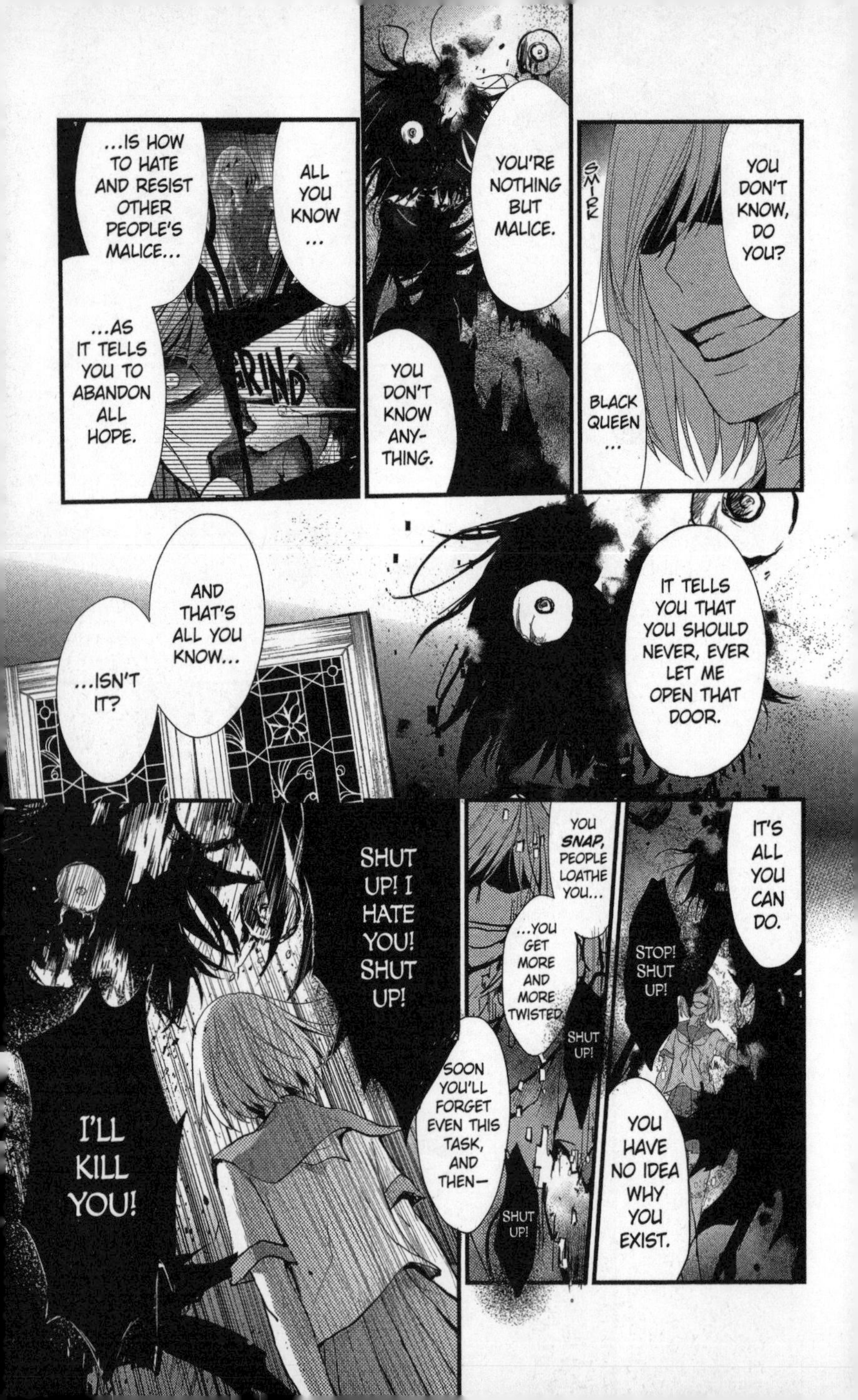
YOU DON'T KNOW, DO YOU?
SMIRK
BLACK QUEEN...
YOU'RE NOTHING BUT MALICE.
YOU DON'T KNOW ANYTHING.
ALL YOU KNOW ...
...IS HOW TO HATE AND RESIST OTHER PEOPLE'S MALICE...
GRIND
...AS IT TELLS YOU TO ABANDON ALL HOPE.
IT TELLS YOU THAT YOU SHOULD NEVER, EVER LET ME OPEN THAT DOOR.
AND THAT'S ALL YOU KNOW...
...ISN'T IT?
IT'S ALL YOU CAN DO.
STOP! SHUT UP!
YOU HAVE NO IDEA WHY YOU EXIST.
YOU SNAP, PEOPLE LOATHE YOU...
...YOU GET MORE AND MORE TWISTED
SHUT UP!
SOON YOU'LL FORGET EVEN THIS TASK, AND THEN—
SHUT UP!
SHUT UP! I HATE YOU! SHUT UP!
I'LL KILL YOU!

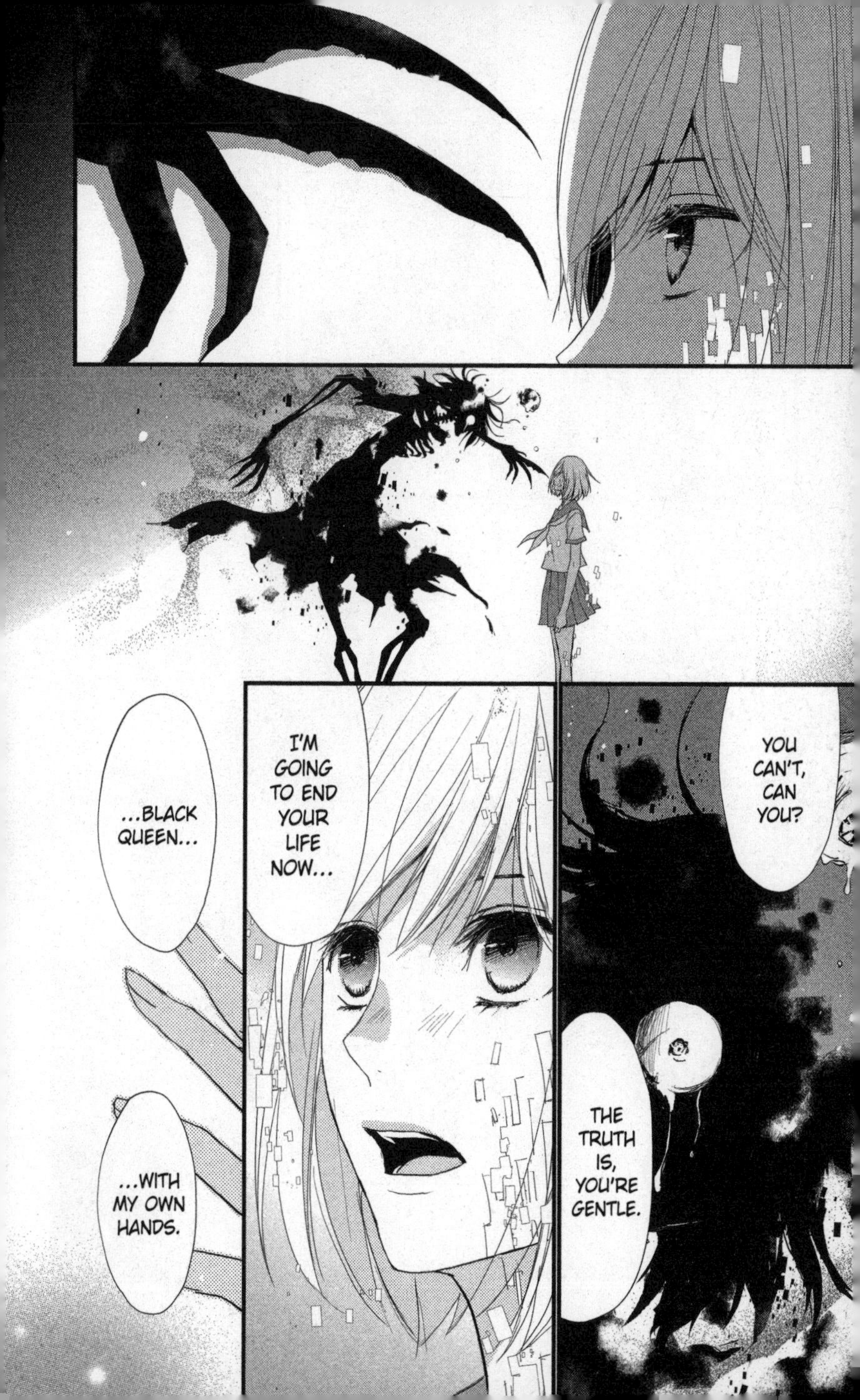
YOU CAN'T, CAN YOU?
THE TRUTH IS, YOU'RE GENTLE.
I'M GOING TO END YOUR LIFE NOW...
...BLACK QUEEN...
...WITH MY OWN HANDS.

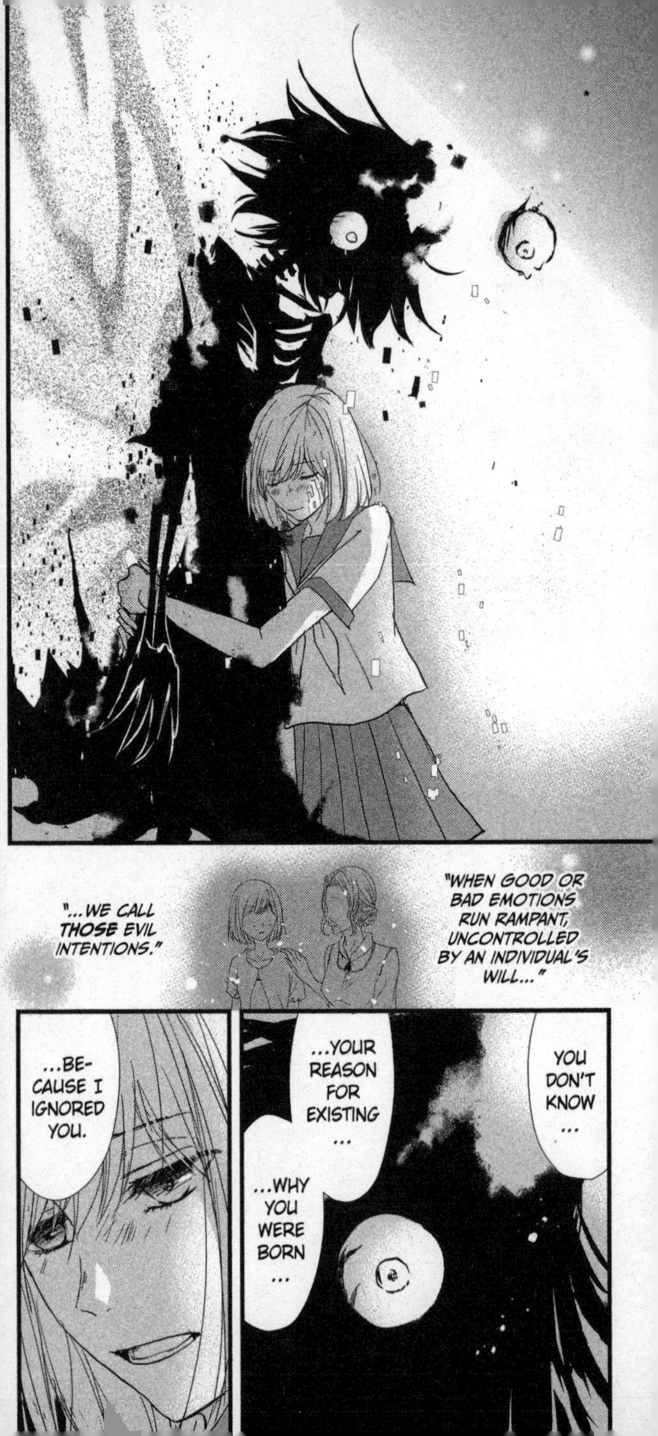
"WHEN GOOD OR BAD EMOTIONS RUN RAMPANT, UNCONTROLLED BY AN INDIVIDUAL'S WILL..."
"...WE CALL THOSE EVIL INTENTIONS."
YOU DON'T KNOW ...
...YOUR REASON FOR EXISTING ...
...WHY YOU WERE BORN ...
...BE- CAUSE I IGNORED YOU.

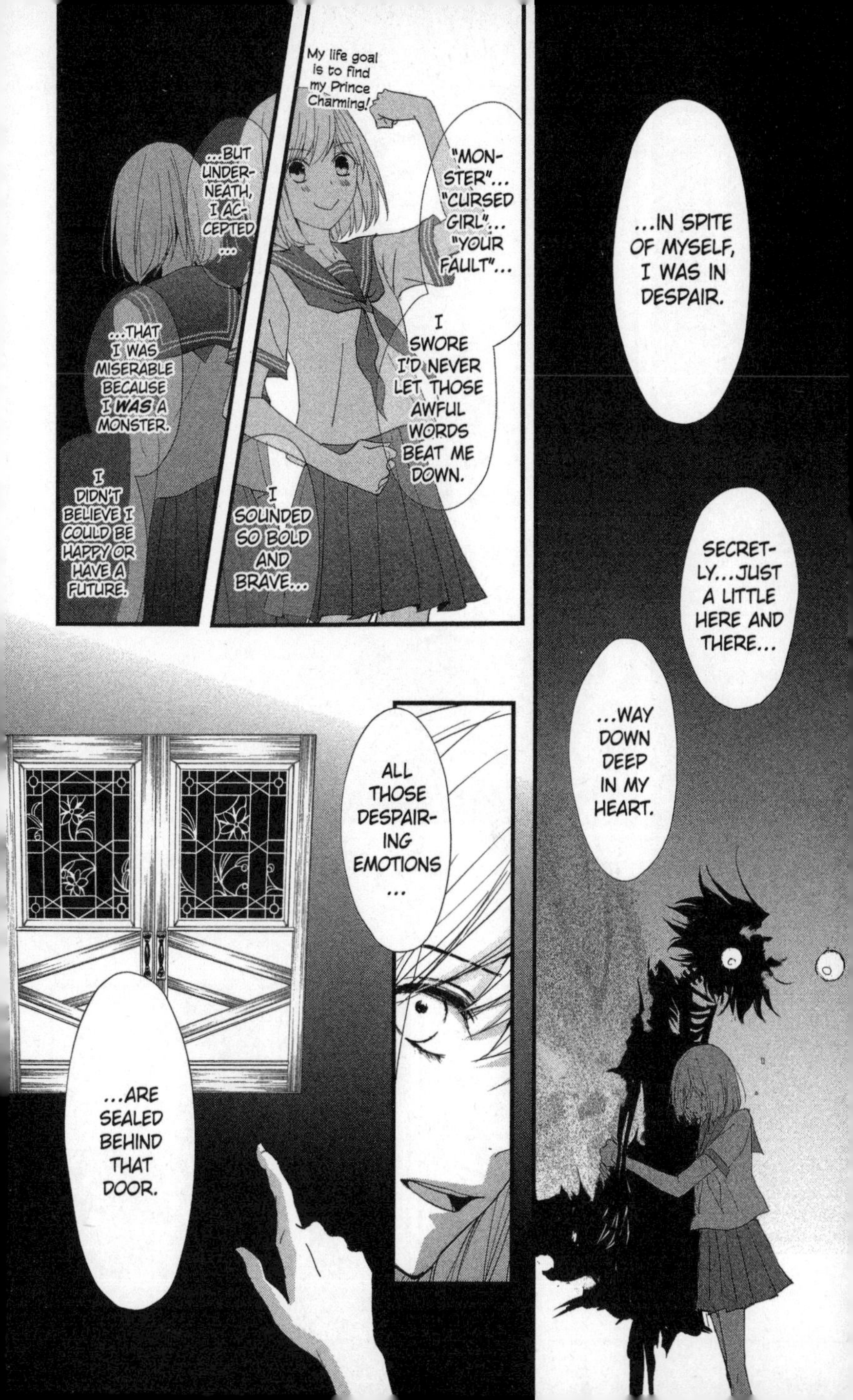
...IN SPITE OF MYSELF, I WAS IN DESPAIR.
SECRETLY...JUST A LITTLE HERE AND THERE...
...WAY DOWN DEEP IN MY HEART.
My life goal is to find my Prince Charming!
"MONSTER"... "CURSED GIRL"... "YOUR FAULT"...
I SWORE I'D NEVER LET THOSE AWFUL WORDS BEAT ME DOWN.
I SOUNDED SO BOLD AND BRAVE...
...BUT UNDERNEATH, I ACCEPTED...
...THAT I WAS MISERABLE BECAUSE I ***WAS*** A MONSTER.
I DIDN'T BELIEVE I COULD BE HAPPY OR HAVE A FUTURE.
ALL THOSE DESPAIRING EMOTIONS...
...ARE SEALED BEHIND THAT DOOR.

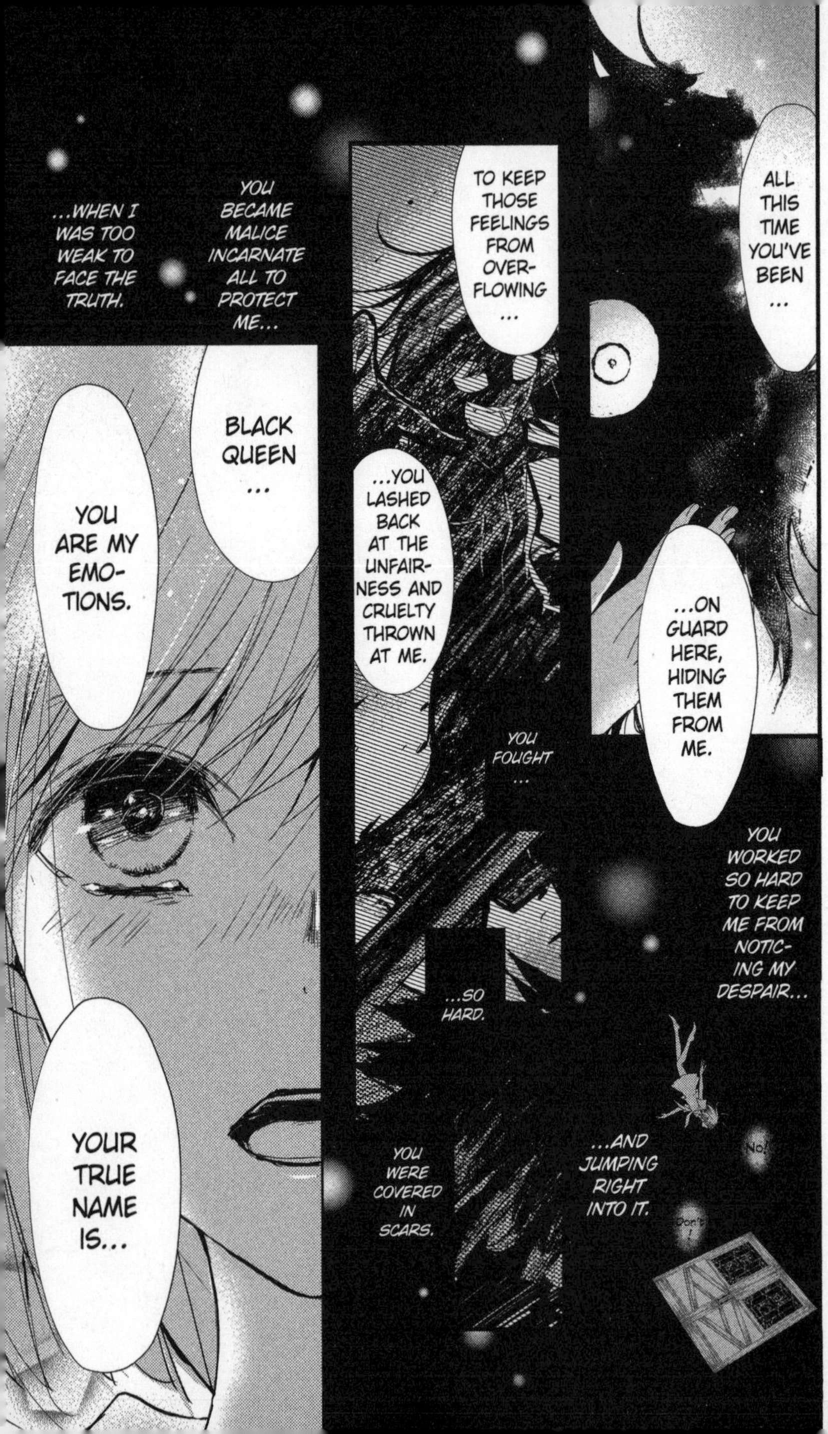
ALL THIS TIME YOU'VE BEEN...
...ON GUARD HERE, HIDING THEM FROM ME.
TO KEEP THOSE FEELINGS FROM OVER-FLOWING...
...YOU LASHED BACK AT THE UNFAIR-NESS AND CRUELTY THROWN AT ME.
YOU FOUGHT...
...SO HARD.
YOU BECAME MALICE INCARNATE ALL TO PROTECT ME...
...WHEN I WAS TOO WEAK TO FACE THE TRUTH.
YOU WORKED SO HARD TO KEEP ME FROM NOTIC-ING MY DESPAIR...
No!
Don't!
...AND JUMPING RIGHT INTO IT.
YOU WERE COVERED IN SCARS.
BLACK QUEEN...
YOU ARE MY EMO-TIONS.
YOUR TRUE NAME IS...

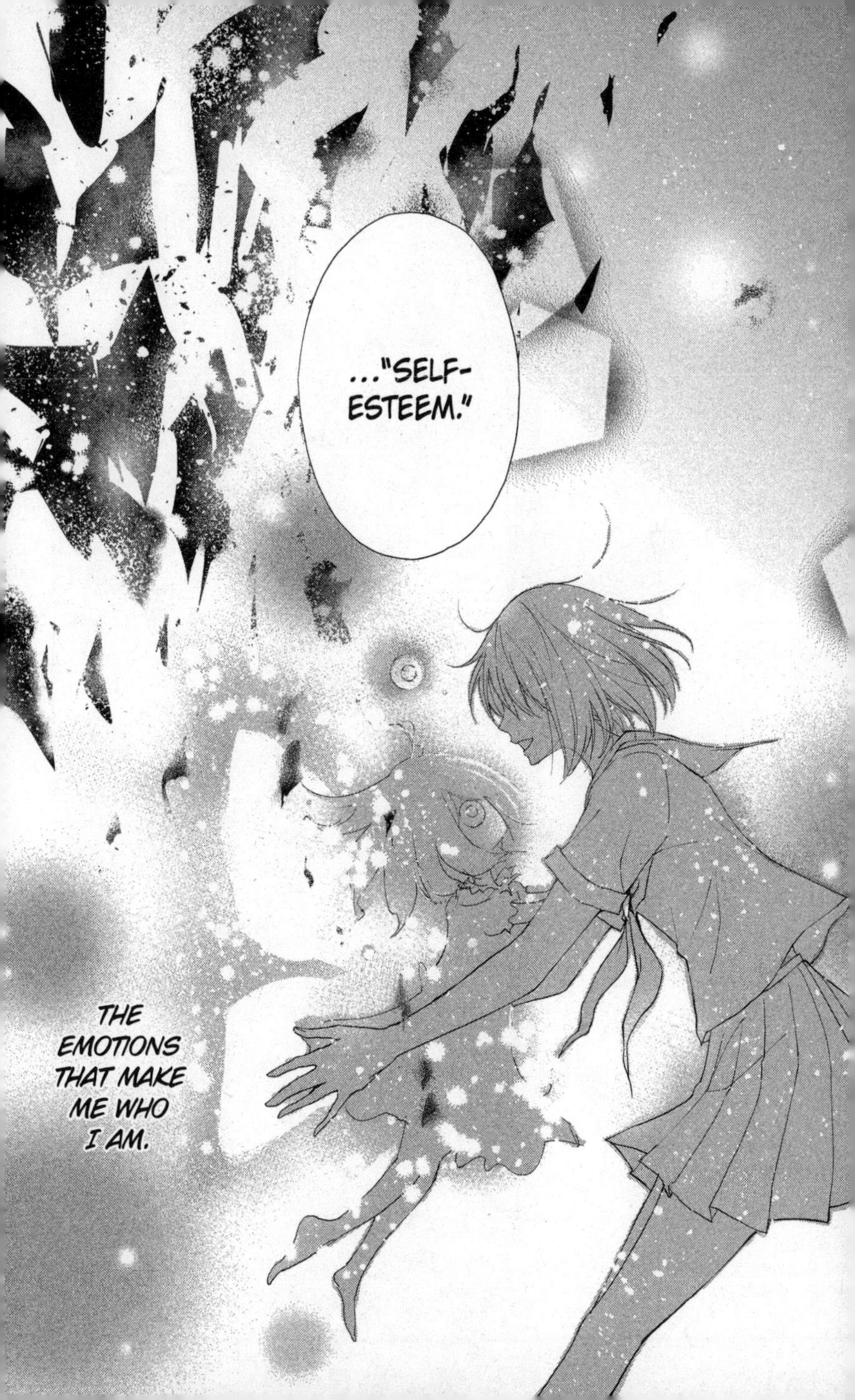
..."SELF-
ESTEEM."
THE
EMOTIONS
THAT MAKE
ME WHO
I AM.

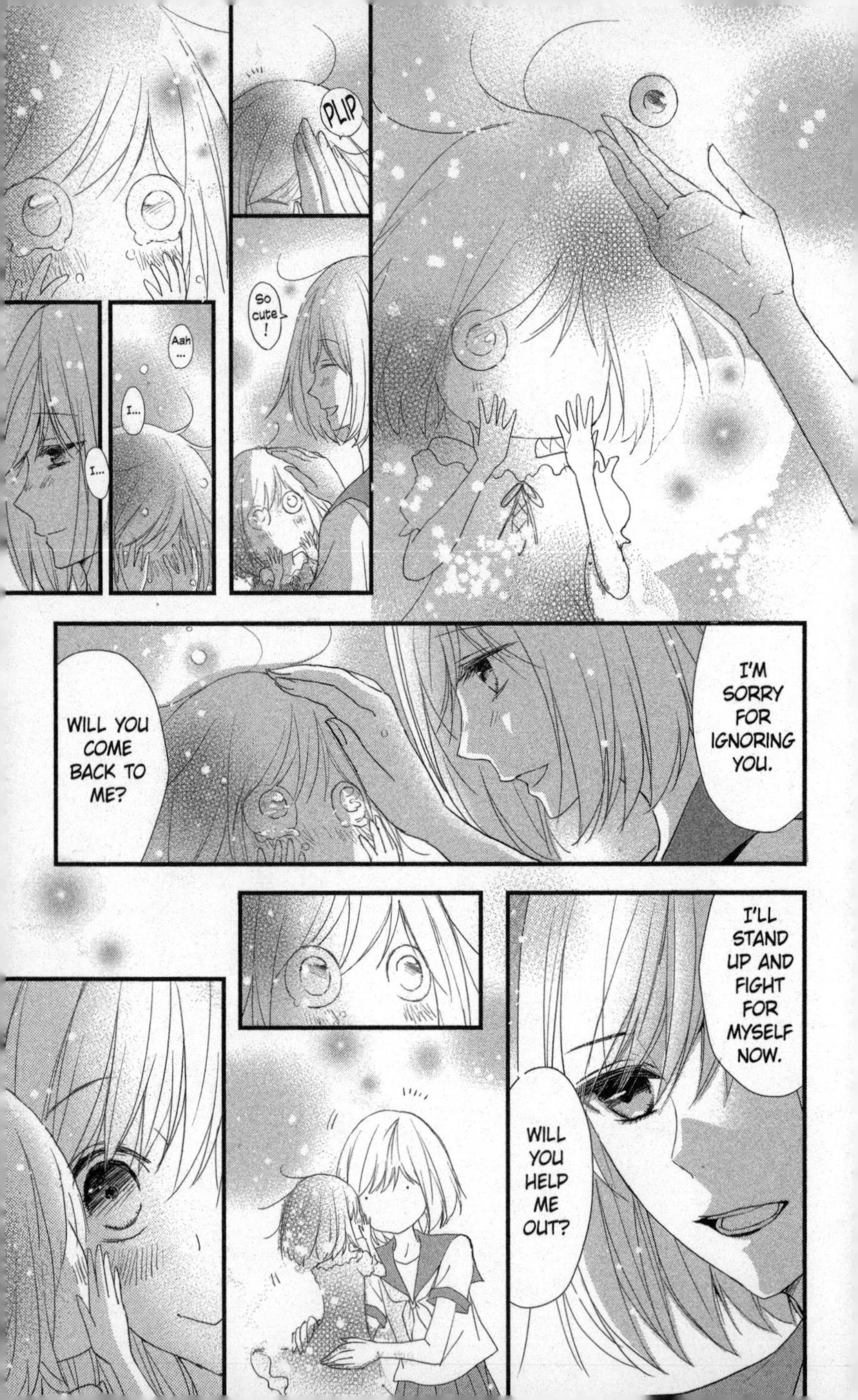
PLIP
So cute!
Aah...
I...
I...
I'M SORRY FOR IGNORING YOU.
WILL YOU COME BACK TO ME?
I'LL STAND UP AND FIGHT FOR MYSELF NOW.
WILL YOU HELP ME OUT?

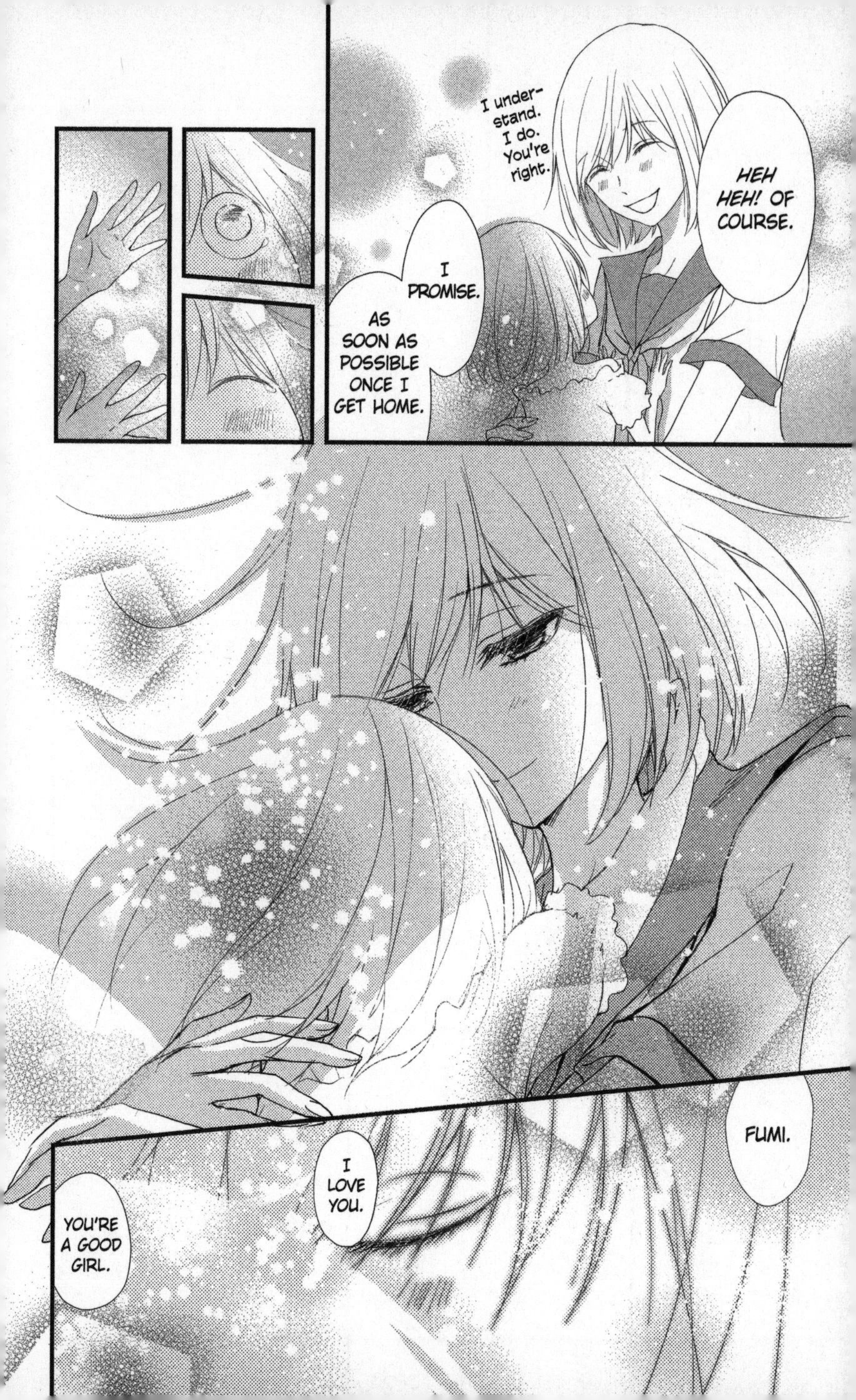
HEH HEH! OF COURSE.
I under-stand. I do. You're right.
I PROMISE.
AS SOON AS POSSIBLE ONCE I GET HOME.
FUMI.
I LOVE YOU.
YOU'RE A GOOD GIRL.

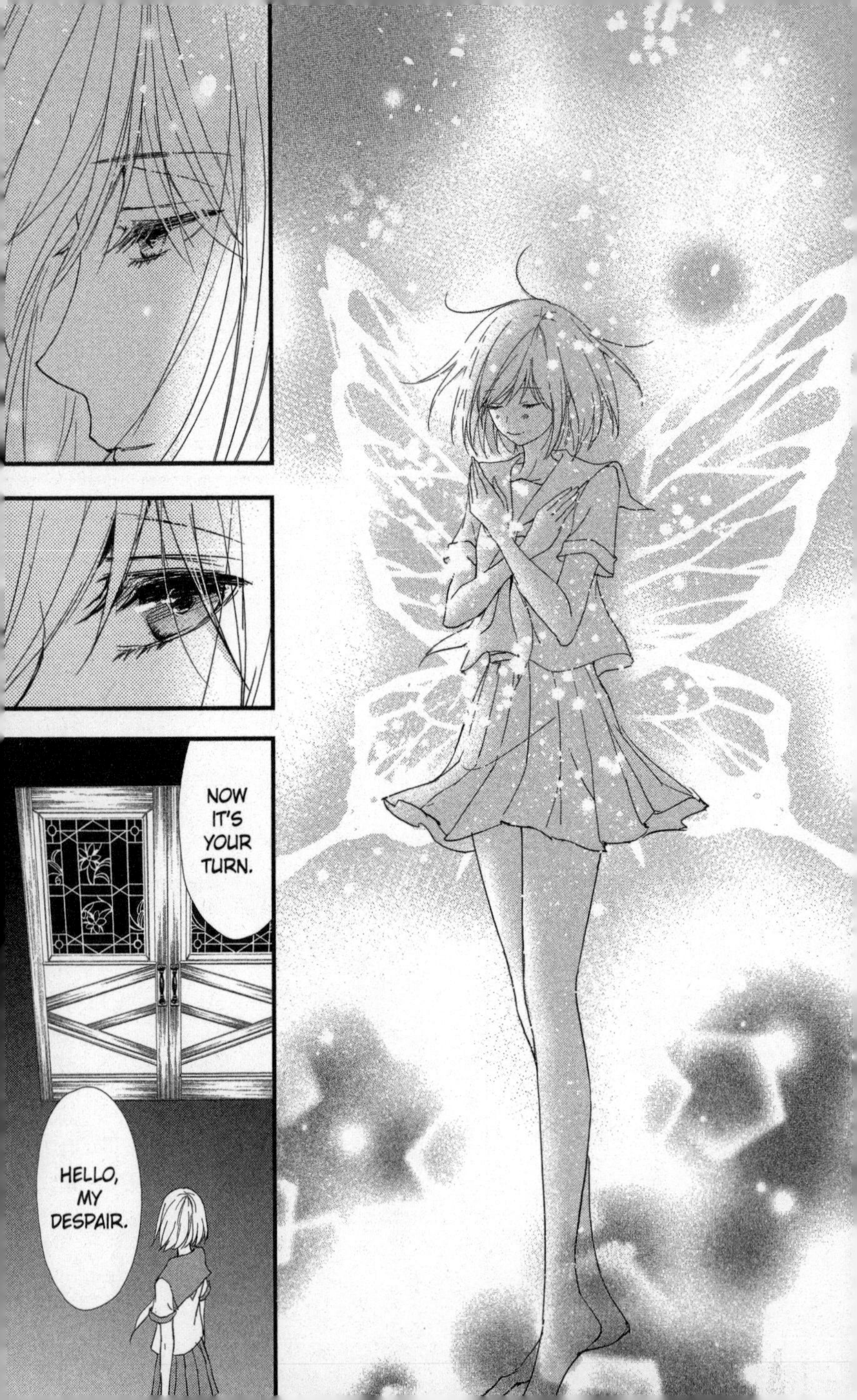
NOW IT'S YOUR TURN.
HELLO, MY DESPAIR.

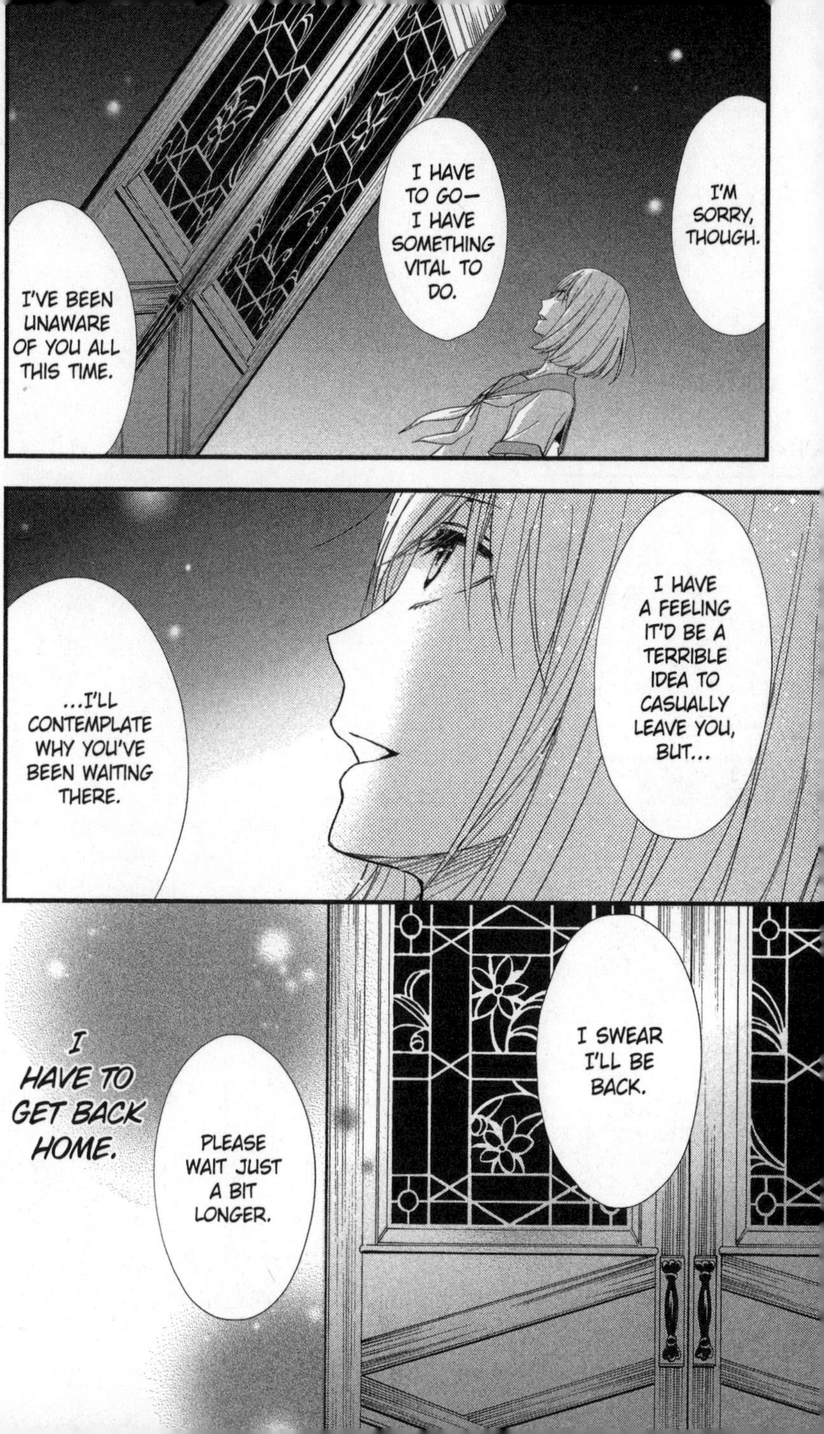
I'M SORRY, THOUGH.
I HAVE TO GO— I HAVE SOMETHING VITAL TO DO.
I'VE BEEN UNAWARE OF YOU ALL THIS TIME.
I HAVE A FEELING IT'D BE A TERRIBLE IDEA TO CASUALLY LEAVE YOU, BUT...
...I'LL CONTEMPLATE WHY YOU'VE BEEN WAITING THERE.
I SWEAR I'LL BE BACK.
PLEASE WAIT JUST A BIT LONGER.
I HAVE TO GET BACK HOME.

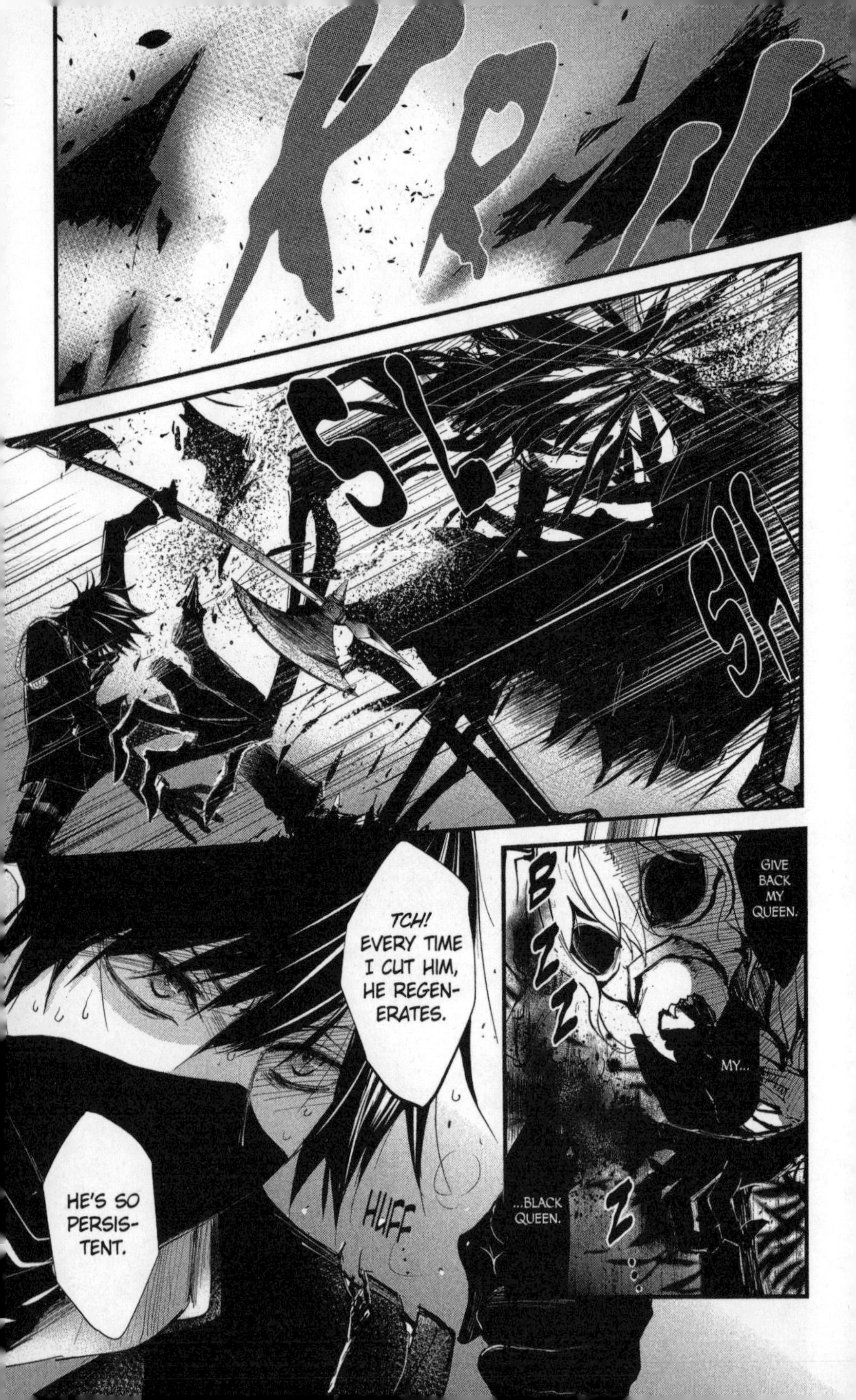
GIVE BACK MY QUEEN.
BZZZ
MY...
...BLACK QUEEN.
TCH! EVERY TIME I CUT HIM, HE REGENERATES.
HE'S SO PERSISTENT.
HUFF

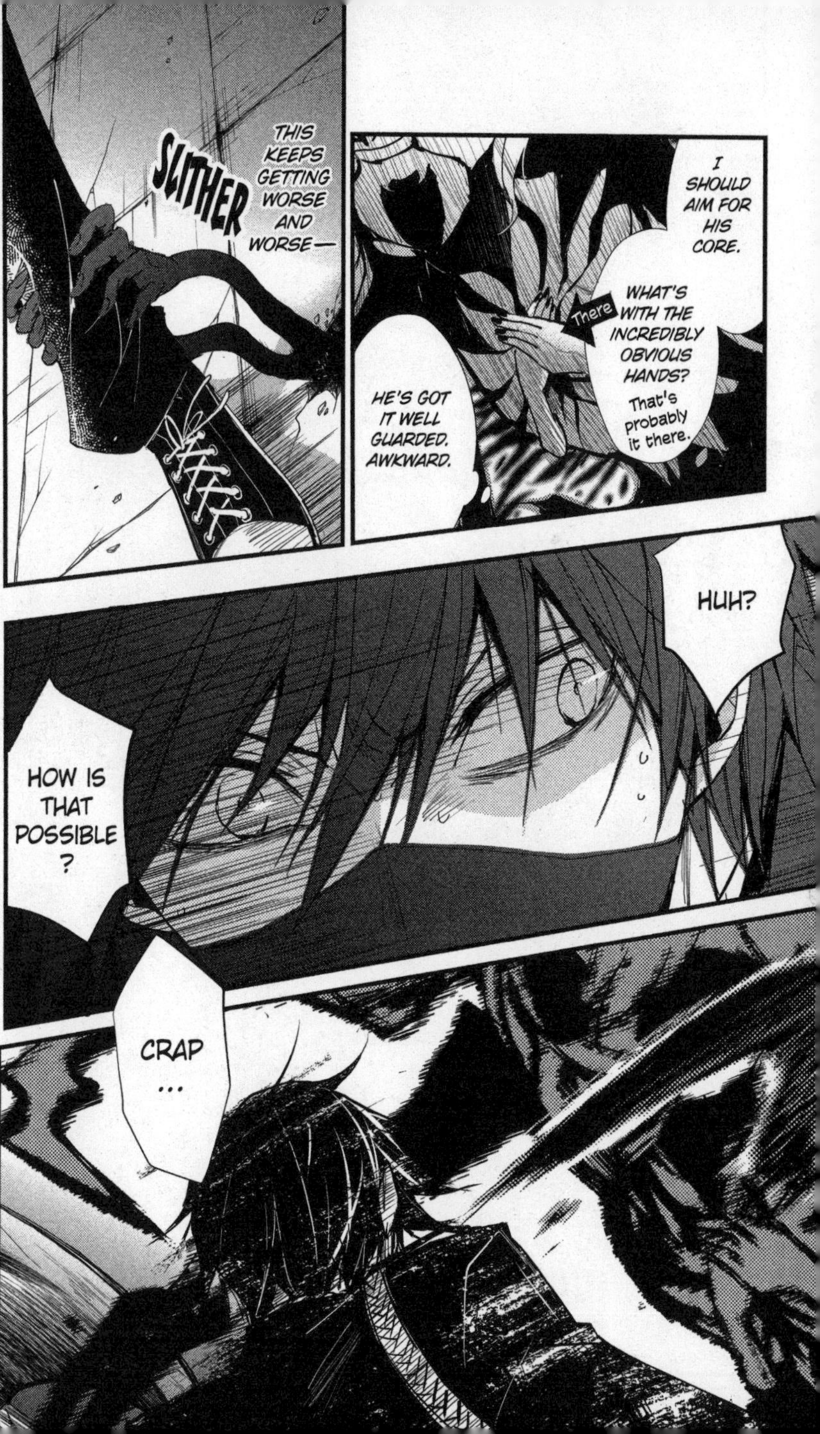
I SHOULD AIM FOR HIS CORE.
There
WHAT'S WITH THE INCREDIBLY OBVIOUS HANDS?
That's probably it there.
HE'S GOT IT WELL GUARDED. AWKWARD.
SLITHER
THIS KEEPS GETTING WORSE AND WORSE—
HUH?
HOW IS THAT POSSIBLE?
CRAP...

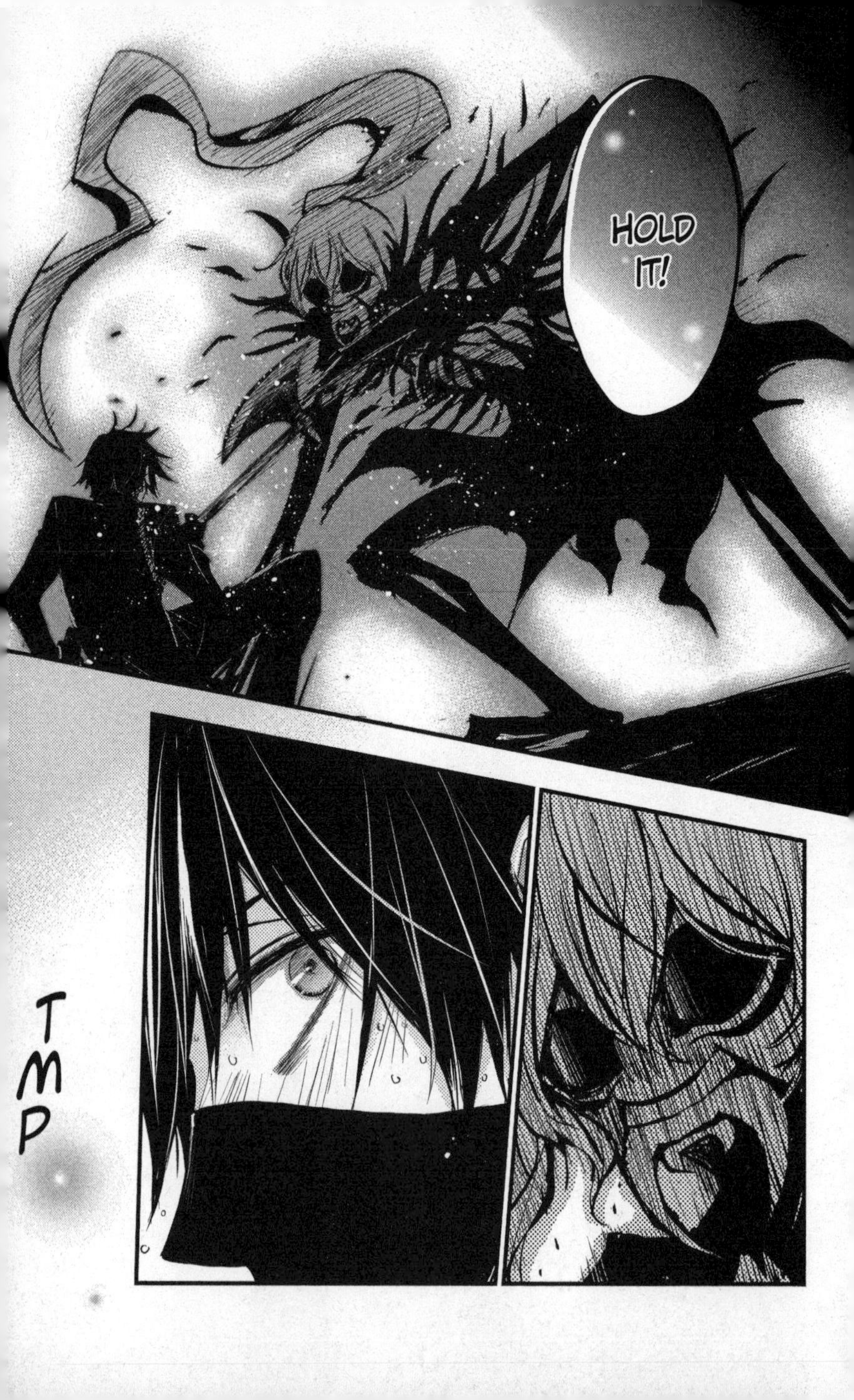
HOLD IT!
TMP

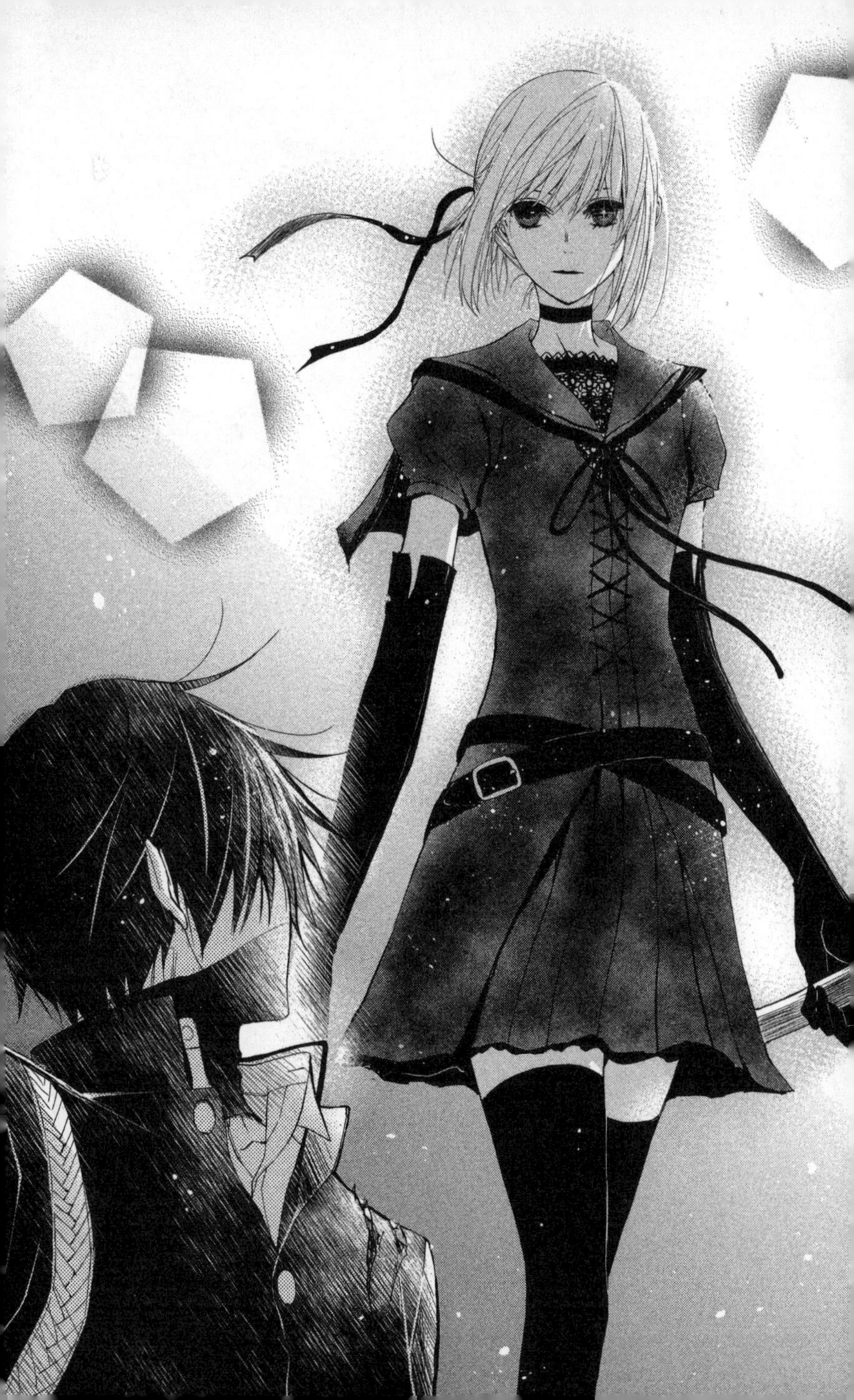

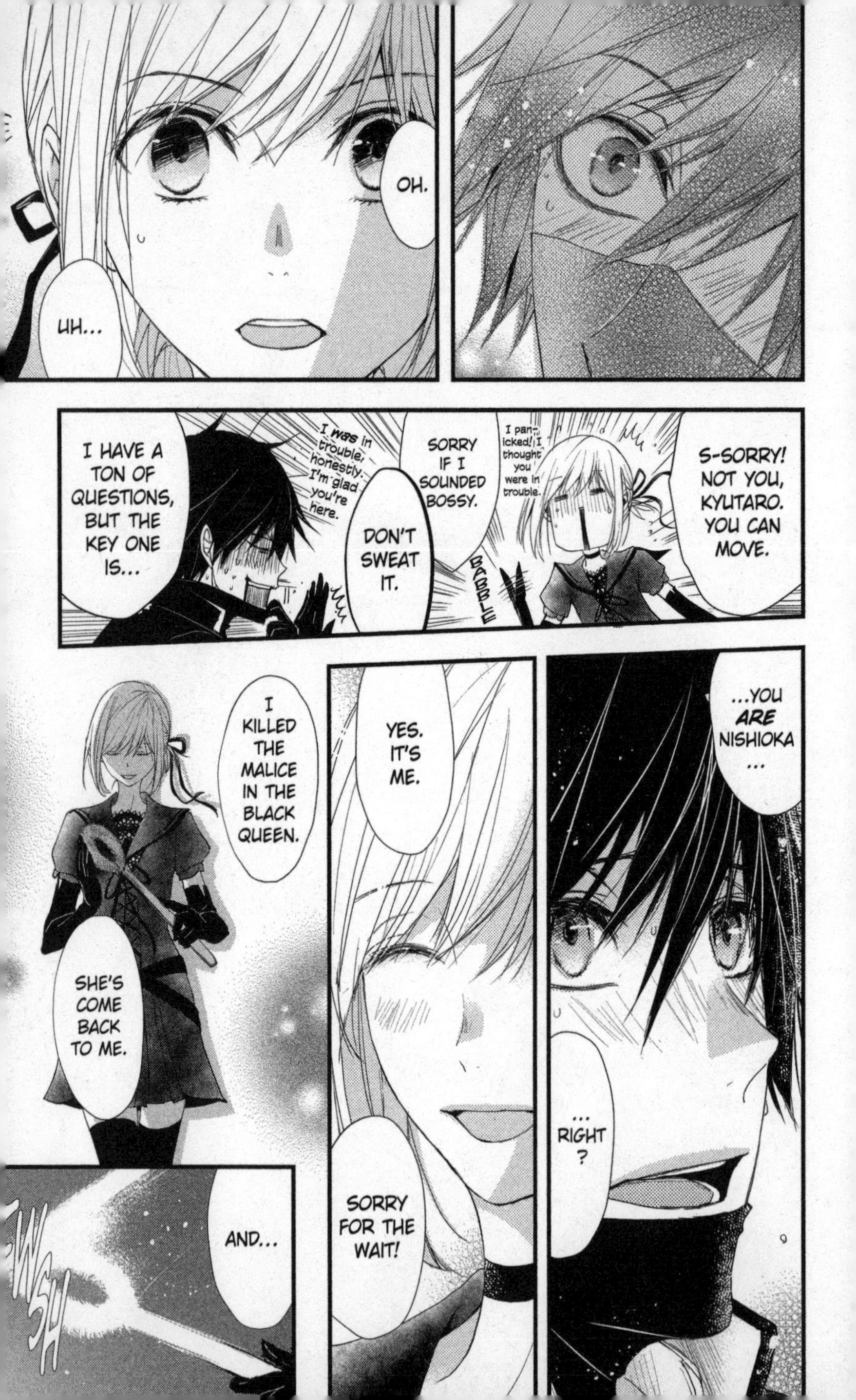
OH.
UH...
S-SORRY! NOT YOU, KYUTARO. YOU CAN MOVE.
I panicked! I thought you were in trouble.
BABBLE
SORRY IF I SOUNDED BOSSY.
DON'T SWEAT IT.
I was in trouble, honestly. I'm glad you're here.
I HAVE A TON OF QUESTIONS, BUT THE KEY ONE IS...
...YOU ARE NISHIOKA...
...RIGHT?
YES. IT'S ME.
SORRY FOR THE WAIT!
I KILLED THE MALICE IN THE BLACK QUEEN.
SHE'S COME BACK TO ME.
AND...

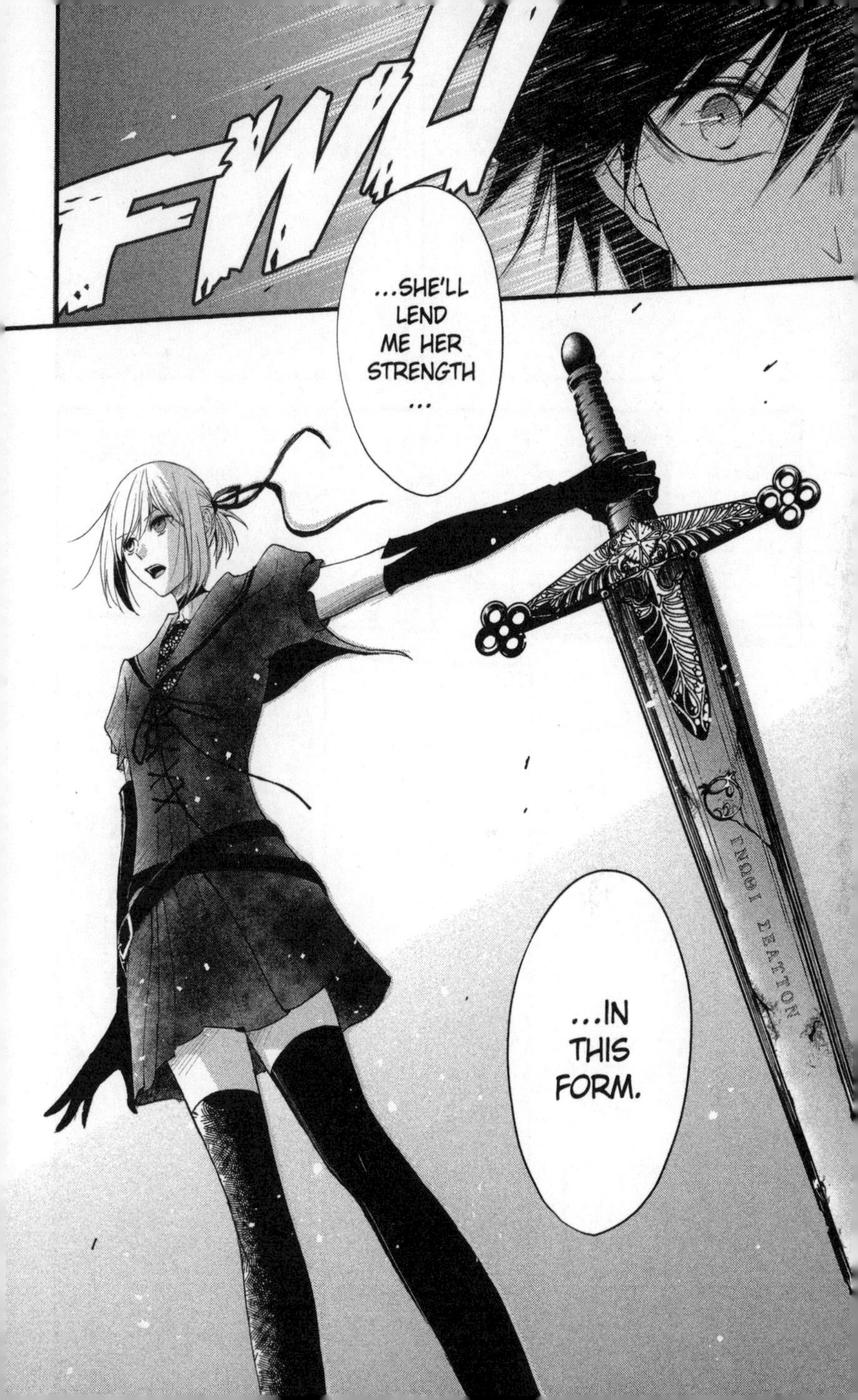
FWI
...SHE'LL LEND ME HER STRENGTH ...
...IN THIS FORM.

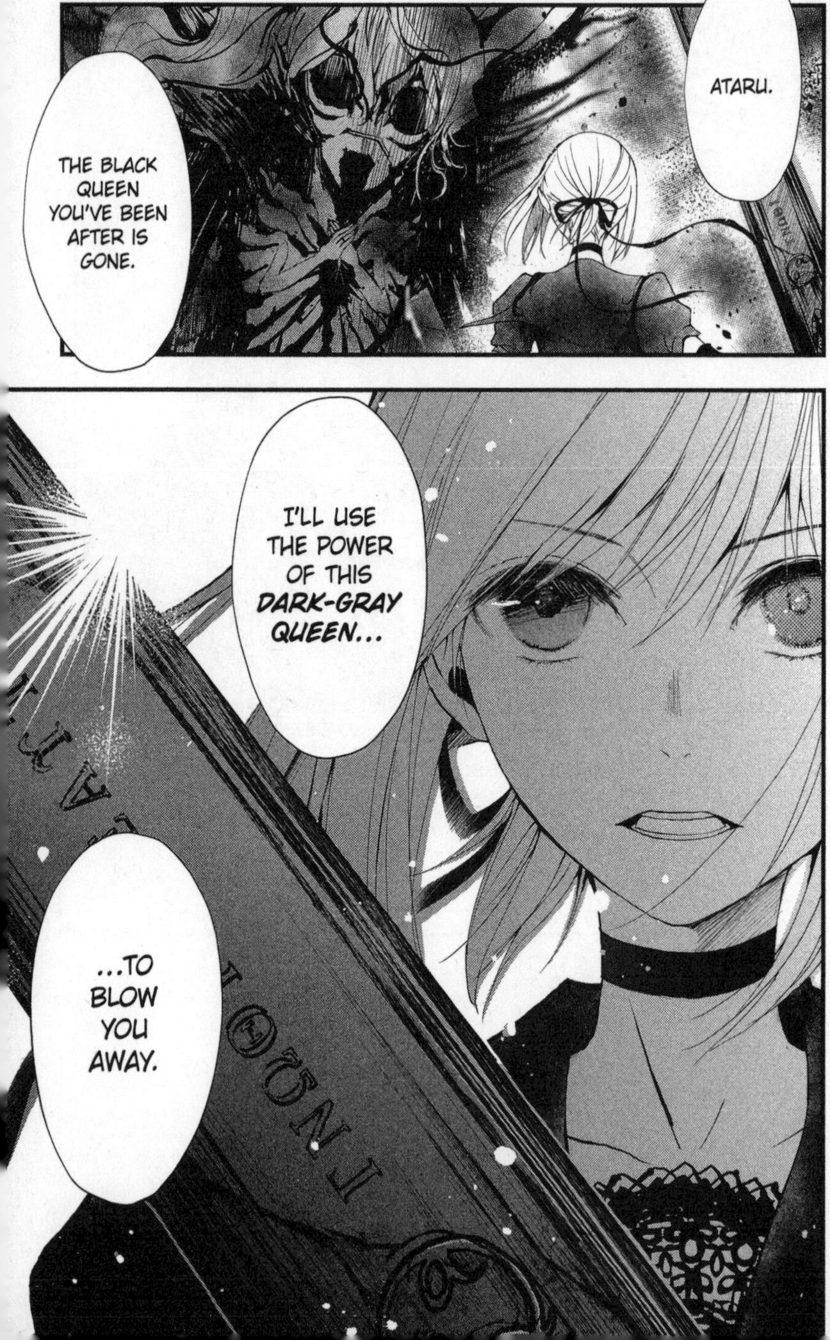
ATARU.
THE BLACK QUEEN YOU'VE BEEN AFTER IS GONE.
I'LL USE THE POWER OF THIS *DARK-GRAY QUEEN*...
...TO BLOW YOU AWAY.

MONTHLY BETSUCOMI SALE DATE NOTICE ON TWITTER

CHAPTER 22

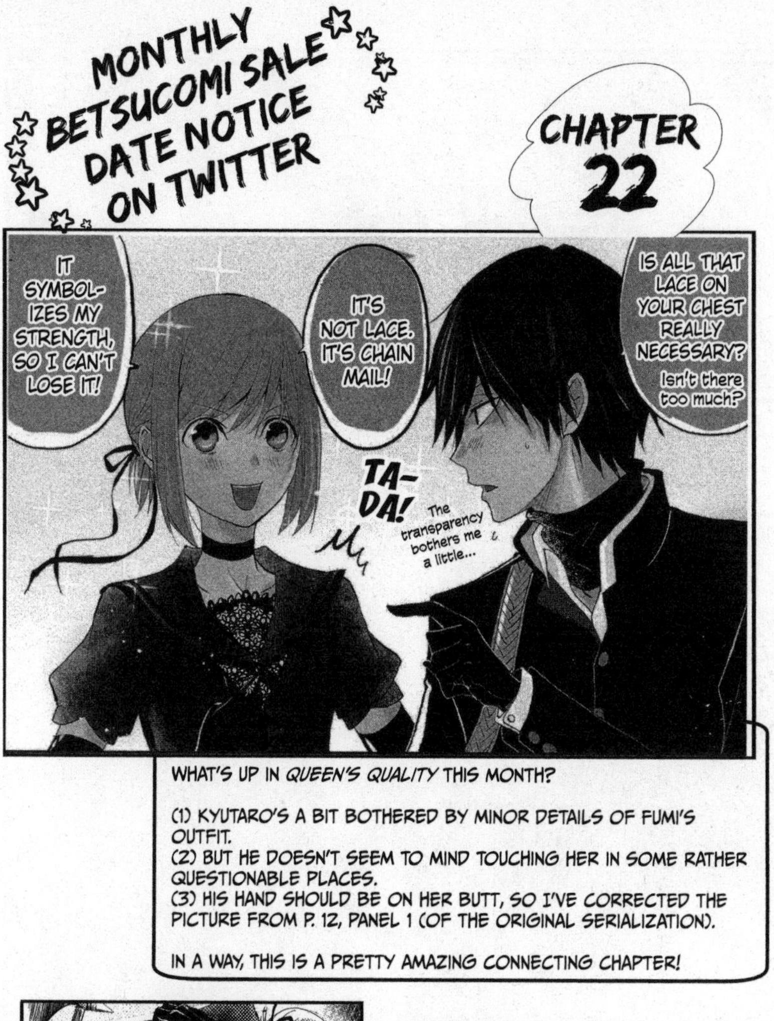
IS ALL THAT LACE ON YOUR CHEST REALLY NECESSARY?
Isn't there too much?
The transparency bothers me a little...
TA-DA!
IT'S NOT LACE. IT'S CHAIN MAIL!
IT SYMBOL-IZES MY STRENGTH, SO I CAN'T LOSE IT!

WHAT'S UP IN *QUEEN'S QUALITY* THIS MONTH?

(1) KYUTARO'S A BIT BOTHERED BY MINOR DETAILS OF FUMI'S OUTFIT.
(2) BUT HE DOESN'T SEEM TO MIND TOUCHING HER IN SOME RATHER QUESTIONABLE PLACES.
(3) HIS HAND SHOULD BE ON HER BUTT, SO I'VE CORRECTED THE PICTURE FROM P. 12, PANEL 1 (OF THE ORIGINAL SERIALIZATION).

IN A WAY, THIS IS A PRETTY AMAZING CONNECTING CHAPTER!

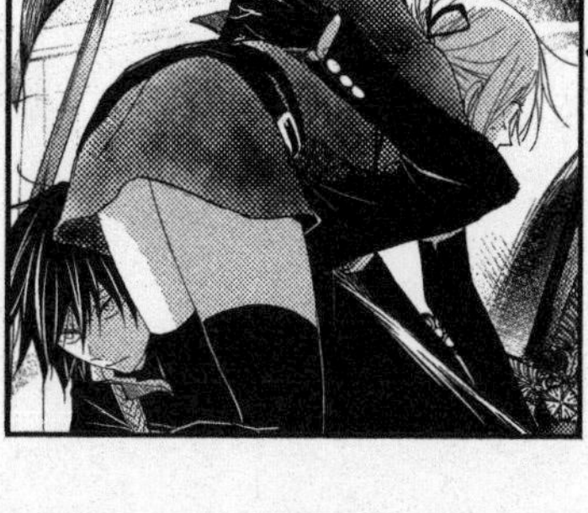

← Before correction. I've adjusted the picture in this chapter to show him holding her by the butt.

Chapter 22

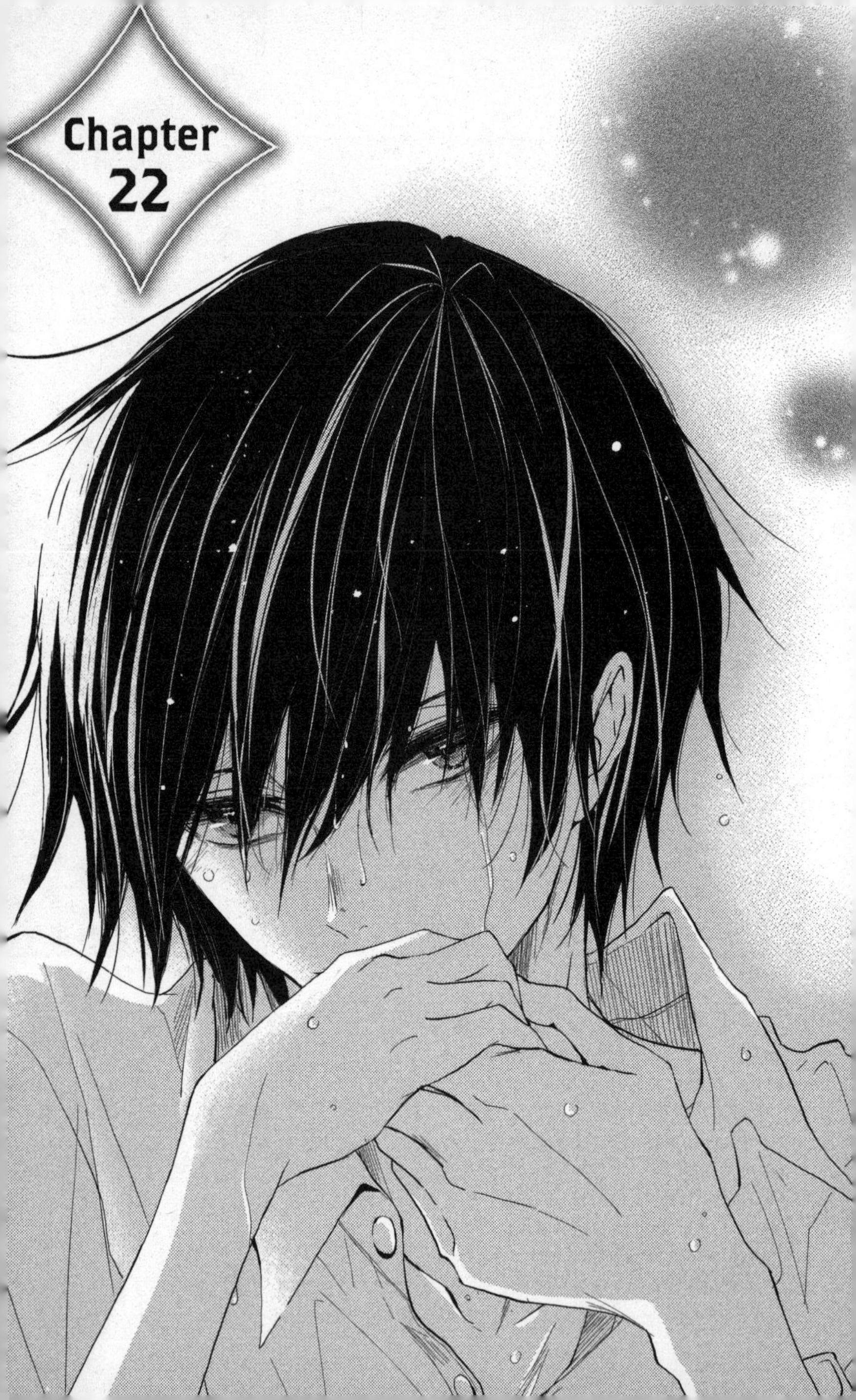

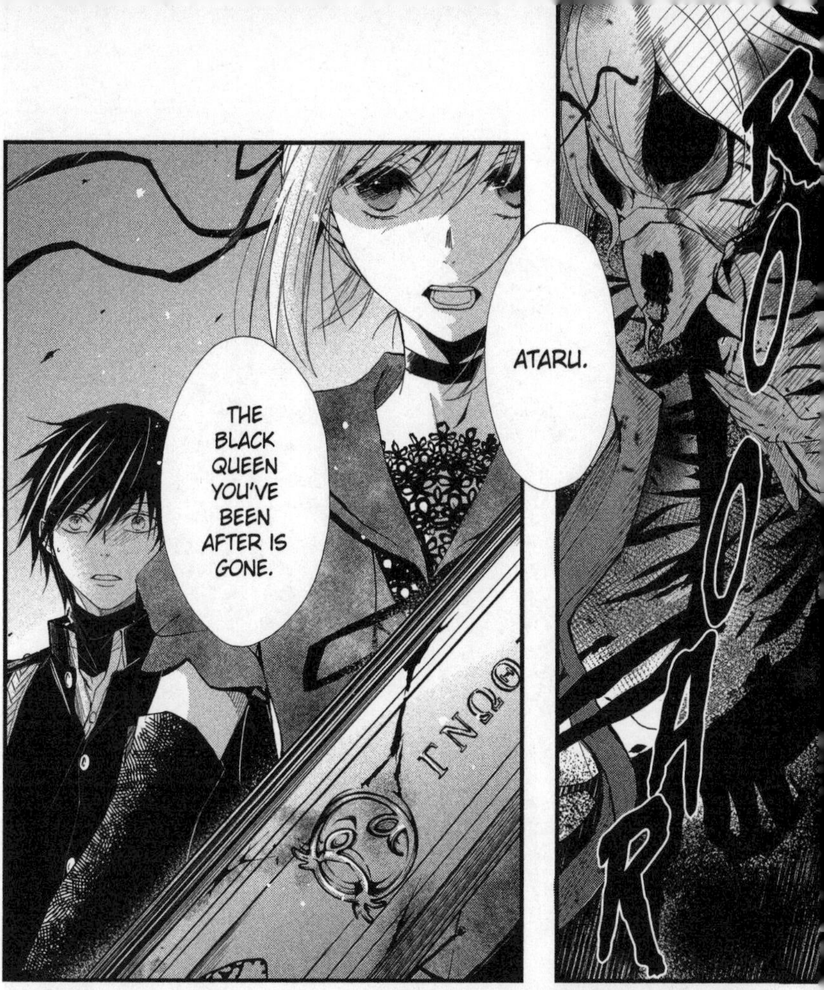
ROOOAR
ATARU.
THE BLACK QUEEN YOU'VE BEEN AFTER IS GONE.

Even after drawing manga for so many years, I find I work too slowly. If I could draw faster I could sleep more, and I could have more time to play *Dragon Quest XI*… In particular, drawing eyes takes forever—especially Kyutaro's. I'd like to show more expression in his eyes, but the more I add, the more I seem to lose the expression I'm going for. Drawing manga is really difficult!

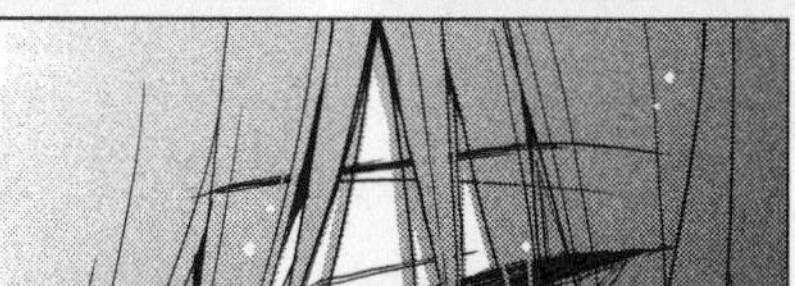

Kyutaro is constantly alert, but there's a certain sadness in his eyes. Alas, as an artist, I have trouble bringing out that sadness the way I'd like.

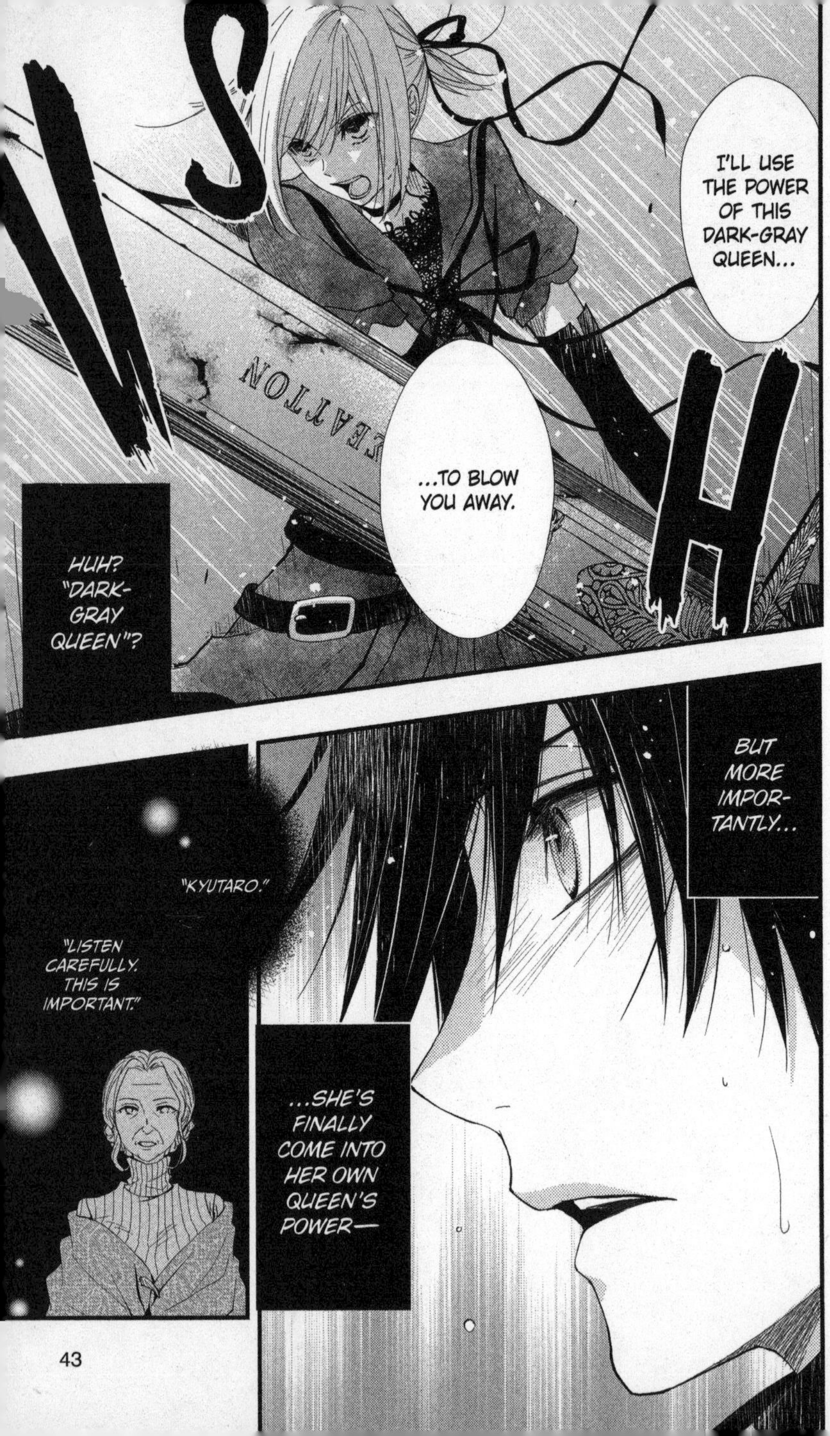
I'LL USE THE POWER OF THIS DARK-GRAY QUEEN...
...TO BLOW YOU AWAY.
HUH? "DARK-GRAY QUEEN"?
BUT MORE IMPOR-TANTLY...
...SHE'S FINALLY COME INTO HER OWN QUEEN'S POWER—
"KYUTARO."
"LISTEN CAREFULLY. THIS IS IMPORTANT."

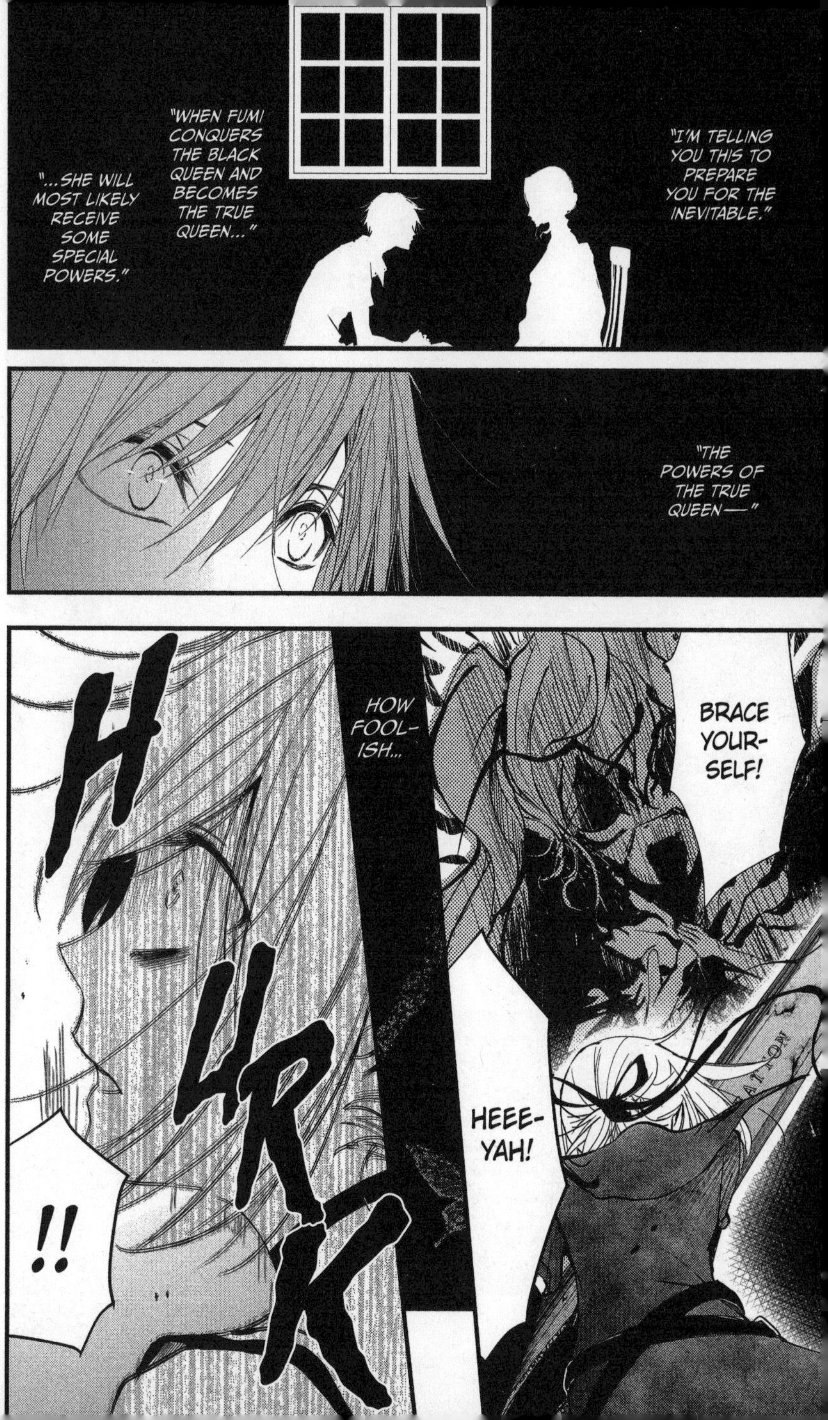
"I'M TELLING YOU THIS TO PREPARE YOU FOR THE INEVITABLE."
"WHEN FUMI CONQUERS THE BLACK QUEEN AND BECOMES THE TRUE QUEEN..."
"...SHE WILL MOST LIKELY RECEIVE SOME SPECIAL POWERS."
"THE POWERS OF THE TRUE QUEEN—"
BRACE YOUR-SELF!
HEEE-YAH!
HOW FOOL-ISH...
HURK
!!

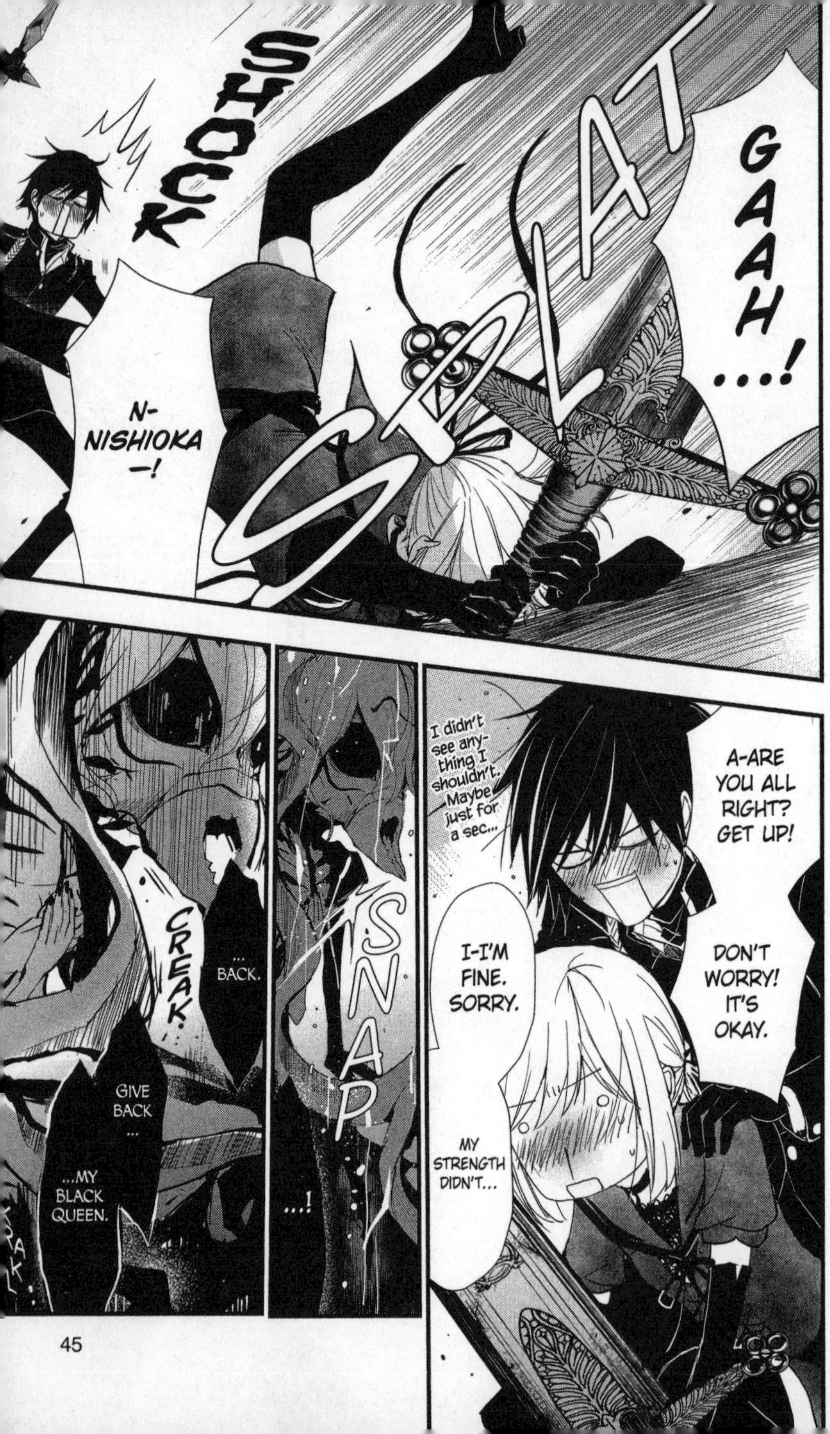
GAAH...!
SHOCK
N-NISHIOKA—!
A-ARE YOU ALL RIGHT? GET UP!
I didn't see anything I shouldn't. Maybe just for a sec...
DON'T WORRY! IT'S OKAY.
I-I'M FINE. SORRY.
MY STRENGTH DIDN'T...
SNAP
...!
CREAK
...BACK.
GIVE BACK...
...MY BLACK QUEEN.

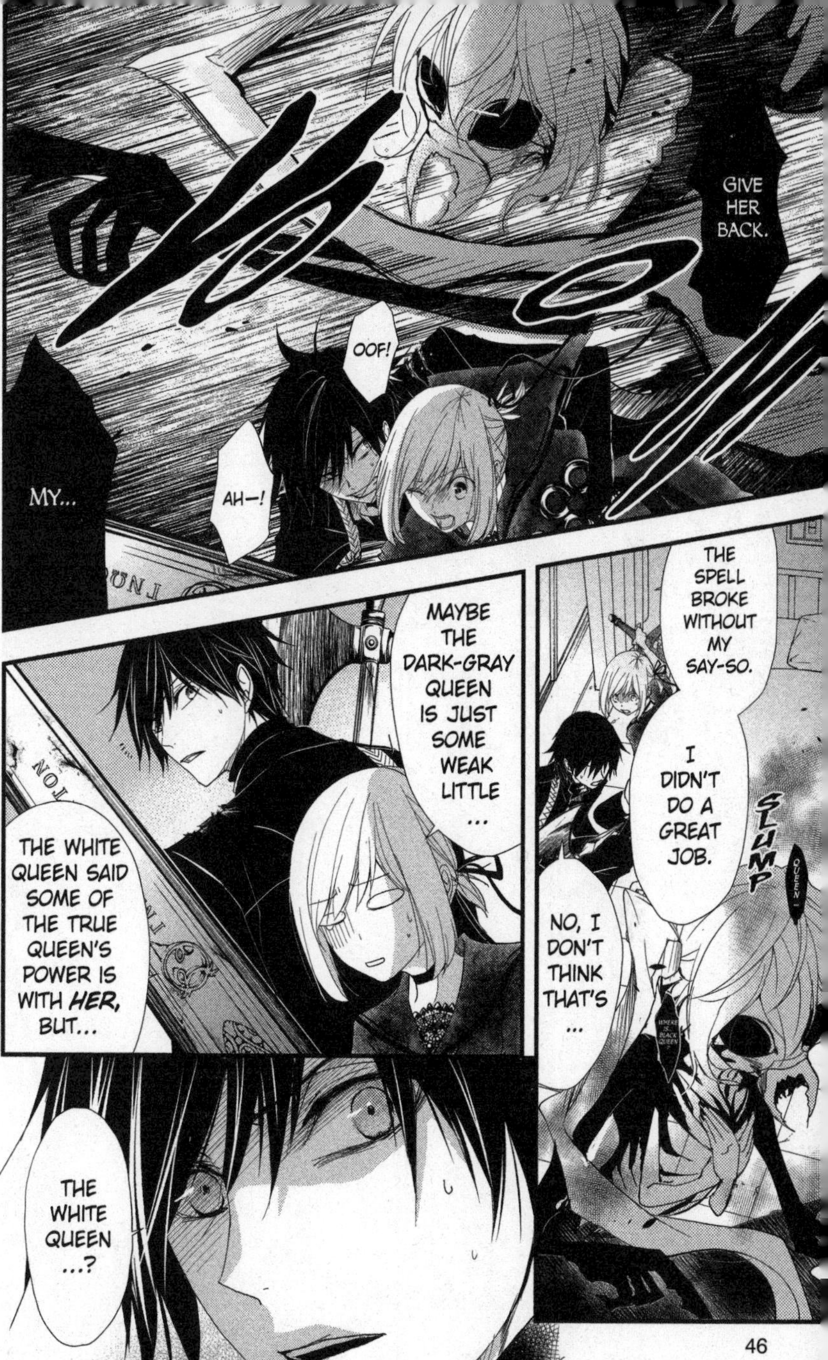

GIVE HER BACK.
OOF!
AH—!
MY...
THE SPELL BROKE WITHOUT MY SAY-SO.
I DIDN'T DO A GREAT JOB.
SLUMP
QUEEN—
NO, I DON'T THINK THAT'S ...
MAYBE THE DARK-GRAY QUEEN IS JUST SOME WEAK LITTLE ...
THE WHITE QUEEN SAID SOME OF THE TRUE QUEEN'S POWER IS WITH *HER*, BUT...
THE WHITE QUEEN ...?

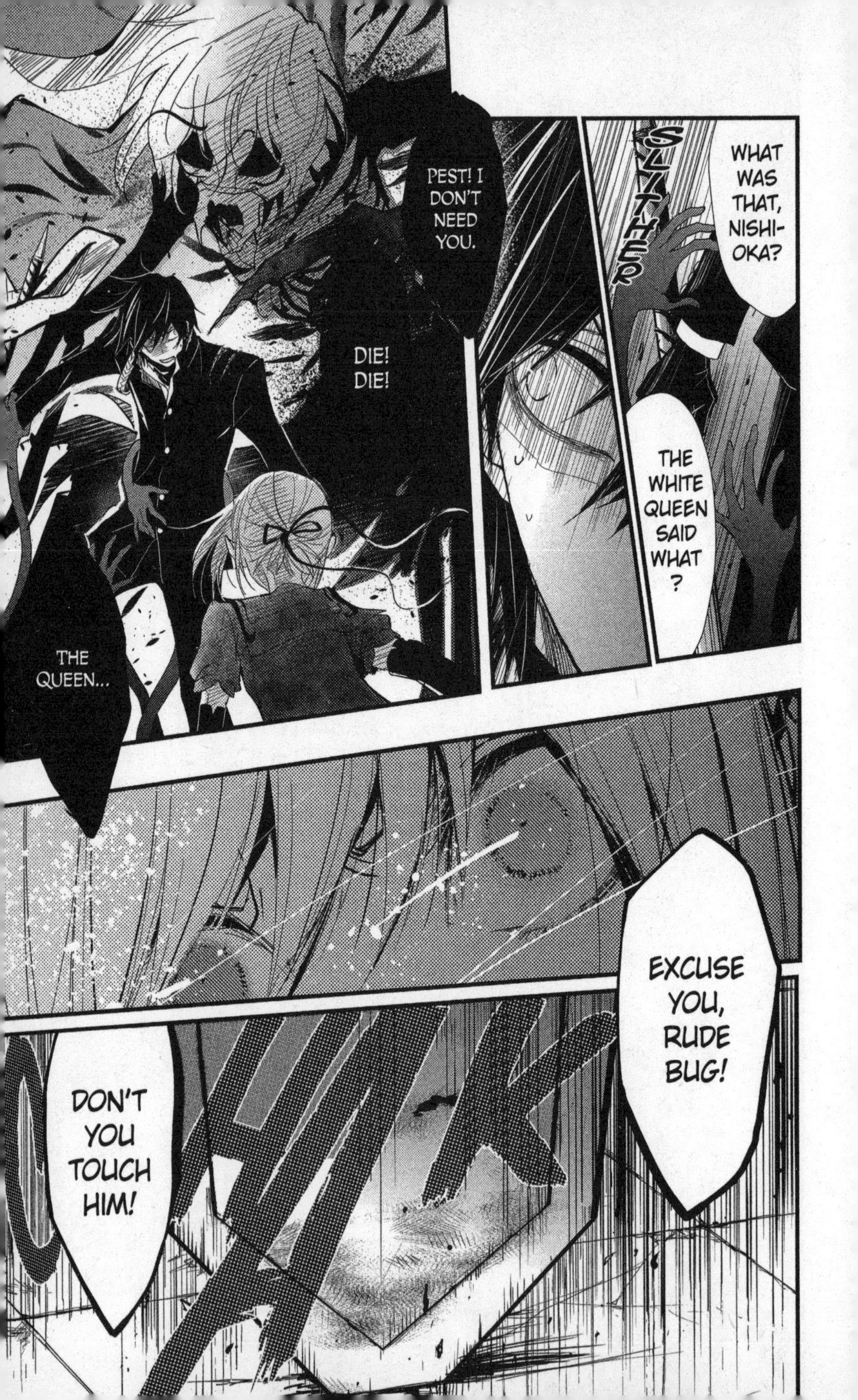
WHAT WAS THAT, NISHI-OKA?
SLITHER
THE WHITE QUEEN SAID WHAT?
PEST! I DON'T NEED YOU.
DIE! DIE!
THE QUEEN...
EXCUSE YOU, RUDE BUG!
DON'T YOU TOUCH HIM!

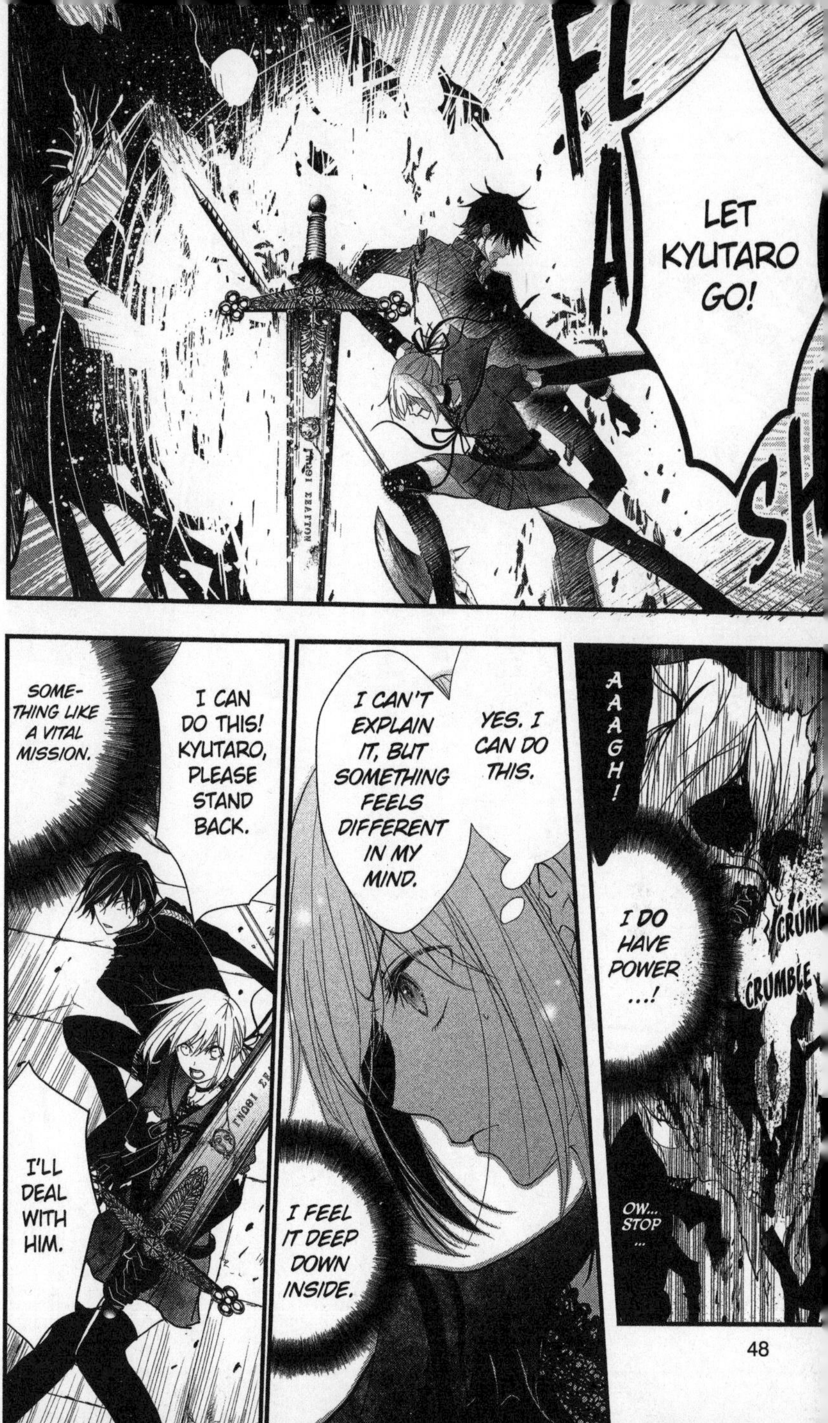
FLASH
LET KYUTARO GO!
AAAGH!
I DO HAVE POWER...!
CRUMB
CRUMBLE
OW... STOP...
YES. I CAN DO THIS.
I CAN'T EXPLAIN IT, BUT SOMETHING FEELS DIFFERENT IN MY MIND.
I FEEL IT DEEP DOWN INSIDE.
I CAN DO THIS! KYUTARO, PLEASE STAND BACK.
SOME-THING LIKE A VITAL MISSION.
I'LL DEAL WITH HIM.

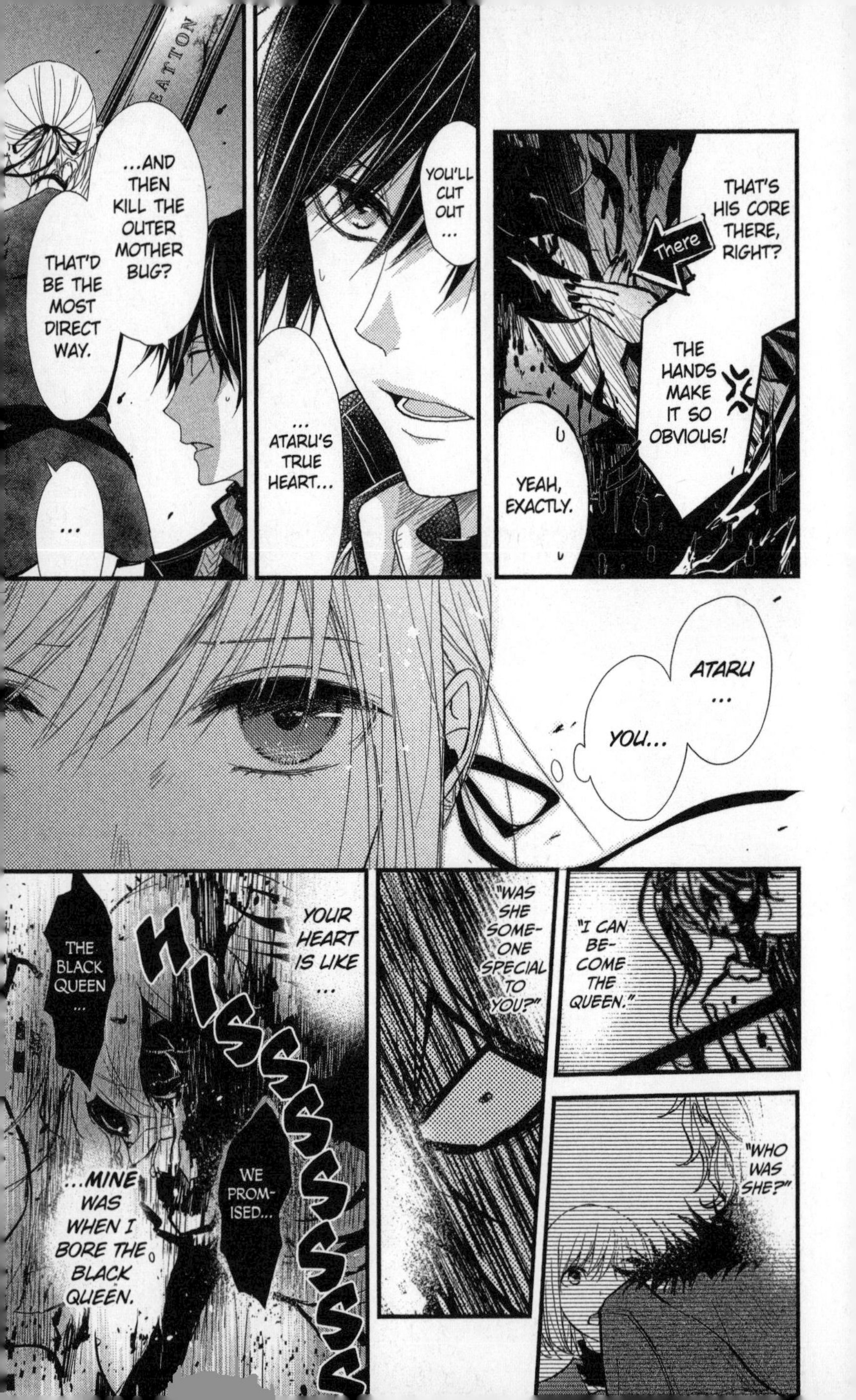
THAT'S HIS CORE THERE, RIGHT?
There
THE HANDS MAKE IT SO OBVIOUS!
YEAH, EXACTLY.
YOU'LL CUT OUT...
...ATARU'S TRUE HEART...
...AND THEN KILL THE OUTER MOTHER BUG?
THAT'D BE THE MOST DIRECT WAY.
...
ATARU... YOU...
"I CAN BECOME THE QUEEN."
"WHO WAS SHE?"
"WAS SHE SOMEONE SPECIAL TO YOU?"
YOUR HEART IS LIKE...
THE BLACK QUEEN...
HISSSSSSS
...MINE WAS WHEN I BORE THE BLACK QUEEN.
WE PROMISED...

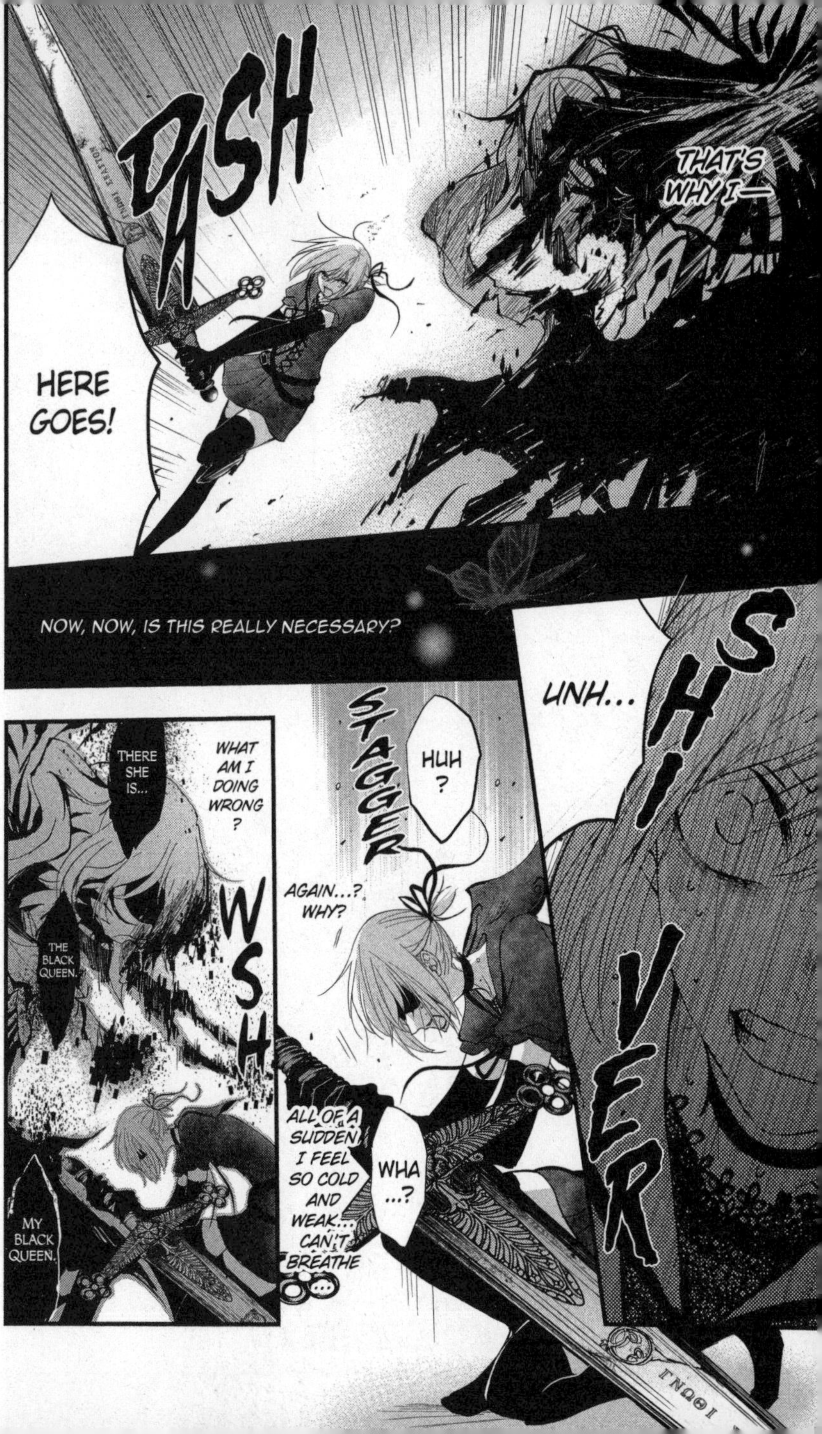
THAT'S WHY I—
DASH
HERE GOES!
NOW, NOW, IS THIS REALLY NECESSARY?
SHIVER
UNH...
HUH?
STAGGER
AGAIN...? WHY?
WHA...?
ALL OF A SUDDEN I FEEL SO COLD AND WEAK... CAN'T BREATHE...
WHAT AM I DOING WRONG?
THERE SHE IS...
WSH
THE BLACK QUEEN.
MY BLACK QUEEN.

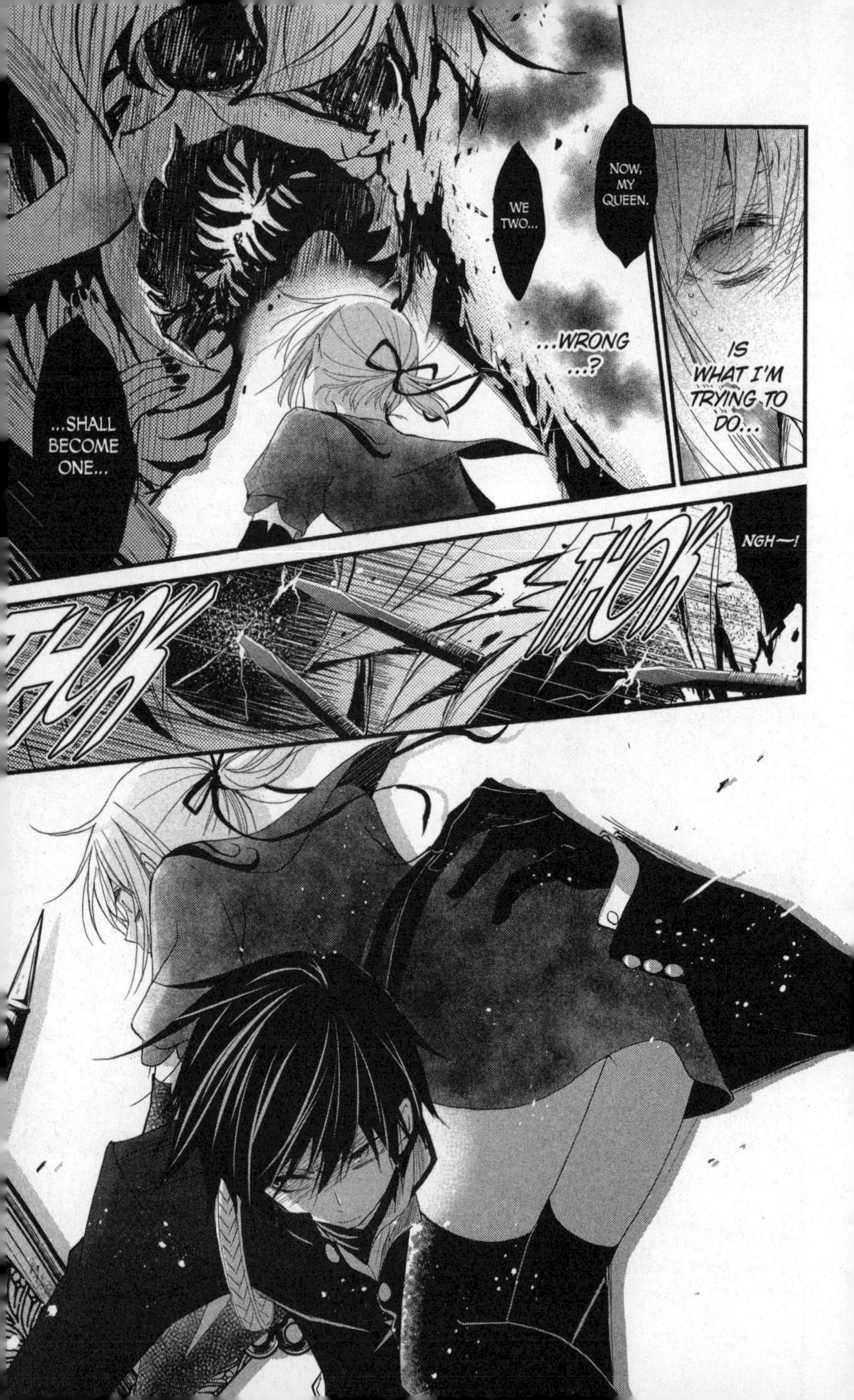
Now, my queen.
We two...
...shall become one...
Is what I'm trying to do...
...wrong ...?
Ngh—!

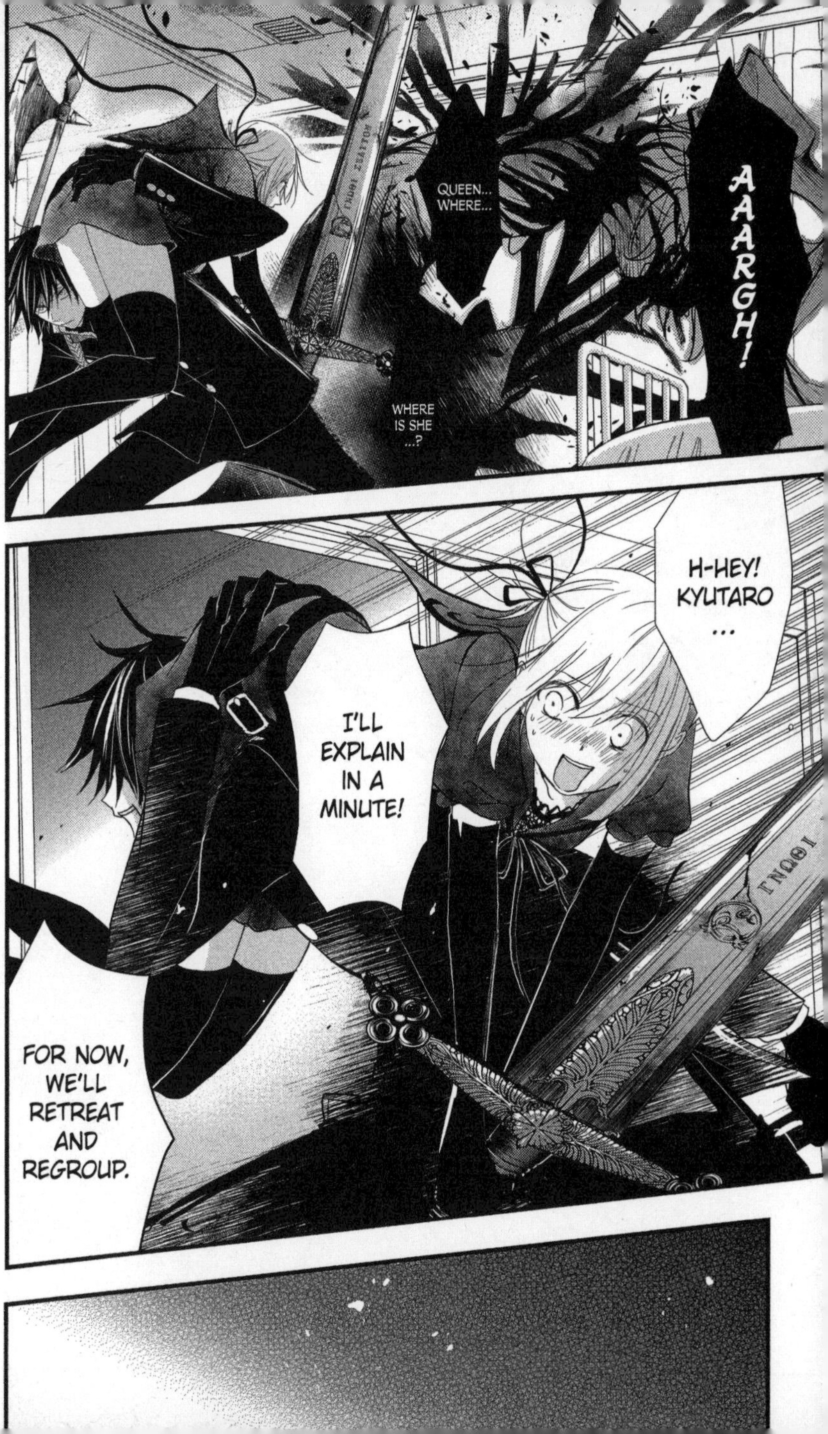
AAAARGH!
QUEEN... WHERE...
WHERE IS SHE ...?
H-HEY! KYUTARO ...
I'LL EXPLAIN IN A MINUTE!
FOR NOW, WE'LL RETREAT AND REGROUP.

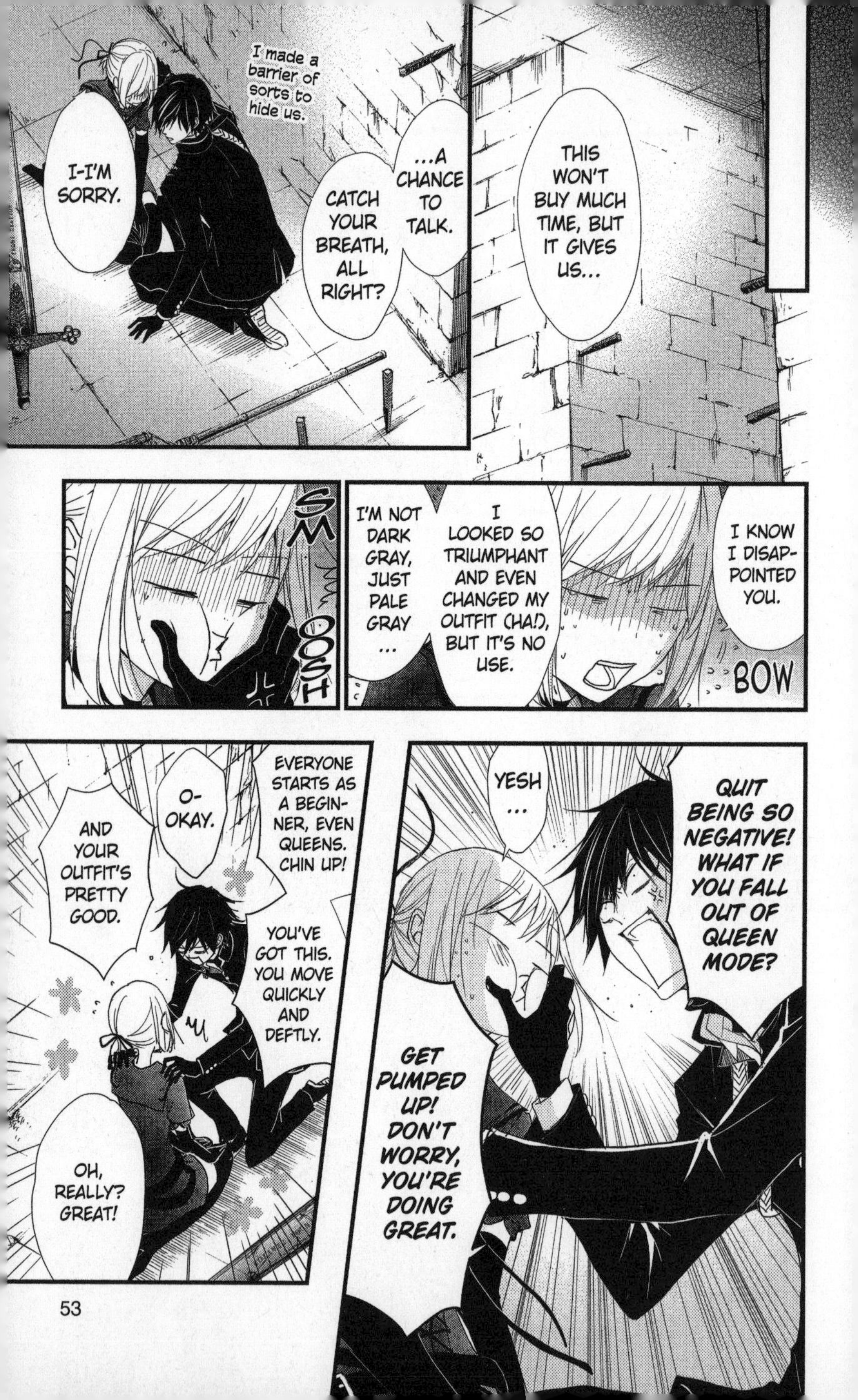
THIS WON'T BUY MUCH TIME, BUT IT GIVES US...
...A CHANCE TO TALK.
CATCH YOUR BREATH, ALL RIGHT?
I made a barrier of sorts to hide us.
I-I'M SORRY.
I KNOW I DISAPPOINTED YOU.
BOW
I LOOKED SO TRIUMPHANT AND EVEN CHANGED MY OUTFIT (HA!), BUT IT'S NO USE.
I'M NOT DARK GRAY, JUST PALE GRAY...
SMOOSH
QUIT BEING SO NEGATIVE! WHAT IF YOU FALL OUT OF QUEEN MODE?
YESH...
GET PUMPED UP! DON'T WORRY, YOU'RE DOING GREAT.
EVERYONE STARTS AS A BEGINNER, EVEN QUEENS. CHIN UP!
O-OKAY.
AND YOUR OUTFIT'S PRETTY GOOD.
YOU'VE GOT THIS. YOU MOVE QUICKLY AND DEFTLY.
OH, REALLY? GREAT!

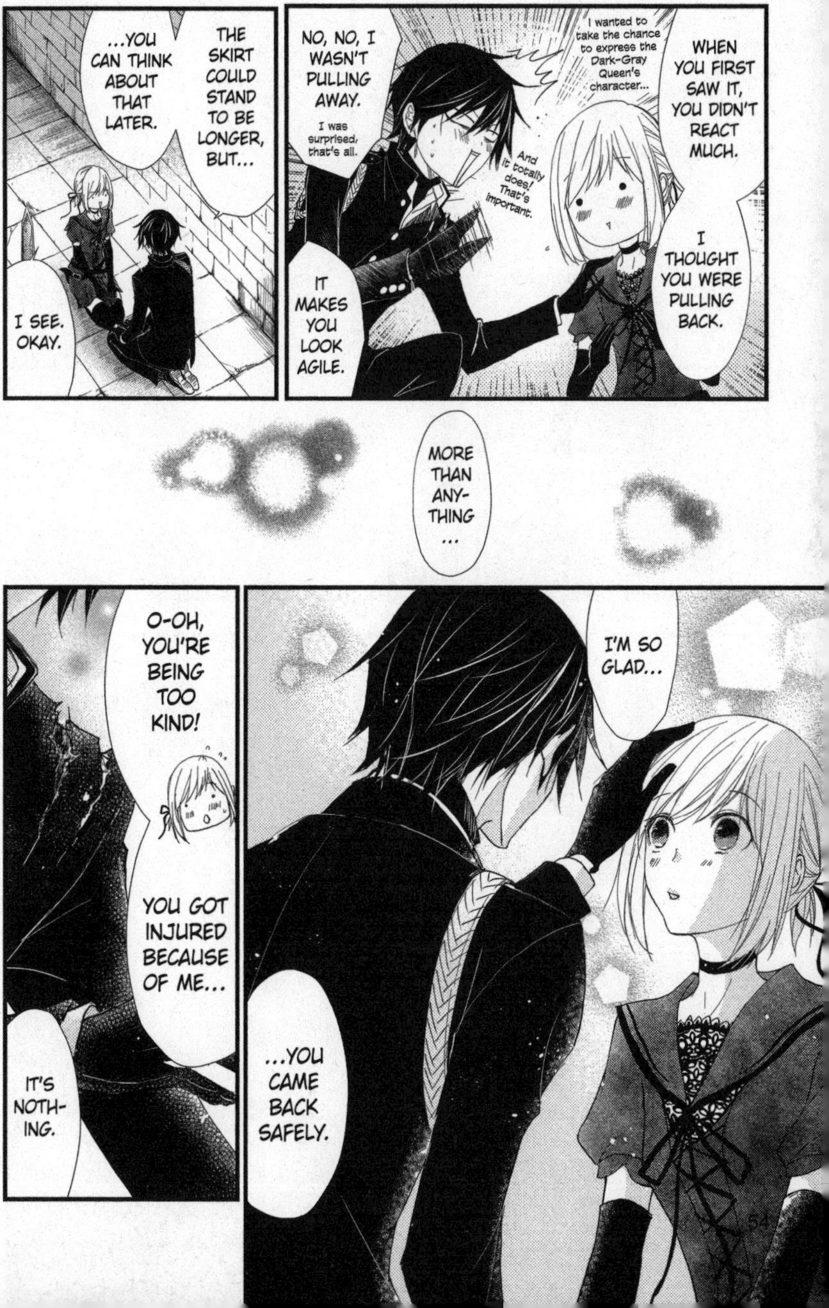
WHEN YOU FIRST SAW IT, YOU DIDN'T REACT MUCH.
I wanted to take the chance to express the Dark-Gray Queen's character...
NO, NO, I WASN'T PULLING AWAY.
I was surprised, that's all.
I THOUGHT YOU WERE PULLING BACK.
And it totally does! That's important.
IT MAKES YOU LOOK AGILE.
THE SKIRT COULD STAND TO BE LONGER, BUT...
...YOU CAN THINK ABOUT THAT LATER.
I SEE. OKAY.
MORE THAN ANYTHING...
I'M SO GLAD...
...YOU CAME BACK SAFELY.
O-OH, YOU'RE BEING TOO KIND!
YOU GOT INJURED BECAUSE OF ME...
IT'S NOTHING.

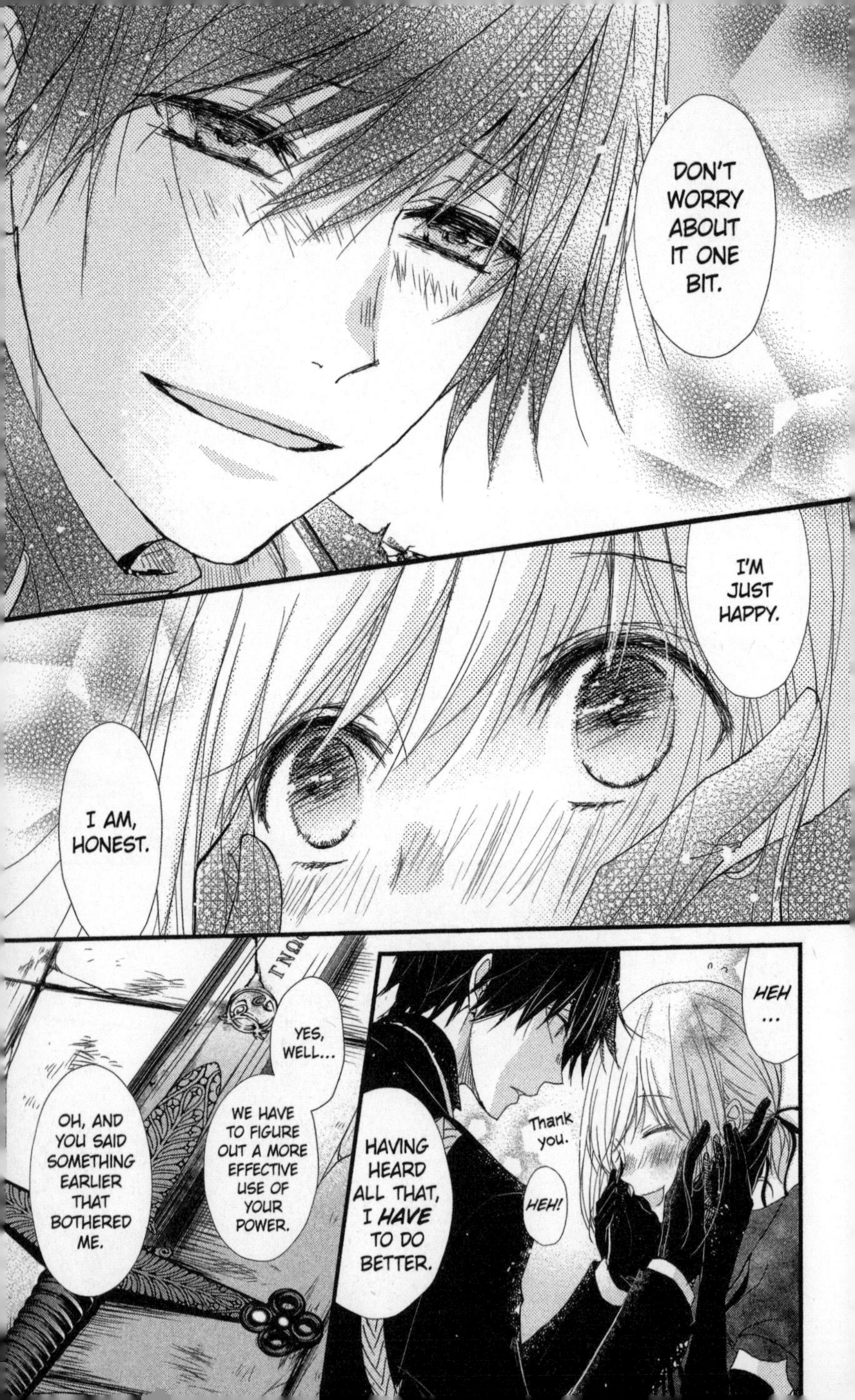
DON'T WORRY ABOUT IT ONE BIT.
I'M JUST HAPPY.
I AM, HONEST.
HEH...
Thank you.
HEH!
HAVING HEARD ALL THAT, I *HAVE* TO DO BETTER.
YES, WELL...
WE HAVE TO FIGURE OUT A MORE EFFECTIVE USE OF YOUR POWER.
OH, AND YOU SAID SOMETHING EARLIER THAT BOTHERED ME.

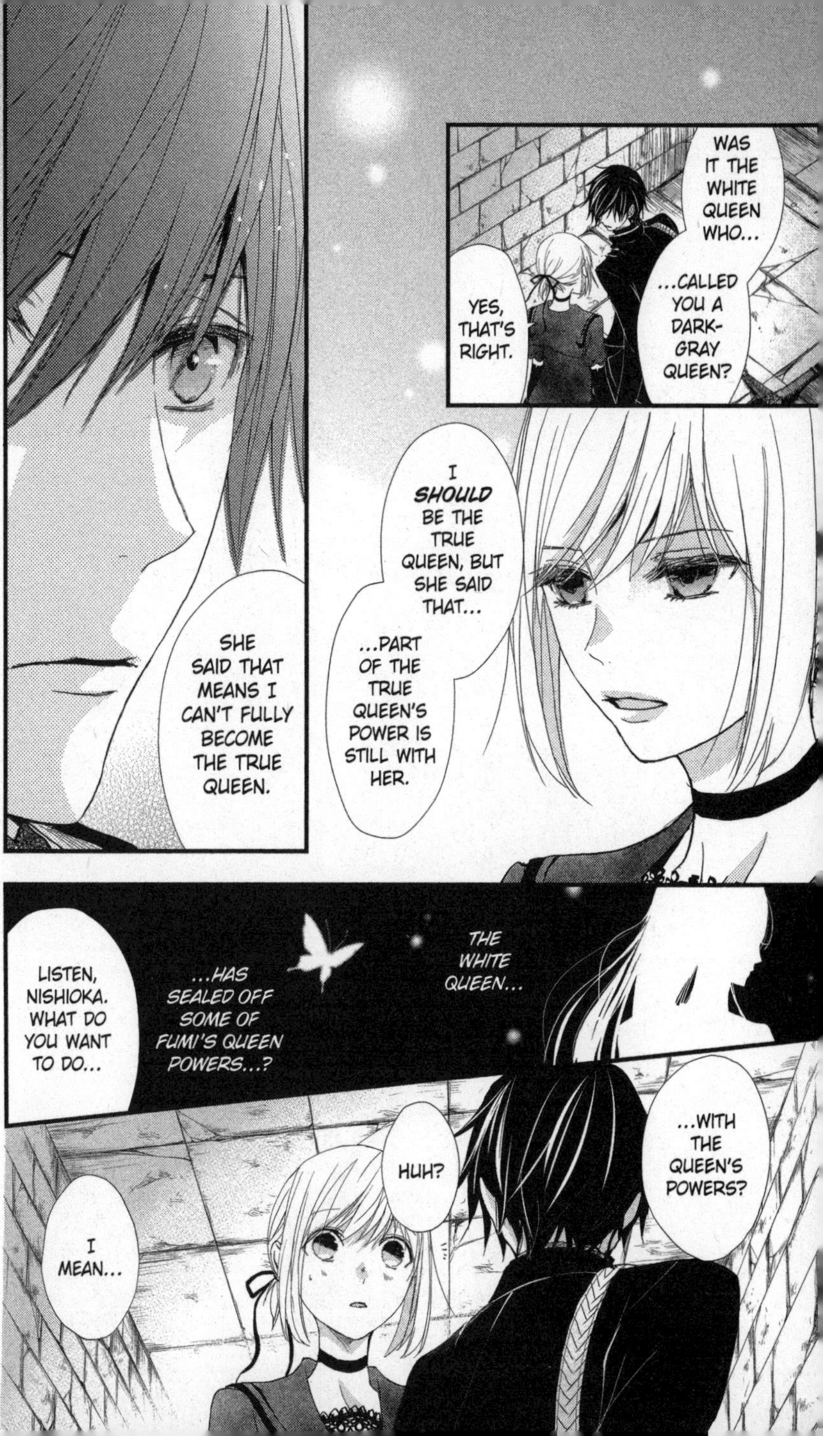
WAS IT THE WHITE QUEEN WHO...
...CALLED YOU A DARK-GRAY QUEEN?
YES, THAT'S RIGHT.
I *SHOULD* BE THE TRUE QUEEN, BUT SHE SAID THAT...
...PART OF THE TRUE QUEEN'S POWER IS STILL WITH HER.
SHE SAID THAT MEANS I CAN'T FULLY BECOME THE TRUE QUEEN.
THE WHITE QUEEN...
...HAS SEALED OFF SOME OF FUMI'S QUEEN POWERS...?
LISTEN, NISHIOKA. WHAT DO YOU WANT TO DO...
...WITH THE QUEEN'S POWERS?
HUH?
I MEAN...

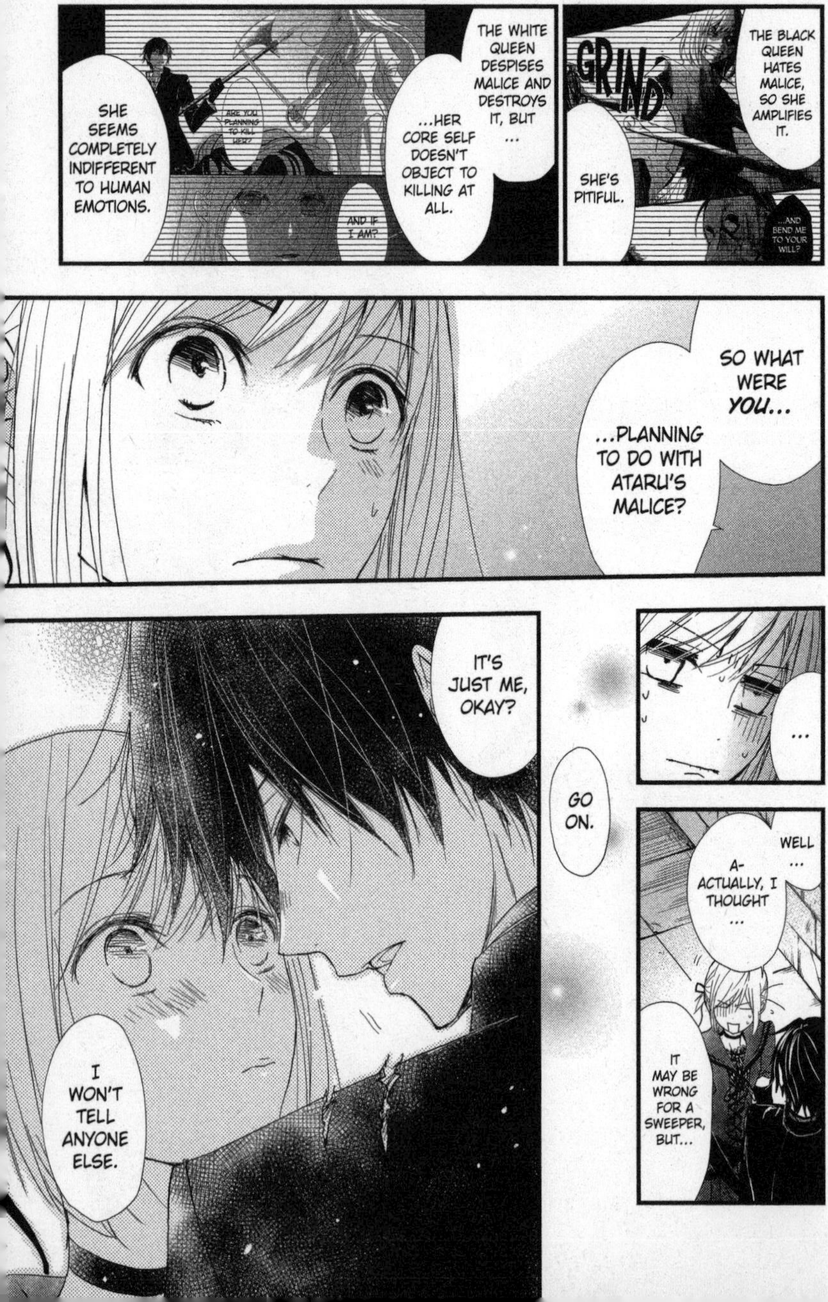
THE BLACK QUEEN HATES MALICE, SO SHE AMPLIFIES IT.
GRIND
...AND BEND ME TO YOUR WILL?
SHE'S PITIFUL.
THE WHITE QUEEN DESPISES MALICE AND DESTROYS IT, BUT ...
...HER CORE SELF DOESN'T OBJECT TO KILLING AT ALL.
ARE YOU PLANNING TO KILL HER?
AND IF I AM?
SHE SEEMS COMPLETELY INDIFFERENT TO HUMAN EMOTIONS.
SO WHAT WERE *YOU*...
...PLANNING TO DO WITH ATARU'S MALICE?
...
WELL ...
A- ACTUALLY, I THOUGHT ...
IT MAY BE WRONG FOR A SWEEPER, BUT...
GO ON.
IT'S JUST ME, OKAY?
I WON'T TELL ANYONE ELSE.

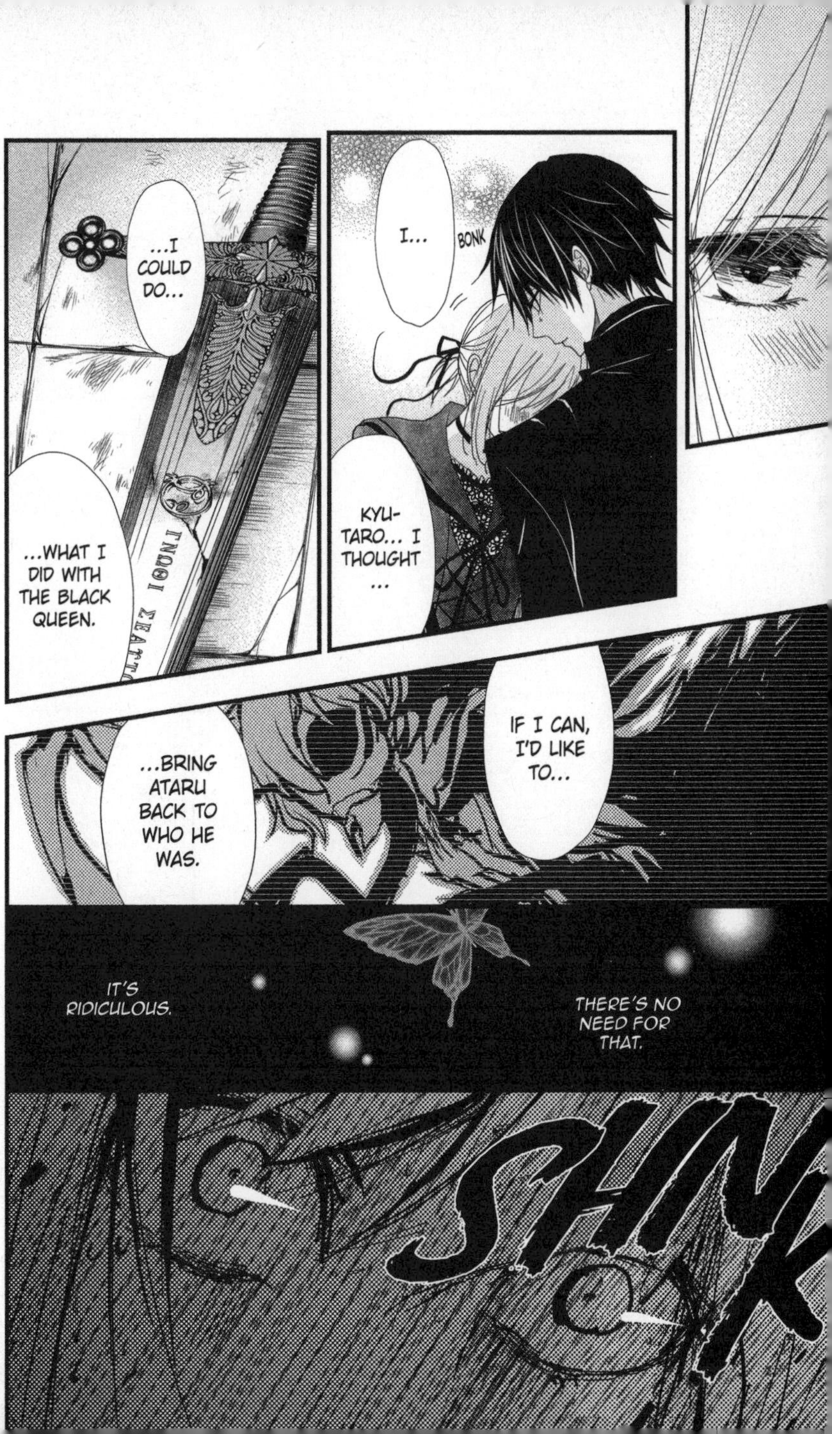
I...
BONK
KYU-TARO... I THOUGHT...
...I COULD DO...
...WHAT I DID WITH THE BLACK QUEEN.
IF I CAN, I'D LIKE TO...
...BRING ATARU BACK TO WHO HE WAS.
THERE'S NO NEED FOR THAT.
IT'S RIDICULOUS.
SHIN

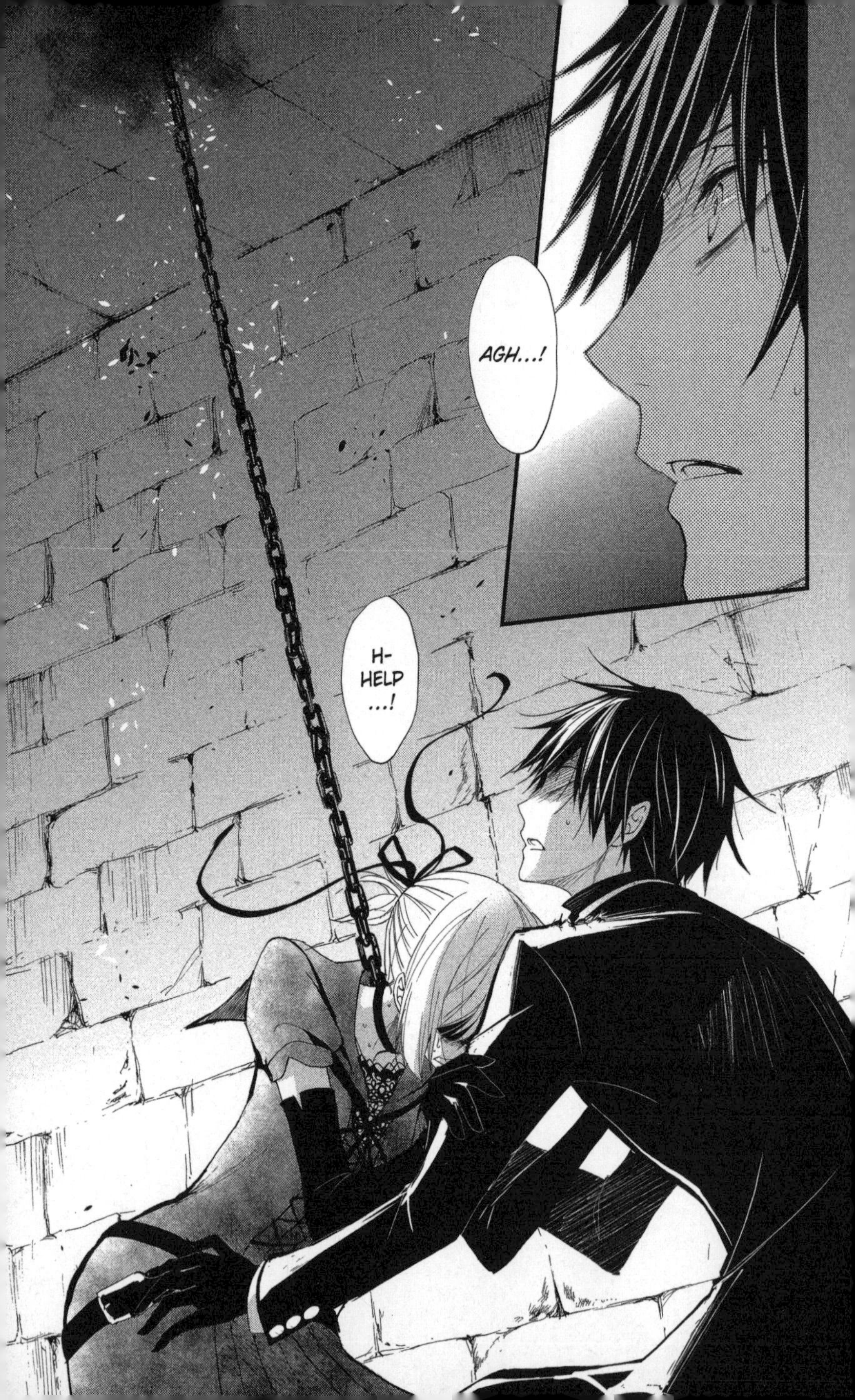
AGH...!
H-HELP ...!

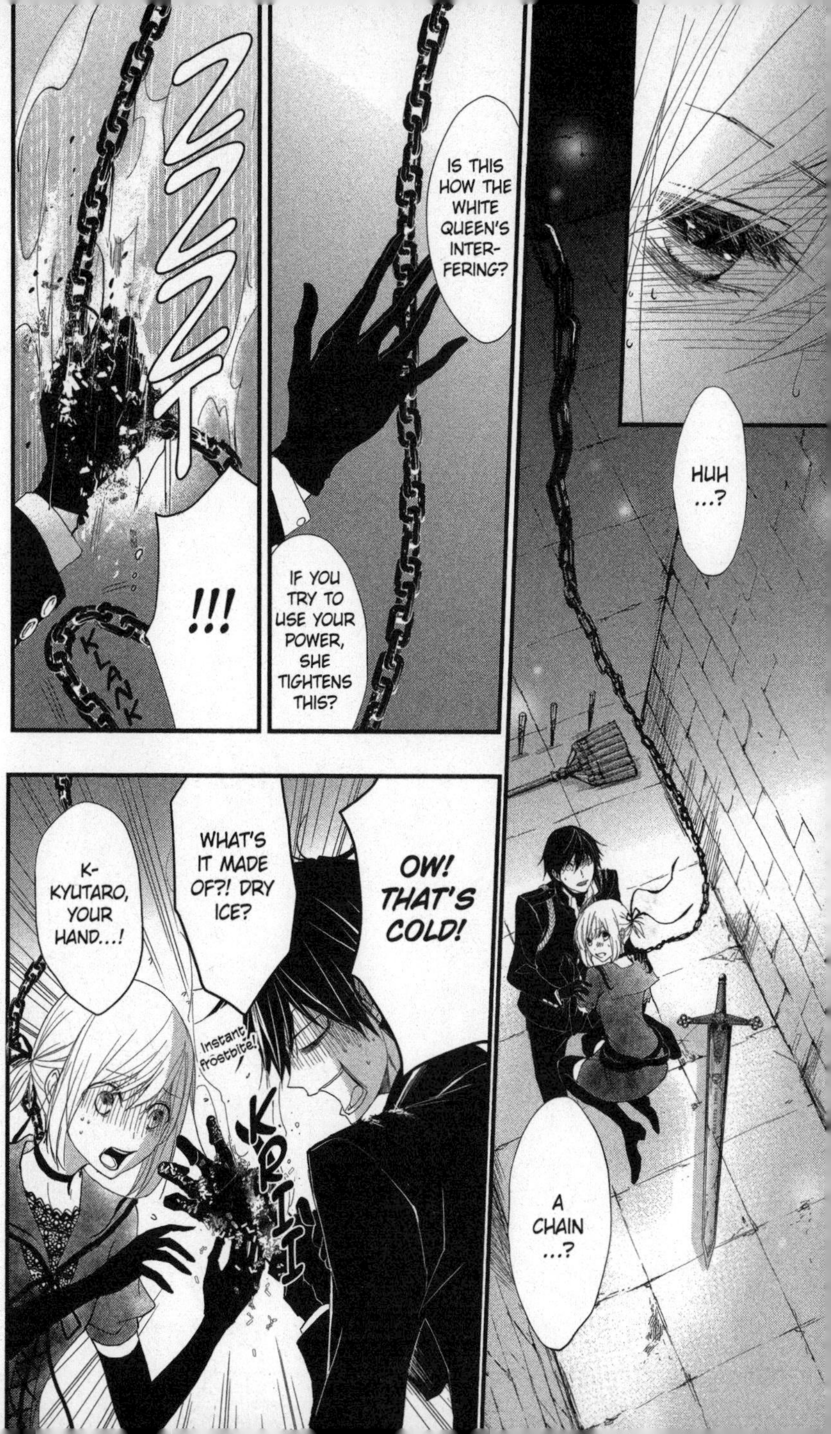
HUH ...?
A CHAIN ...?
IS THIS HOW THE WHITE QUEEN'S INTERFERING?
IF YOU TRY TO USE YOUR POWER, SHE TIGHTENS THIS?
ZZZT
!!!
KLACK
OW! THAT'S COLD!
WHAT'S IT MADE OF?! DRY ICE?
K-KYUTARO, YOUR HAND...!
Instant frostbite!
KRII

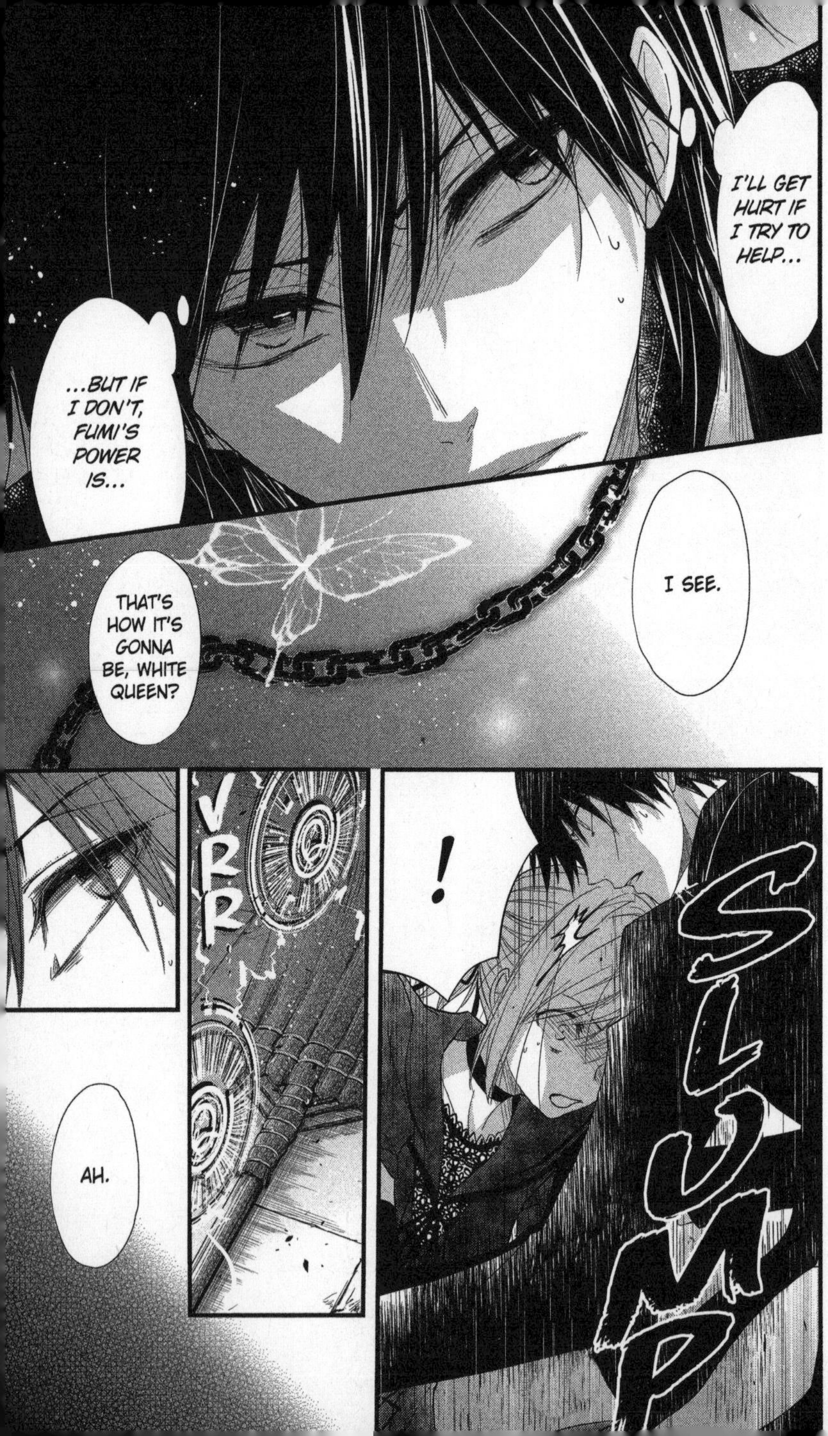
I'LL GET HURT IF I TRY TO HELP...
...BUT IF I DON'T, FUMI'S POWER IS...
I SEE.
THAT'S HOW IT'S GONNA BE, WHITE QUEEN?
SLUMP
!
VRR
AH.

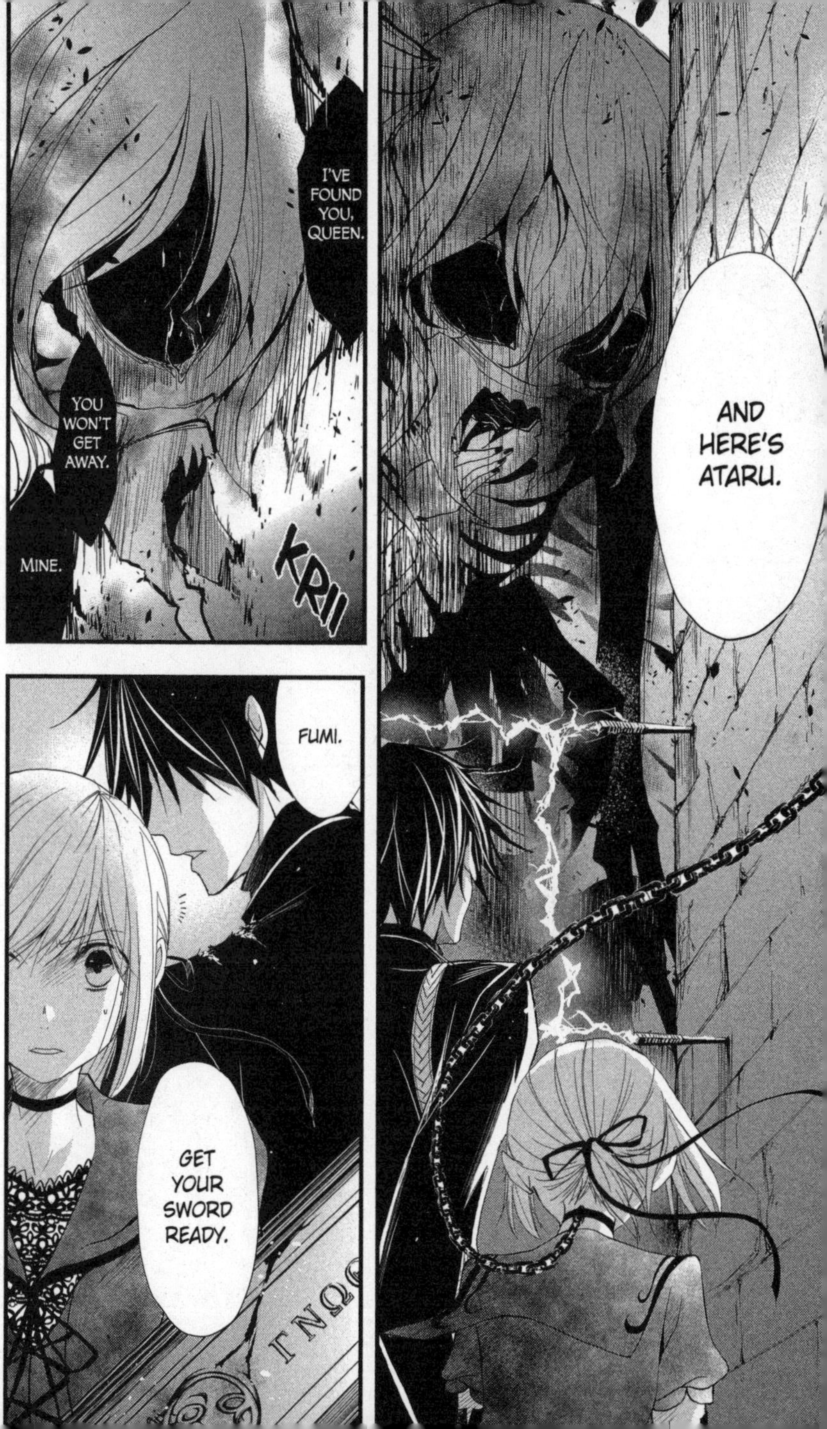
AND HERE'S ATARU.
I'VE FOUND YOU, QUEEN.
YOU WON'T GET AWAY.
MINE.
KRII
FUMI.
GET YOUR SWORD READY.

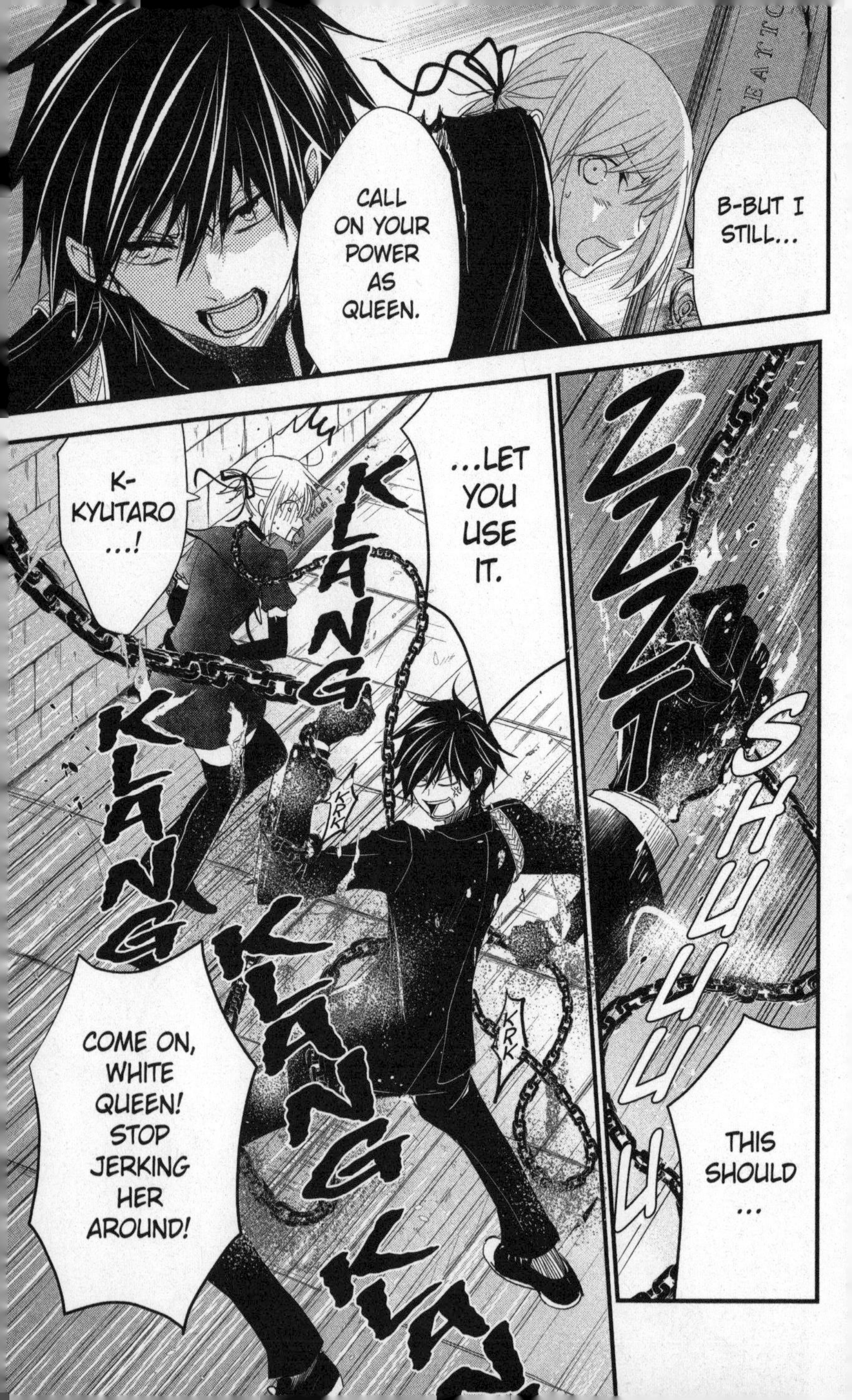
B-BUT I STILL...
CALL ON YOUR POWER AS QUEEN.
ZZZZT
SHUUUUU
THIS SHOULD ...
...LET YOU USE IT.
K-KYUTARO ...!
KLANG
KRK
KLANG
KLANG
KRK
COME ON, WHITE QUEEN! STOP JERKING HER AROUND!
KLA

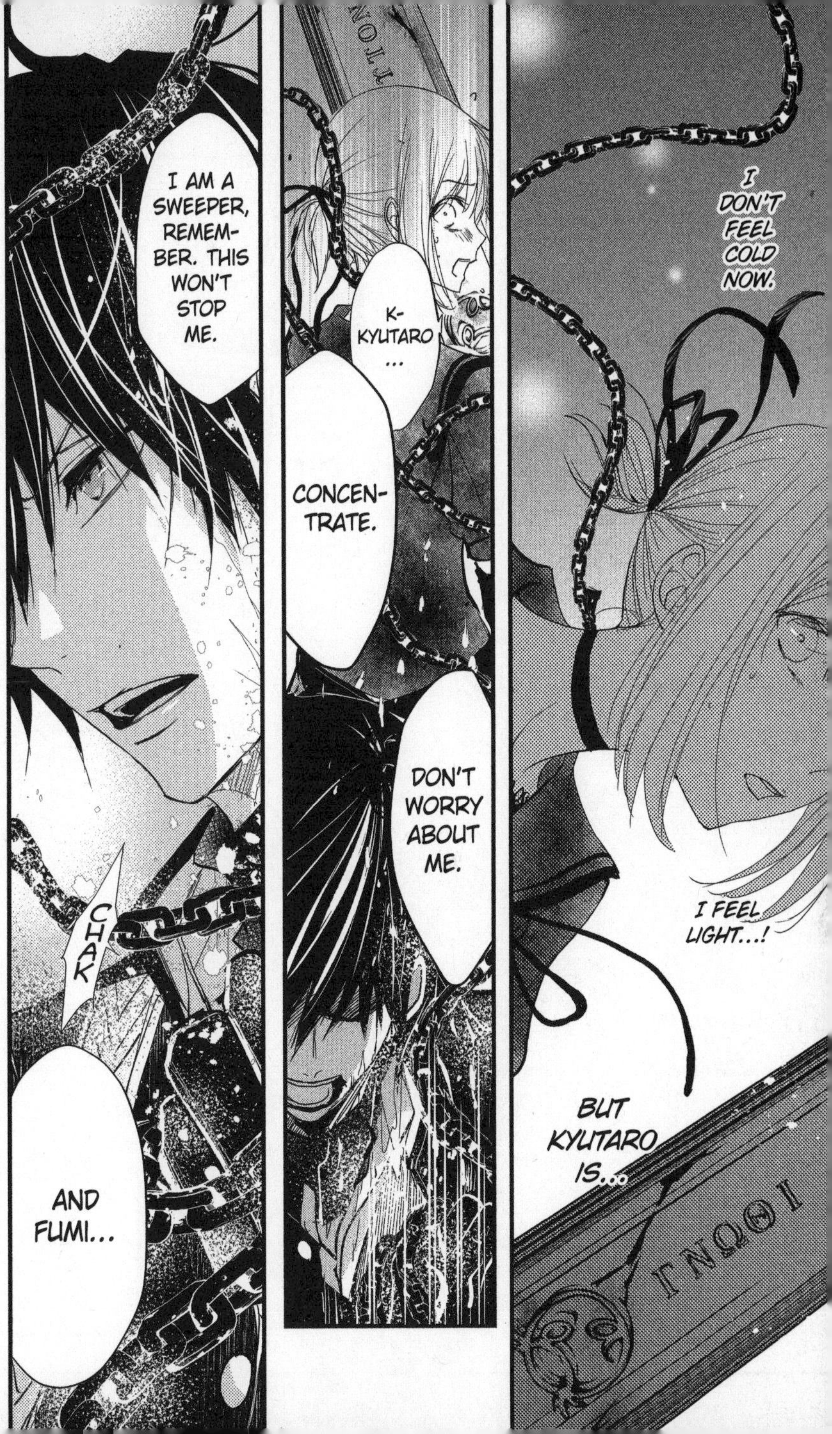
I DON'T FEEL COLD NOW.
I FEEL LIGHT...!
BUT KYUTARO IS...
K-KYUTARO...
CONCENTRATE.
DON'T WORRY ABOUT ME.
I AM A SWEEPER, REMEMBER. THIS WON'T STOP ME.
CHAK
AND FUMI...

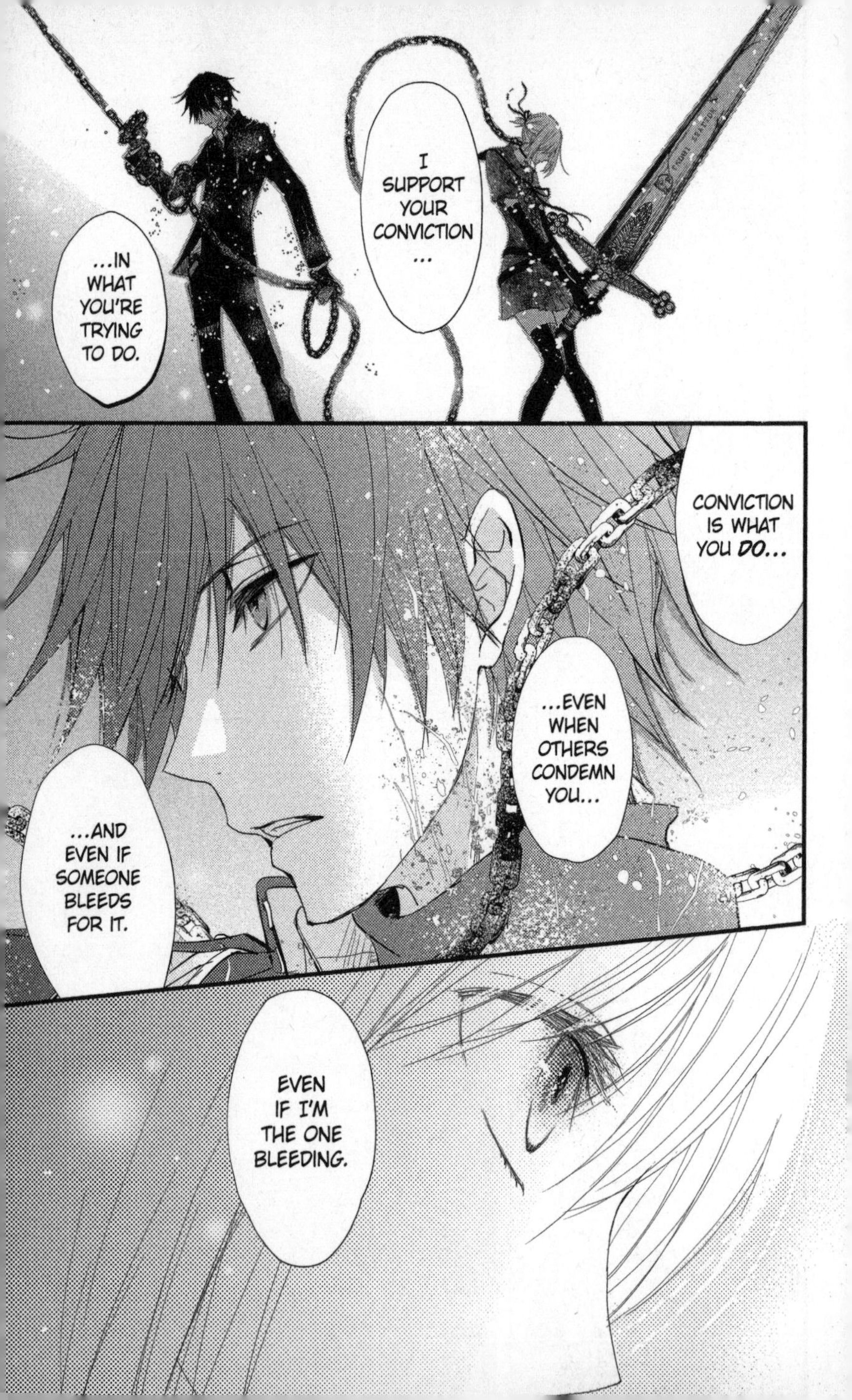
I SUPPORT YOUR CONVICTION...
...IN WHAT YOU'RE TRYING TO DO.
CONVICTION IS WHAT YOU ***DO***...
...EVEN WHEN OTHERS CONDEMN YOU...
...AND EVEN IF SOMEONE BLEEDS FOR IT.
EVEN IF I'M THE ONE BLEEDING.

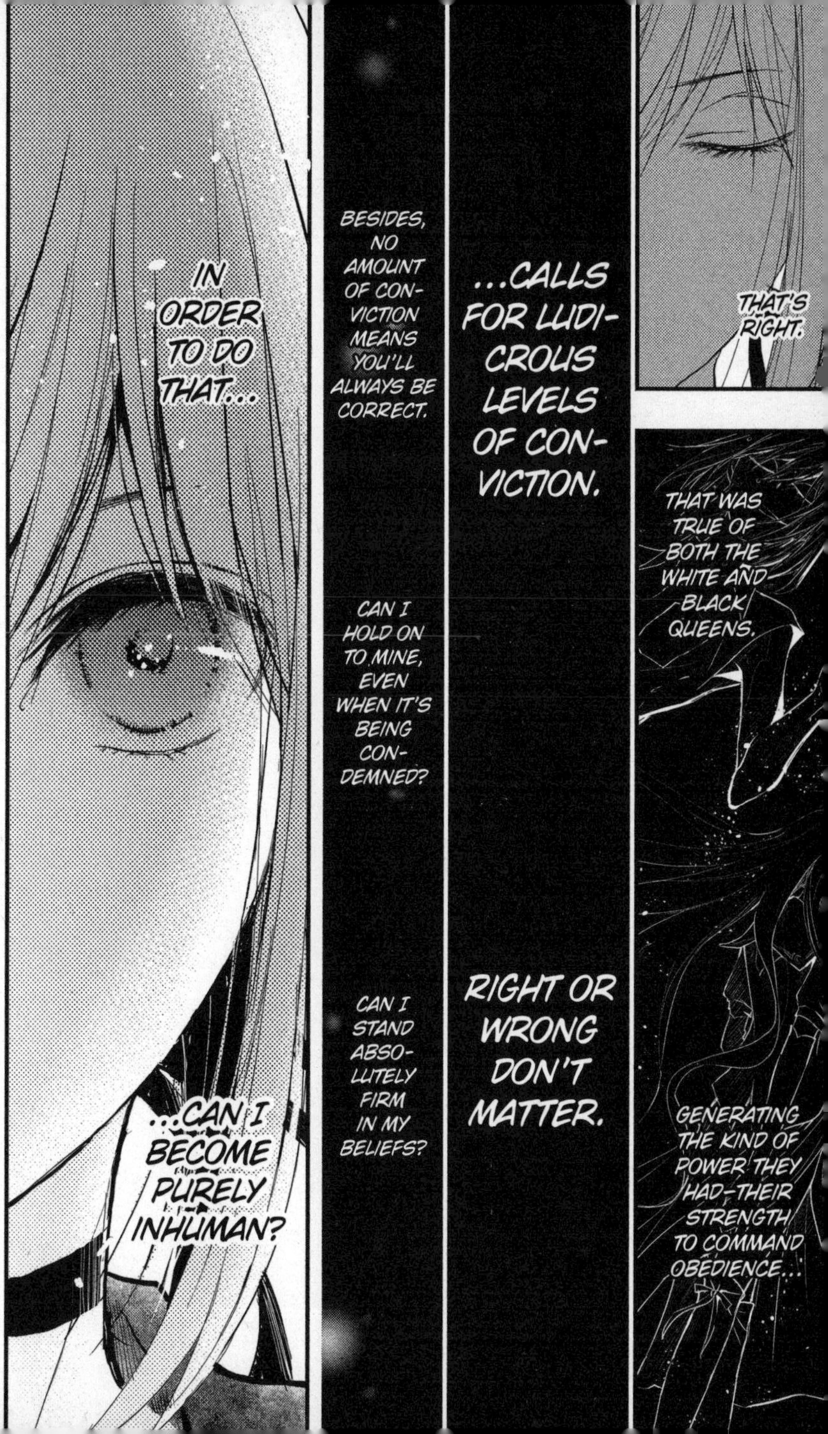
THAT'S RIGHT.
THAT WAS TRUE OF BOTH THE WHITE AND BLACK QUEENS.
GENERATING THE KIND OF POWER THEY HAD—THEIR STRENGTH TO COMMAND OBEDIENCE...
...CALLS FOR LUDICROUS LEVELS OF CONVICTION.
RIGHT OR WRONG DON'T MATTER.
BESIDES, NO AMOUNT OF CONVICTION MEANS YOU'LL ALWAYS BE CORRECT.
CAN I HOLD ON TO MINE, EVEN WHEN IT'S BEING CONDEMNED?
CAN I STAND ABSOLUTELY FIRM IN MY BELIEFS?
IN ORDER TO DO THAT...
...CAN I BECOME PURELY INHUMAN?

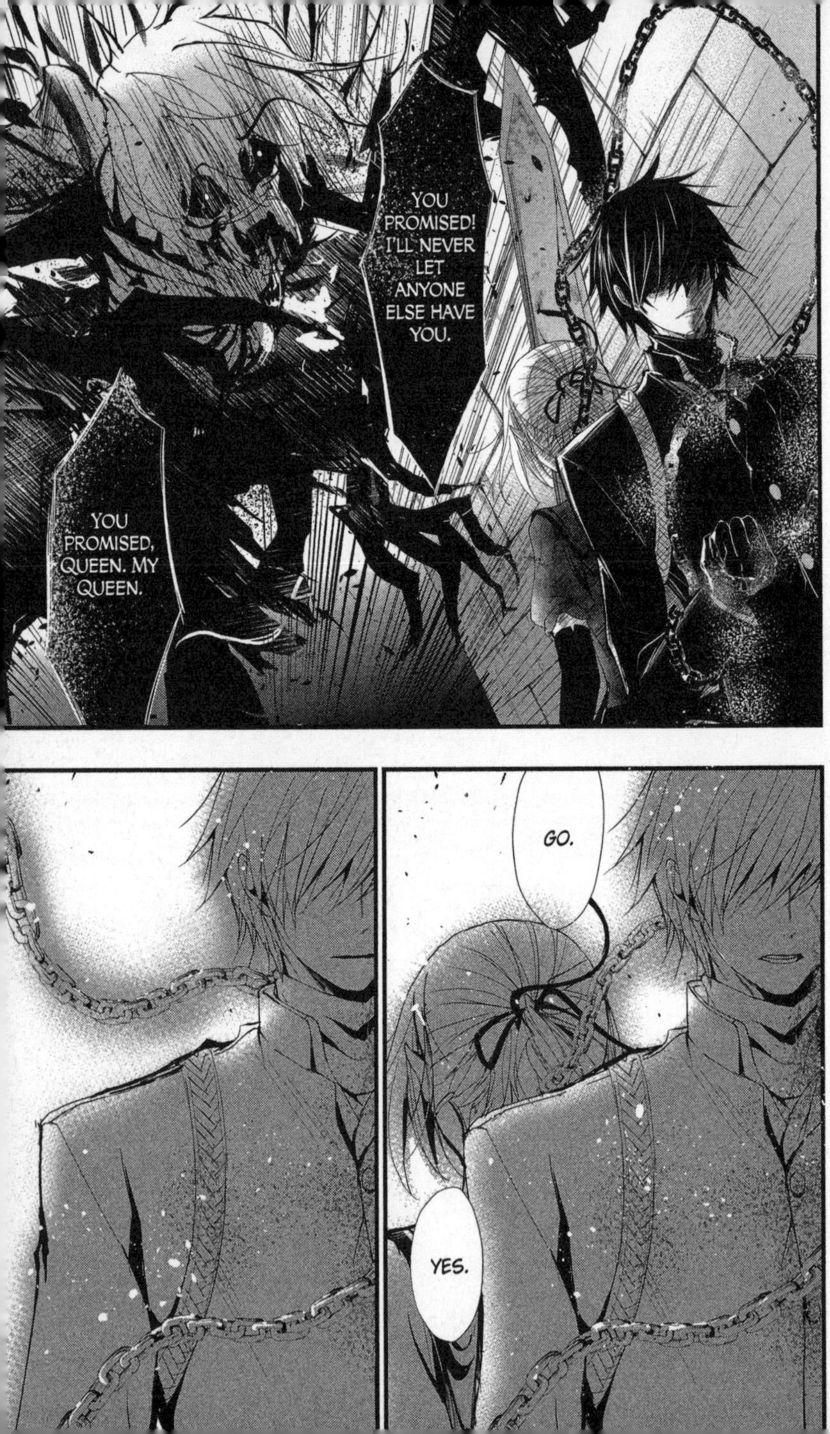
YOU PROMISED! I'LL NEVER LET ANYONE ELSE HAVE YOU.
YOU PROMISED, QUEEN. MY QUEEN.
GO.
YES.

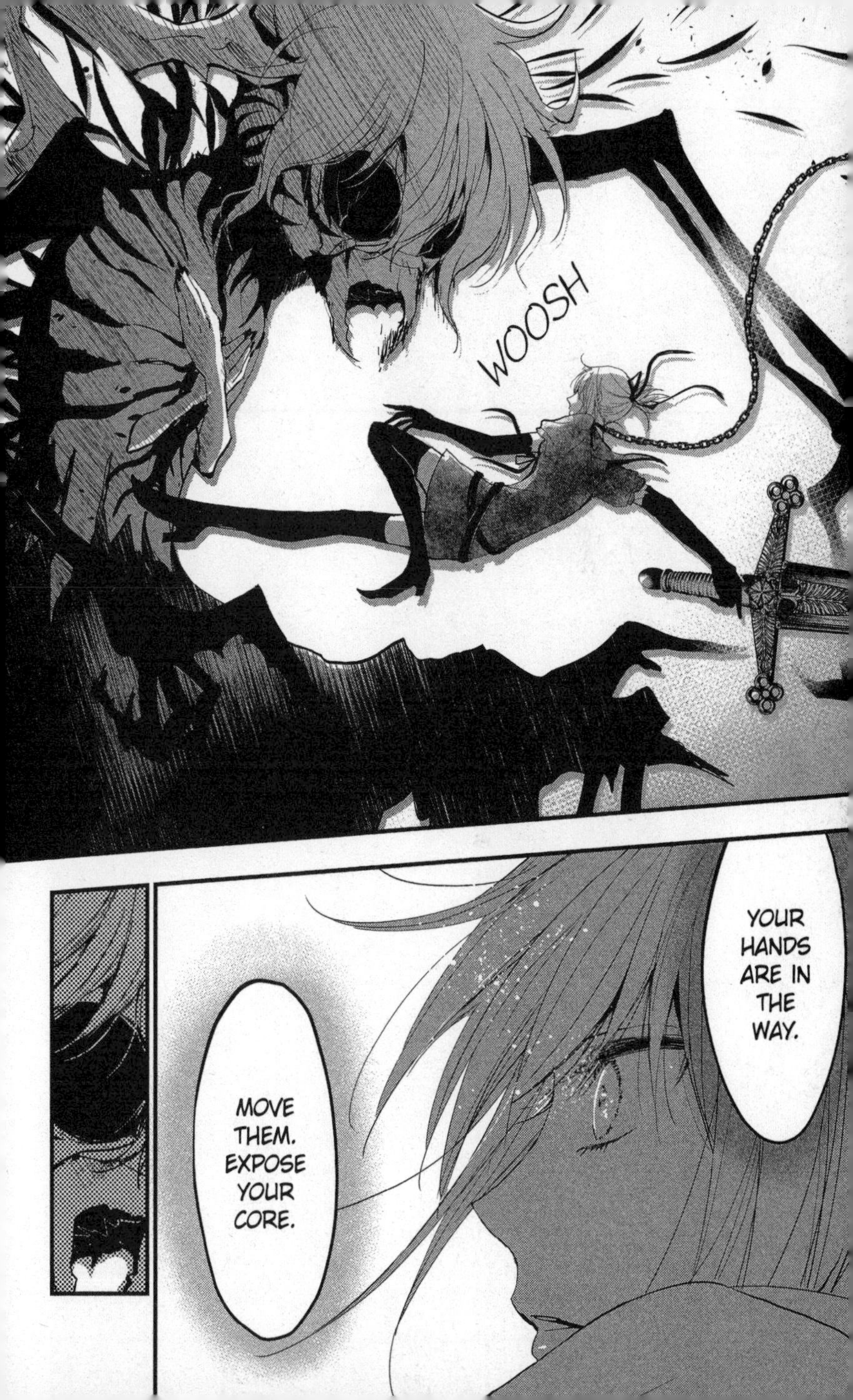
WOOSH
YOUR HANDS ARE IN THE WAY.
MOVE THEM. EXPOSE YOUR CORE.

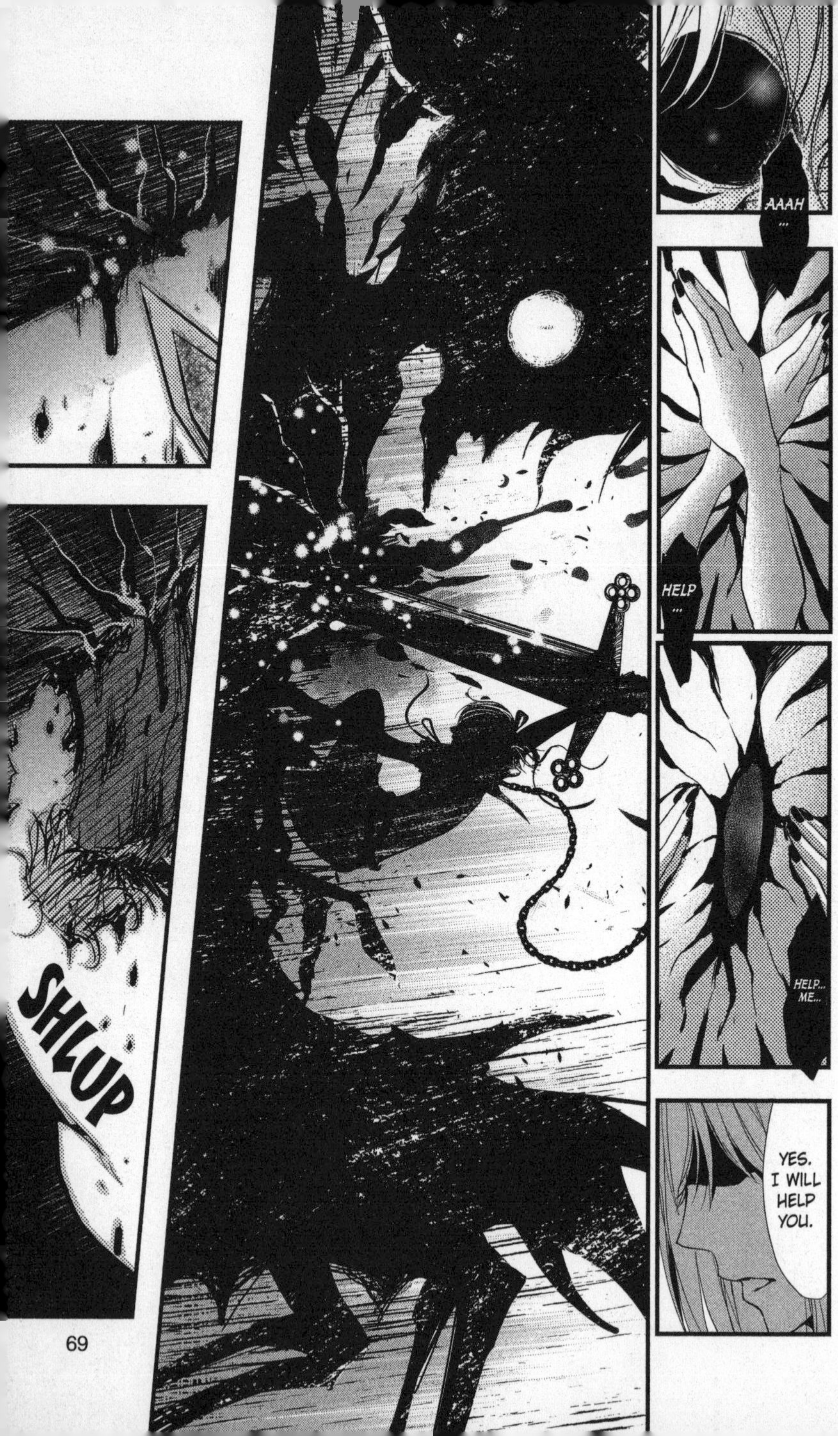
AAAH ...
HELP ...
HELP... ME...
YES. I WILL HELP YOU.
SHLUP

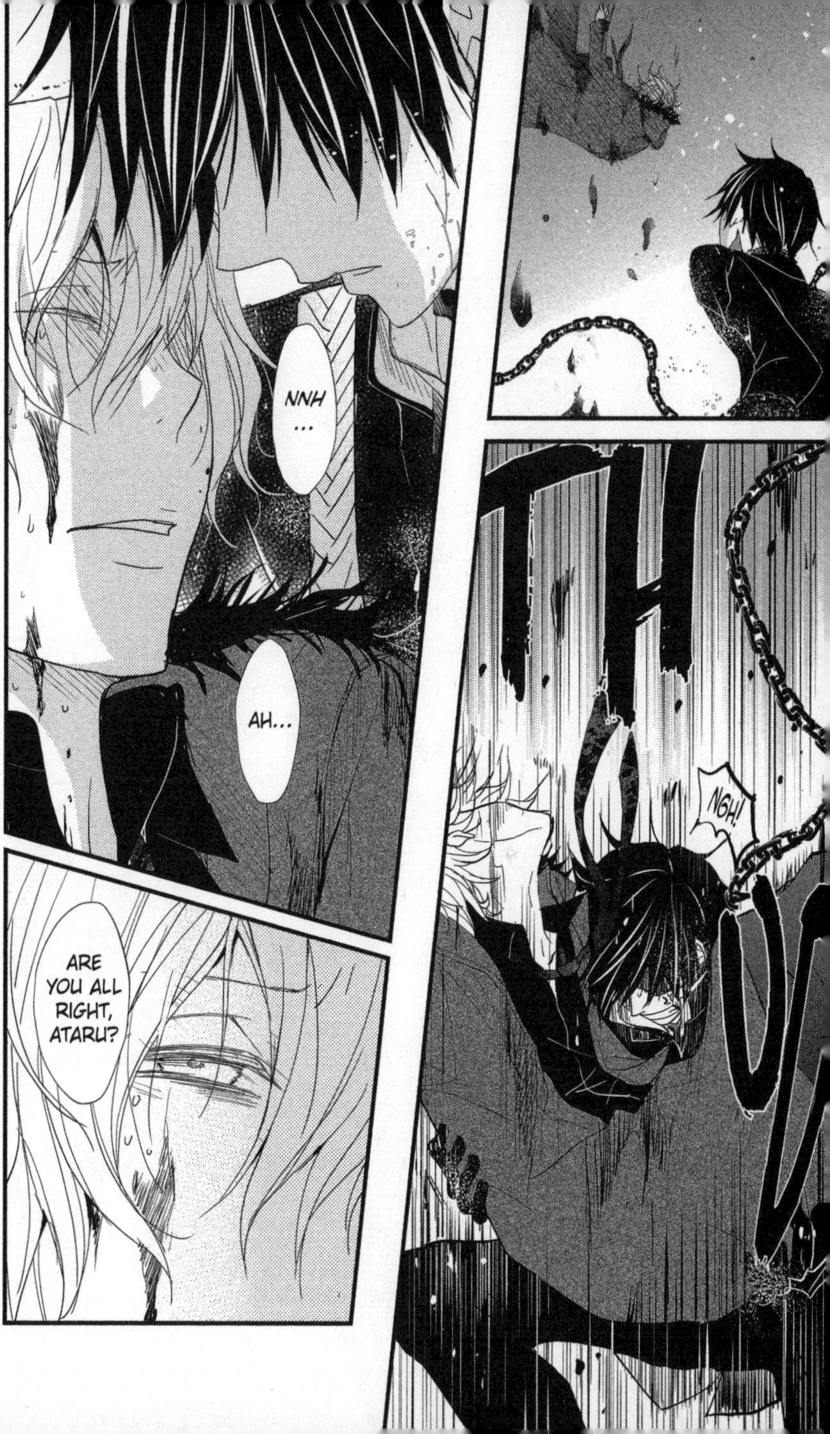
NGH!
NNH ...
AH...
ARE YOU ALL RIGHT, ATARU?

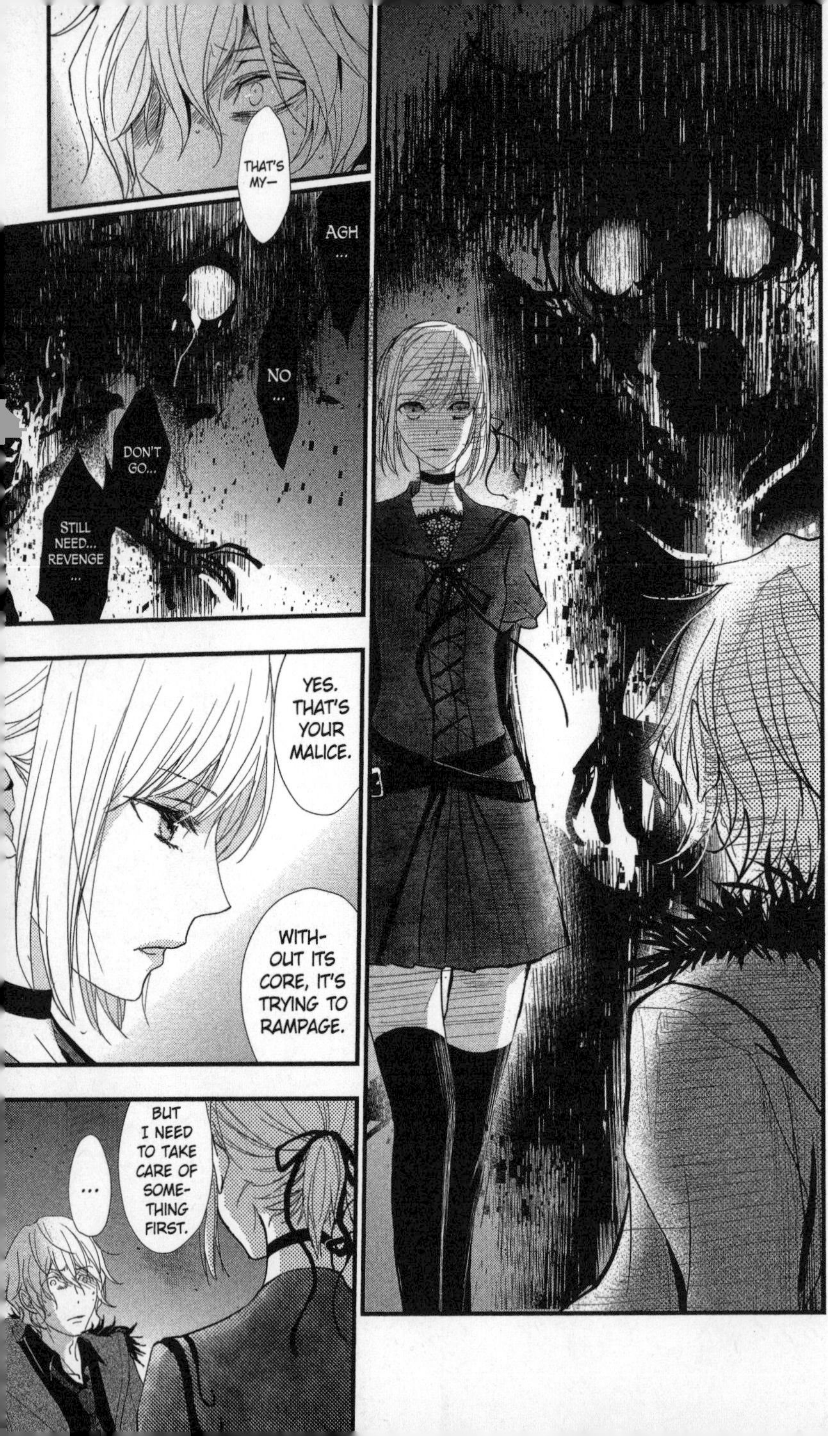
THAT'S MY—
AGH ...
NO ...
DON'T GO...
STILL NEED... REVENGE ...
YES. THAT'S YOUR MALICE.
WITH-OUT ITS CORE, IT'S TRYING TO RAMPAGE.
BUT I NEED TO TAKE CARE OF SOME-THING FIRST.
...

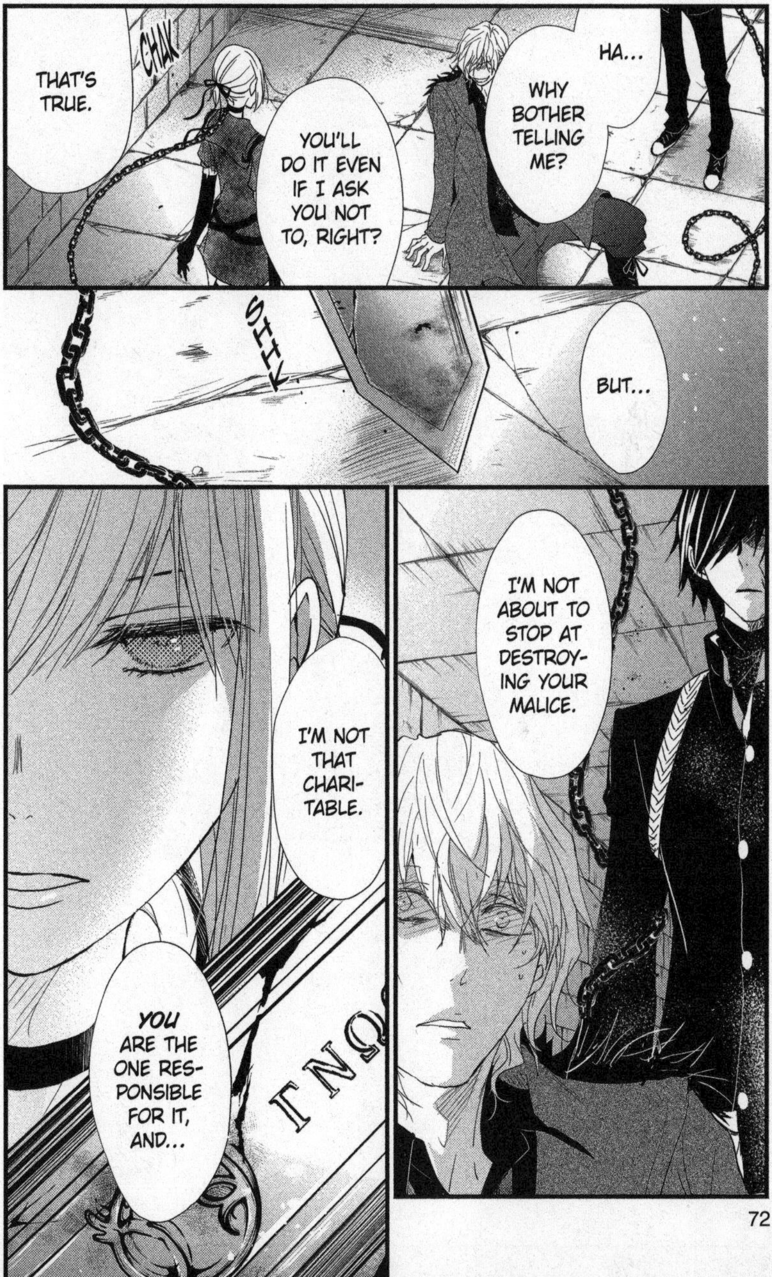
HA...
WHY BOTHER TELLING ME?
YOU'LL DO IT EVEN IF I ASK YOU NOT TO, RIGHT?
CHAK
THAT'S TRUE.
BUT...
SHHK
I'M NOT ABOUT TO STOP AT DESTROYING YOUR MALICE.
I'M NOT THAT CHARITABLE.
YOU ARE THE ONE RESPONSIBLE FOR IT, AND...

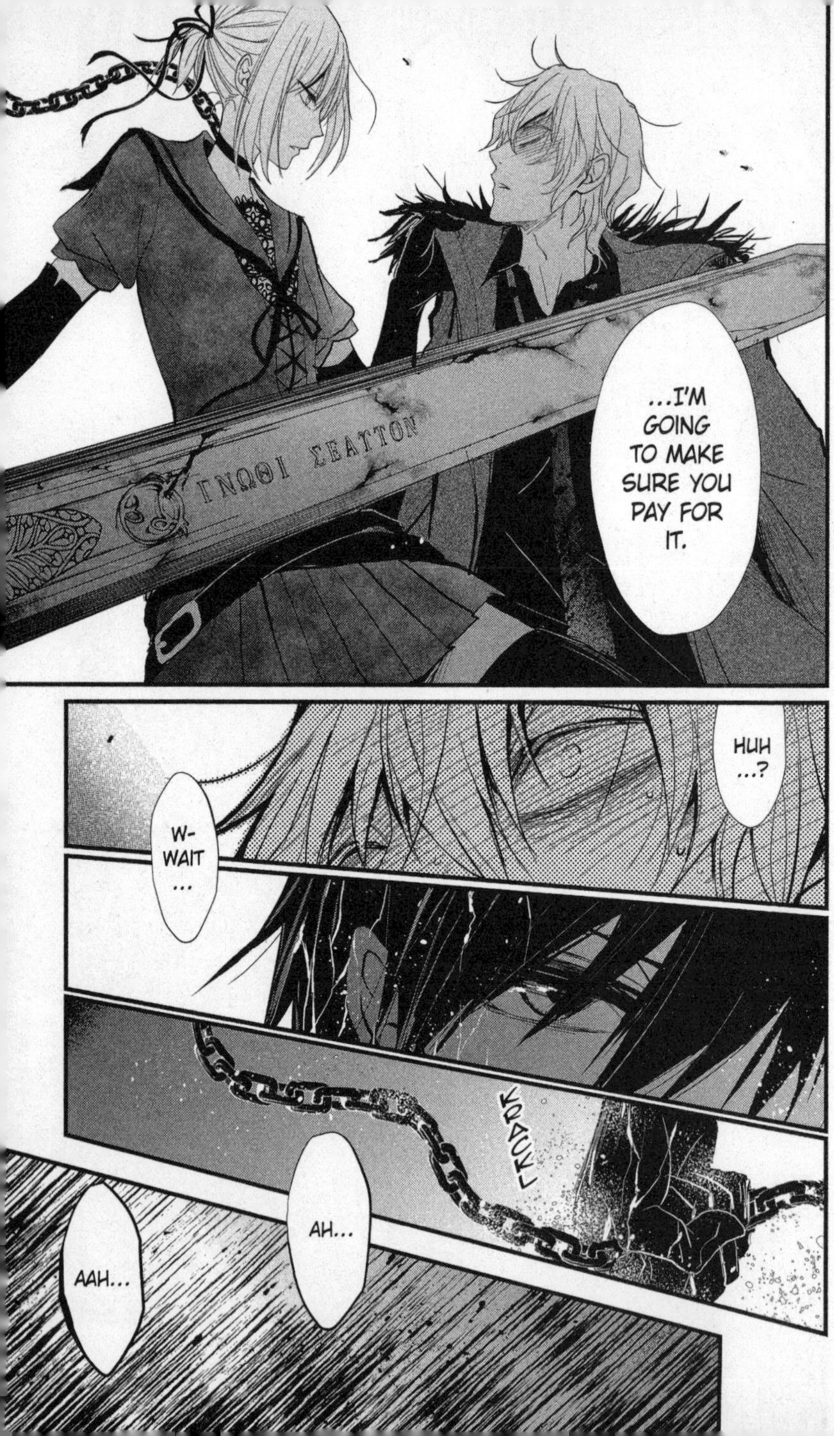
...I'M GOING TO MAKE SURE YOU PAY FOR IT.
ΓΝΩΘΙ ΣΕΑΥΤΟΝ
HUH ...?
W-WAIT ...
KRACK!
AH...
AAH...

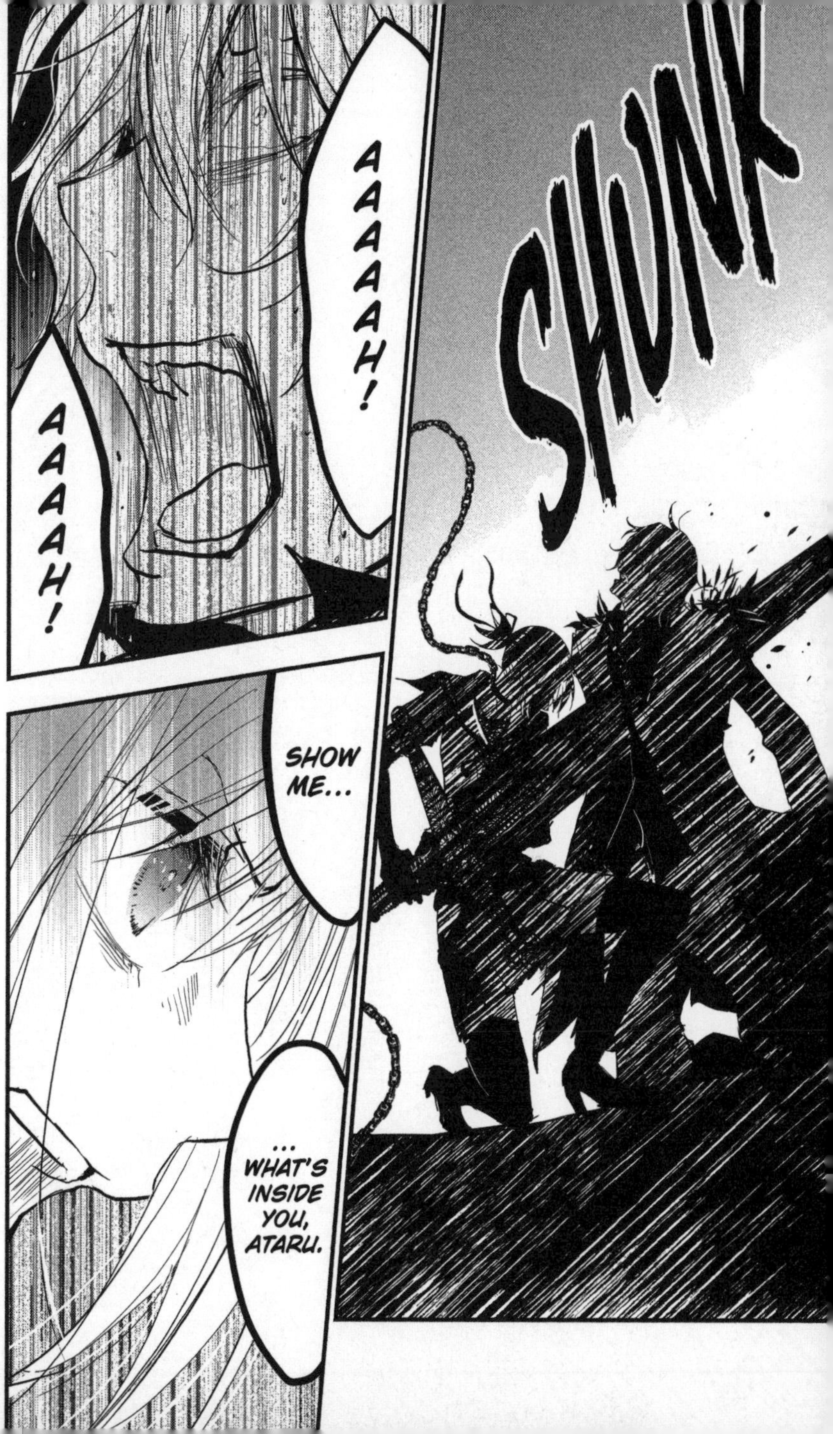
SHUNK
AAAAAH!
AAAAAH!
SHOW ME...
...WHAT'S INSIDE YOU, ATARU.

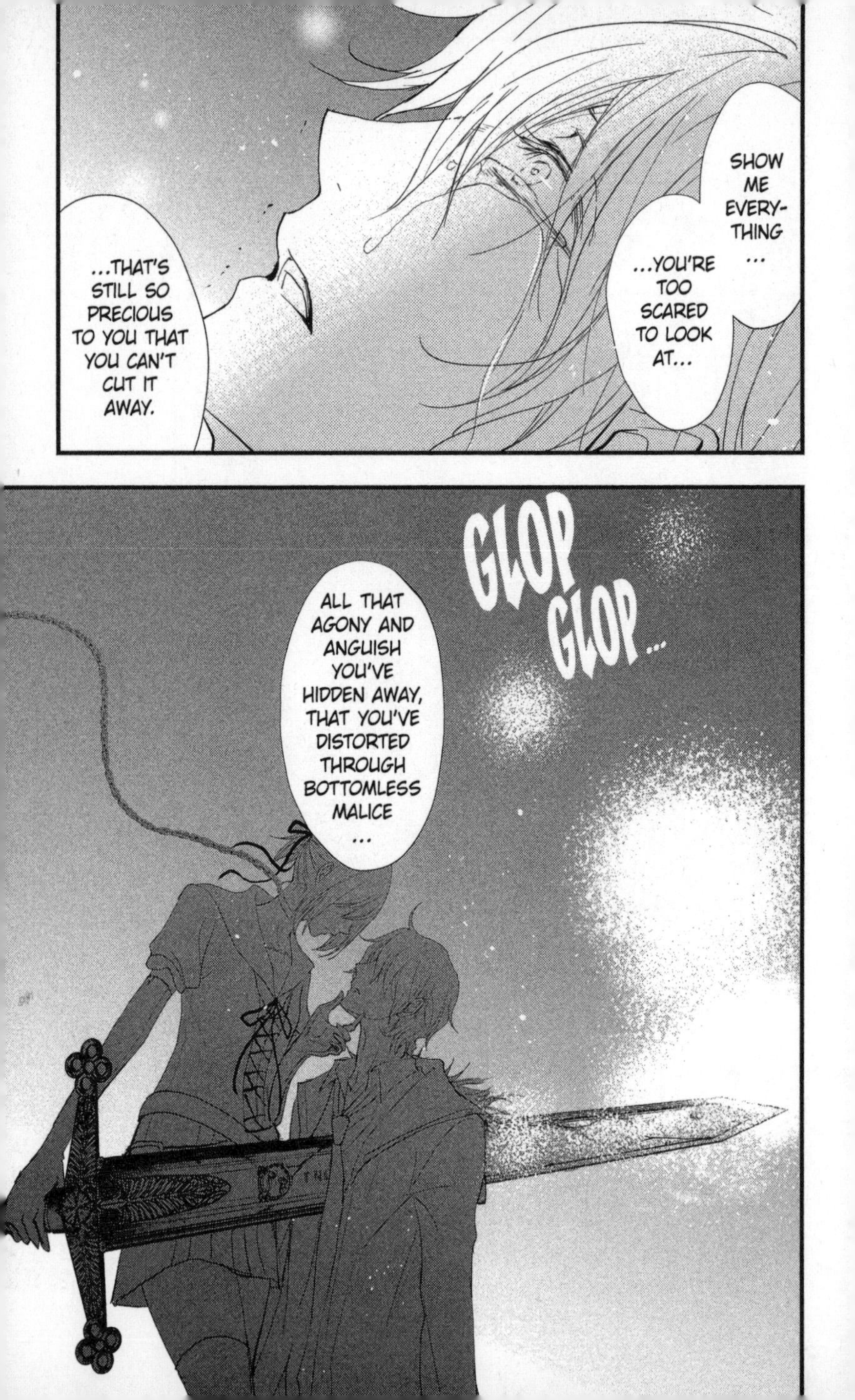
SHOW ME EVERYTHING...
...YOU'RE TOO SCARED TO LOOK AT...
...THAT'S STILL SO PRECIOUS TO YOU THAT YOU CAN'T CUT IT AWAY.
GLOP GLOP...
ALL THAT AGONY AND ANGUISH YOU'VE HIDDEN AWAY, THAT YOU'VE DISTORTED THROUGH BOTTOMLESS MALICE...

MONTHLY BETSUCOMI SALE DATE NOTICE ON TWITTER

CHAPTER 23

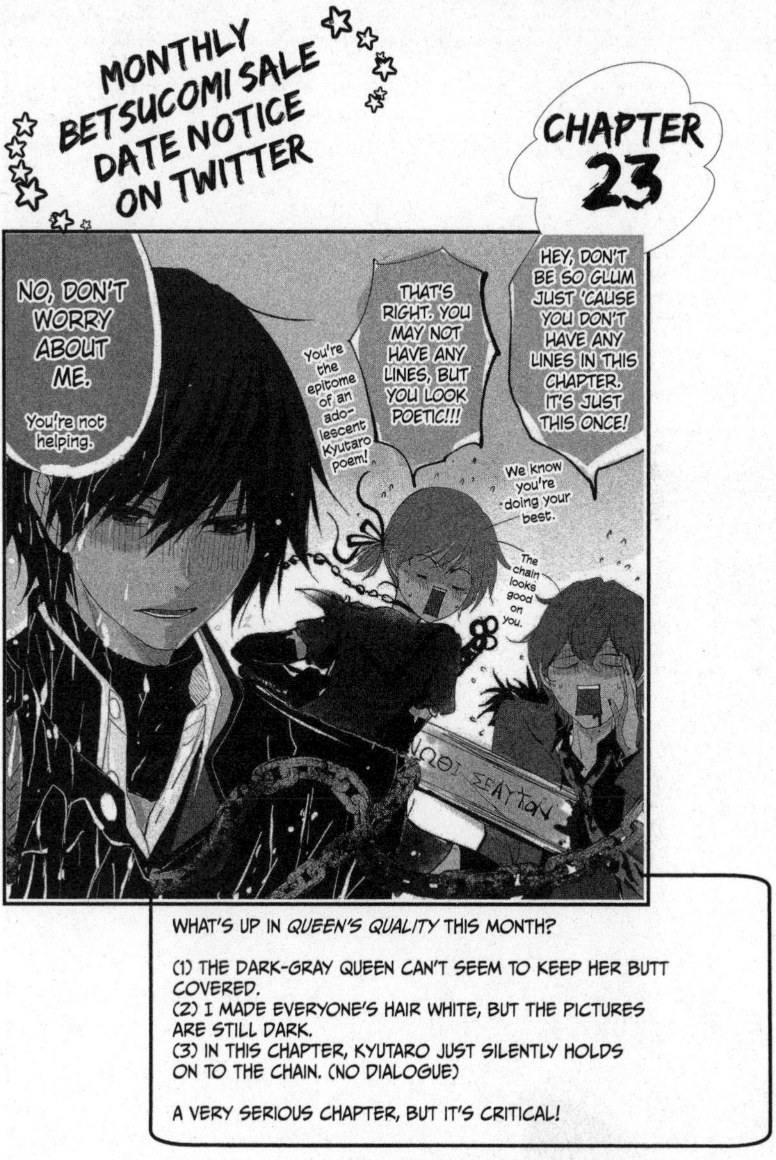
HEY, DON'T BE SO GLUM JUST 'CAUSE YOU DON'T HAVE ANY LINES IN THIS CHAPTER. IT'S JUST THIS ONCE!
We know you're doing your best.
THAT'S RIGHT. YOU MAY NOT HAVE ANY LINES, BUT YOU LOOK POETIC!!!
You're the epitome of an adolescent Kyutaro poem!
The chain looks good on you.
NO, DON'T WORRY ABOUT ME.
You're not helping.

WHAT'S UP IN *QUEEN'S QUALITY* THIS MONTH?

(1) THE DARK-GRAY QUEEN CAN'T SEEM TO KEEP HER BUTT COVERED.
(2) I MADE EVERYONE'S HAIR WHITE, BUT THE PICTURES ARE STILL DARK.
(3) IN THIS CHAPTER, KYUTARO JUST SILENTLY HOLDS ON TO THE CHAIN. (NO DIALOGUE)

A VERY SERIOUS CHAPTER, BUT IT'S CRITICAL!

FOR SOMEONE WITH POOR COMMUNICATION SKILLS, HIS HEART PROBABLY CHILLED MORE FROM BEING ASSURED THAT HE LOOKED LIKE A POEM (HA!) THAN FROM NOT HAVING ANY LINES.

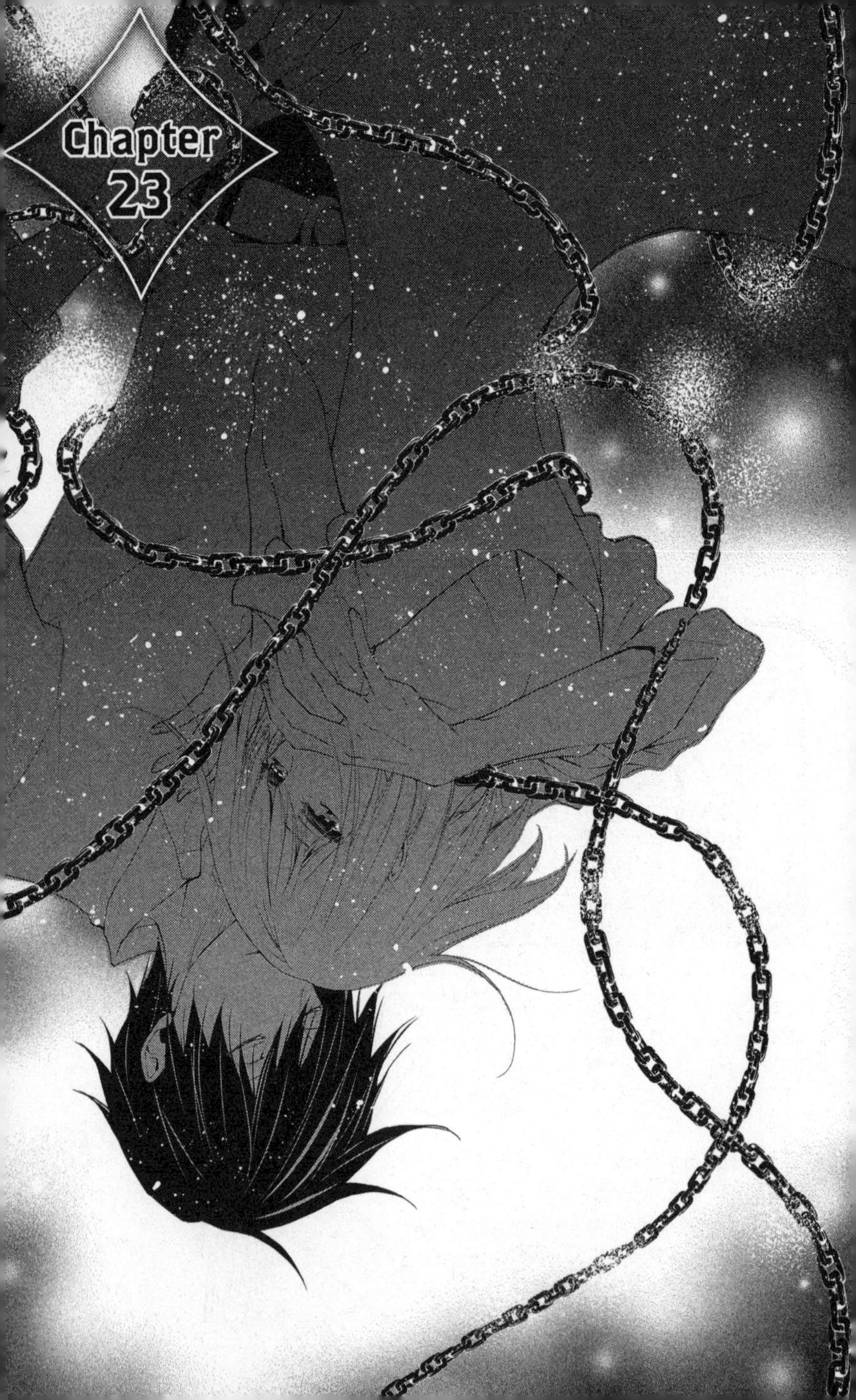
Chapter
23

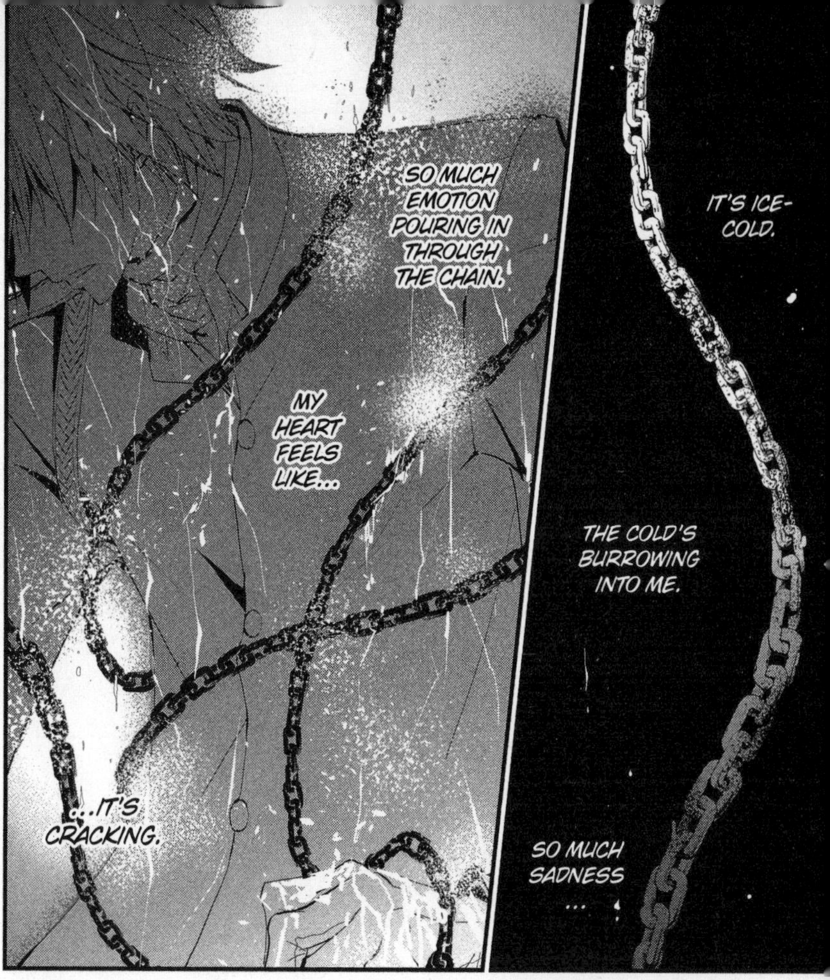
IT'S ICE-COLD.
THE COLD'S BURROWING INTO ME.
SO MUCH SADNESS ...
SO MUCH EMOTION POURING IN THROUGH THE CHAIN.
MY HEART FEELS LIKE...
...IT'S CRACKING.

The great sword that is the incarnation of the Black Queen is Fumi's new protection.

ΓΝΩΘΙ ΣΑΥΤΟΝ (Gnothi Seauton)

The characters on it are ancient Greek for "know thyself." I use that here as the theme of both Fumi's life and Queen's Quality. Greek is pretty cool, isn't it?

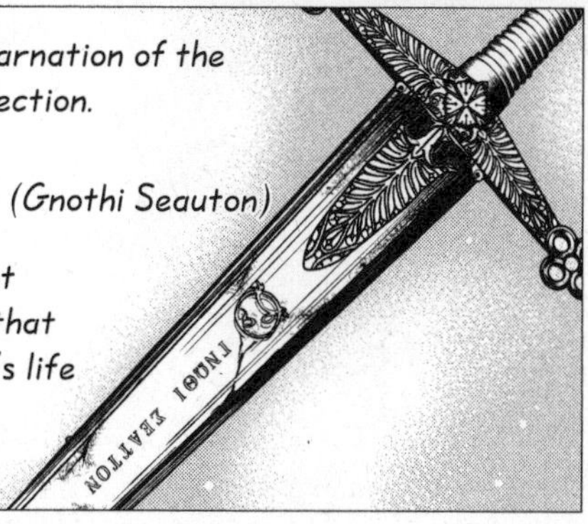

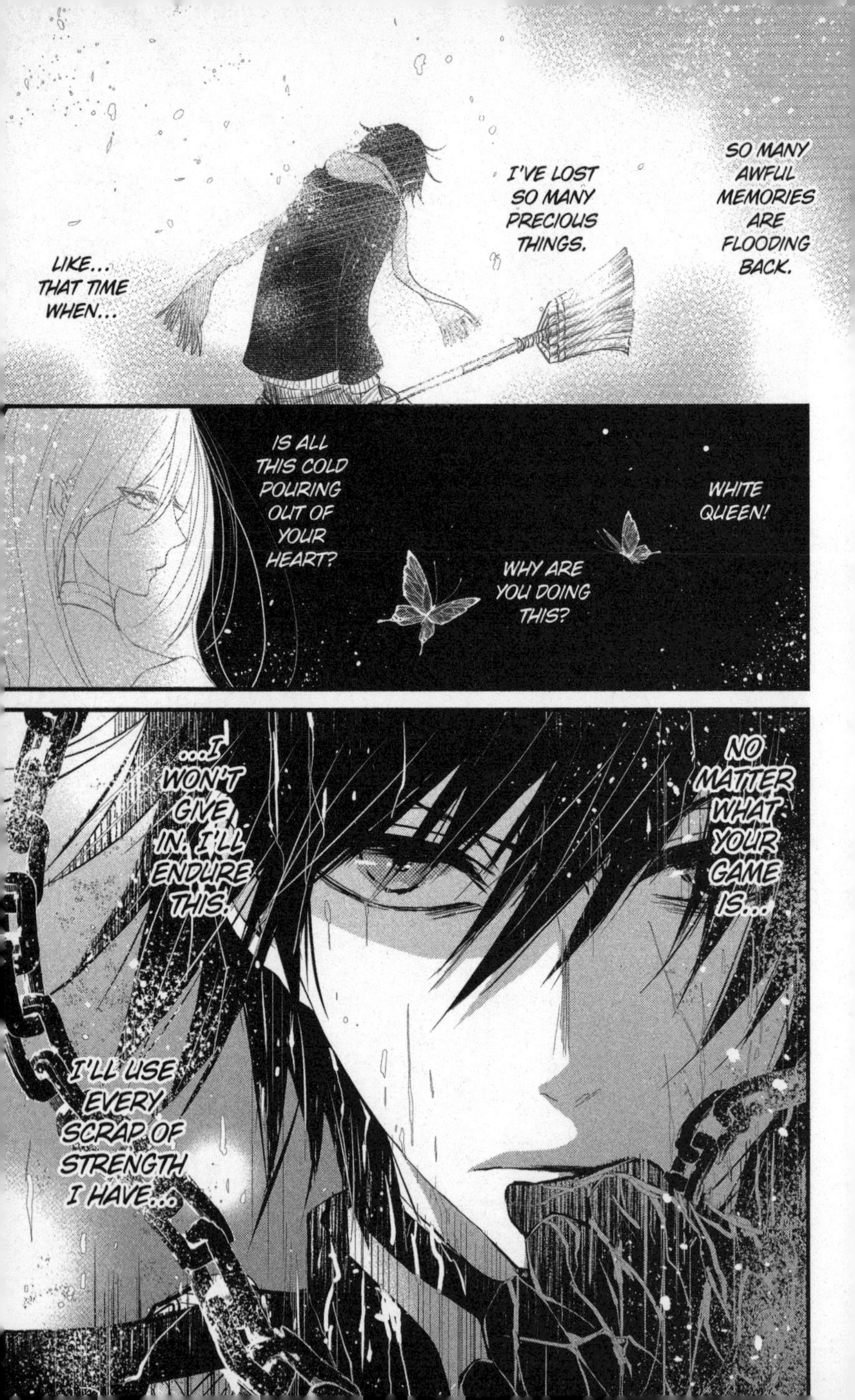
SO MANY AWFUL MEMORIES ARE FLOODING BACK.
I'VE LOST SO MANY PRECIOUS THINGS.
LIKE... THAT TIME WHEN...
WHITE QUEEN!
WHY ARE YOU DOING THIS?
IS ALL THIS COLD POURING OUT OF YOUR HEART?
NO MATTER WHAT YOUR GAME IS...
...I WON'T GIVE IN. I'LL ENDURE THIS.
I'LL USE EVERY SCRAP OF STRENGTH I HAVE...

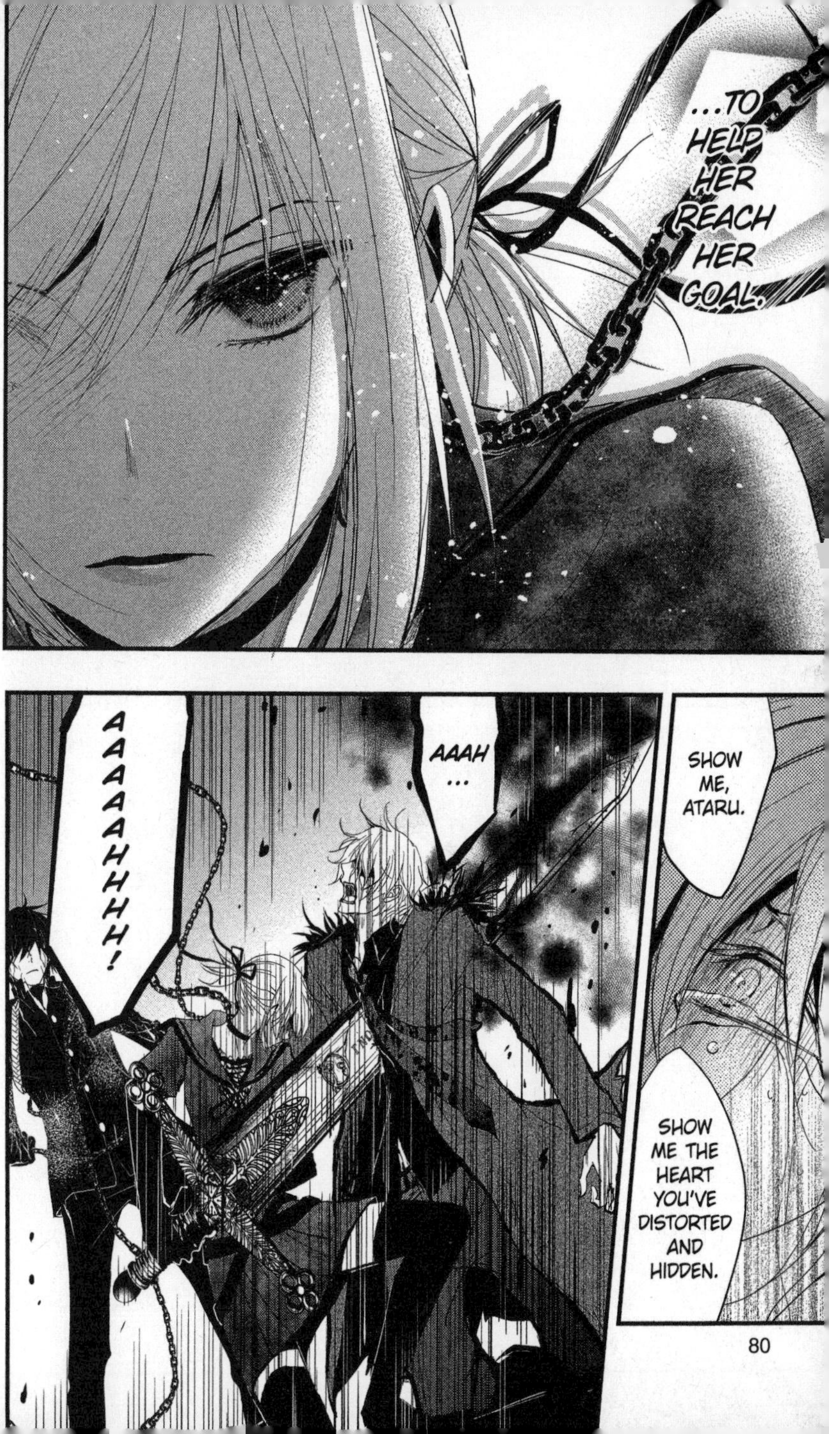
...TO HELP HER REACH HER GOAL.
SHOW ME, ATARU.
SHOW ME THE HEART YOU'VE DISTORTED AND HIDDEN.
AAAH...
AAAAAAAHHHHH!

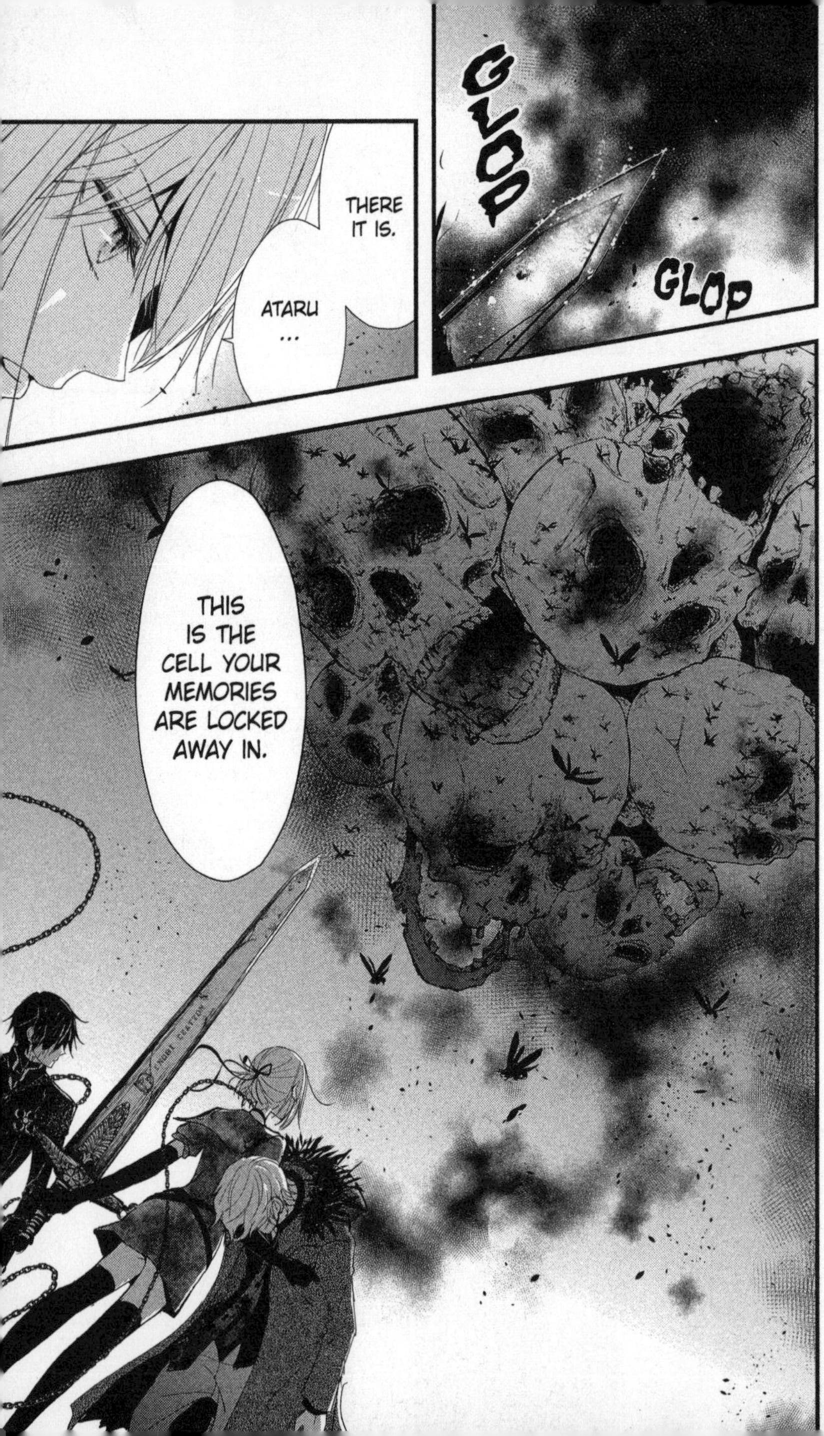
GLOP
GLOP
THERE IT IS.
ATARU ...
THIS IS THE CELL YOUR MEMORIES ARE LOCKED AWAY IN.

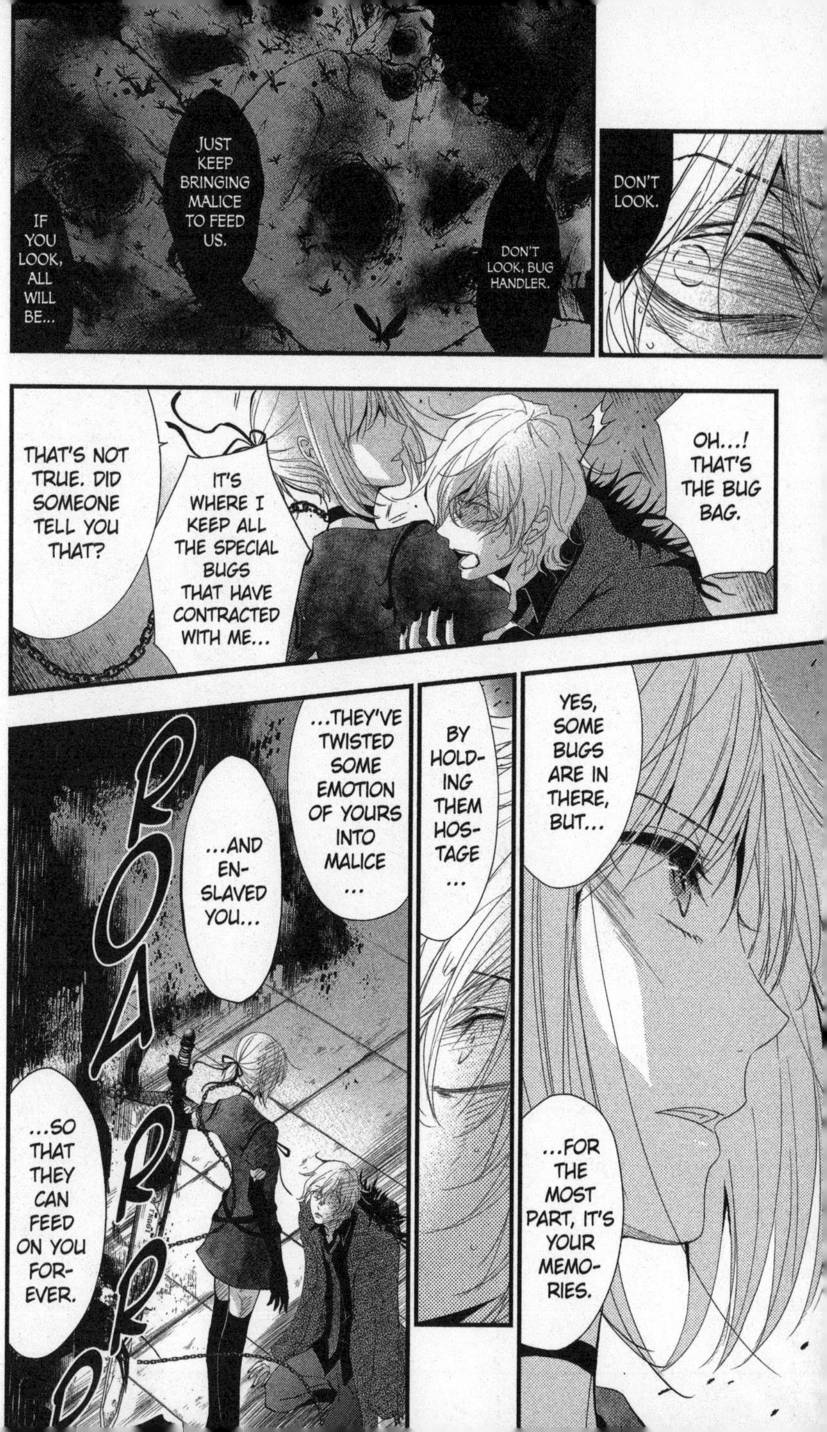
DON'T LOOK.
DON'T LOOK, BUG HANDLER.
JUST KEEP BRINGING MALICE TO FEED US.
IF YOU LOOK, ALL WILL BE...
OH...! THAT'S THE BUG BAG.
IT'S WHERE I KEEP ALL THE SPECIAL BUGS THAT HAVE CONTRACTED WITH ME...
THAT'S NOT TRUE. DID SOMEONE TELL YOU THAT?
YES, SOME BUGS ARE IN THERE, BUT...
...FOR THE MOST PART, IT'S YOUR MEMORIES.
BY HOLDING THEM HOSTAGE...
...THEY'VE TWISTED SOME EMOTION OF YOURS INTO MALICE...
...AND ENSLAVED YOU...
...SO THAT THEY CAN FEED ON YOU FOREVER.

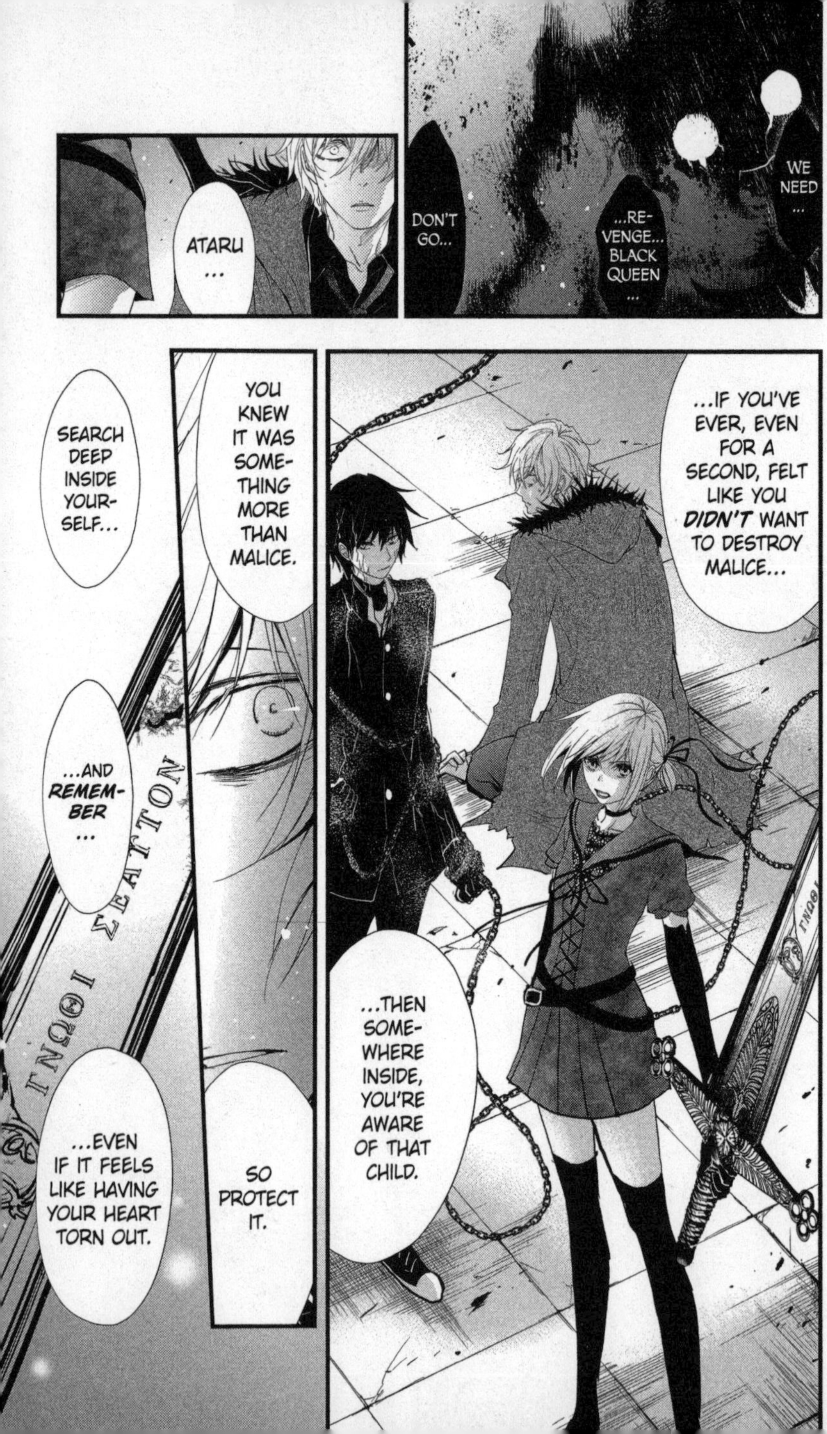
WE NEED ...
...RE-VENGE... BLACK QUEEN ...
DON'T GO...
ATARU ...
...IF YOU'VE EVER, EVEN FOR A SECOND, FELT LIKE YOU *DIDN'T* WANT TO DESTROY MALICE...
...THEN SOME-WHERE INSIDE, YOU'RE AWARE OF THAT CHILD.
YOU KNEW IT WAS SOME-THING MORE THAN MALICE.
SO PROTECT IT.
SEARCH DEEP INSIDE YOUR-SELF...
...AND *REMEM-BER* ...
...EVEN IF IT FEELS LIKE HAVING YOUR HEART TORN OUT.

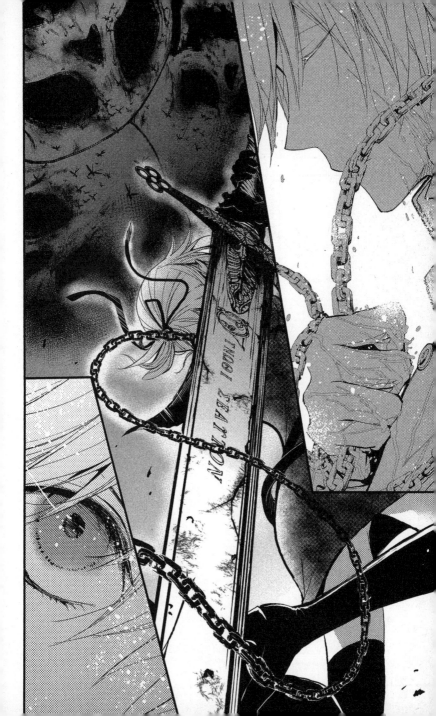

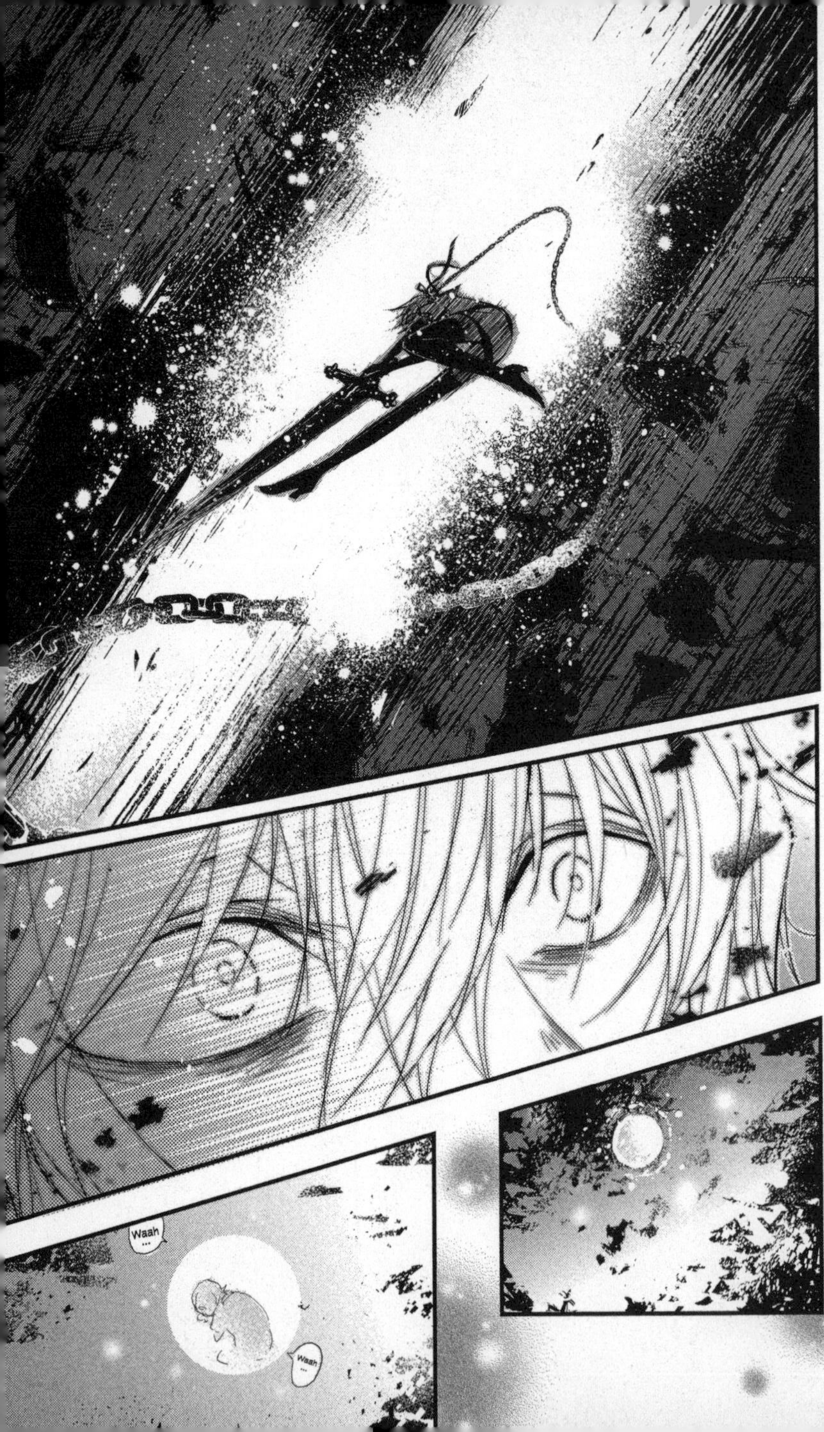
Waah...
Waah...

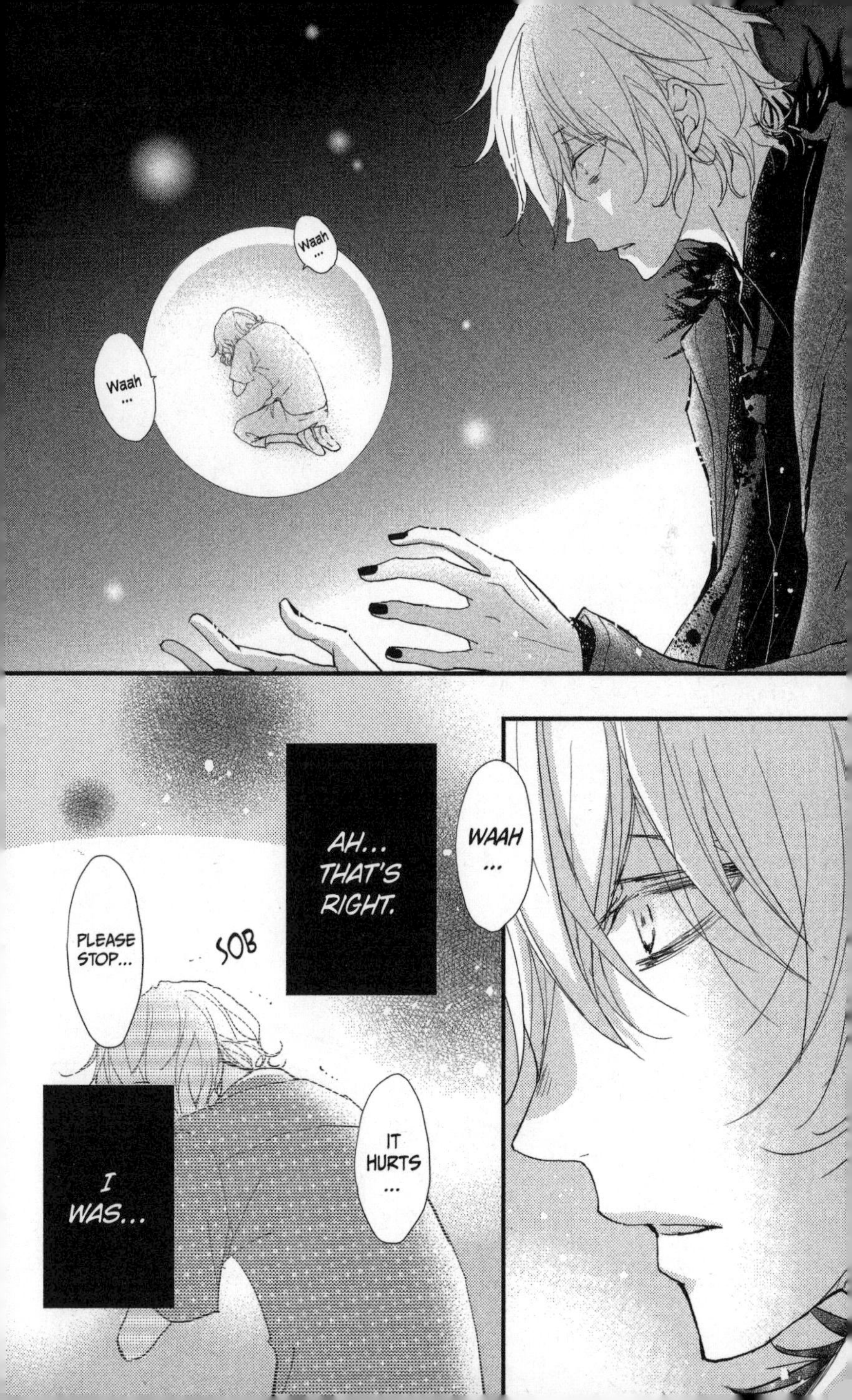
Waah...
Waah...
WAAH...
AH... THAT'S RIGHT.
SOB
PLEASE STOP...
IT HURTS...
I WAS...

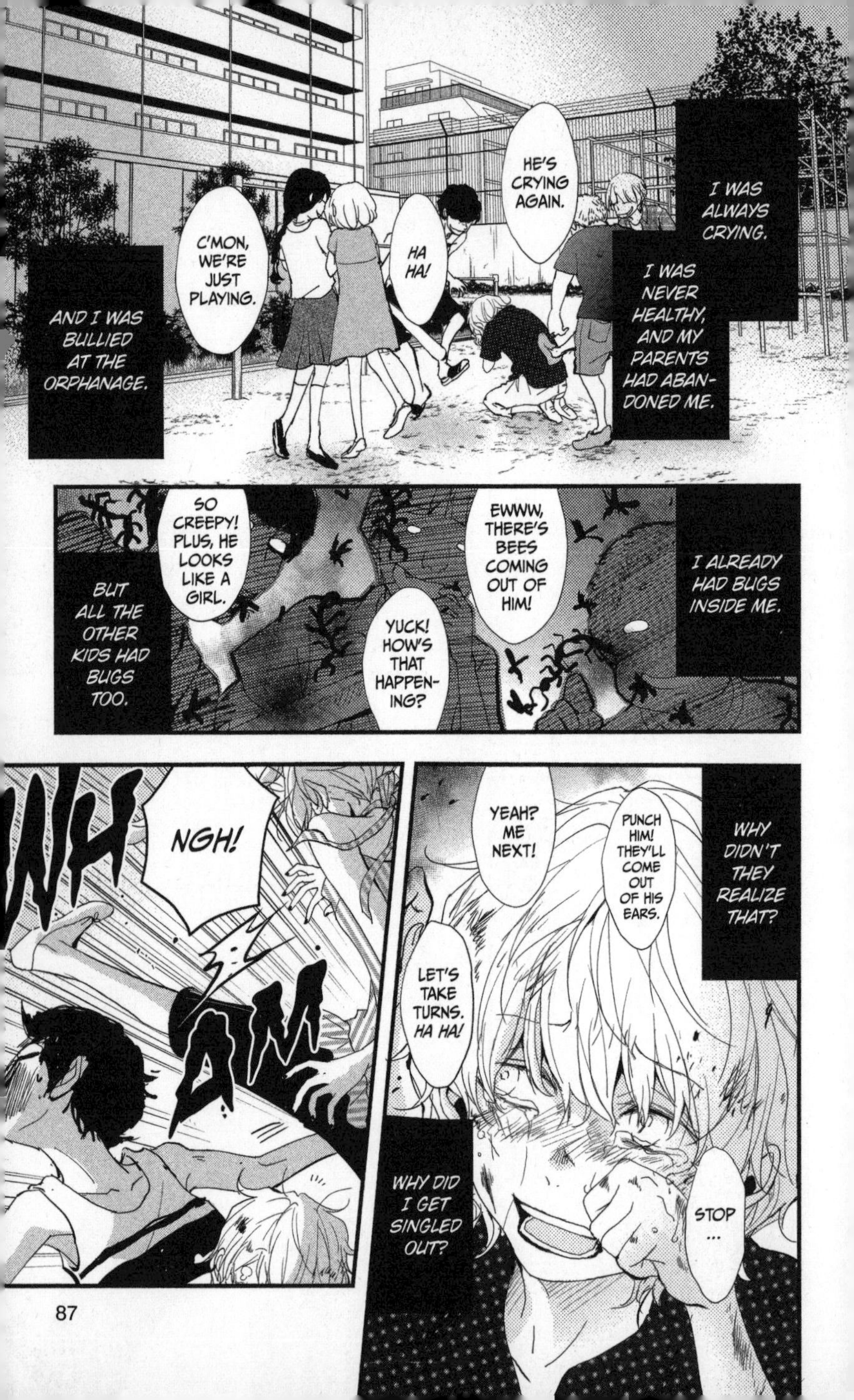
I WAS ALWAYS CRYING.
I WAS NEVER HEALTHY, AND MY PARENTS HAD ABANDONED ME.
HE'S CRYING AGAIN.
HA HA!
C'MON, WE'RE JUST PLAYING.
AND I WAS BULLIED AT THE ORPHANAGE.
I ALREADY HAD BUGS INSIDE ME.
EWWW, THERE'S BEES COMING OUT OF HIM!
YUCK! HOW'S THAT HAPPENING?
SO CREEPY! PLUS, HE LOOKS LIKE A GIRL.
BUT ALL THE OTHER KIDS HAD BUGS TOO.
WHY DIDN'T THEY REALIZE THAT?
PUNCH HIM! THEY'LL COME OUT OF HIS EARS.
YEAH? ME NEXT!
LET'S TAKE TURNS. HA HA!
STOP ...
WHY DID I GET SINGLED OUT?
NGH!

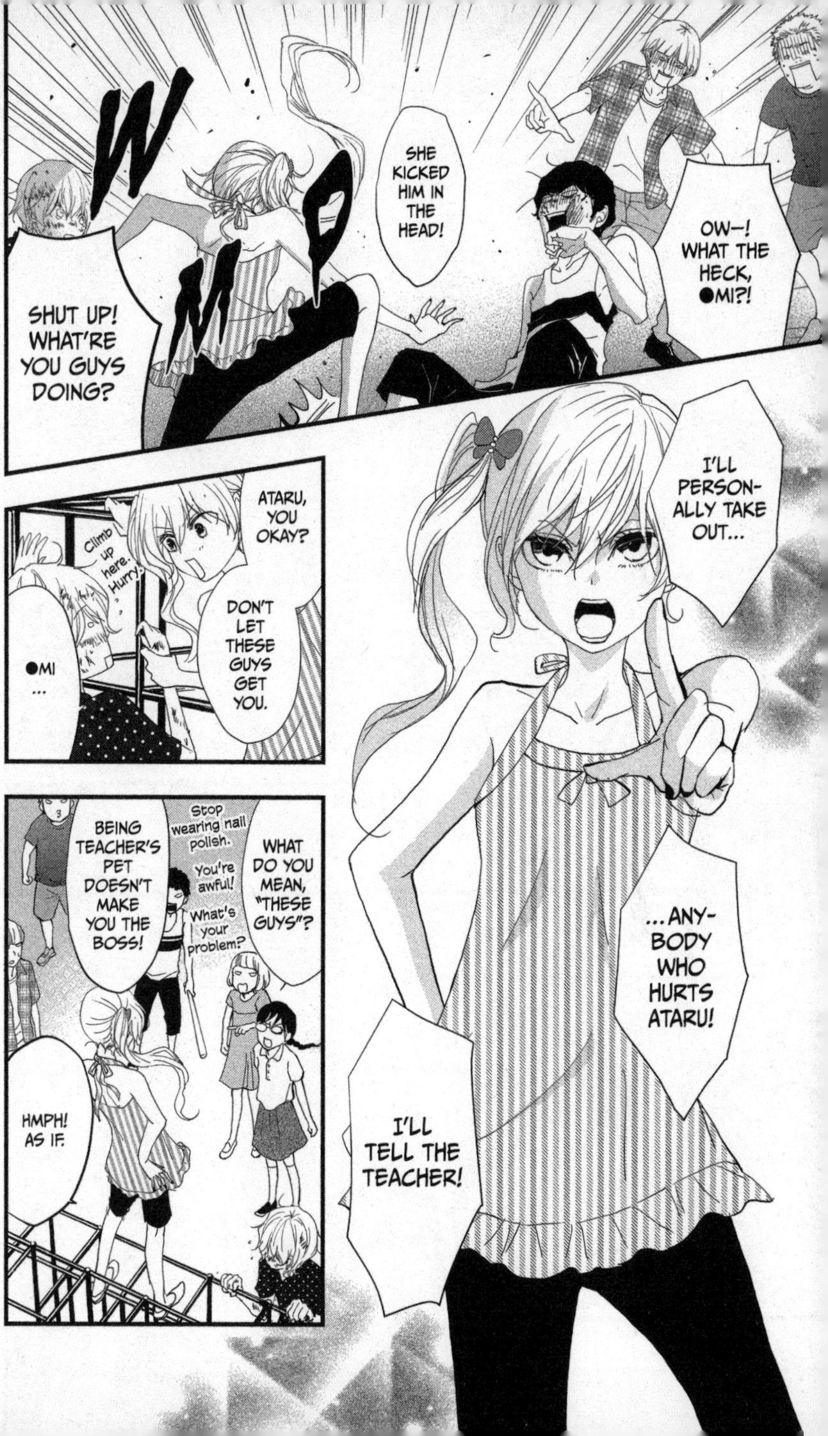
OW—! WHAT THE HECK, [redacted]MI?!
SHE KICKED HIM IN THE HEAD!
WMP
SHUT UP! WHAT'RE YOU GUYS DOING?
I'LL PERSONALLY TAKE OUT...
...ANYBODY WHO HURTS ATARU!
I'LL TELL THE TEACHER!
ATARU, YOU OKAY?
DON'T LET THESE GUYS GET YOU.
Climb up here. Hurry.
[redacted]MI ...
WHAT DO YOU MEAN, "THESE GUYS"?
Stop wearing nail polish.
You're awful!
What's your problem?
BEING TEACHER'S PET DOESN'T MAKE YOU THE BOSS!
HMPH! AS IF.

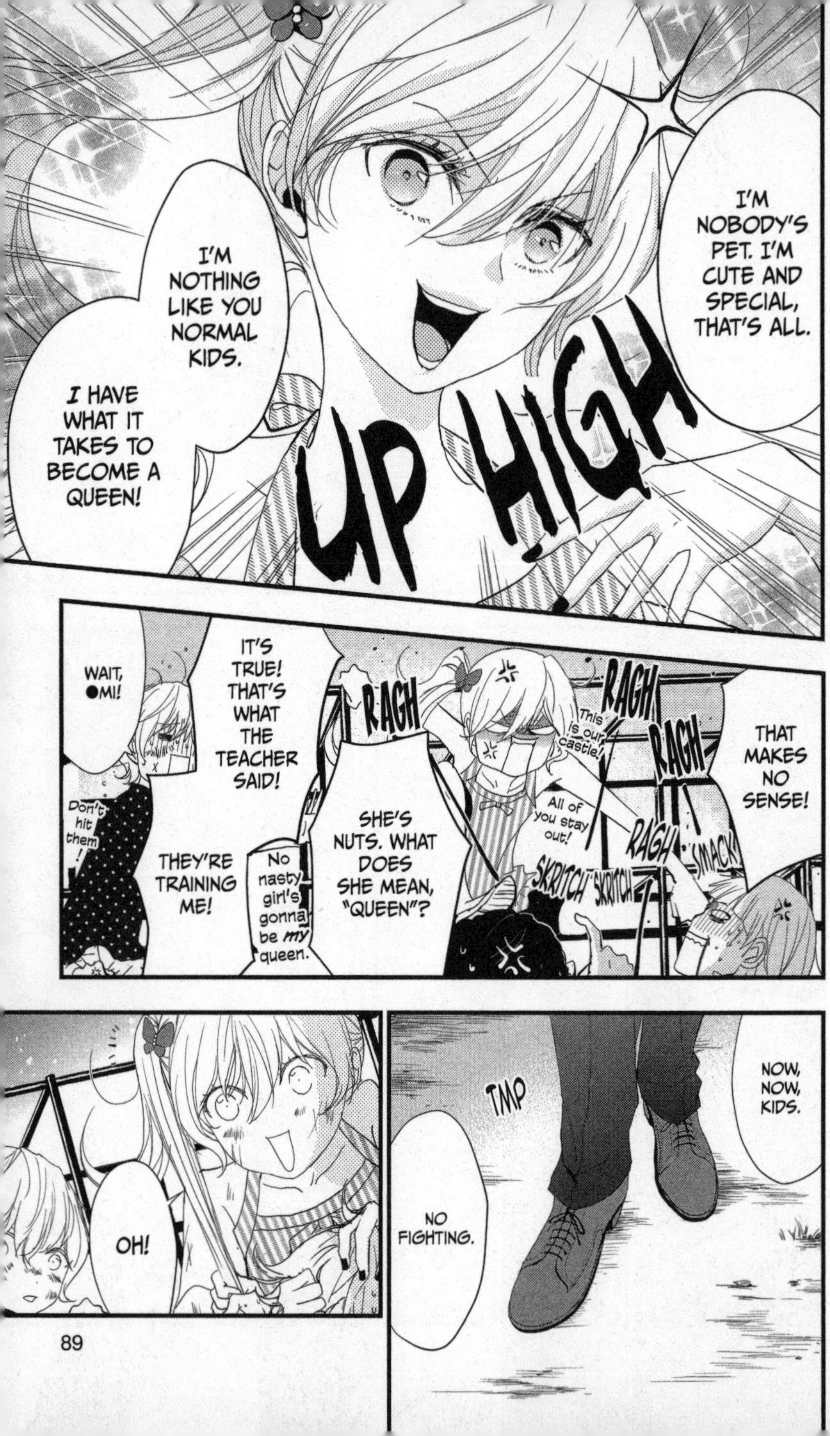
I'M NOBODY'S PET. I'M CUTE AND SPECIAL, THAT'S ALL.
UP HIGH
I'M NOTHING LIKE YOU NORMAL KIDS.
I HAVE WHAT IT TAKES TO BECOME A QUEEN!
THAT MAKES NO SENSE!
RAGH
RAGH
This is our castle!
All of you stay out!
RAGH
SMACK
SKRITCH
SKRITCH
RAGH
SHE'S NUTS. WHAT DOES SHE MEAN, "QUEEN"?
No nasty girl's gonna be my queen.
IT'S TRUE! THAT'S WHAT THE TEACHER SAID!
THEY'RE TRAINING ME!
WAIT, OMI!
Don't hit them!
NOW, NOW, KIDS.
TMP
NO FIGHTING.
OH!

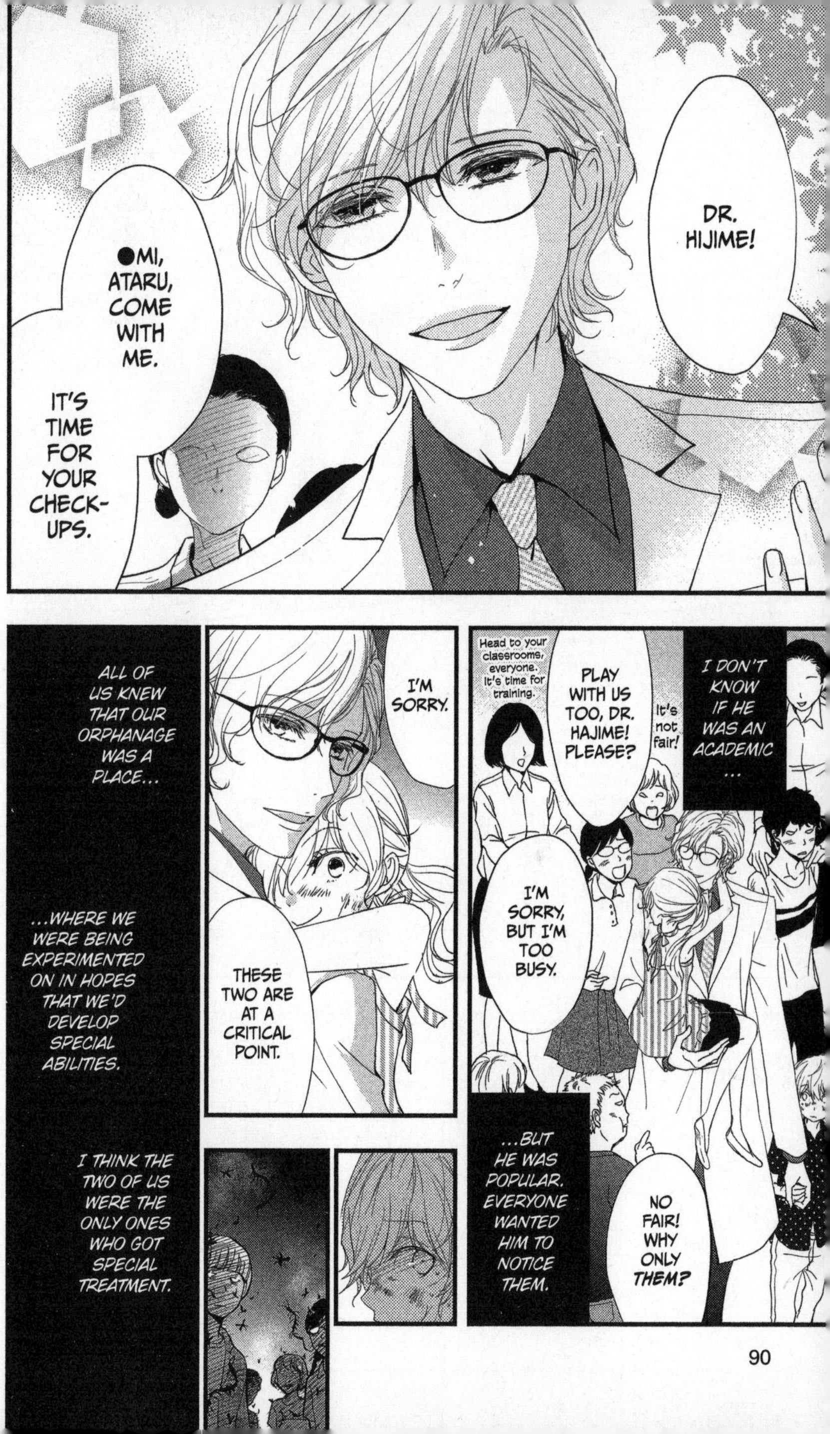
DR. HIJIME!
●MI, ATARU, COME WITH ME.
IT'S TIME FOR YOUR CHECK-UPS.
I DON'T KNOW IF HE WAS AN ACADEMIC...
Head to your classrooms, everyone. It's time for training.
PLAY WITH US TOO, DR. HAJIME! PLEASE?
It's not fair!
I'M SORRY, BUT I'M TOO BUSY.
...BUT HE WAS POPULAR. EVERYONE WANTED HIM TO NOTICE THEM.
NO FAIR! WHY ONLY THEM?
I'M SORRY.
THESE TWO ARE AT A CRITICAL POINT.
ALL OF US KNEW THAT OUR ORPHANAGE WAS A PLACE...
...WHERE WE WERE BEING EXPERIMENTED ON IN HOPES THAT WE'D DEVELOP SPECIAL ABILITIES.
I THINK THE TWO OF US WERE THE ONLY ONES WHO GOT SPECIAL TREATMENT.

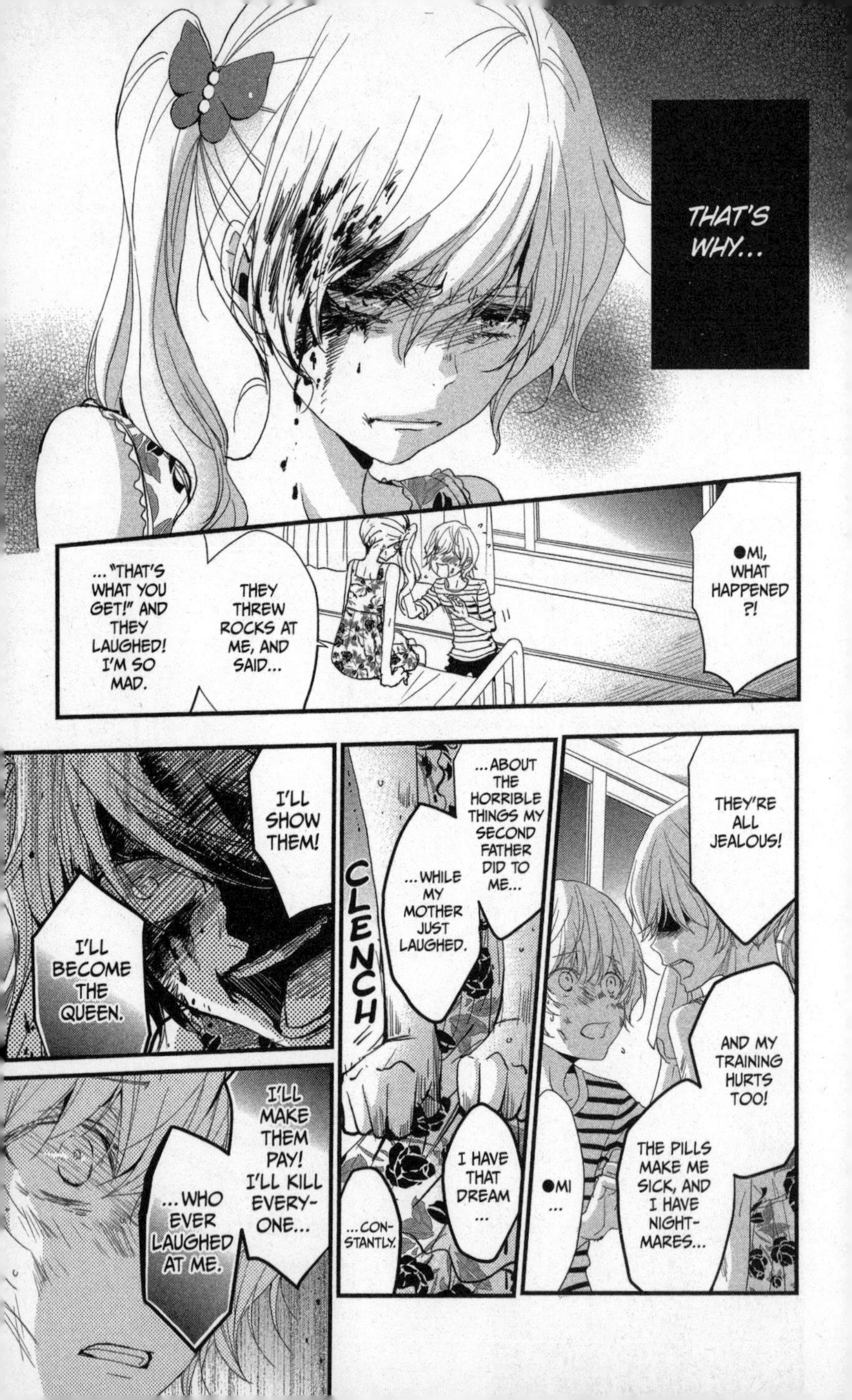
THAT'S WHY...
●MI, WHAT HAPPENED?!
THEY THREW ROCKS AT ME, AND SAID...
..."THAT'S WHAT YOU GET!" AND THEY LAUGHED! I'M SO MAD.
THEY'RE ALL JEALOUS!
AND MY TRAINING HURTS TOO!
THE PILLS MAKE ME SICK, AND I HAVE NIGHT-MARES...
●MI...
I HAVE THAT DREAM...
...CON-STANTLY.
...ABOUT THE HORRIBLE THINGS MY SECOND FATHER DID TO ME...
...WHILE MY MOTHER JUST LAUGHED.
CLENCH
I'LL SHOW THEM!
I'LL BECOME THE QUEEN.
I'LL MAKE THEM PAY! I'LL KILL EVERY-ONE...
...WHO EVER LAUGHED AT ME.

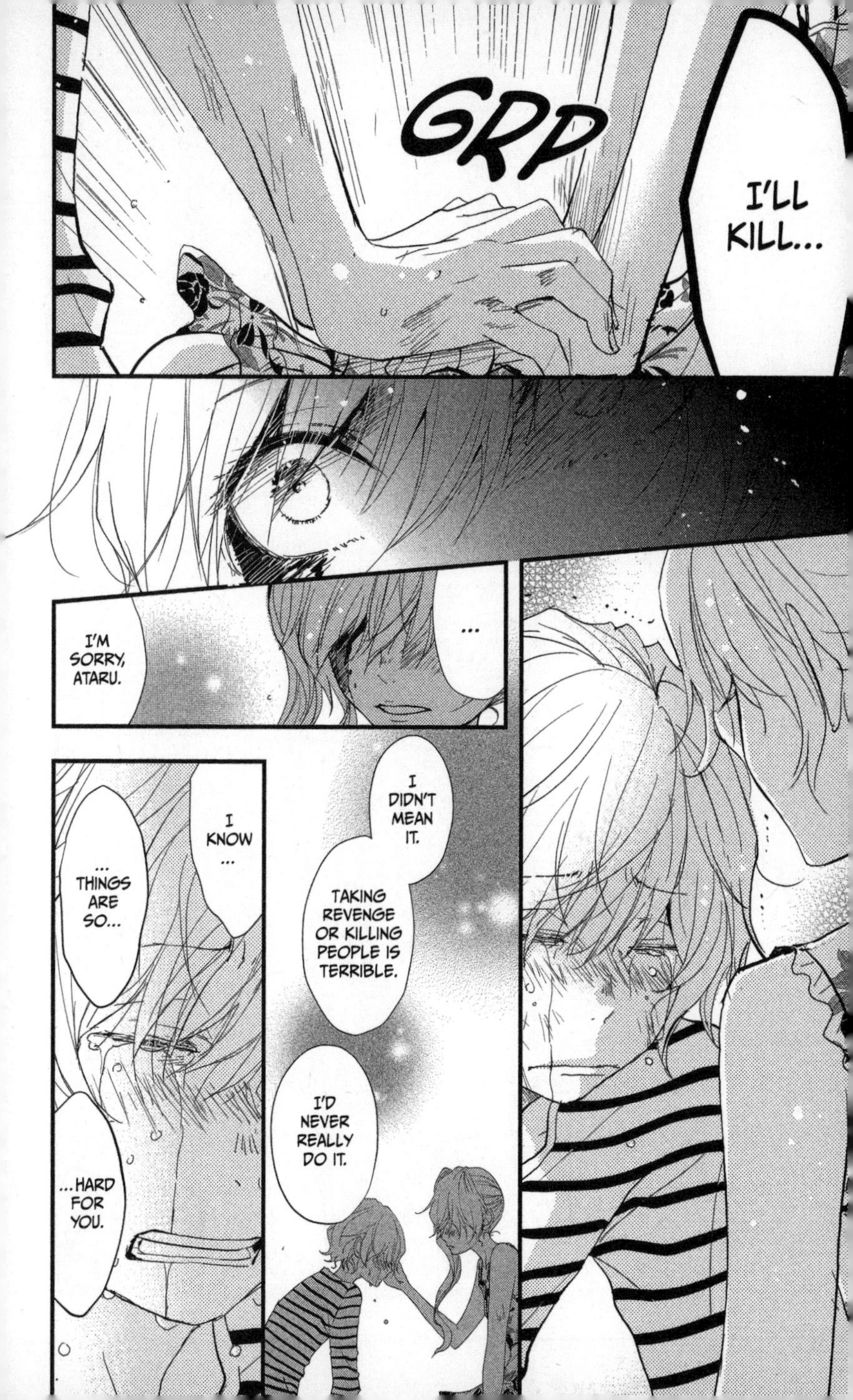

I'LL KILL...
GRP
...
...
I'M SORRY, ATARU.
I DIDN'T MEAN IT.
TAKING REVENGE OR KILLING PEOPLE IS TERRIBLE.
I'D NEVER REALLY DO IT.
I KNOW...
...THINGS ARE SO...
...HARD FOR YOU.

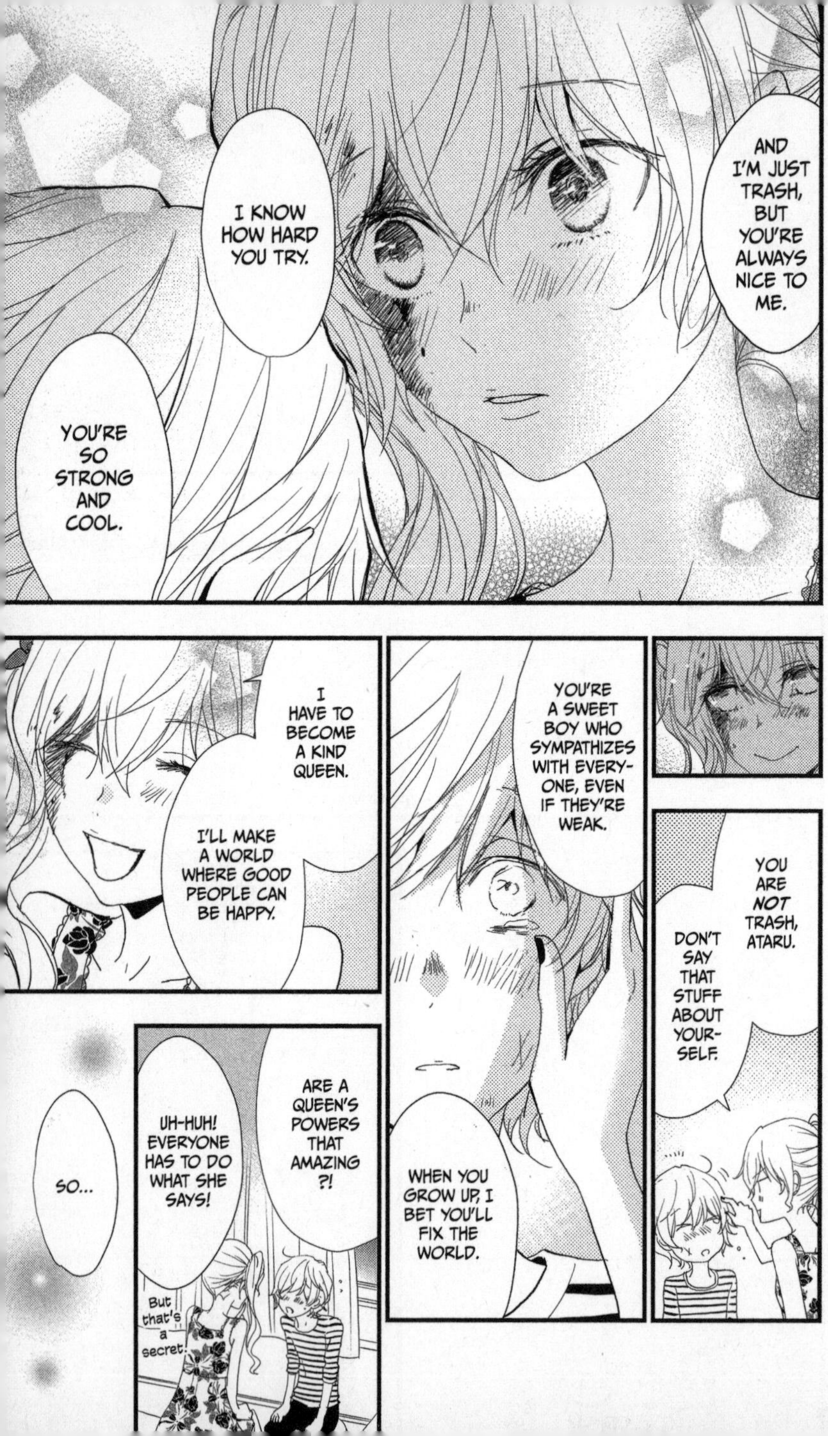
AND I'M JUST TRASH, BUT YOU'RE ALWAYS NICE TO ME.
I KNOW HOW HARD YOU TRY.
YOU'RE SO STRONG AND COOL.
YOU ARE *NOT* TRASH, ATARU.
DON'T SAY THAT STUFF ABOUT YOURSELF.
YOU'RE A SWEET BOY WHO SYMPATHIZES WITH EVERYONE, EVEN IF THEY'RE WEAK.
WHEN YOU GROW UP, I BET YOU'LL FIX THE WORLD.
I HAVE TO BECOME A KIND QUEEN.
I'LL MAKE A WORLD WHERE GOOD PEOPLE CAN BE HAPPY.
ARE A QUEEN'S POWERS THAT AMAZING?!
UH-HUH! EVERYONE HAS TO DO WHAT SHE SAYS!
But that's a secret!
SO...

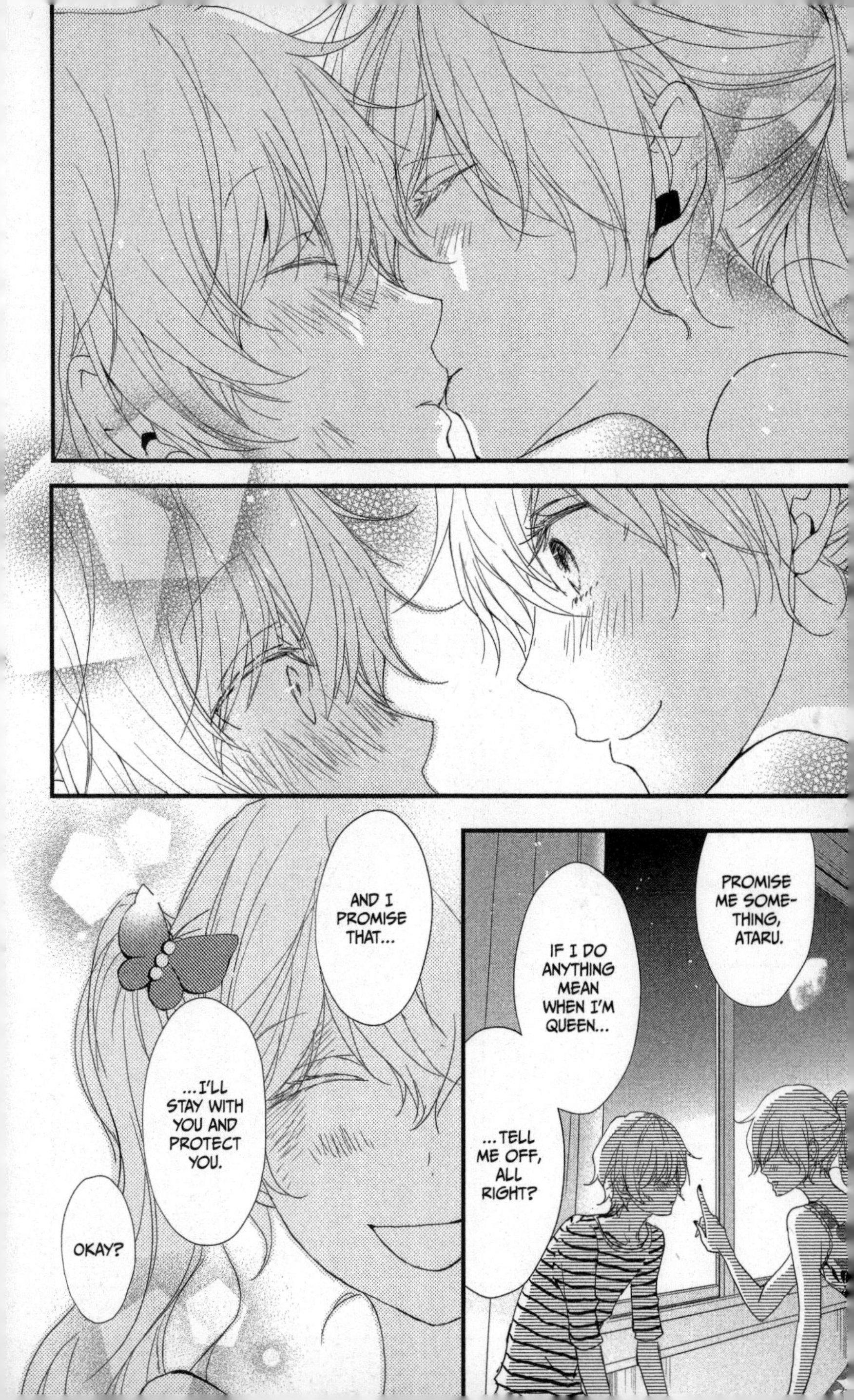
PROMISE ME SOME-THING, ATARU.
IF I DO ANYTHING MEAN WHEN I'M QUEEN...
...TELL ME OFF, ALL RIGHT?
AND I PROMISE THAT...
...I'LL STAY WITH YOU AND PROTECT YOU.
OKAY?

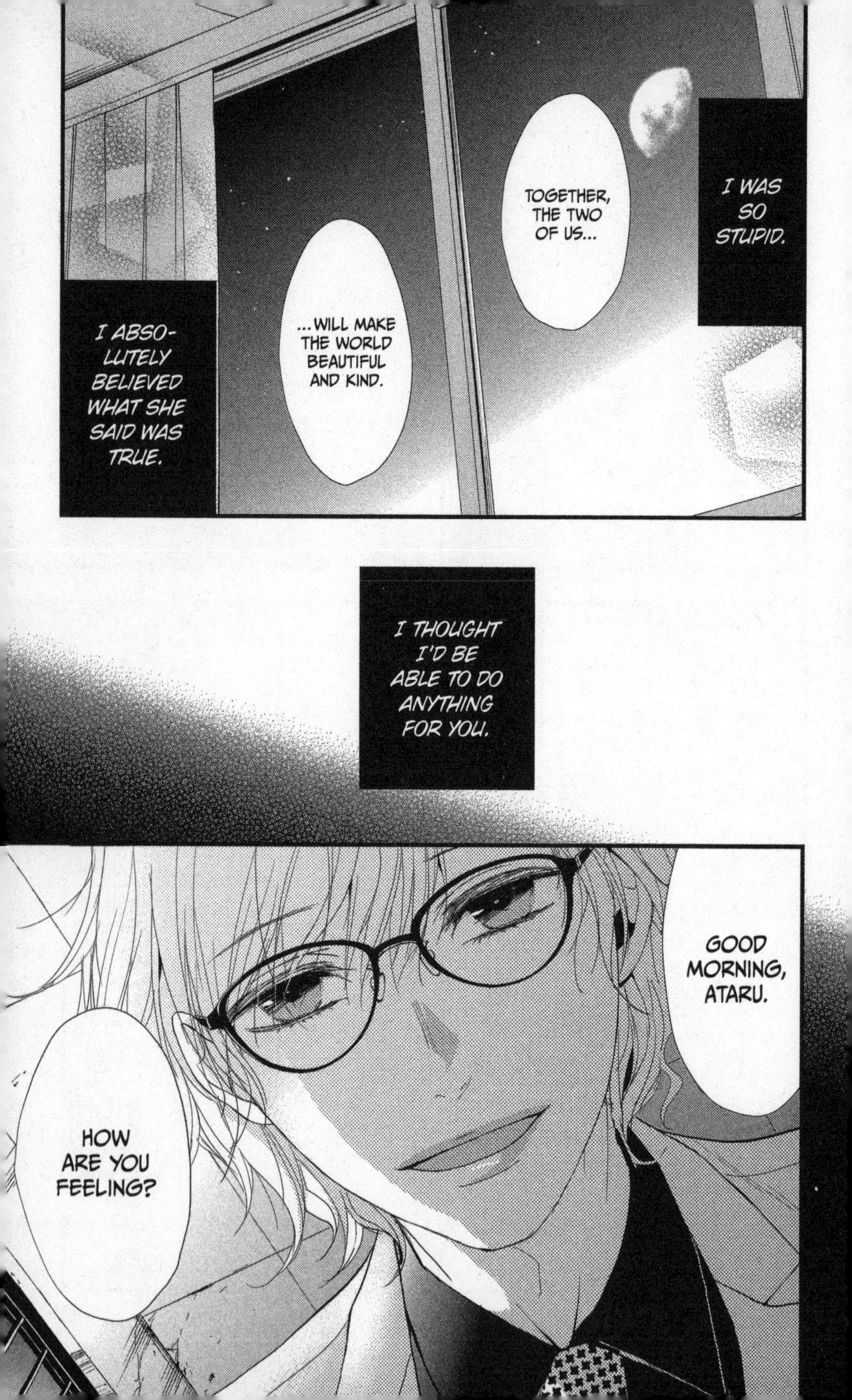
I WAS SO STUPID.
TOGETHER, THE TWO OF US...
...WILL MAKE THE WORLD BEAUTIFUL AND KIND.
I ABSO-LUTELY BELIEVED WHAT SHE SAID WAS TRUE.
I THOUGHT I'D BE ABLE TO DO ANYTHING FOR YOU.
GOOD MORNING, ATARU.
HOW ARE YOU FEELING?

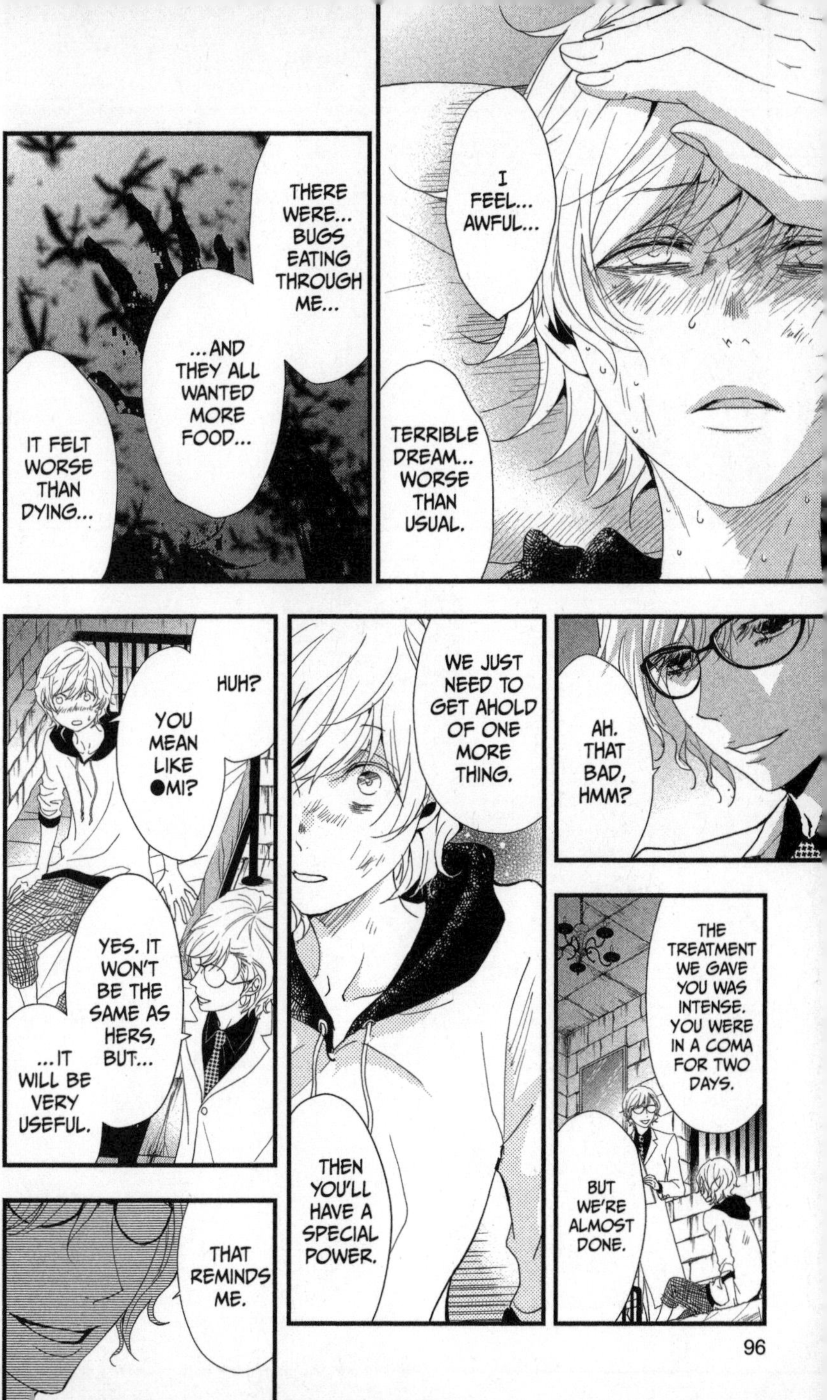
I FEEL... AWFUL...
TERRIBLE DREAM... WORSE THAN USUAL.
THERE WERE... BUGS EATING THROUGH ME...
...AND THEY ALL WANTED MORE FOOD...
IT FELT WORSE THAN DYING...
AH. THAT BAD, HMM?
THE TREATMENT WE GAVE YOU WAS INTENSE. YOU WERE IN A COMA FOR TWO DAYS.
BUT WE'RE ALMOST DONE.
WE JUST NEED TO GET AHOLD OF ONE MORE THING.
THEN YOU'LL HAVE A SPECIAL POWER.
HUH?
YOU MEAN LIKE ●MI?
YES. IT WON'T BE THE SAME AS HERS, BUT...
...IT WILL BE VERY USEFUL.
THAT REMINDS ME.

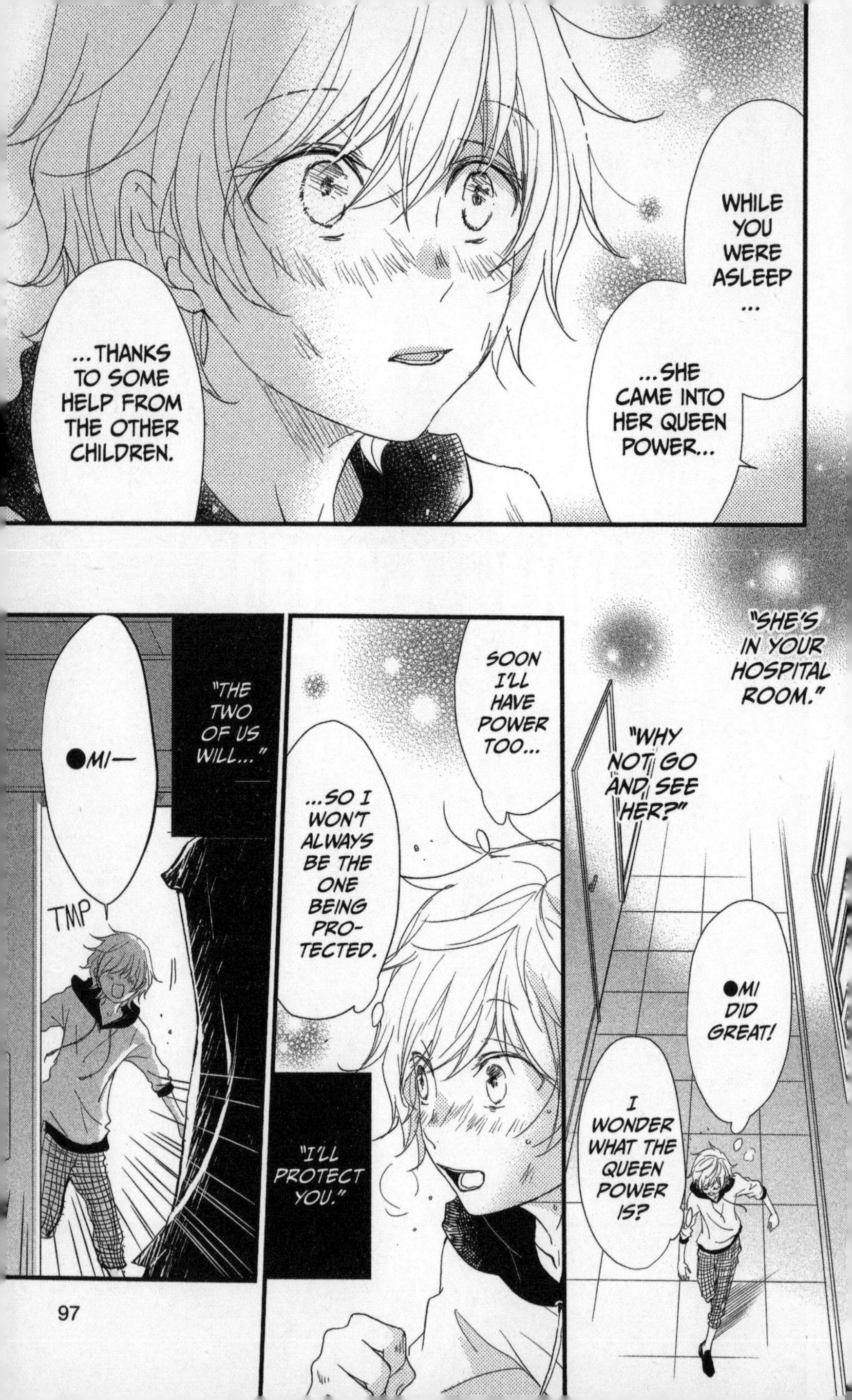
WHILE YOU WERE ASLEEP...
...SHE CAME INTO HER QUEEN POWER...
...THANKS TO SOME HELP FROM THE OTHER CHILDREN.
"SHE'S IN YOUR HOSPITAL ROOM."
"WHY NOT GO AND SEE HER?"
●MI DID GREAT!
I WONDER WHAT THE QUEEN POWER IS?
SOON I'LL HAVE POWER TOO...
...SO I WON'T ALWAYS BE THE ONE BEING PRO-TECTED.
"I'LL PROTECT YOU."
"THE TWO OF US WILL..."
●MI—
TMP

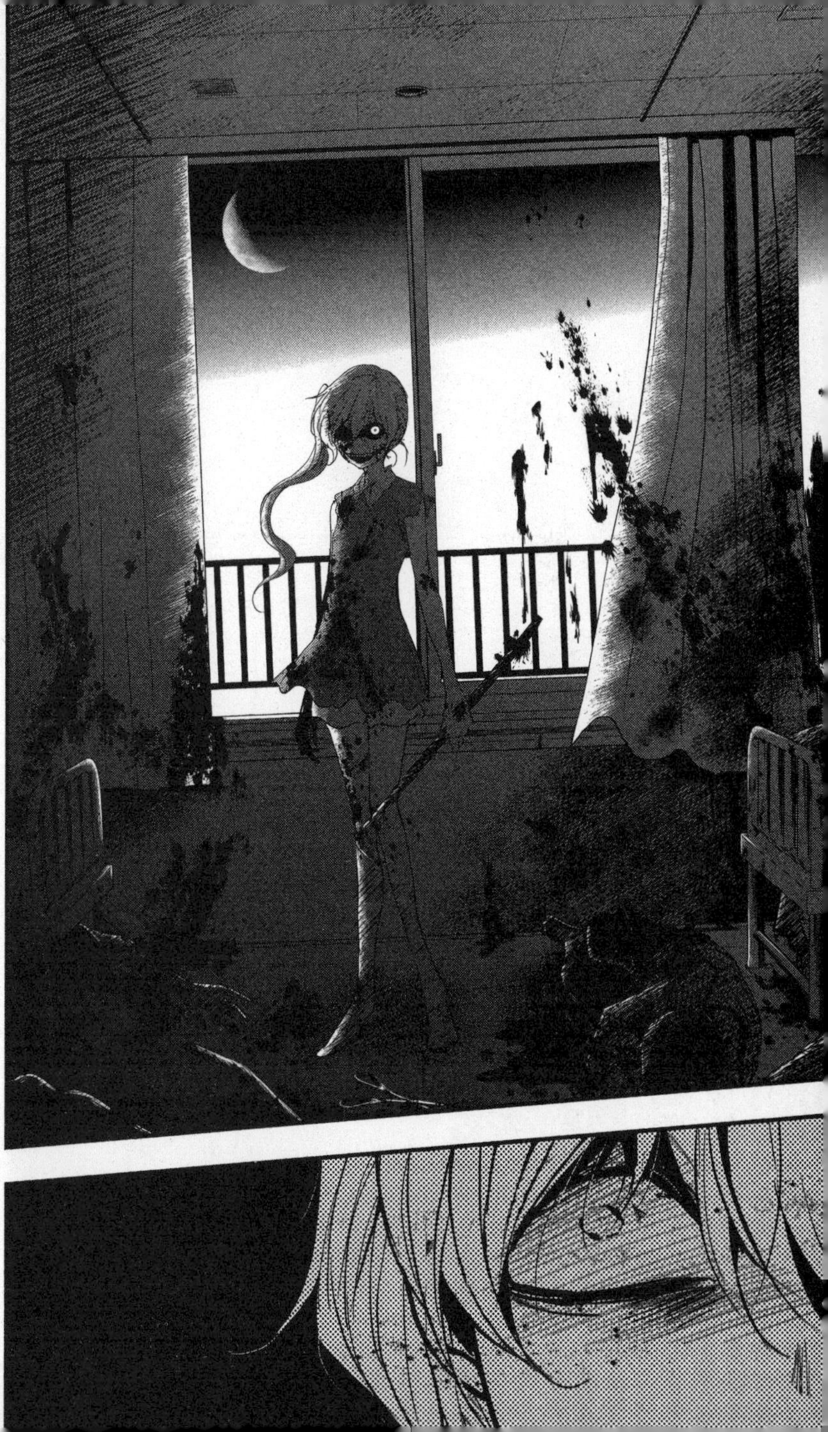

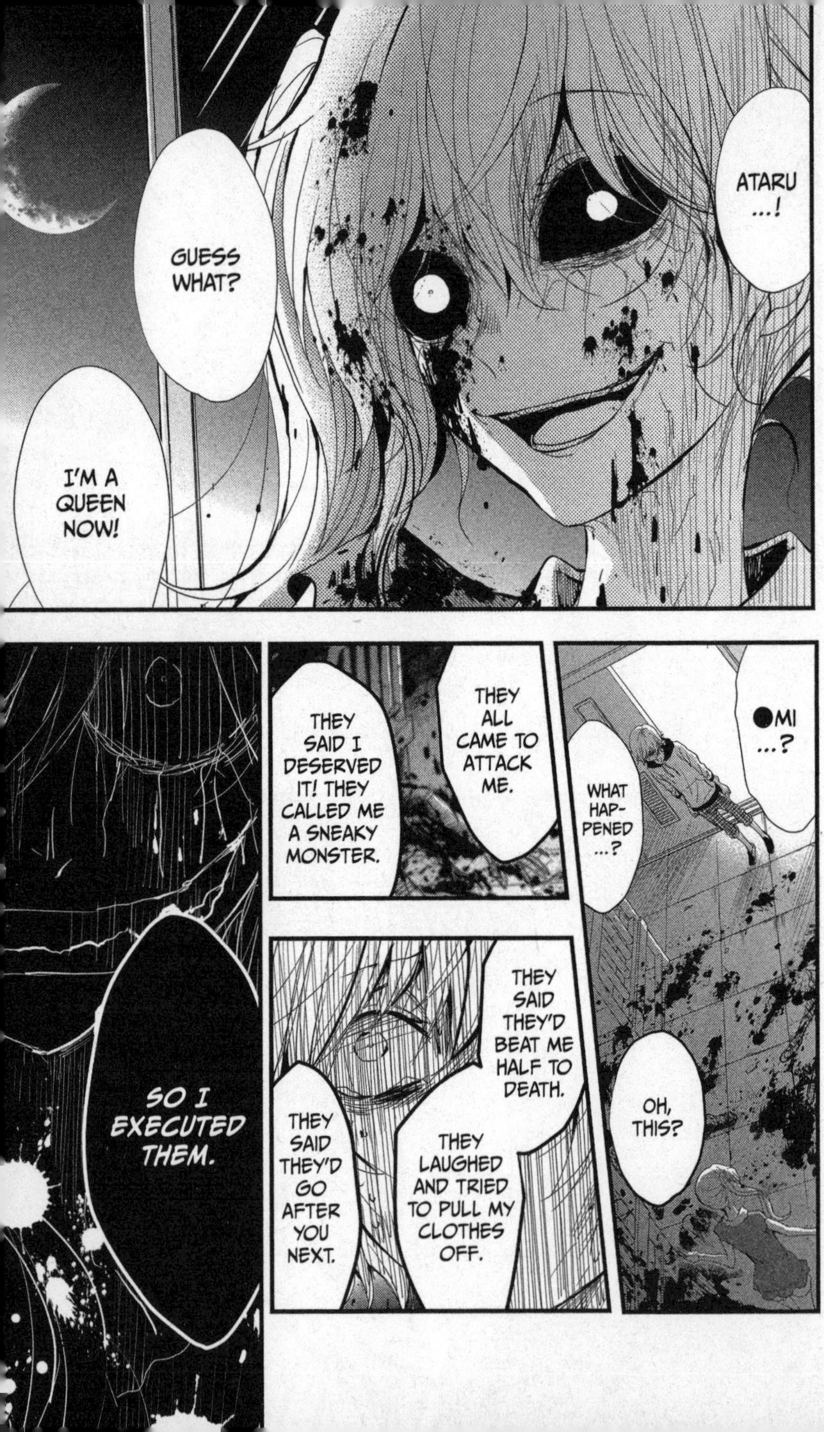
ATARU ...!
GUESS WHAT?
I'M A QUEEN NOW!
[redacted]MI ...?
WHAT HAP-PENED ...?
OH, THIS?
THEY ALL CAME TO ATTACK ME.
THEY SAID I DESERVED IT! THEY CALLED ME A SNEAKY MONSTER.
THEY SAID THEY'D BEAT ME HALF TO DEATH.
THEY LAUGHED AND TRIED TO PULL MY CLOTHES OFF.
THEY SAID THEY'D GO AFTER YOU NEXT.
SO I EXECUTED THEM.

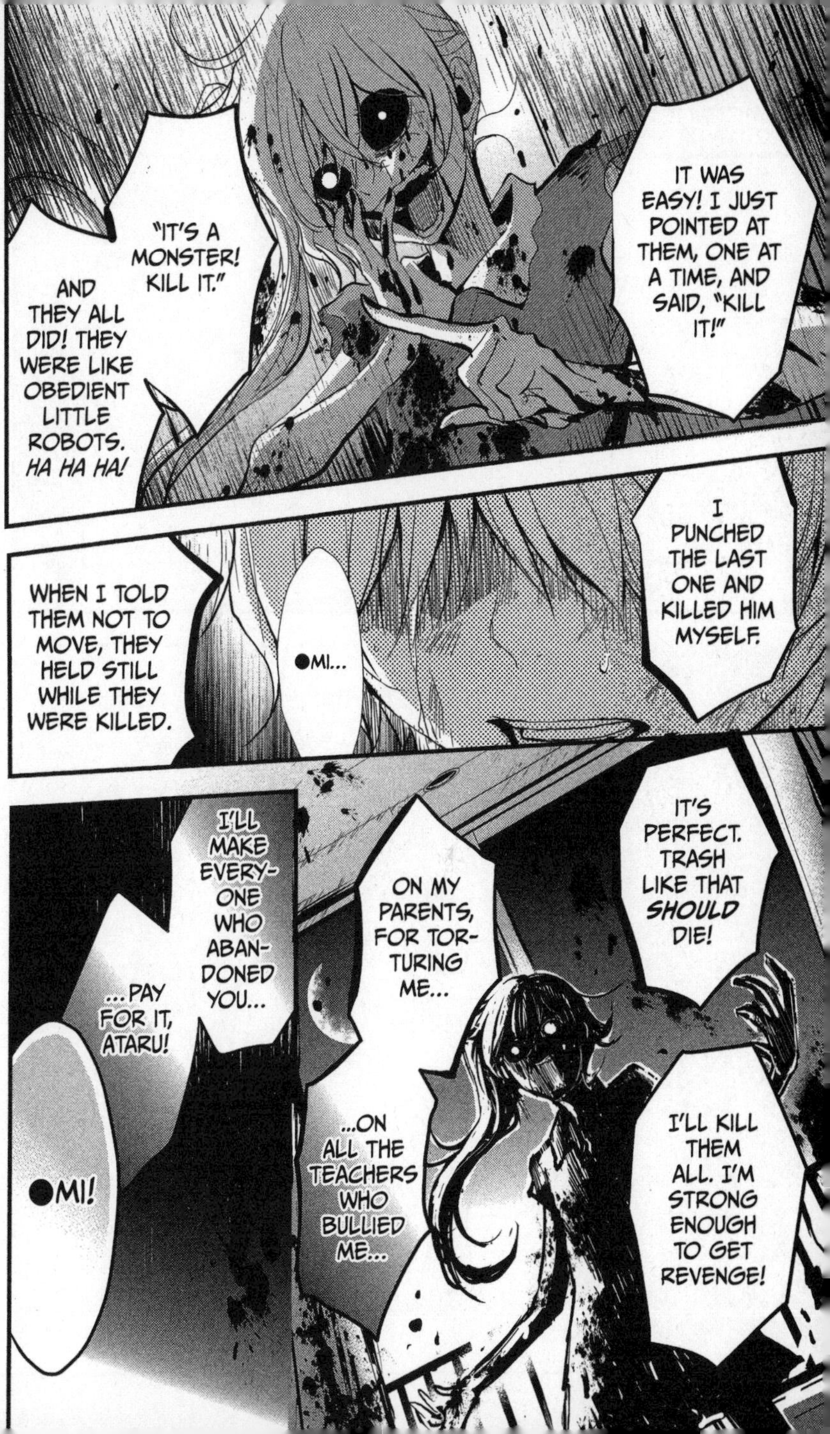
IT WAS EASY! I JUST POINTED AT THEM, ONE AT A TIME, AND SAID, "KILL IT!"
"IT'S A MONSTER! KILL IT."
AND THEY ALL DID! THEY WERE LIKE OBEDIENT LITTLE ROBOTS. *HA HA HA!*
I PUNCHED THE LAST ONE AND KILLED HIM MYSELF.
●MI...
WHEN I TOLD THEM NOT TO MOVE, THEY HELD STILL WHILE THEY WERE KILLED.
IT'S PERFECT. TRASH LIKE THAT ***SHOULD*** DIE!
I'LL KILL THEM ALL. I'M STRONG ENOUGH TO GET REVENGE!
ON MY PARENTS, FOR TOR-TURING ME...
...ON ALL THE TEACHERS WHO BULLIED ME...
I'LL MAKE EVERY-ONE WHO ABAN-DONED YOU...
...PAY FOR IT, ATARU!
●MI!

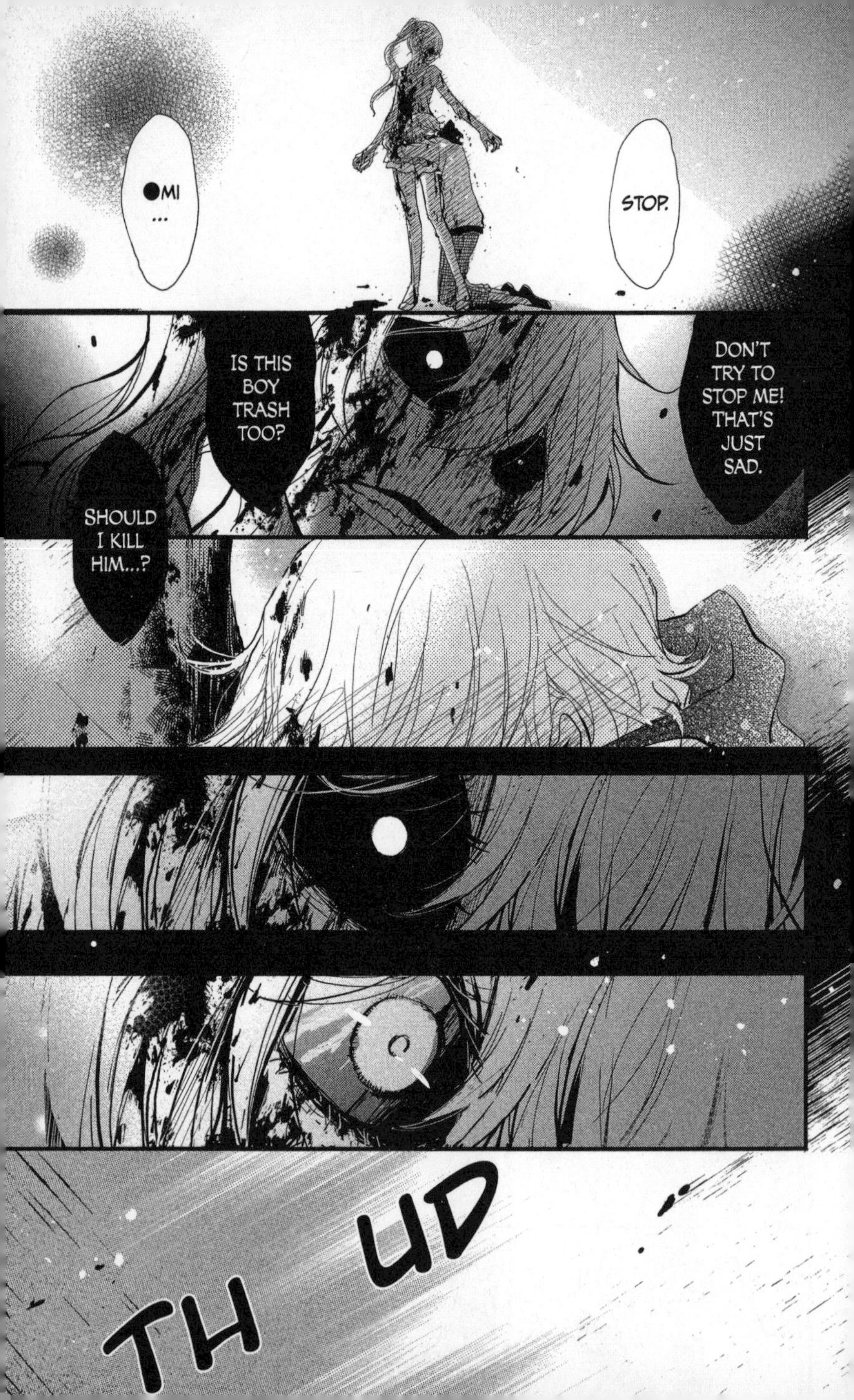
STOP.
●MI ...
DON'T TRY TO STOP ME! THAT'S JUST SAD.
IS THIS BOY TRASH TOO?
SHOULD I KILL HIM...?
THUD

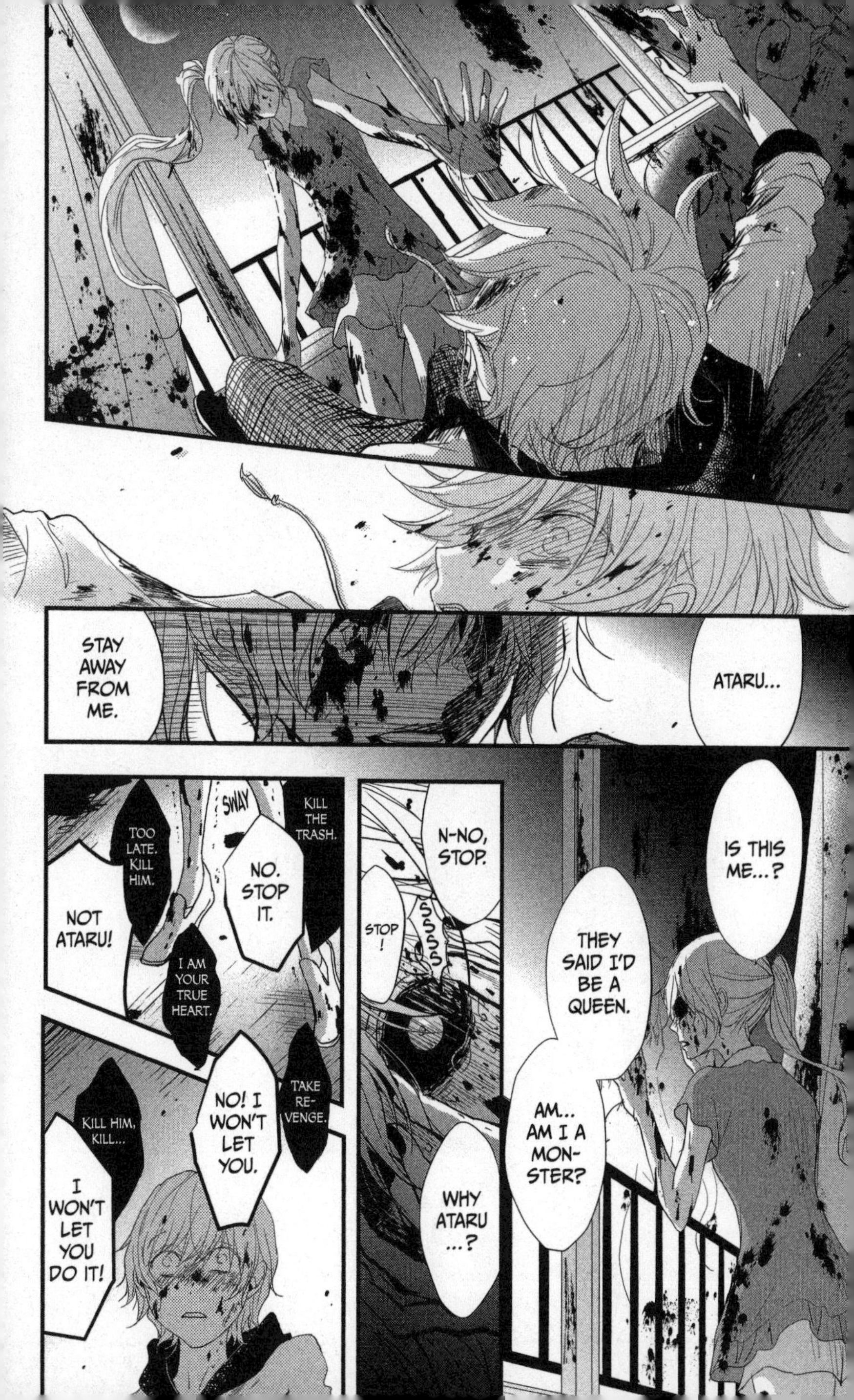

ATARU...
STAY AWAY FROM ME.
IS THIS ME...?
THEY SAID I'D BE A QUEEN.
AM... AM I A MONSTER?
N-NO, STOP.
STOP!
WHY ATARU ...?
KILL THE TRASH.
SWAY
NO. STOP IT.
TOO LATE. KILL HIM.
NOT ATARU!
I AM YOUR TRUE HEART.
TAKE RE-VENGE.
NO! I WON'T LET YOU.
KILL HIM, KILL...
I WON'T LET YOU DO IT!

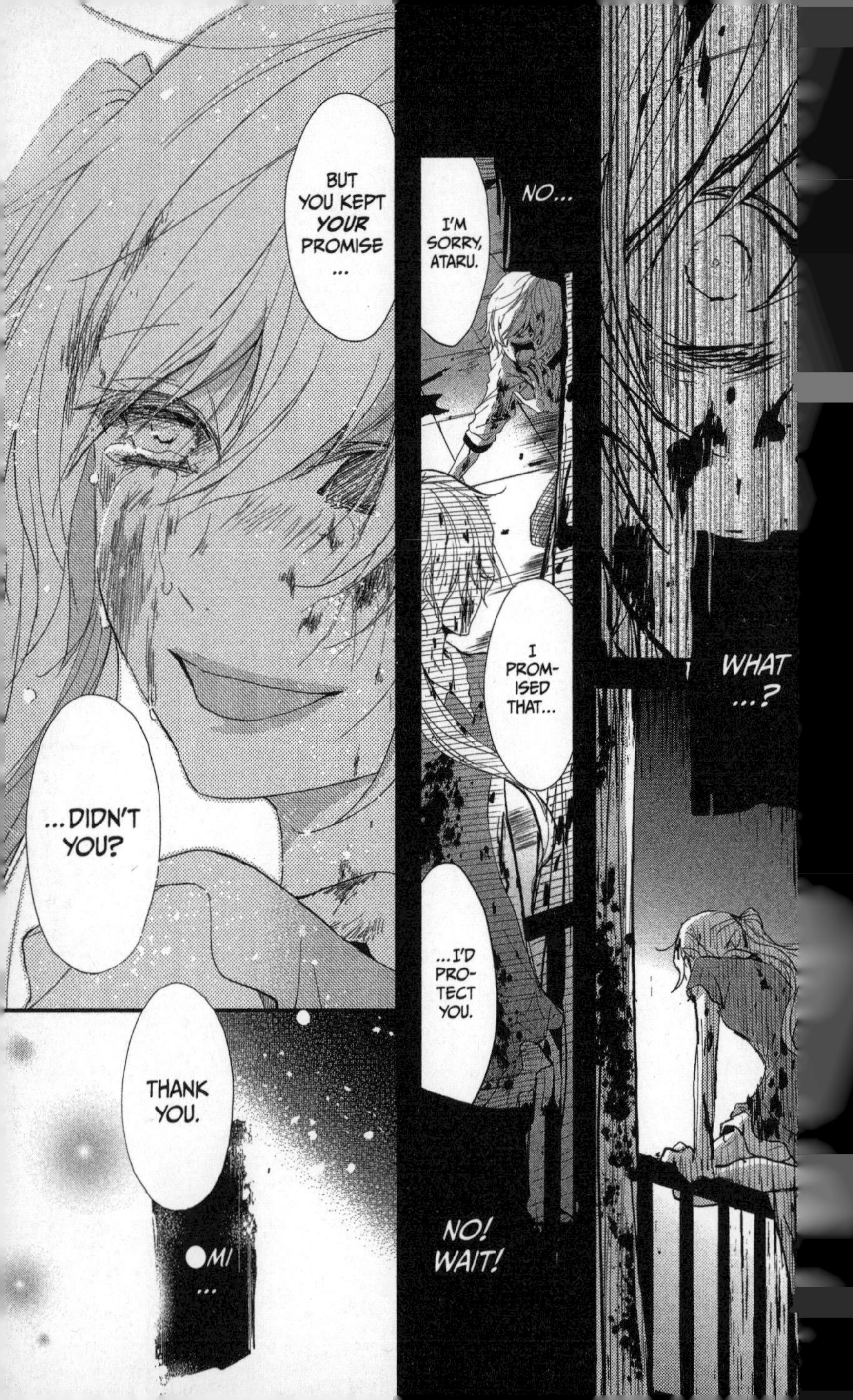
WHAT ...?
NO...
I'M SORRY, ATARU.
I PROMISED THAT...
...I'D PROTECT YOU.
NO! WAIT!
BUT YOU KEPT *YOUR* PROMISE ...
...DIDN'T YOU?
THANK YOU.
MI ...

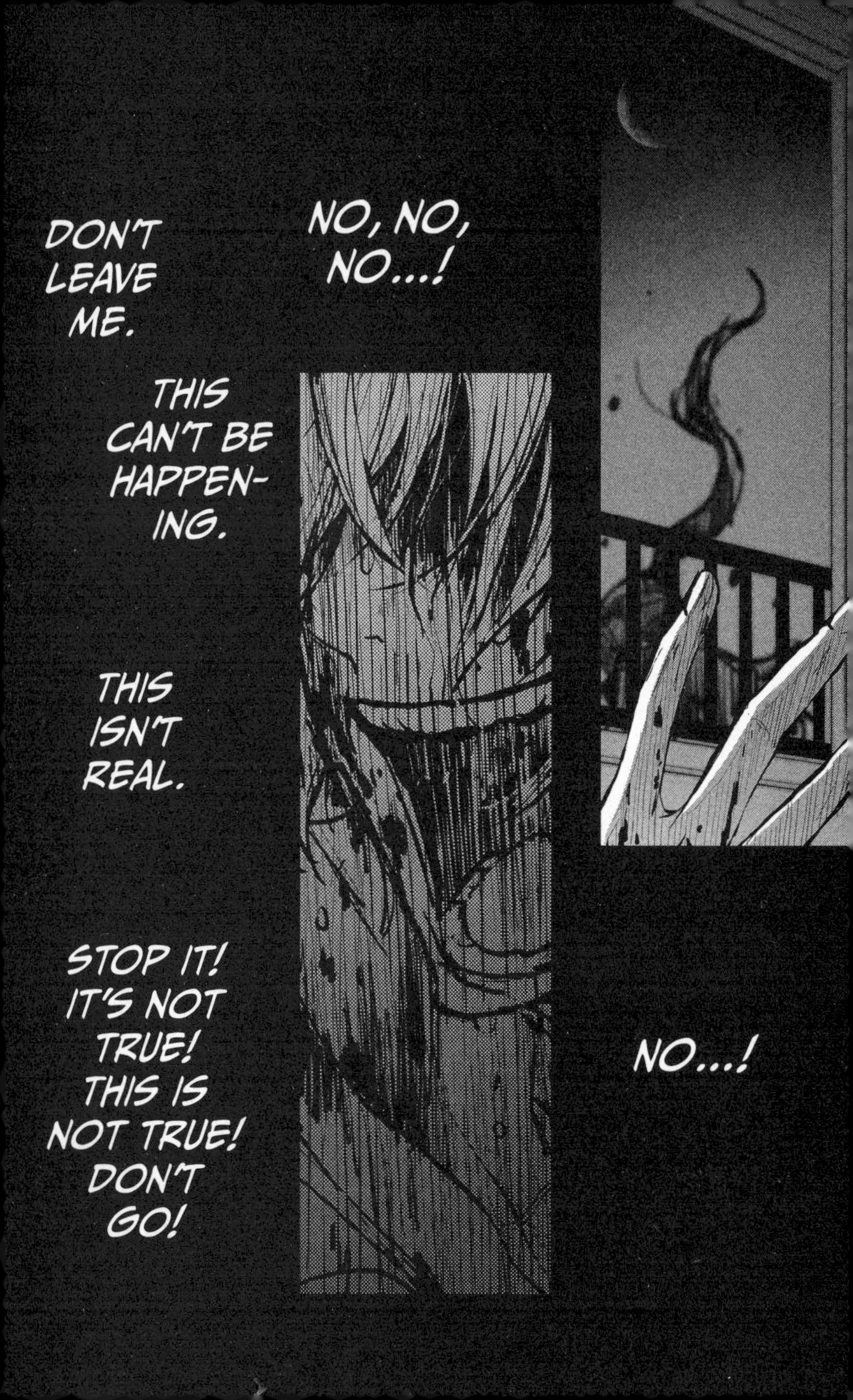
NO, NO, NO...!
DON'T LEAVE ME.
THIS CAN'T BE HAPPEN-ING.
THIS ISN'T REAL.
NO...!
STOP IT! IT'S NOT TRUE! THIS IS NOT TRUE! DON'T GO!

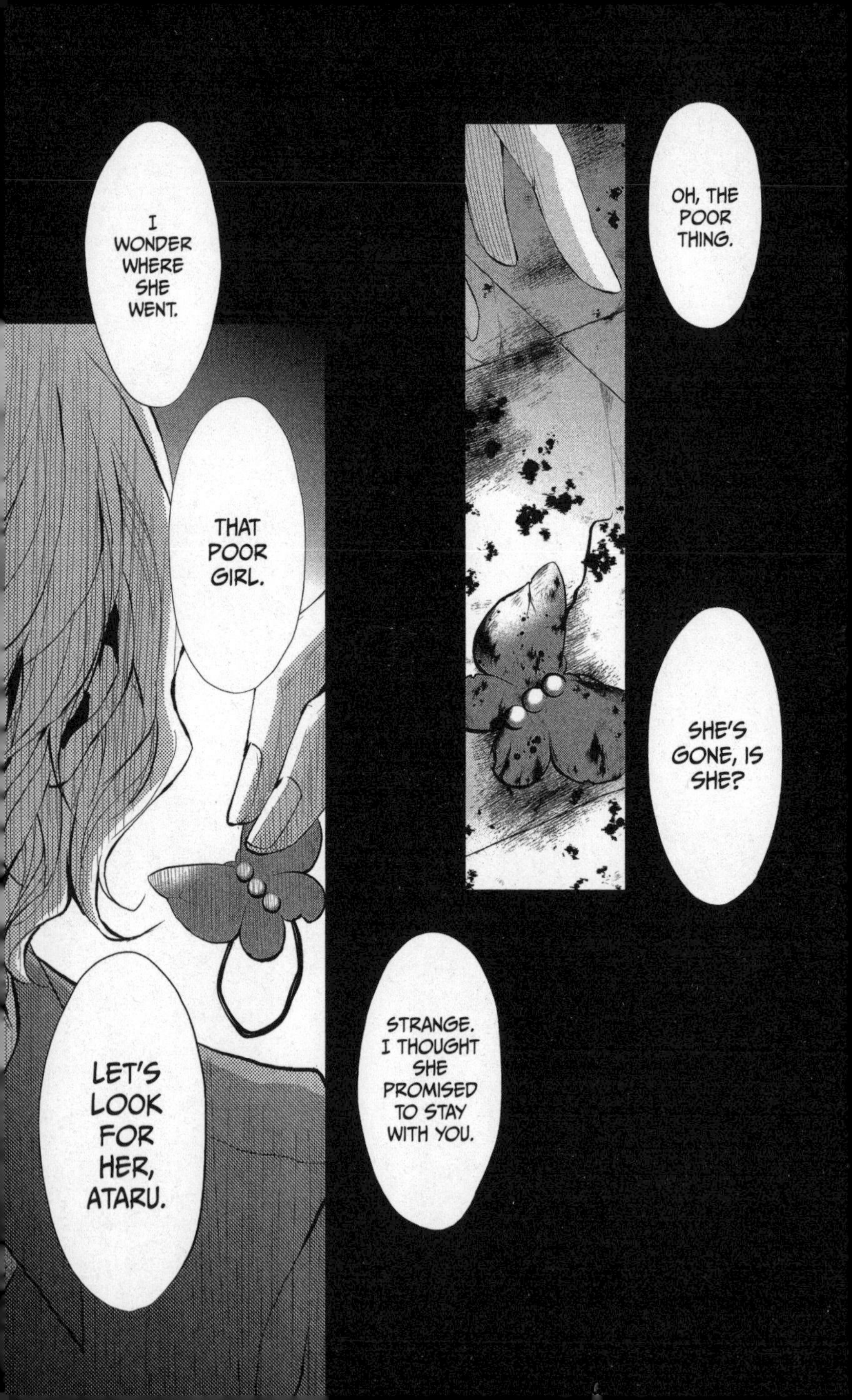
OH, THE POOR THING.
SHE'S GONE, IS SHE?
STRANGE. I THOUGHT SHE PROMISED TO STAY WITH YOU.
I WONDER WHERE SHE WENT.
THAT POOR GIRL.
LET'S LOOK FOR HER, ATARU.

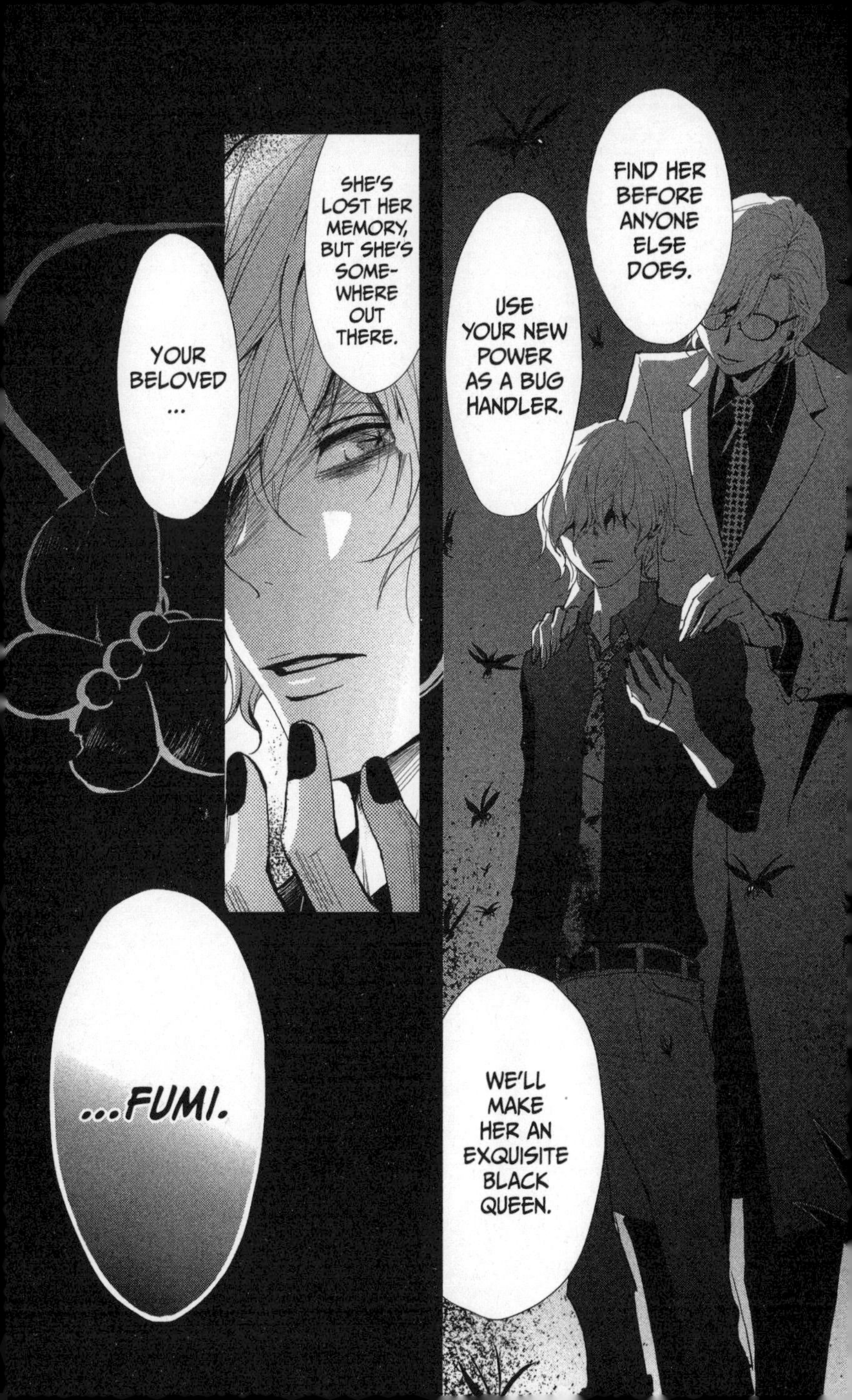
FIND HER BEFORE ANYONE ELSE DOES.
USE YOUR NEW POWER AS A BUG HANDLER.
WE'LL MAKE HER AN EXQUISITE BLACK QUEEN.
SHE'S LOST HER MEMORY, BUT SHE'S SOME-WHERE OUT THERE.
YOUR BELOVED ...
...FUMI.

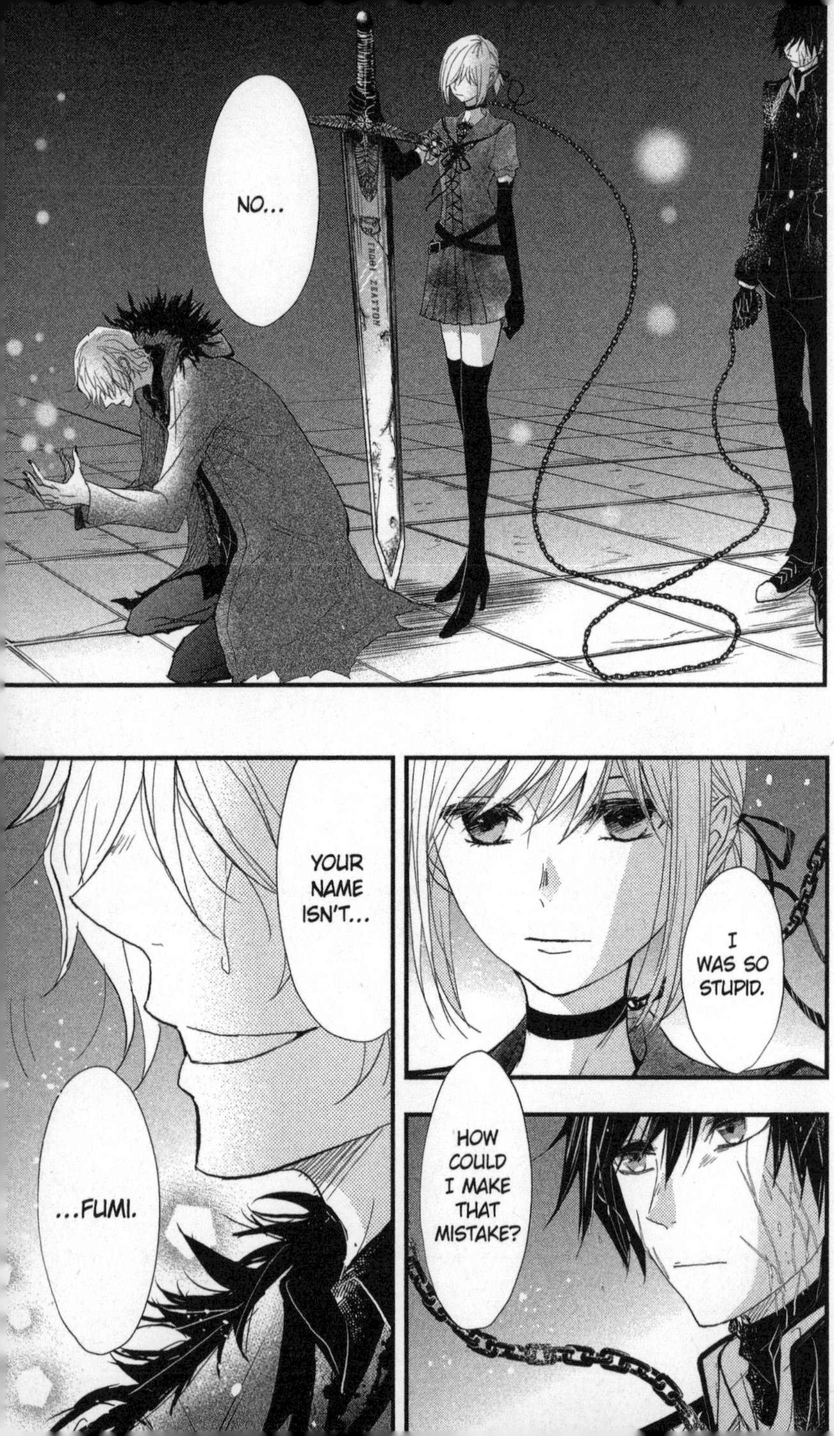
NO...
I WAS SO STUPID.
HOW COULD I MAKE THAT MISTAKE?
YOUR NAME ISN'T...
...FUMI.

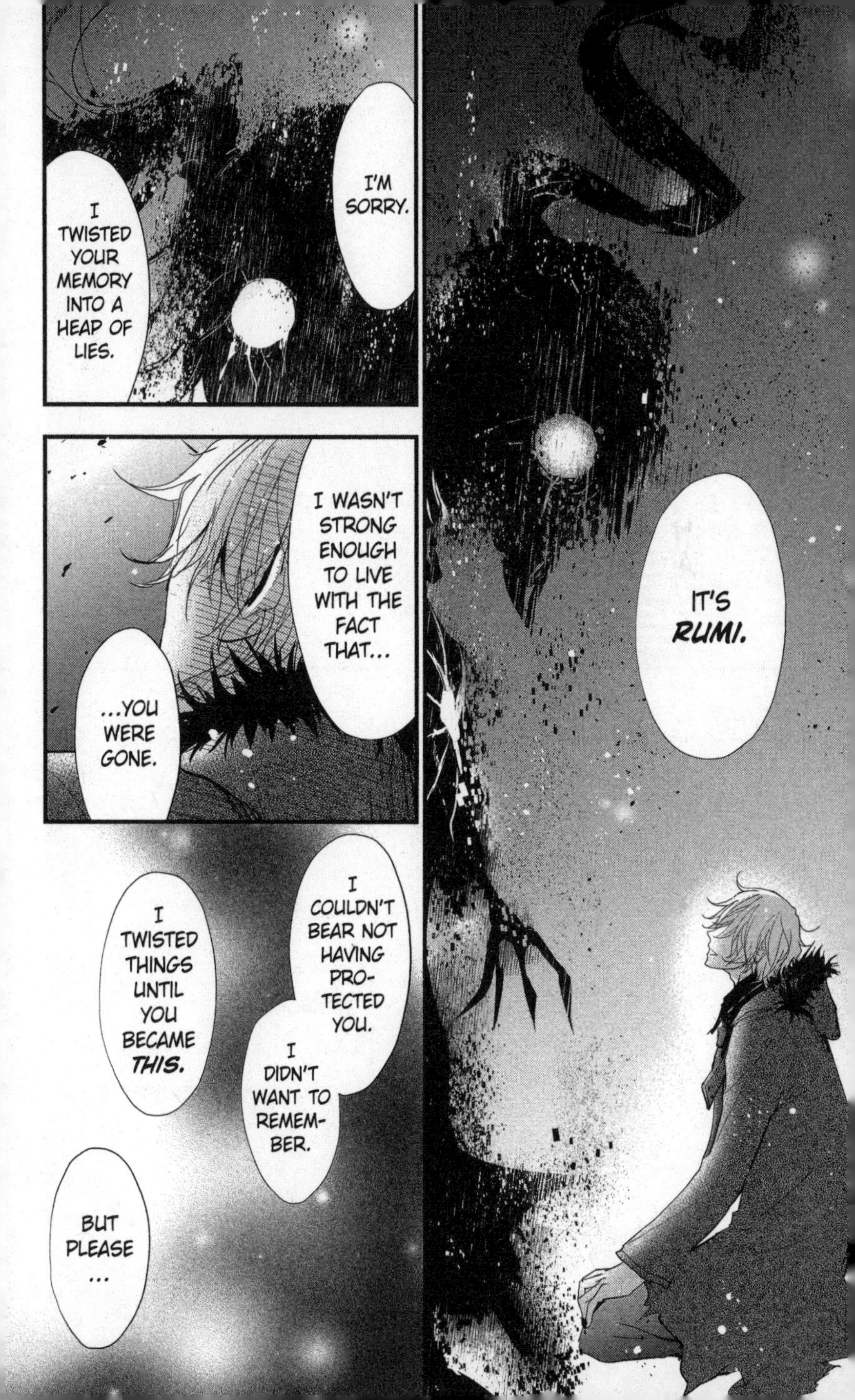
IT'S *RUMI.*
I'M SORRY.
I TWISTED YOUR MEMORY INTO A HEAP OF LIES.
I WASN'T STRONG ENOUGH TO LIVE WITH THE FACT THAT...
...YOU WERE GONE.
I COULDN'T BEAR NOT HAVING PRO-TECTED YOU.
I TWISTED THINGS UNTIL YOU BECAME *THIS.*
I DIDN'T WANT TO REMEM-BER.
BUT PLEASE...

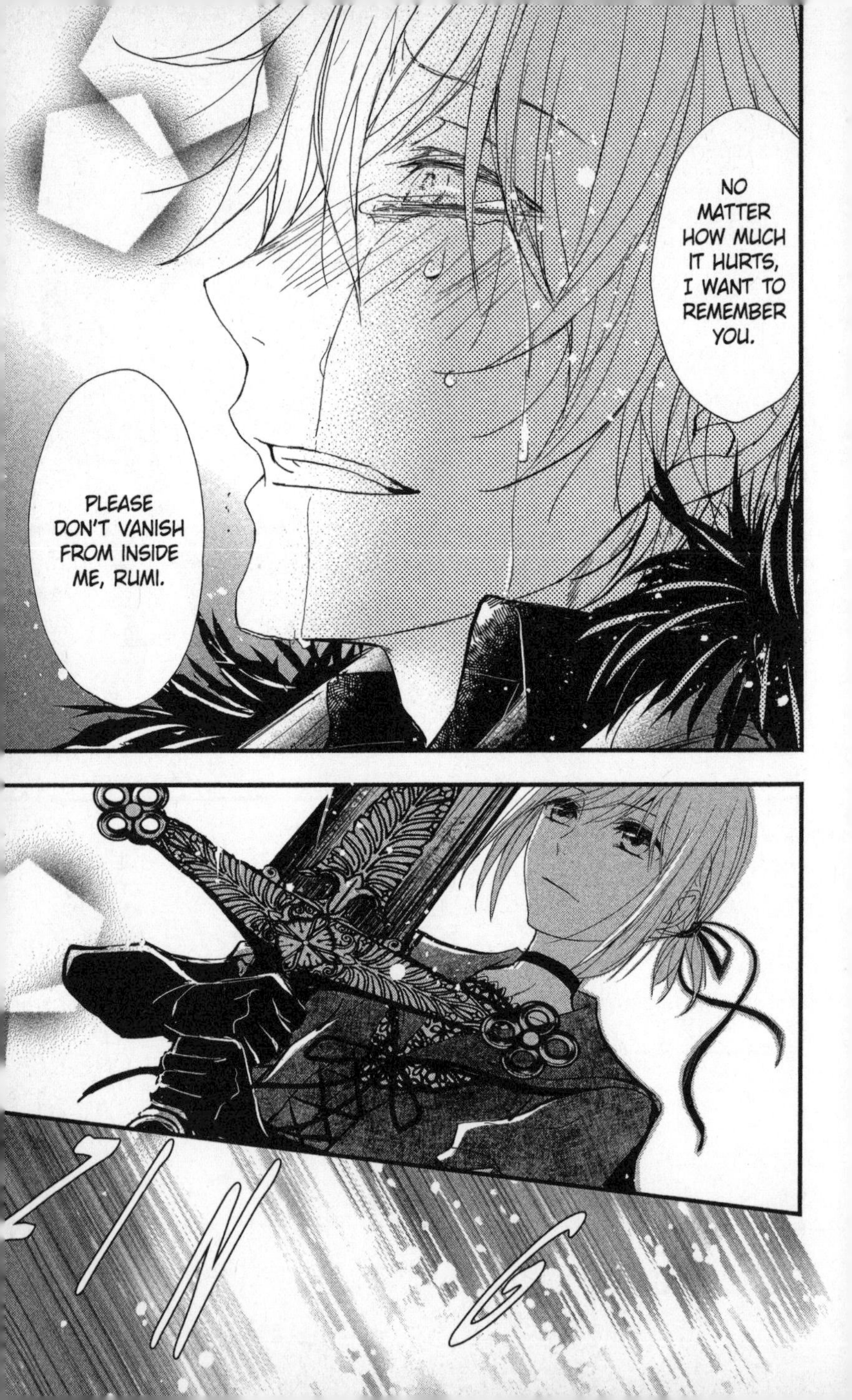
NO MATTER HOW MUCH IT HURTS, I WANT TO REMEMBER YOU.
PLEASE DON'T VANISH FROM INSIDE ME, RUMI.
ZING

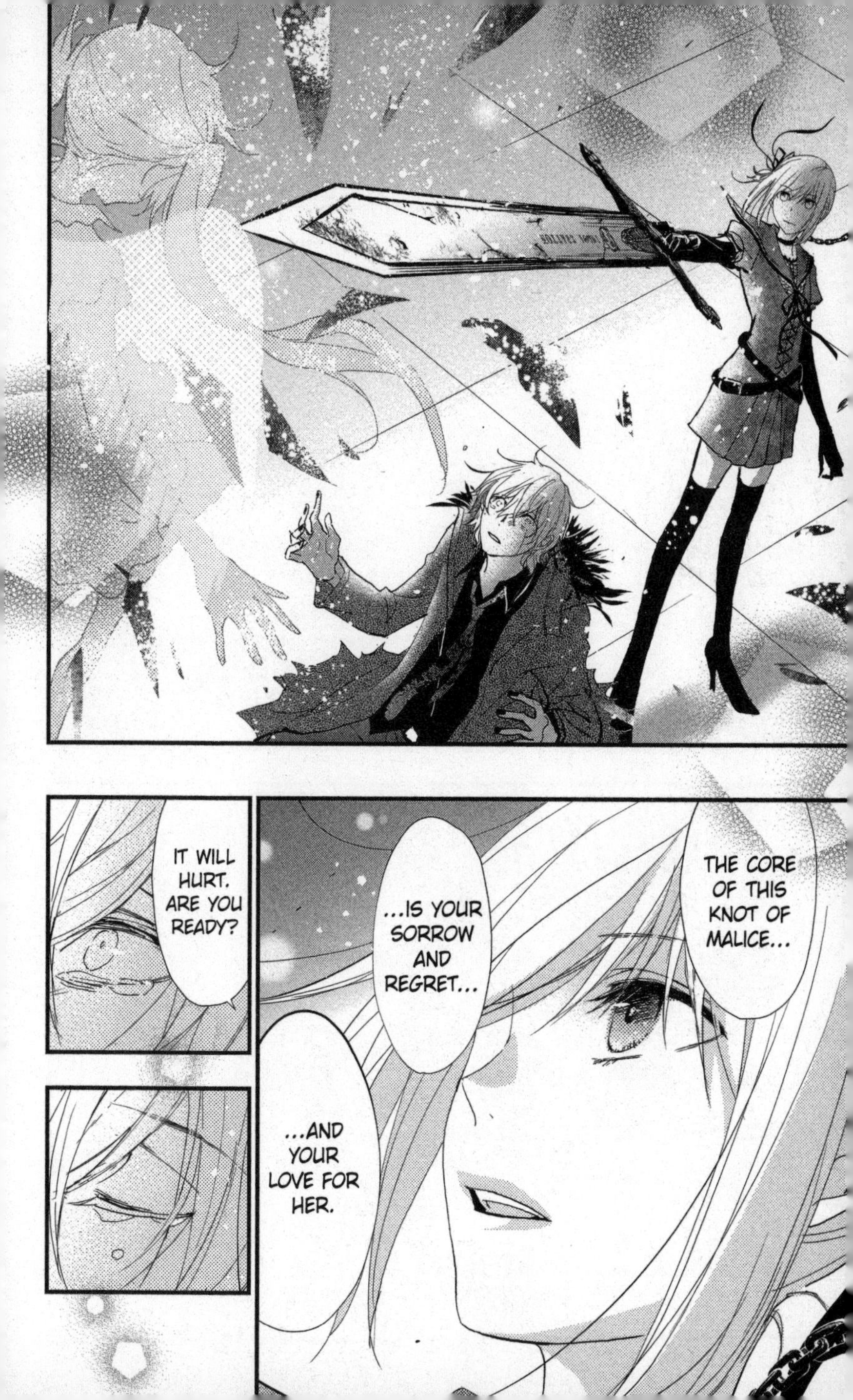
THE CORE OF THIS KNOT OF MALICE...
...IS YOUR SORROW AND REGRET...
...AND YOUR LOVE FOR HER.
IT WILL HURT. ARE YOU READY?

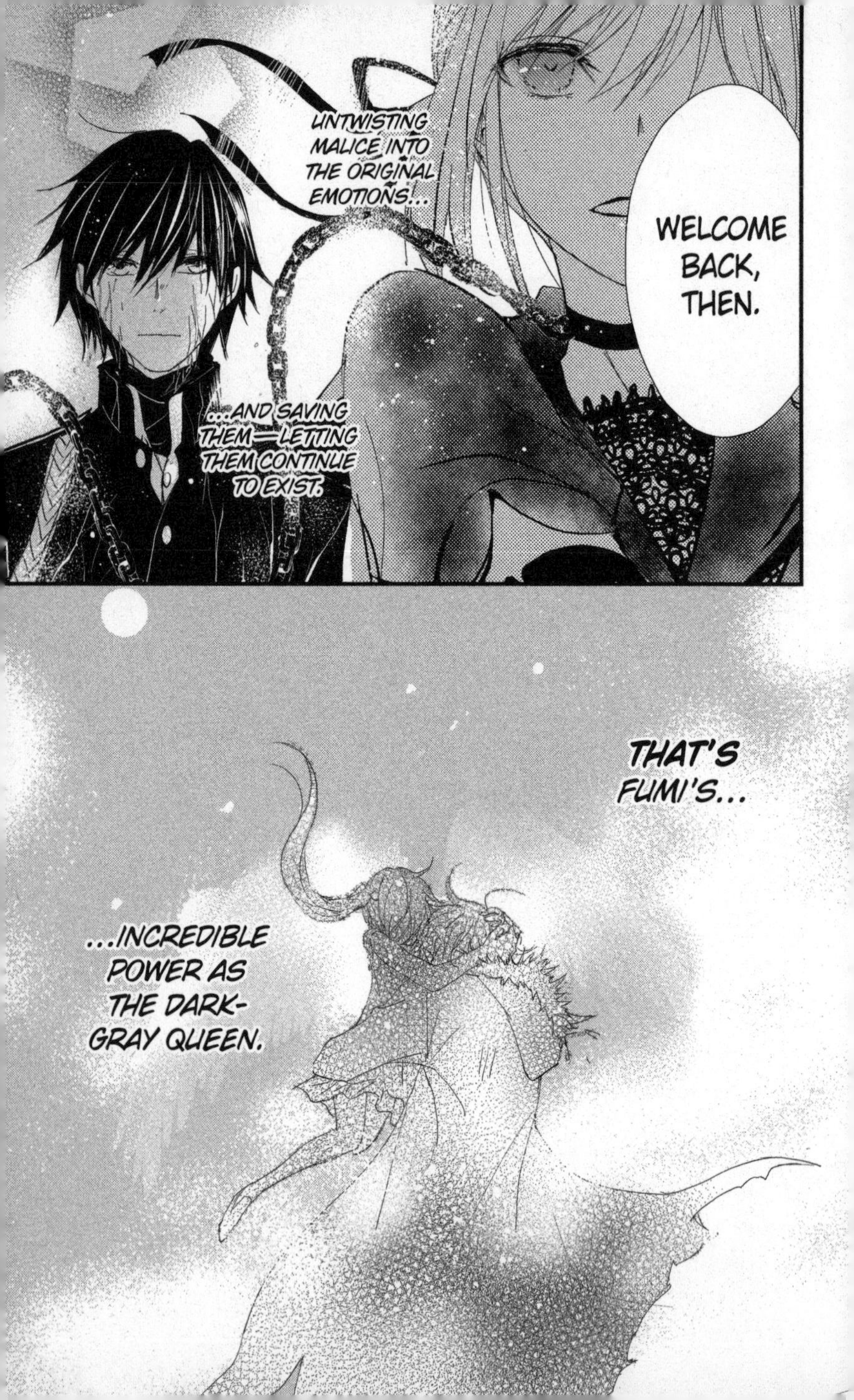
WELCOME BACK, THEN.
UNTWISTING MALICE INTO THE ORIGINAL EMOTIONS...
...AND SAVING THEM—LETTING THEM CONTINUE TO EXIST.
THAT'S FUMI'S...
...INCREDIBLE POWER AS THE DARK-GRAY QUEEN.

MONTHLY BETSUCOMI SALE DATE NOTICE ON TWITTER

CHAPTER 24

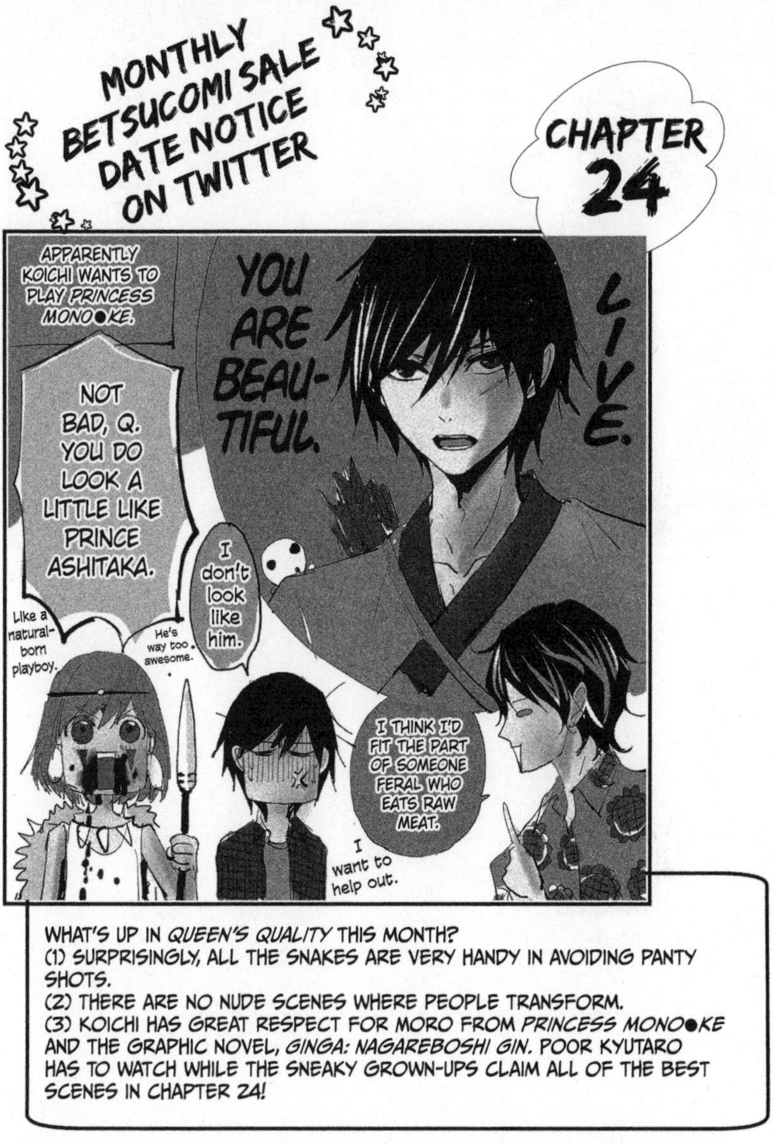
LIVE.
YOU ARE BEAU-TIFUL.
APPARENTLY KOICHI WANTS TO PLAY PRINCESS MONO●KE.
NOT BAD, Q. YOU DO LOOK A LITTLE LIKE PRINCE ASHITAKA.
I don't look like him.
He's way too awesome.
Like a natural-born playboy.
I THINK I'D FIT THE PART OF SOMEONE FERAL WHO EATS RAW MEAT.
I want to help out.

WHAT'S UP IN *QUEEN'S QUALITY* THIS MONTH?
(1) SURPRISINGLY, ALL THE SNAKES ARE VERY HANDY IN AVOIDING PANTY SHOTS.
(2) THERE ARE NO NUDE SCENES WHERE PEOPLE TRANSFORM.
(3) KOICHI HAS GREAT RESPECT FOR MORO FROM *PRINCESS MONO●KE* AND THE GRAPHIC NOVEL, *GINGA: NAGAREBOSHI GIN*. POOR KYUTARO HAS TO WATCH WHILE THE SNEAKY GROWN-UPS CLAIM ALL OF THE BEST SCENES IN CHAPTER 24!

I'VE MENTIONED VARIOUS POPULAR ANIME AND MANGA IN THIS MONTH'S NOTICE. MY FAVORITE CHARACTERS ARE LADY EBOSHI IN *PRINCESS MONO●KE* AND BEN AND BENIZAKURA IN *GINGA*.

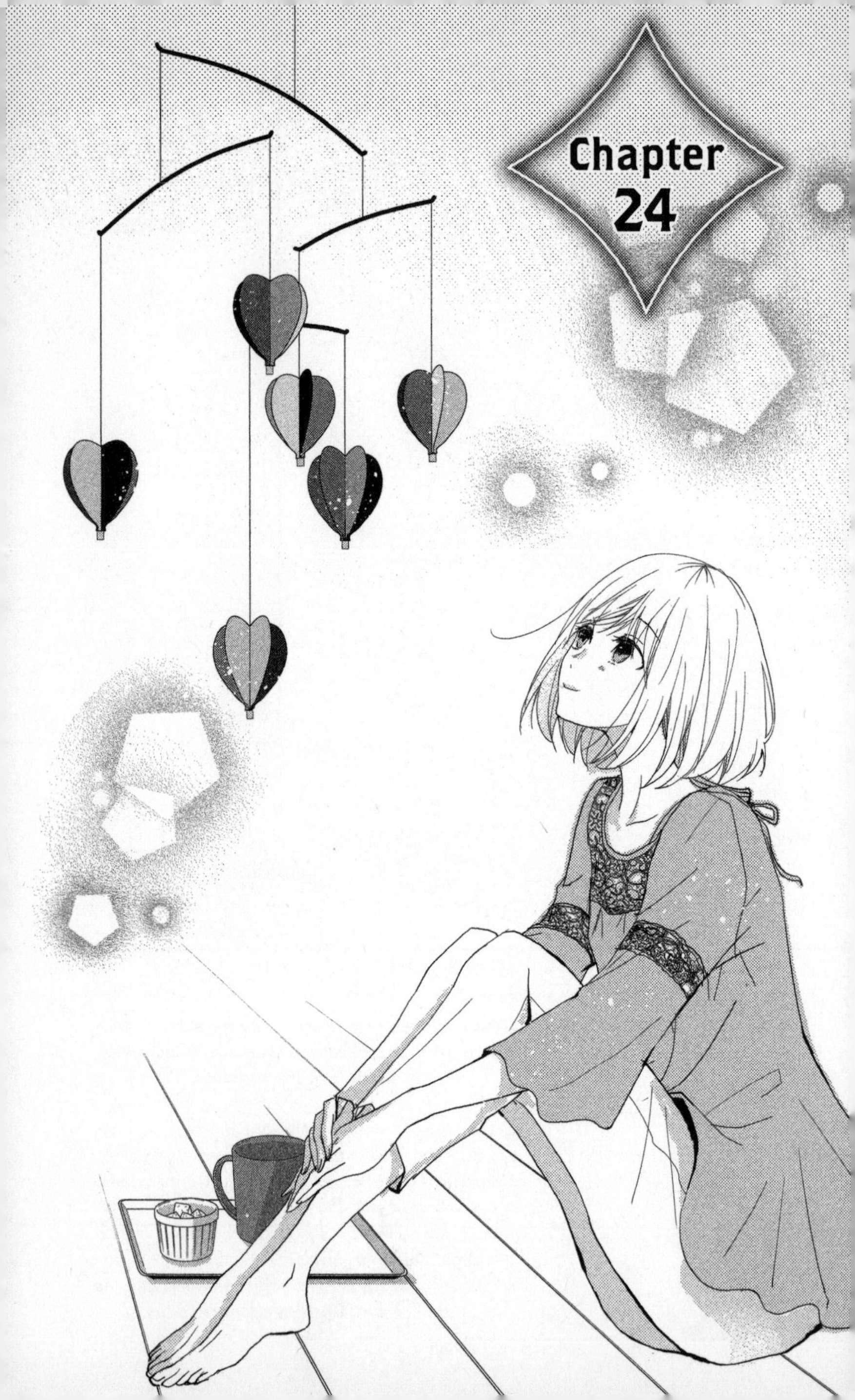
Chapter
24

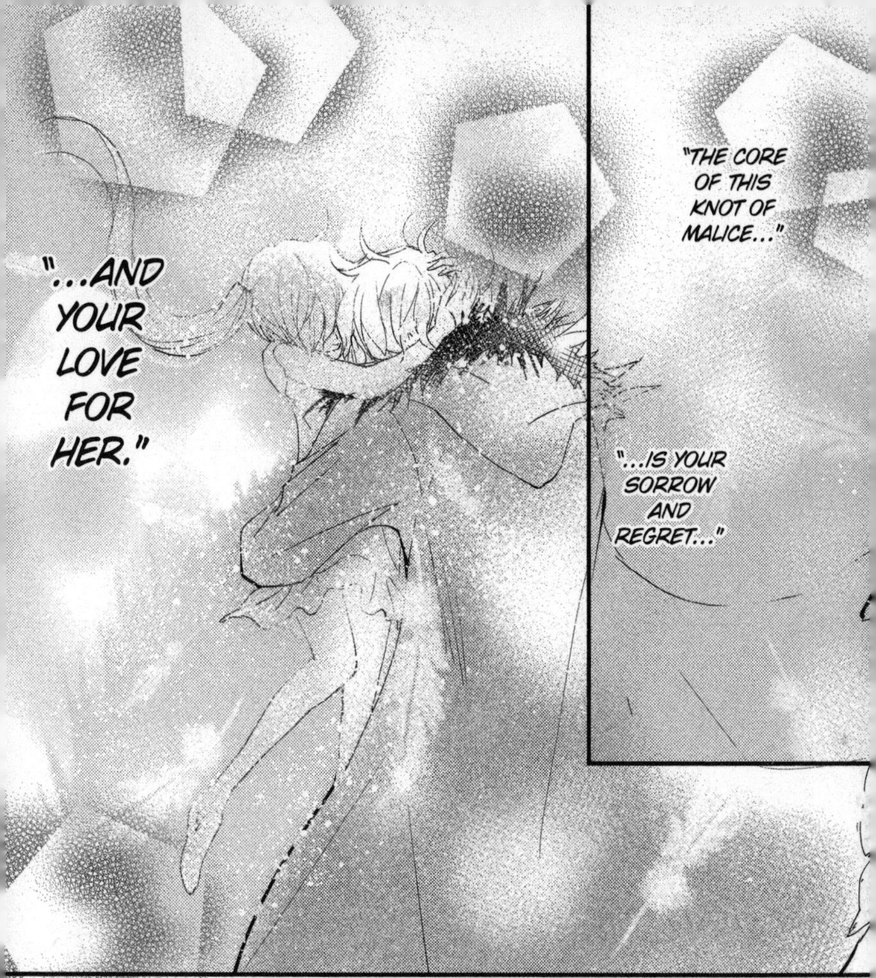
"THE CORE OF THIS KNOT OF MALICE..."
"...IS YOUR SORROW AND REGRET..."
"...AND YOUR LOVE FOR HER."

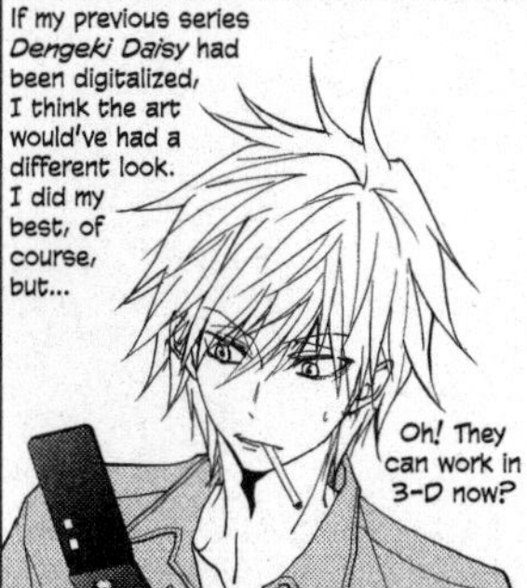
If my previous series *Dengeki Daisy* had been digitalized, I think the art would've had a different look. I did my best, of course, but...
Oh! They can work in 3-D now?

In this volume, there are so many scenes with chains that it makes you wonder if the chain is the actual protagonist.

Because we compose the art digitally, what we call the "chain brush" is extremely useful. Chaining Kyutaro up is so easy. It only takes a second digitally. But even with such handy tools, I don't finish my work any faster. It's so strange. But drawing on the computer is so much fun, and it's perfect for someone like me since I'm constantly redoing scenes.

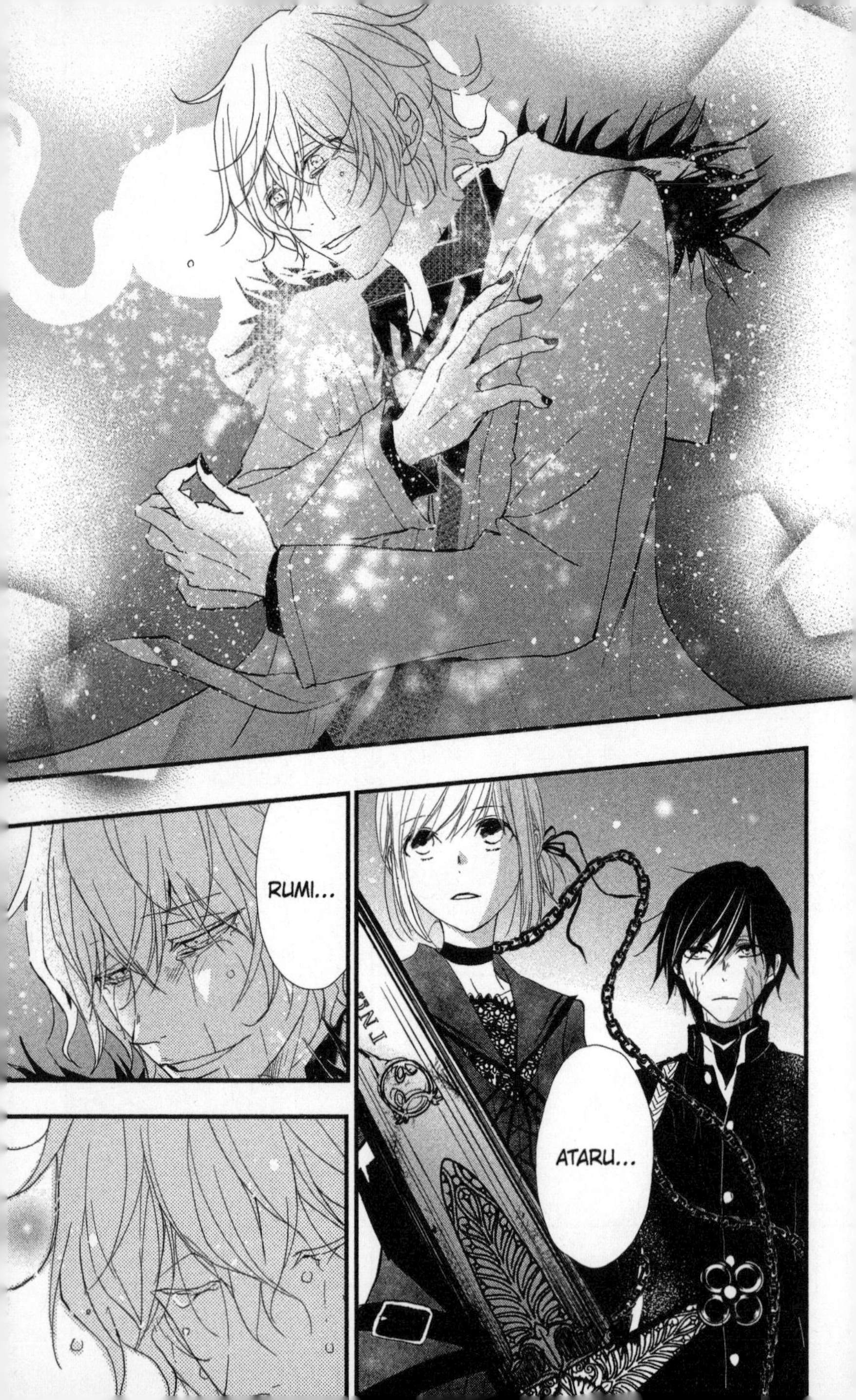
ATARU...
RUMI...

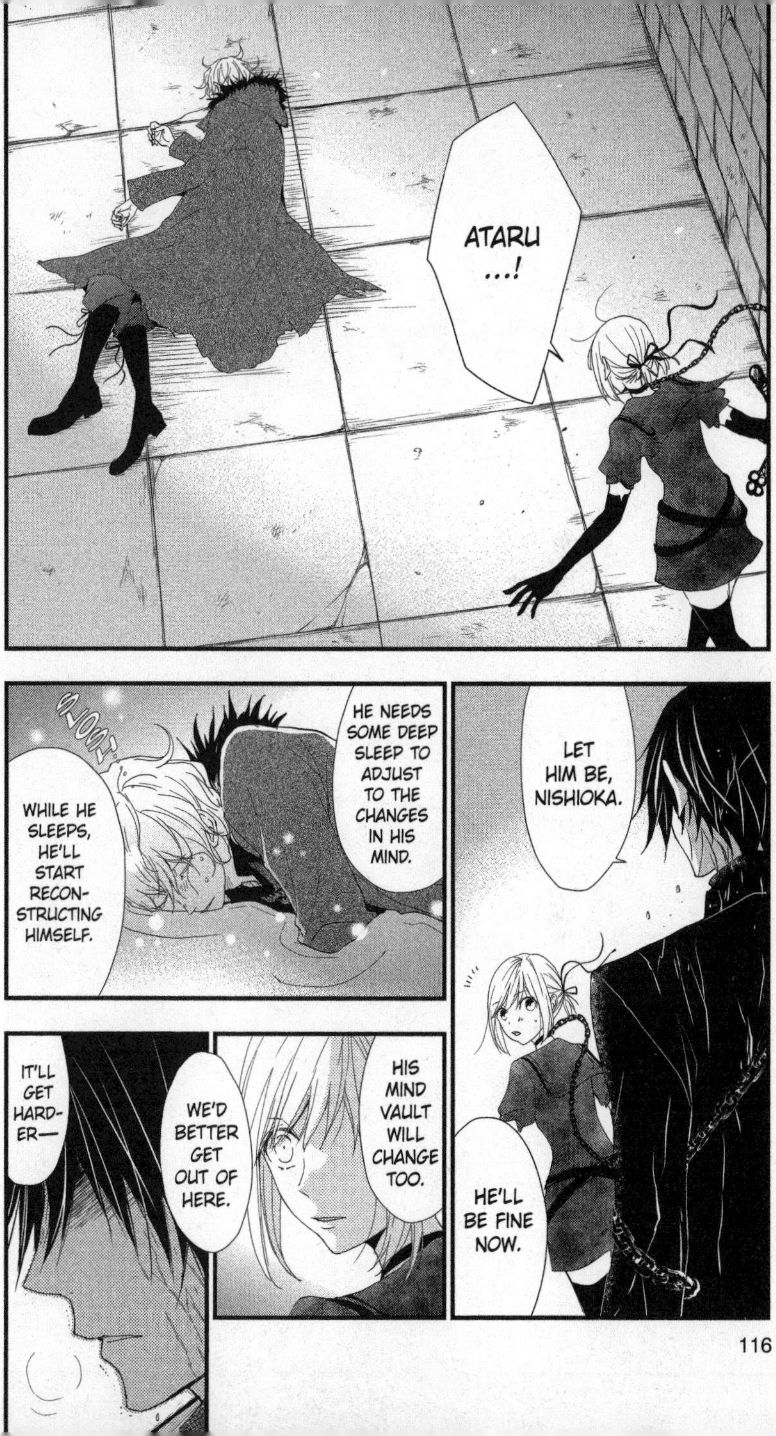
ATARU ...!
LET HIM BE, NISHIOKA.
HE'LL BE FINE NOW.
HE NEEDS SOME DEEP SLEEP TO ADJUST TO THE CHANGES IN HIS MIND.
WHILE HE SLEEPS, HE'LL START RECON-STRUCTING HIMSELF.
HIS MIND VAULT WILL CHANGE TOO.
WE'D BETTER GET OUT OF HERE.
IT'LL GET HARD-ER—

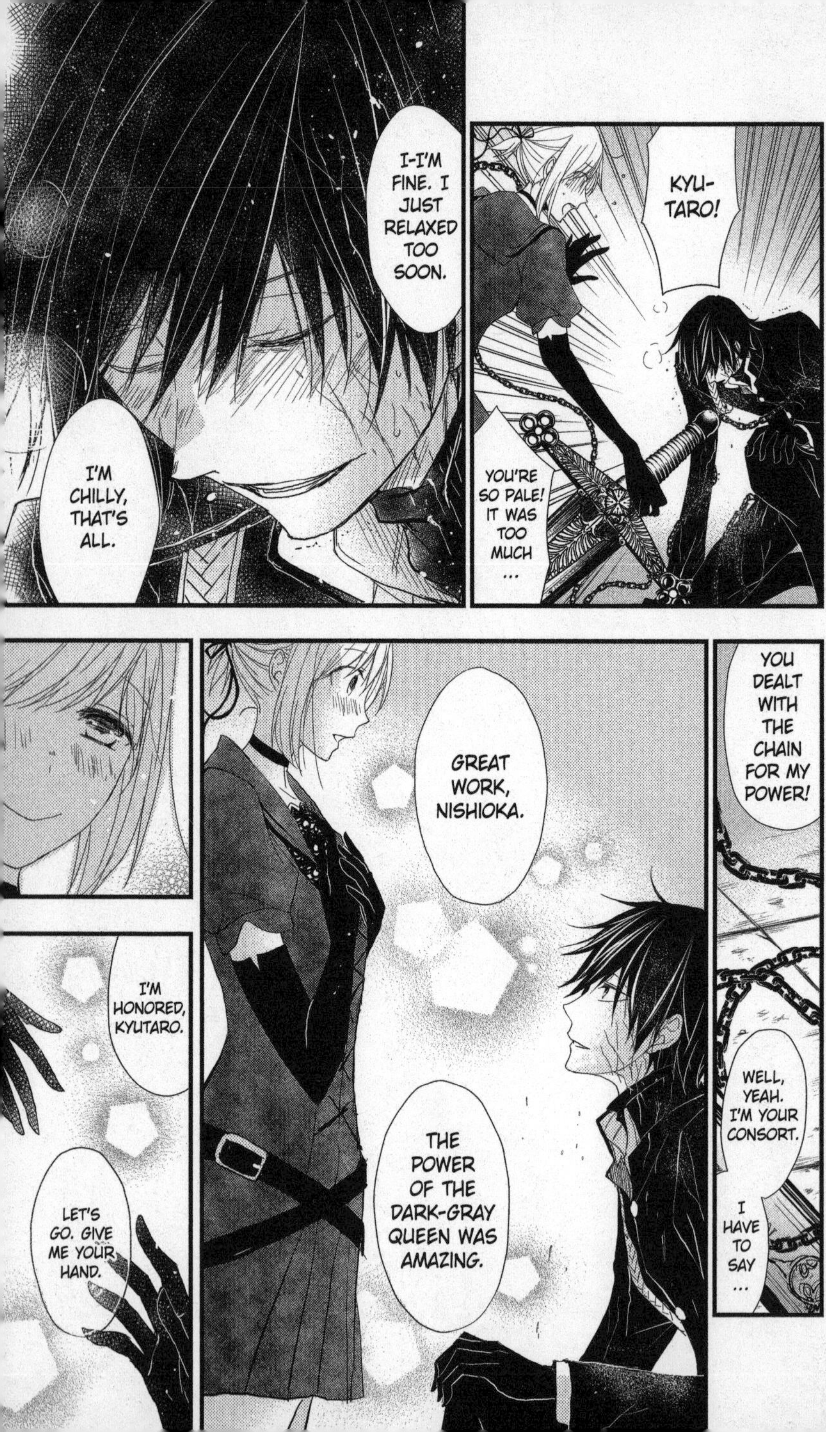
KYU-TARO!
YOU'RE SO PALE! IT WAS TOO MUCH ...
I-I'M FINE. I JUST RELAXED TOO SOON.
I'M CHILLY, THAT'S ALL.
YOU DEALT WITH THE CHAIN FOR MY POWER!
WELL, YEAH. I'M YOUR CONSORT.
I HAVE TO SAY ...
GREAT WORK, NISHIOKA.
THE POWER OF THE DARK-GRAY QUEEN WAS AMAZING.
I'M HONORED, KYUTARO.
LET'S GO. GIVE ME YOUR HAND.

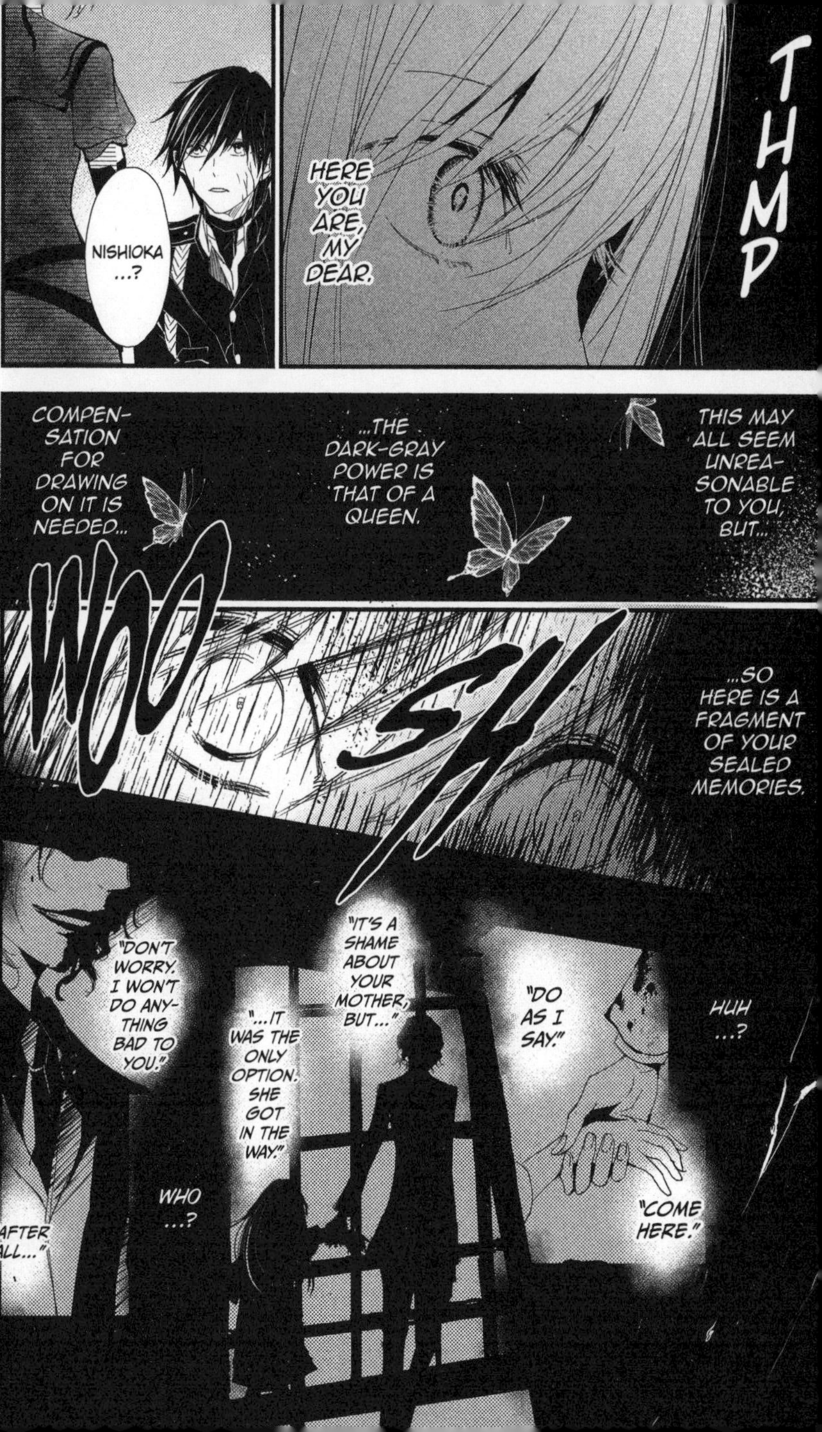
THMP
HERE YOU ARE, MY DEAR.
NISHIOKA ...?
THIS MAY ALL SEEM UNREASONABLE TO YOU, BUT...
...THE DARK-GRAY POWER IS THAT OF A QUEEN.
COMPENSATION FOR DRAWING ON IT IS NEEDED...
WOOSH
...SO HERE IS A FRAGMENT OF YOUR SEALED MEMORIES.
HUH ...?
"COME HERE."
"DO AS I SAY."
"IT'S A SHAME ABOUT YOUR MOTHER, BUT..."
"...IT WAS THE ONLY OPTION. SHE GOT IN THE WAY."
WHO ...?
"DON'T WORRY. I WON'T DO ANYTHING BAD TO YOU."
"AFTER ALL..."

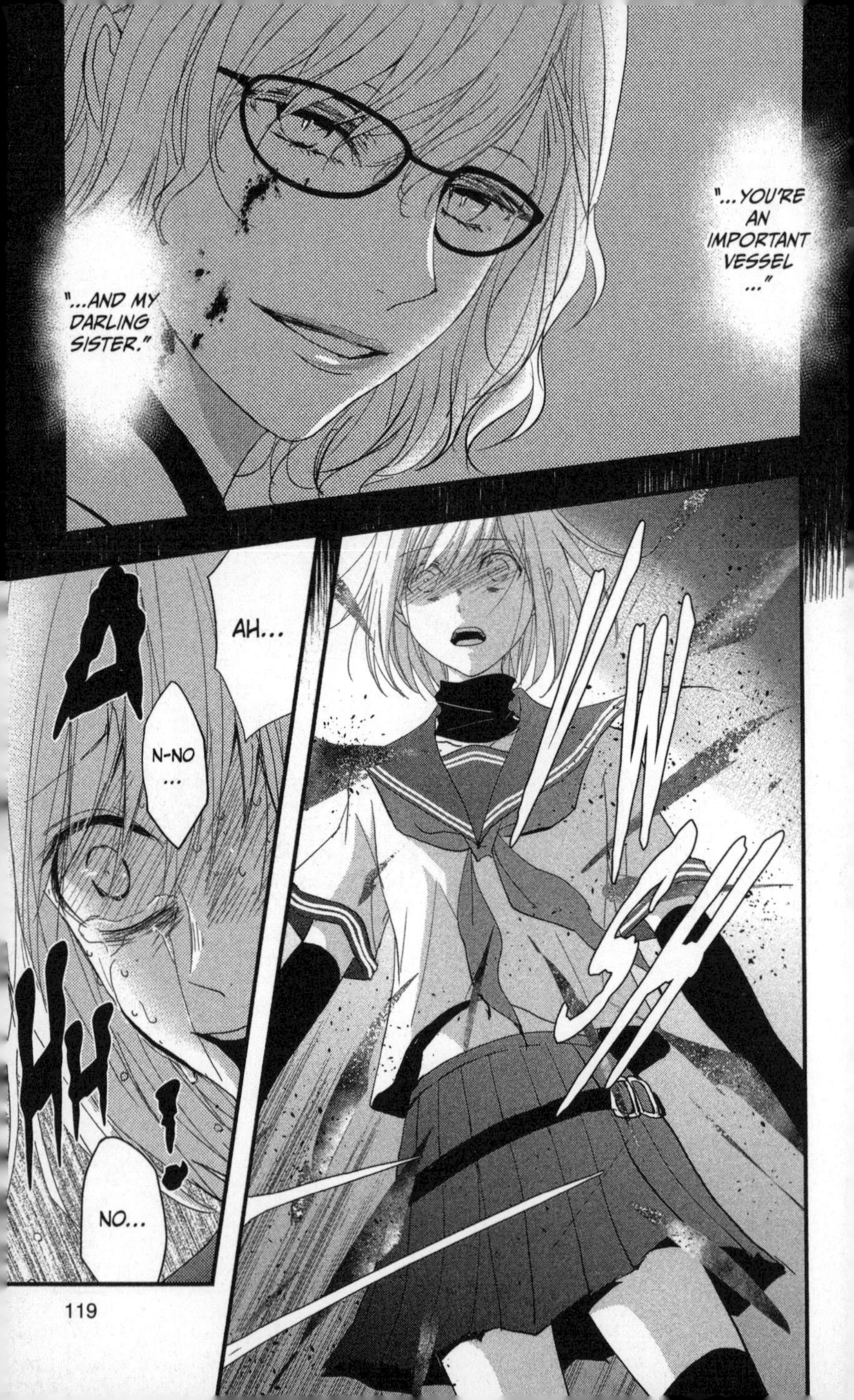
"...YOU'RE AN IMPORTANT VESSEL ..."
"...AND MY DARLING SISTER."
AH...
N-NO ...
AHH!
NO...

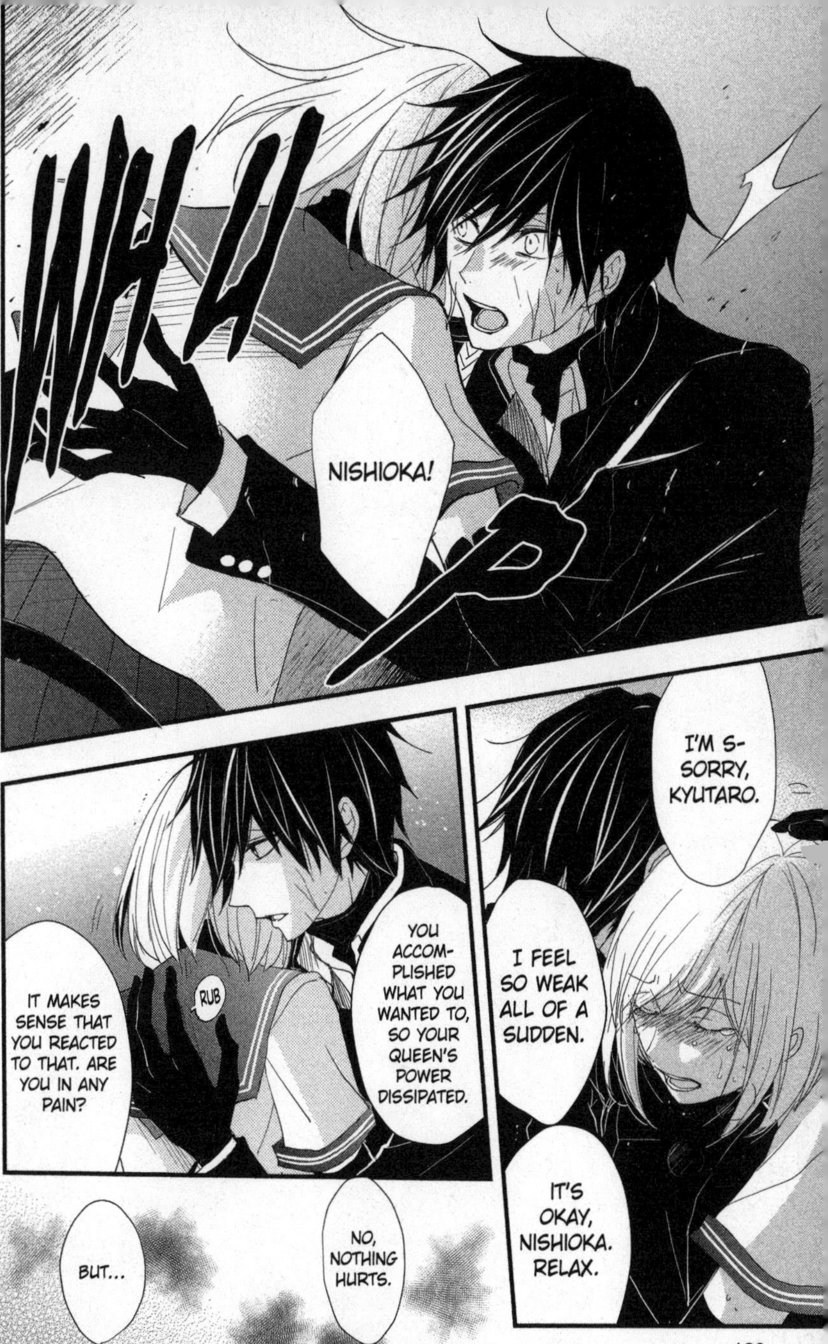
NISHIOKA!
I'M S-SORRY, KYUTARO.
I FEEL SO WEAK ALL OF A SUDDEN.
IT'S OKAY, NISHIOKA. RELAX.
YOU ACCOMPLISHED WHAT YOU WANTED TO, SO YOUR QUEEN'S POWER DISSIPATED.
RUB
IT MAKES SENSE THAT YOU REACTED TO THAT. ARE YOU IN ANY PAIN?
NO, NOTHING HURTS.
BUT...

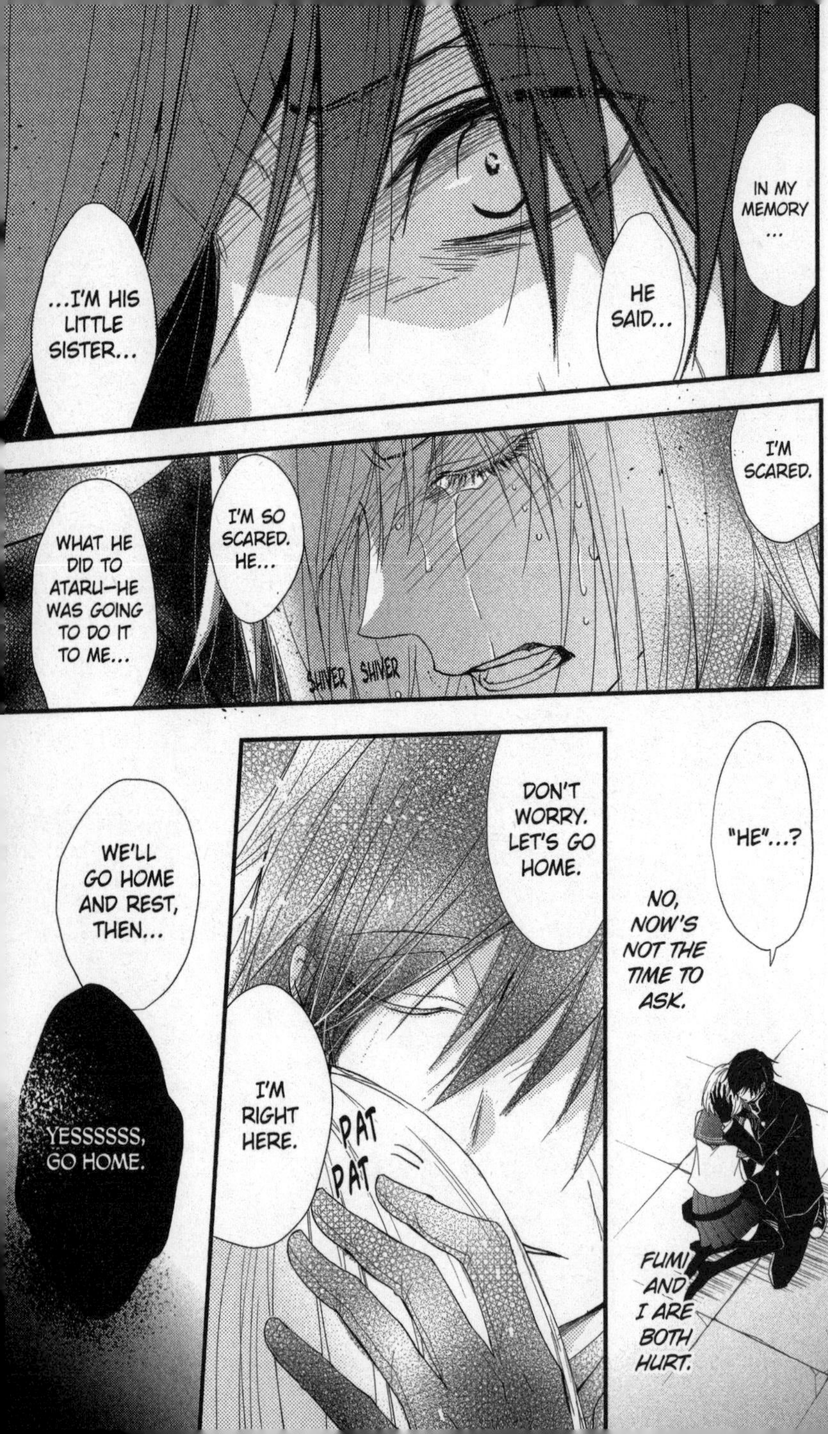
IN MY MEMORY ...
HE SAID...
...I'M HIS LITTLE SISTER...
I'M SCARED.
I'M SO SCARED. HE...
WHAT HE DID TO ATARU—HE WAS GOING TO DO IT TO ME...
SHIVER SHIVER
"HE"...?
NO, NOW'S NOT THE TIME TO ASK.
FUMI AND I ARE BOTH HURT.
DON'T WORRY. LET'S GO HOME.
I'M RIGHT HERE.
PAT PAT
WE'LL GO HOME AND REST, THEN...
YESSSSSS, GO HOME.

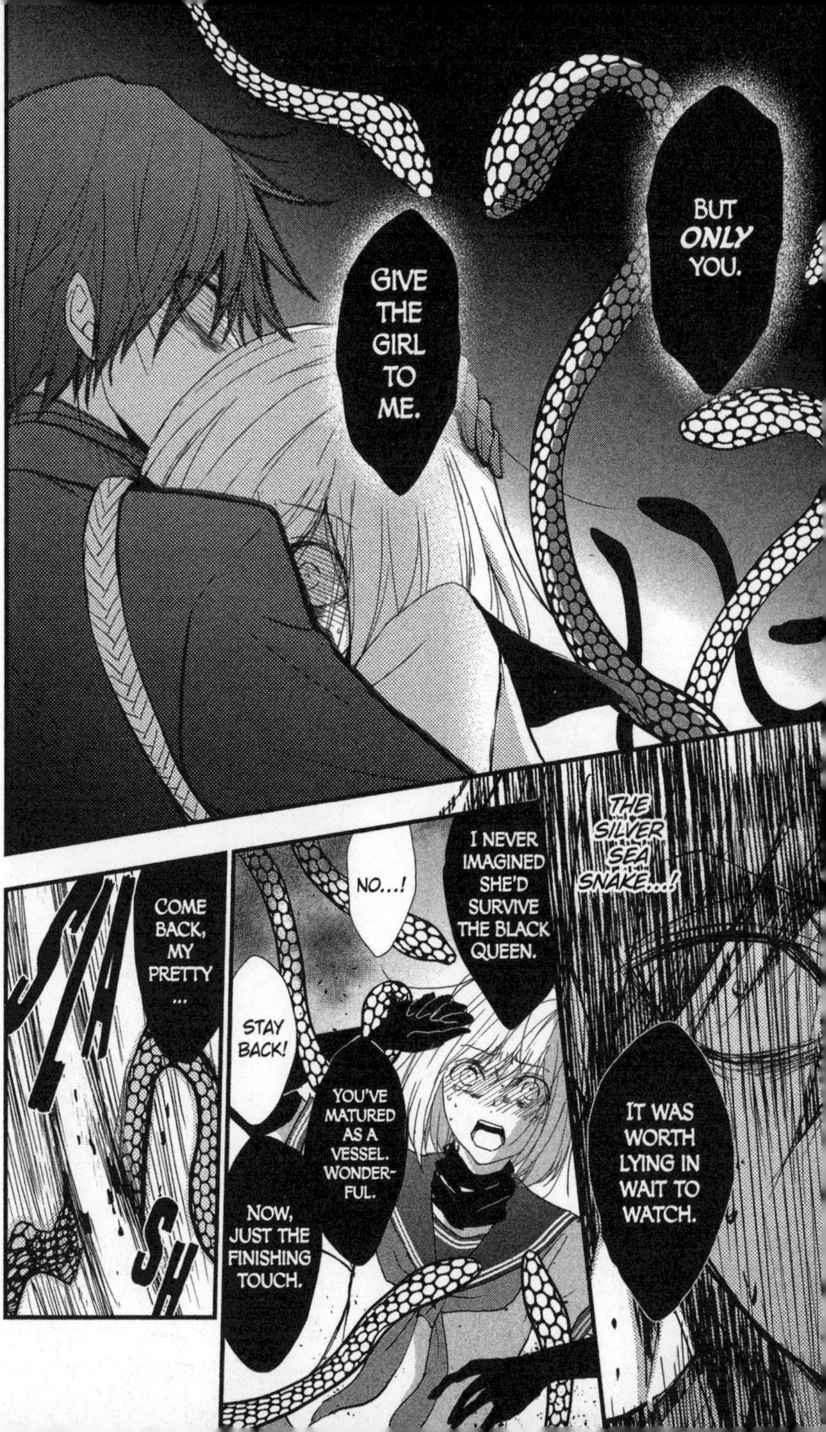
BUT ONLY YOU.
GIVE THE GIRL TO ME.
THE SILVER SEA SNAKE...!
IT WAS WORTH LYING IN WAIT TO WATCH.
I NEVER IMAGINED SHE'D SURVIVE THE BLACK QUEEN.
NO...!
YOU'VE MATURED AS A VESSEL. WONDER-FUL.
STAY BACK!
NOW, JUST THE FINISHING TOUCH.
COME BACK, MY PRETTY ...
SH

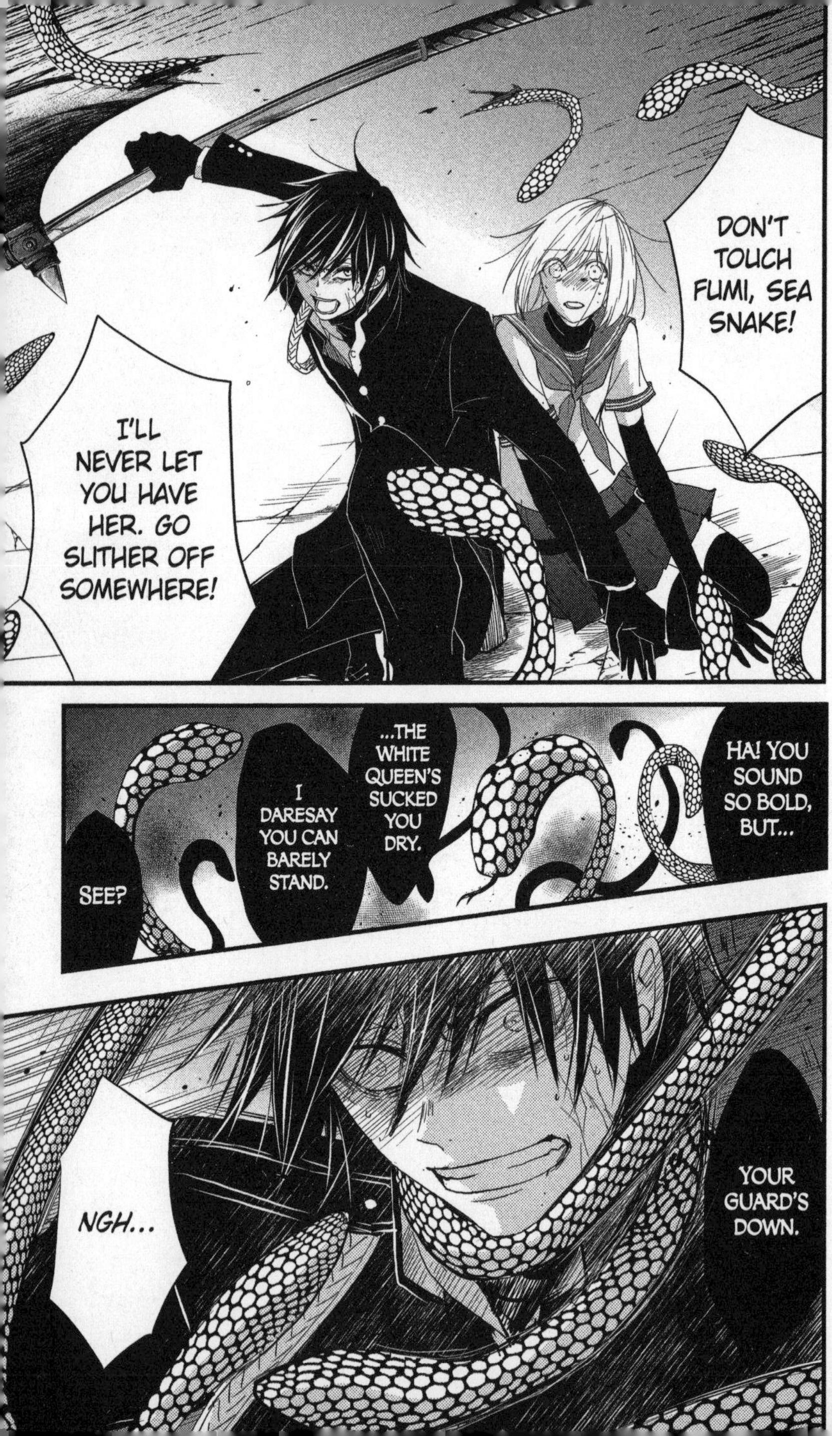
DON'T TOUCH FUMI, SEA SNAKE!
I'LL NEVER LET YOU HAVE HER. GO SLITHER OFF SOMEWHERE!
HA! YOU SOUND SO BOLD, BUT...
...THE WHITE QUEEN'S SUCKED YOU DRY.
I DARESAY YOU CAN BARELY STAND.
SEE?
YOUR GUARD'S DOWN.
NGH...

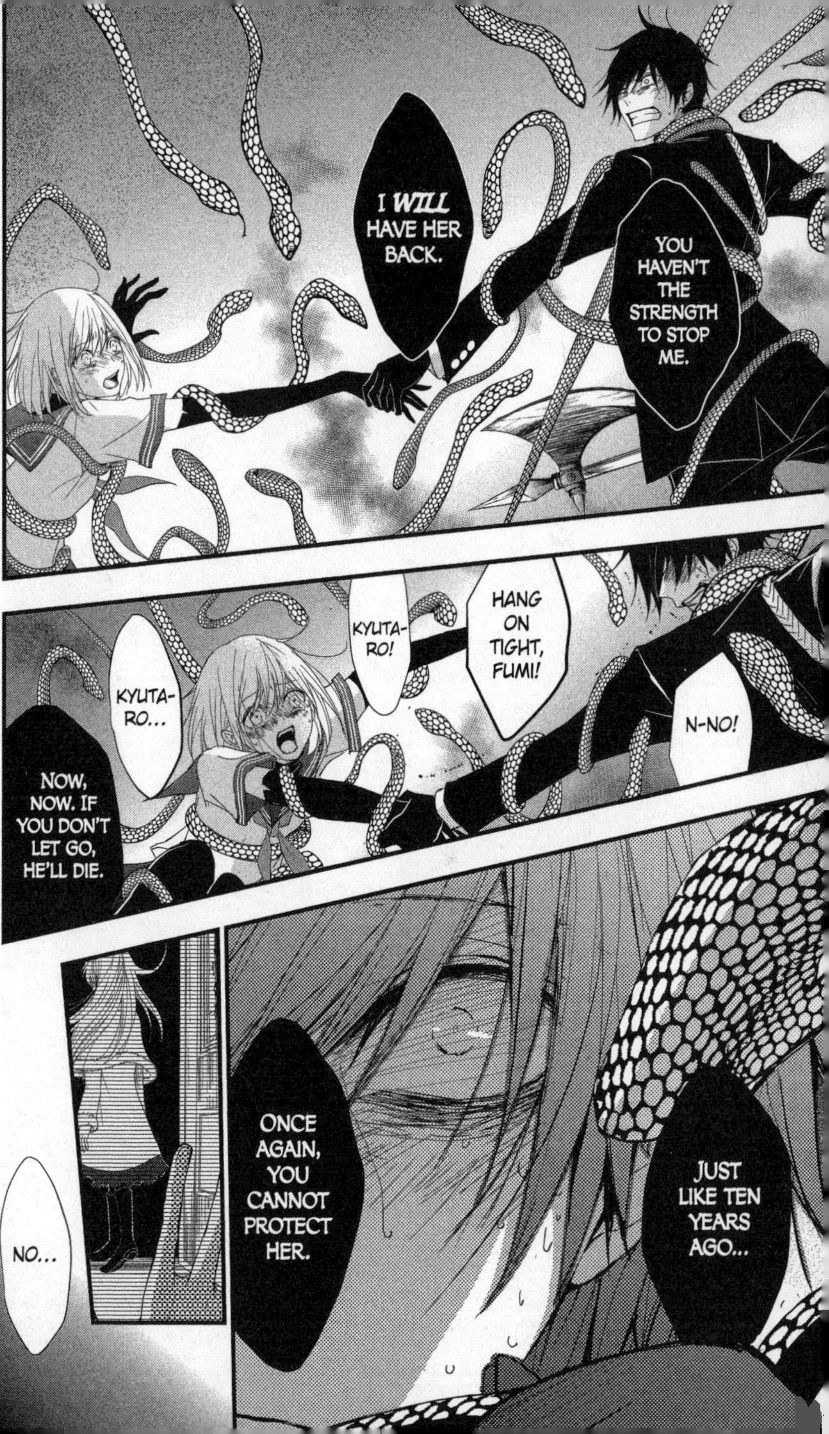
YOU HAVEN'T THE STRENGTH TO STOP ME.
I *WILL* HAVE HER BACK.
N-NO!
HANG ON TIGHT, FUMI!
KYUTA-RO!
KYUTA-RO...
NOW, NOW. IF YOU DON'T LET GO, HE'LL DIE.
JUST LIKE TEN YEARS AGO...
ONCE AGAIN, YOU CANNOT PROTECT HER.
NO...

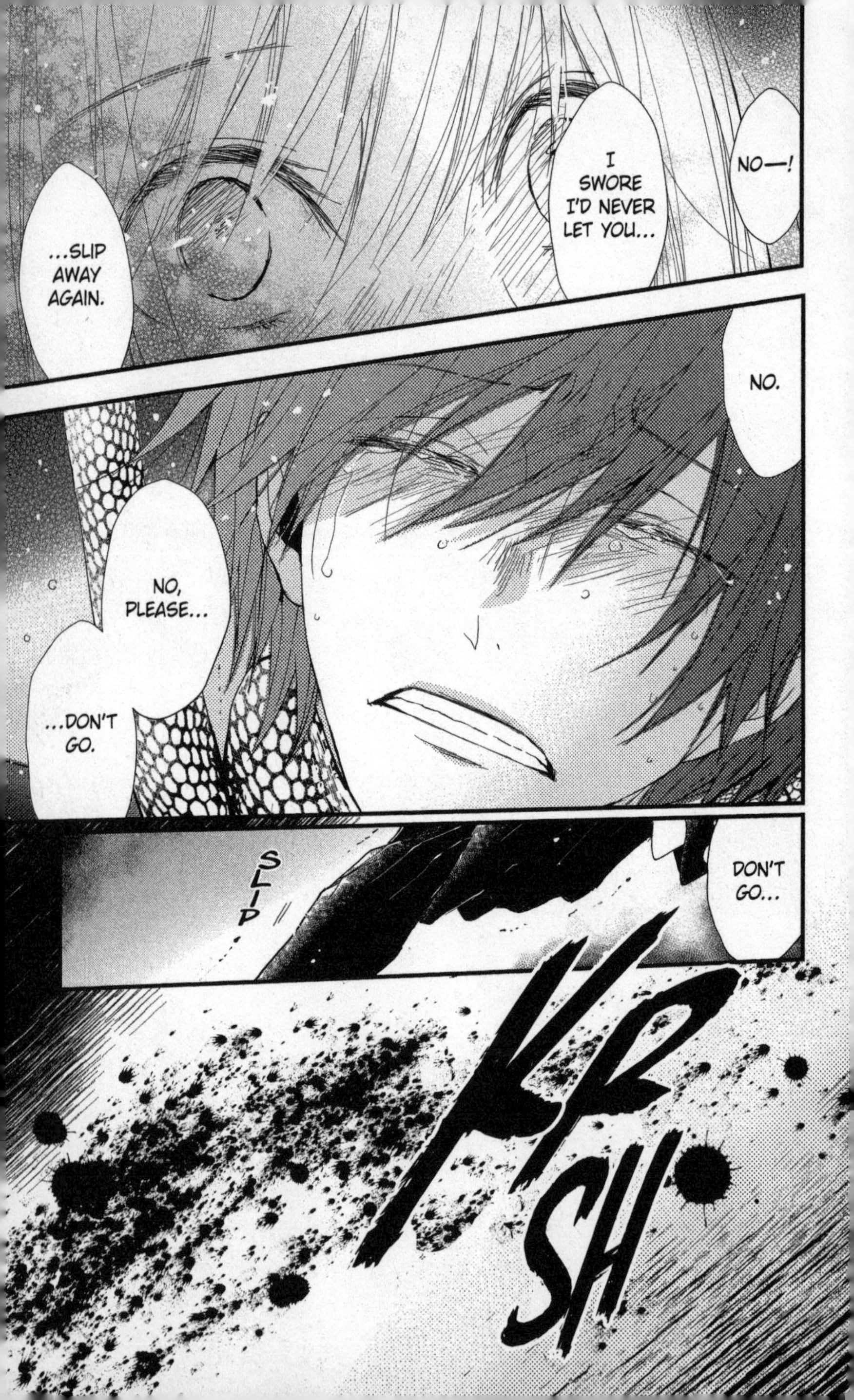
NO—!
I SWORE I'D NEVER LET YOU...
...SLIP AWAY AGAIN.
NO.
NO, PLEASE...
...DON'T GO.
DON'T GO...
SLIP...
KRSH

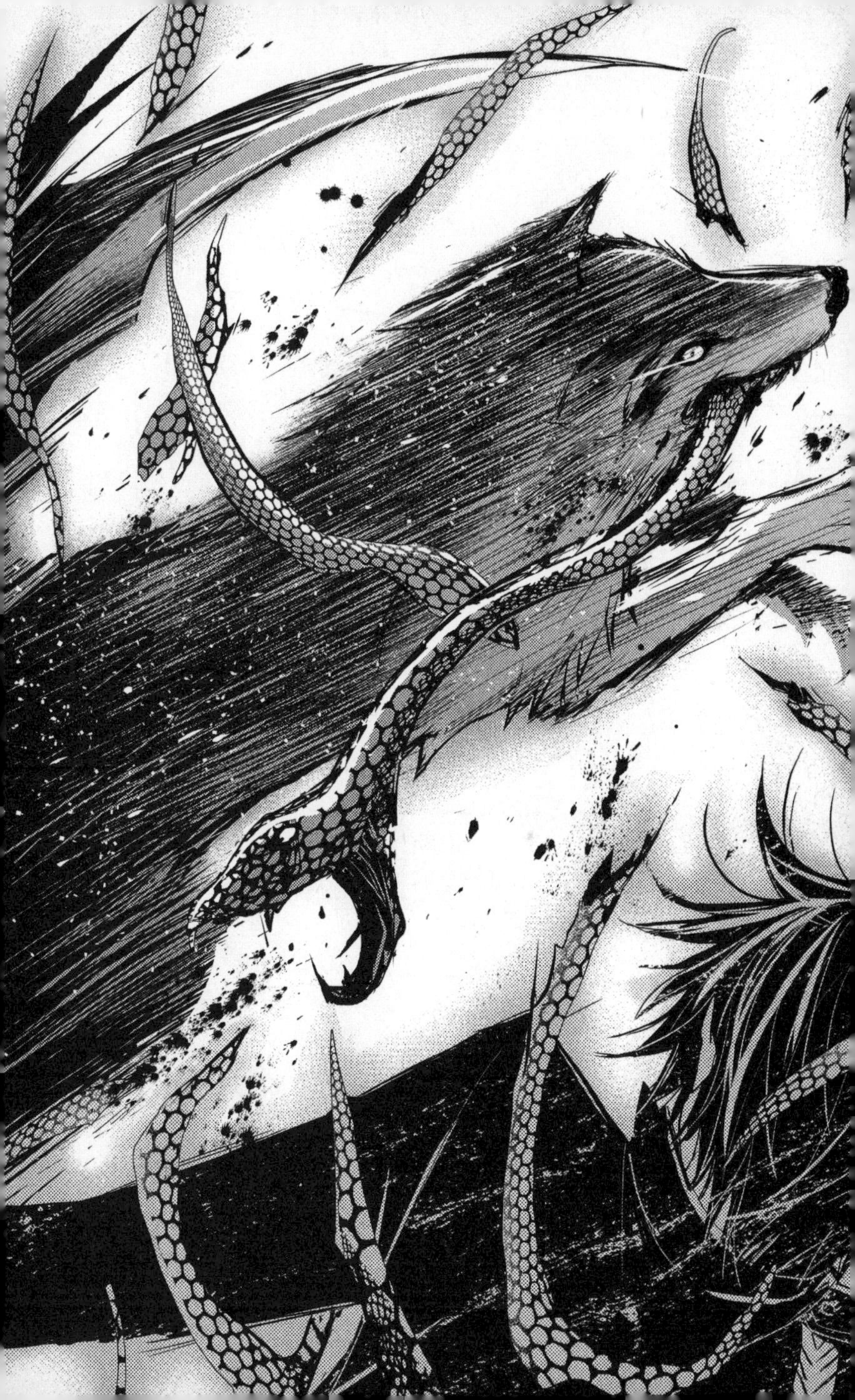

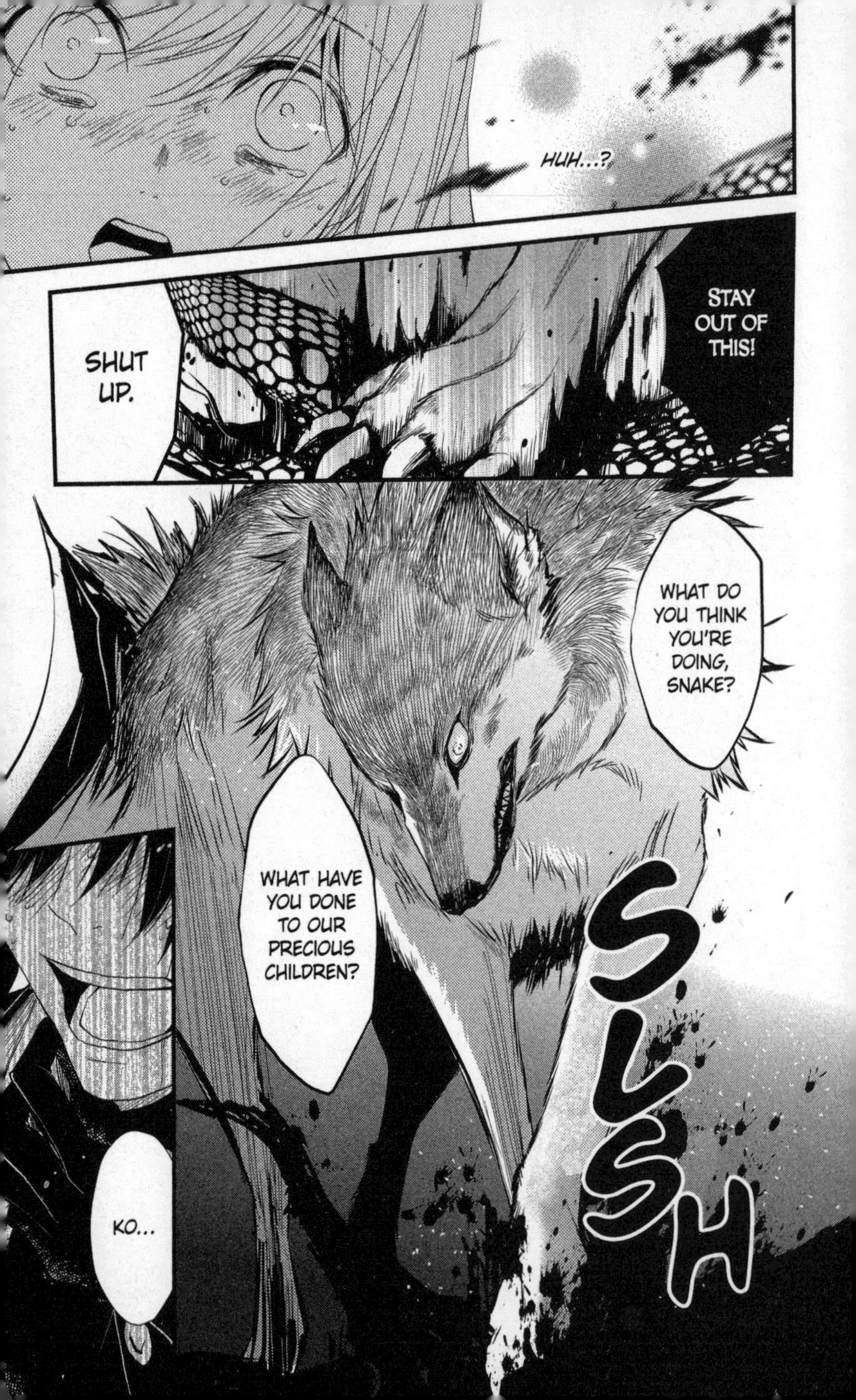
HUH...?
STAY OUT OF THIS!
SHUT UP.
WHAT DO YOU THINK YOU'RE DOING, SNAKE?
SLSH
WHAT HAVE YOU DONE TO OUR PRECIOUS CHILDREN?
KO...

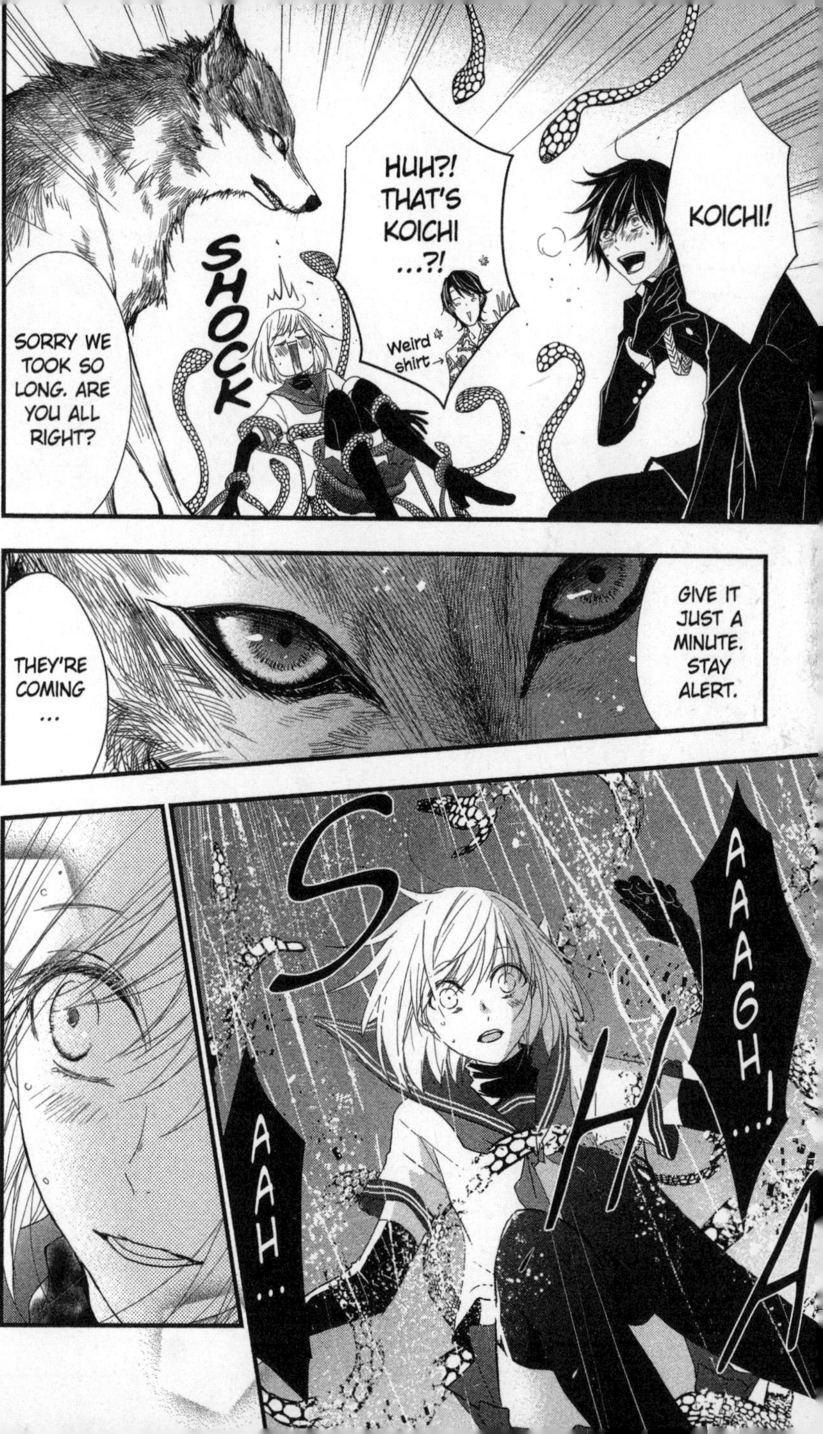
KOICHI!
HUH?! THAT'S KOICHI ...?!
Weird shirt →
SHOCK
SORRY WE TOOK SO LONG. ARE YOU ALL RIGHT?
GIVE IT JUST A MINUTE. STAY ALERT.
THEY'RE COMING ...
AAAGH!...
SH
AAH...

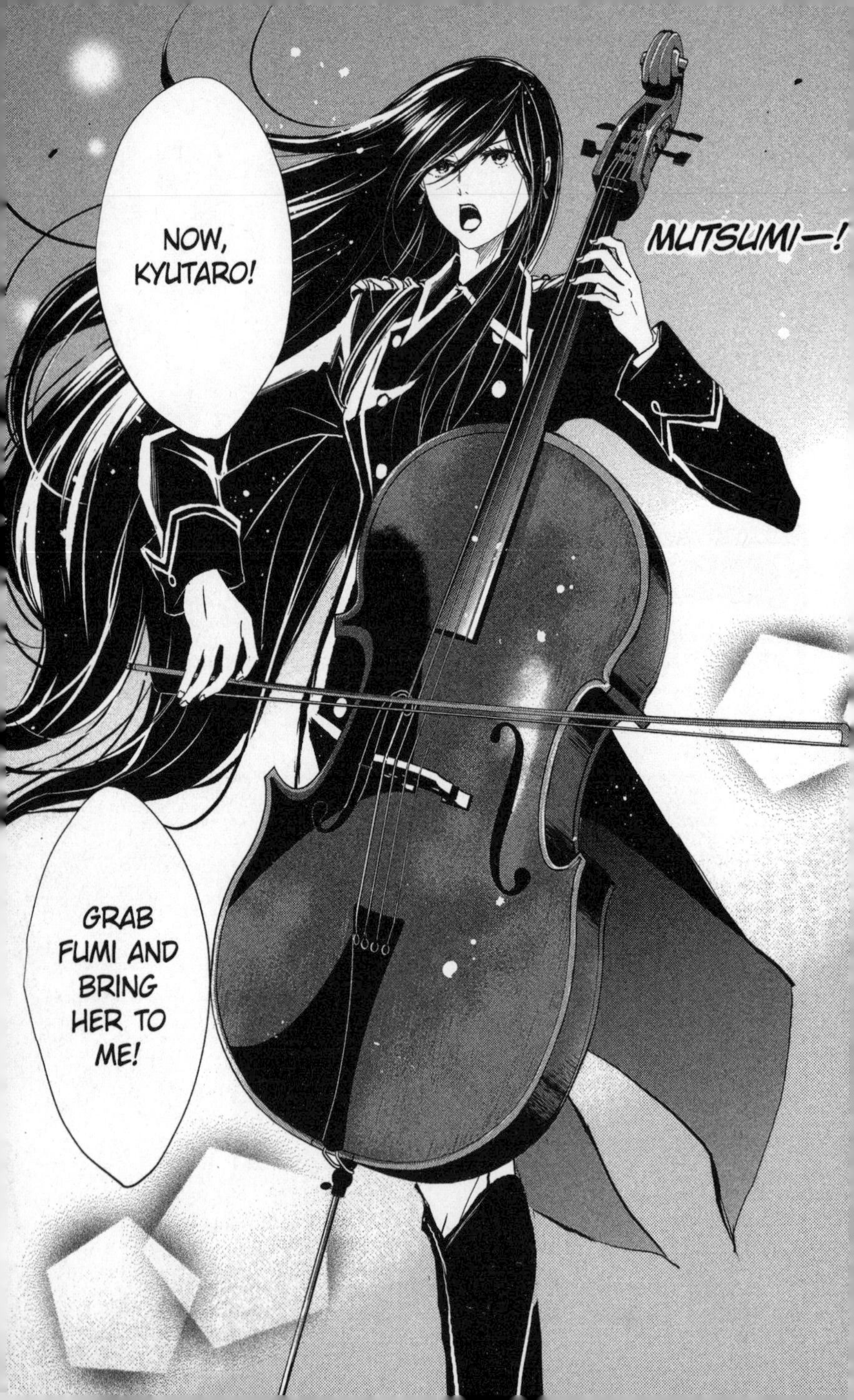
MUTSUMI—!
NOW, KYUTARO!
GRAB FUMI AND BRING HER TO ME!

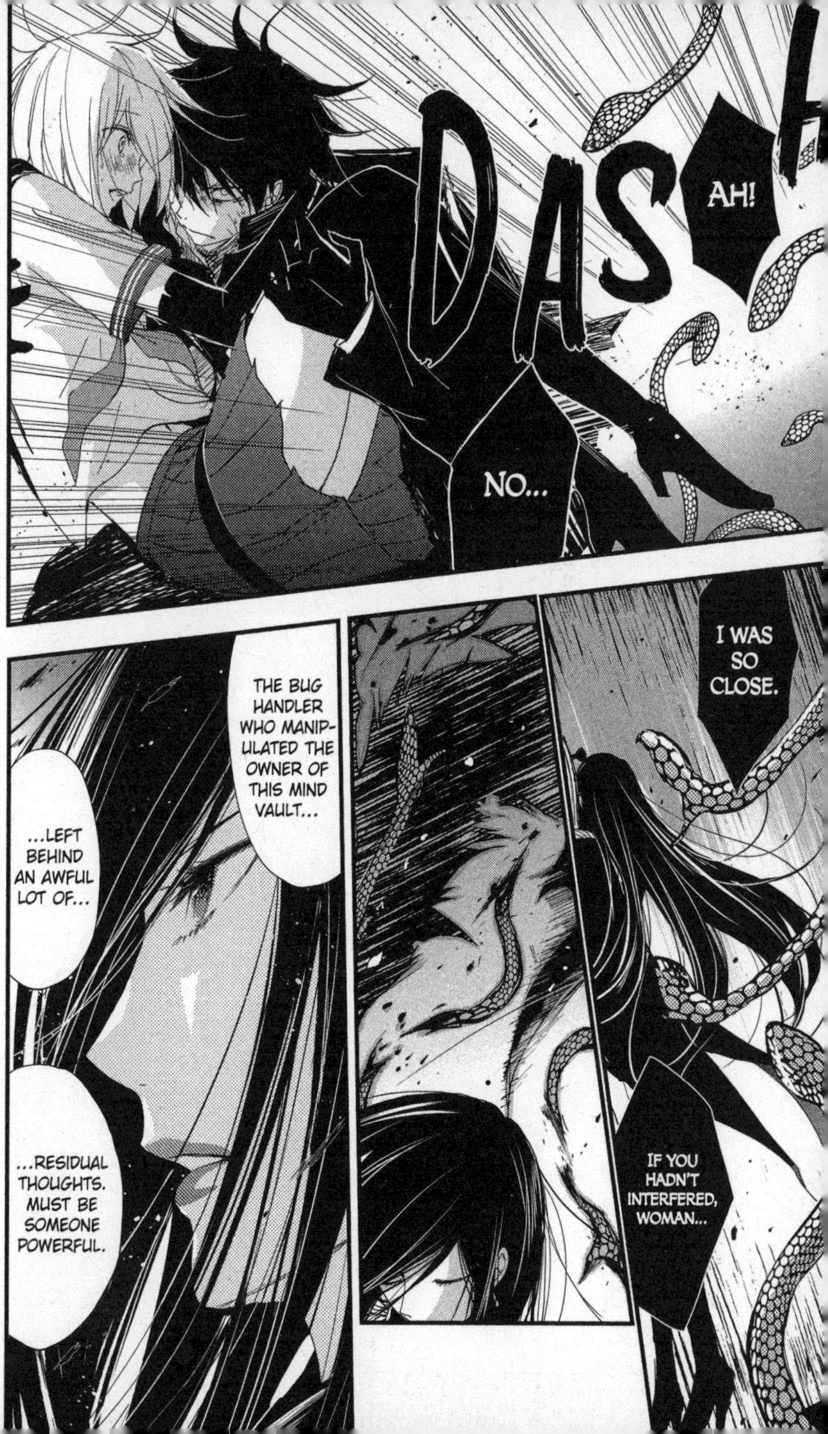
AH!
DAS
NO...
I WAS SO CLOSE.
IF YOU HADN'T INTERFERED, WOMAN...
THE BUG HANDLER WHO MANIP-ULATED THE OWNER OF THIS MIND VAULT...
...LEFT BEHIND AN AWFUL LOT OF...
...RESIDUAL THOUGHTS. MUST BE SOMEONE POWERFUL.

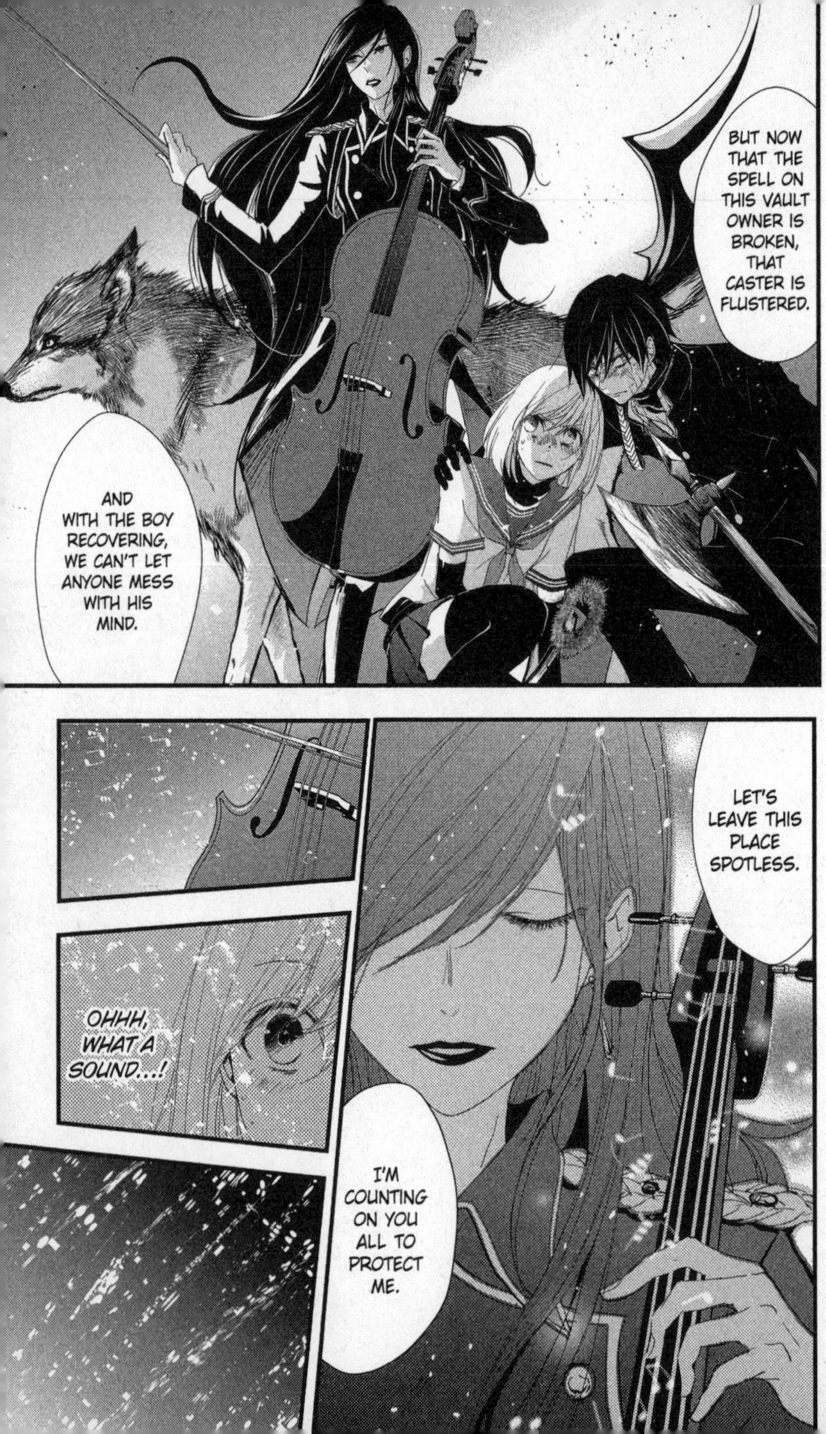
BUT NOW THAT THE SPELL ON THIS VAULT OWNER IS BROKEN, THAT CASTER IS FLUSTERED.
AND WITH THE BOY RECOVERING, WE CAN'T LET ANYONE MESS WITH HIS MIND.
LET'S LEAVE THIS PLACE SPOTLESS.
I'M COUNTING ON YOU ALL TO PROTECT ME.
OHHH, WHAT A SOUND...!

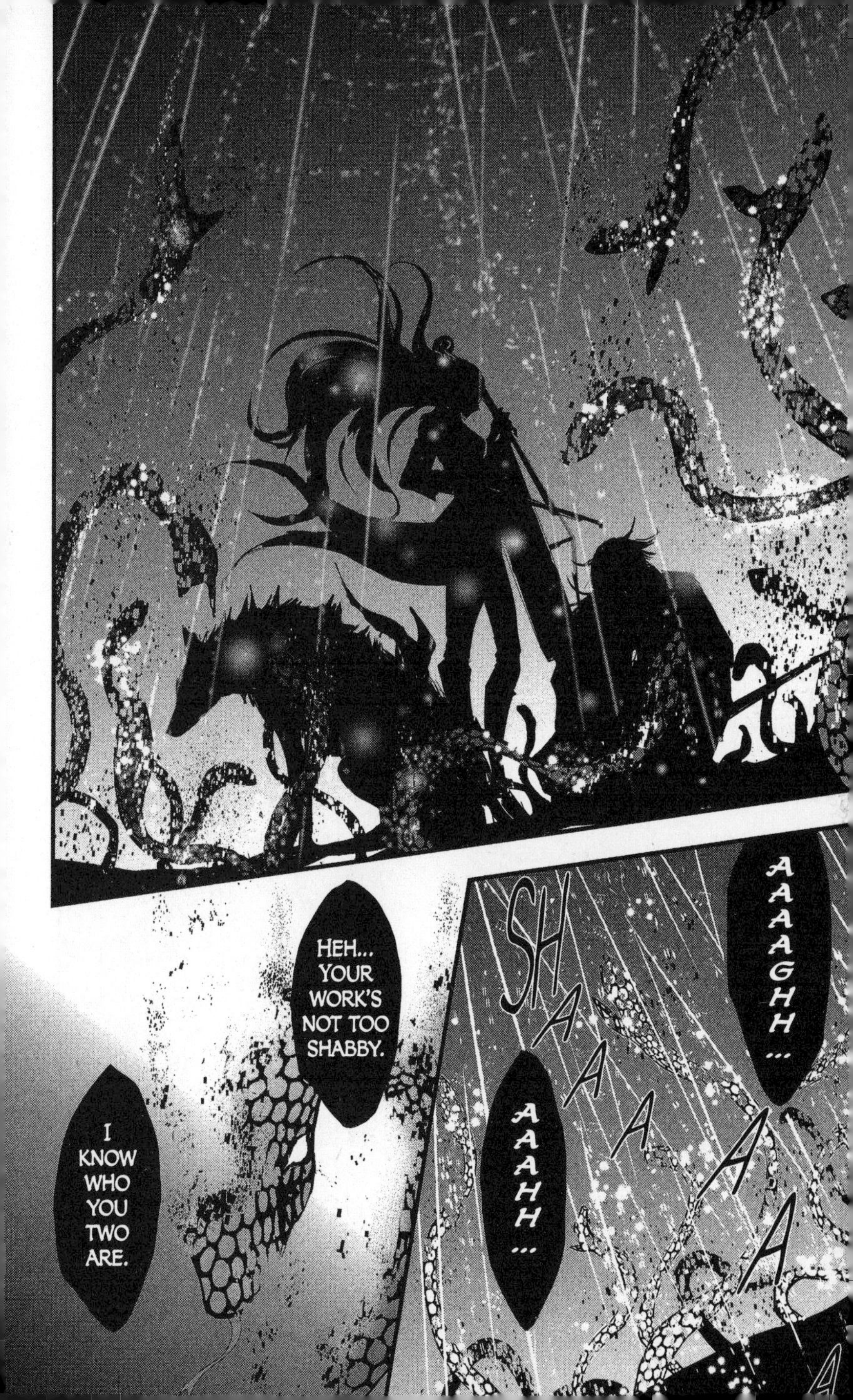
AAAAGHH...
SHAAAAAAA
AAAHH...
HEH... YOUR WORK'S NOT TOO SHABBY.
I KNOW WHO YOU TWO ARE.

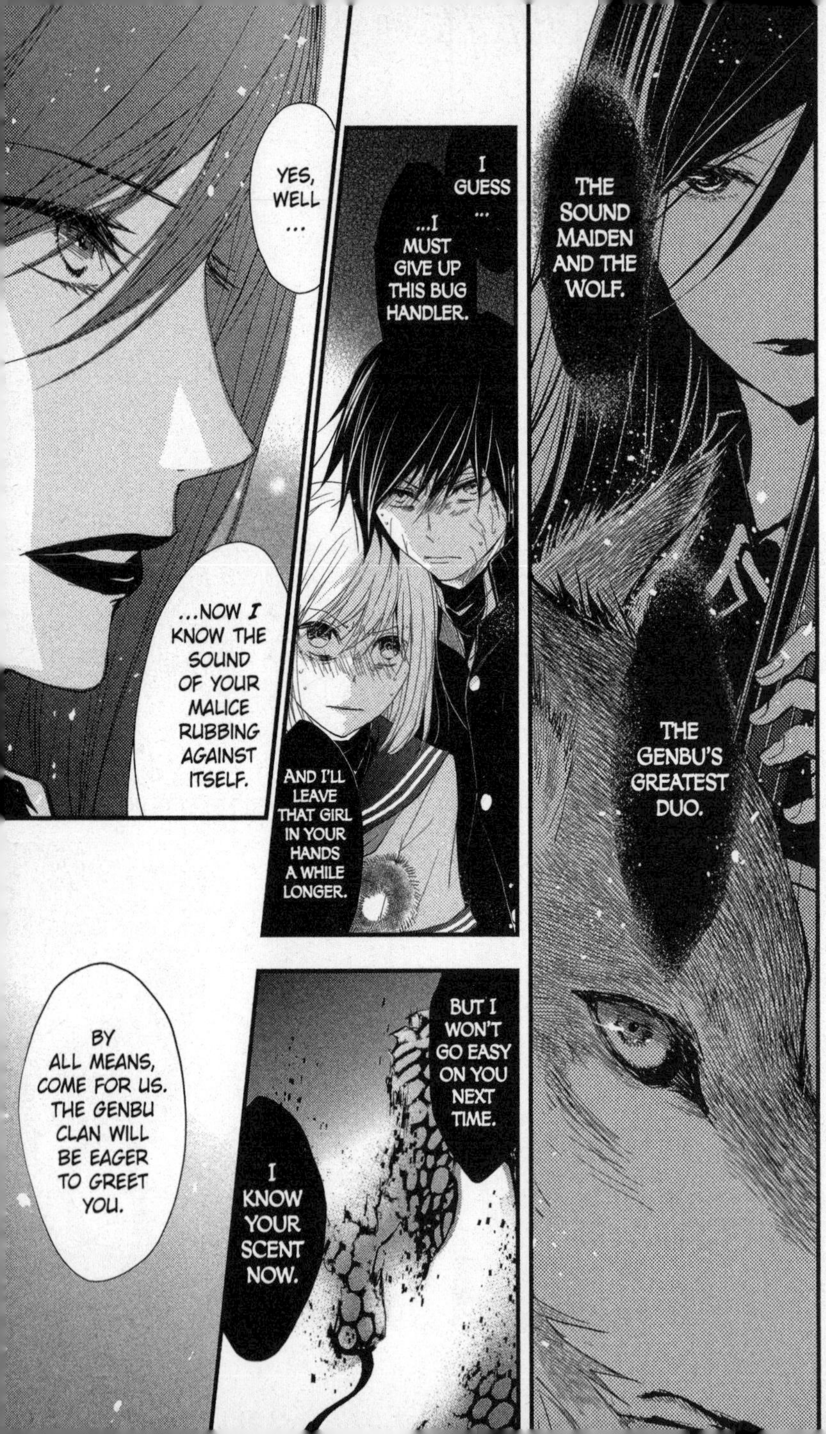
THE SOUND MAIDEN AND THE WOLF.
THE GENBU'S GREATEST DUO.
I GUESS ...
...I MUST GIVE UP THIS BUG HANDLER.
YES, WELL ...
...NOW *I* KNOW THE SOUND OF YOUR MALICE RUBBING AGAINST ITSELF.
AND I'LL LEAVE THAT GIRL IN YOUR HANDS A WHILE LONGER.
BUT I WON'T GO EASY ON YOU NEXT TIME.
I KNOW YOUR SCENT NOW.
BY ALL MEANS, COME FOR US. THE GENBU CLAN WILL BE EAGER TO GREET YOU.

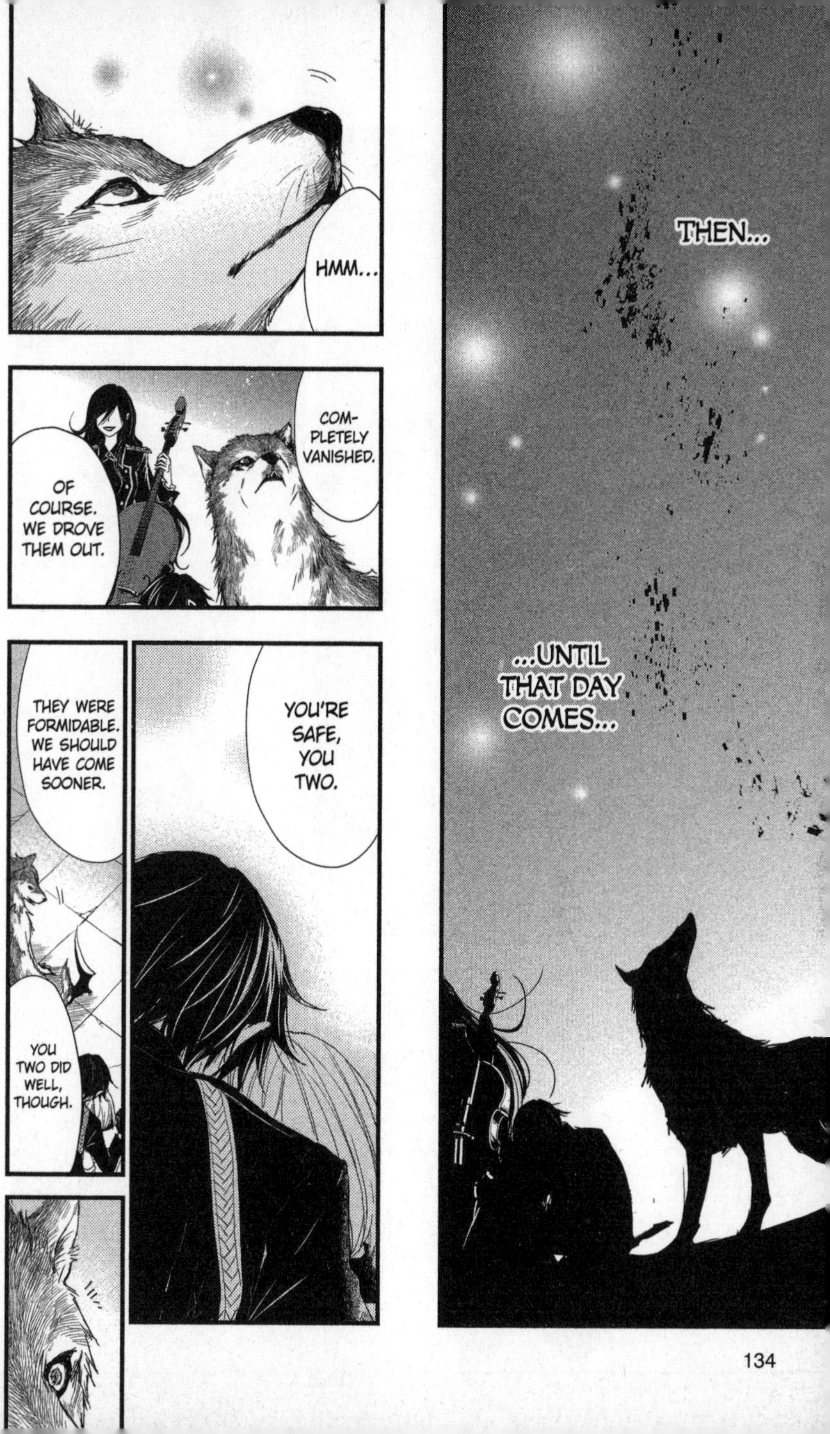
THEN...
...UNTIL THAT DAY COMES...
HMM...
COM-PLETELY VANISHED.
OF COURSE. WE DROVE THEM OUT.
YOU'RE SAFE, YOU TWO.
THEY WERE FORMIDABLE. WE SHOULD HAVE COME SOONER.
YOU TWO DID WELL, THOUGH.

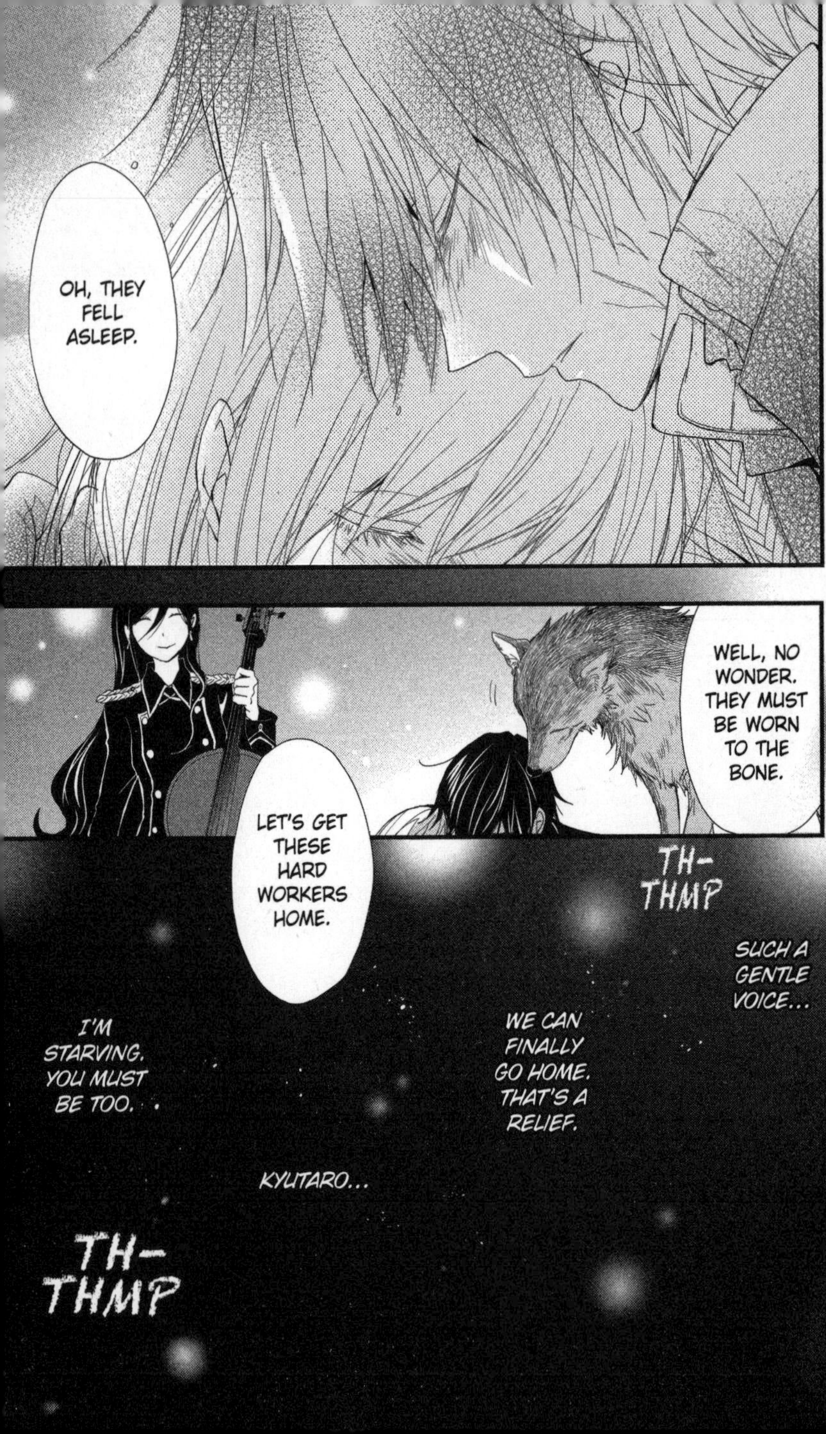
OH, THEY FELL ASLEEP.
WELL, NO WONDER. THEY MUST BE WORN TO THE BONE.
LET'S GET THESE HARD WORKERS HOME.
TH- THMP
SUCH A GENTLE VOICE...
WE CAN FINALLY GO HOME. THAT'S A RELIEF.
I'M STARVING. YOU MUST BE TOO.
KYUTARO...
TH- THMP

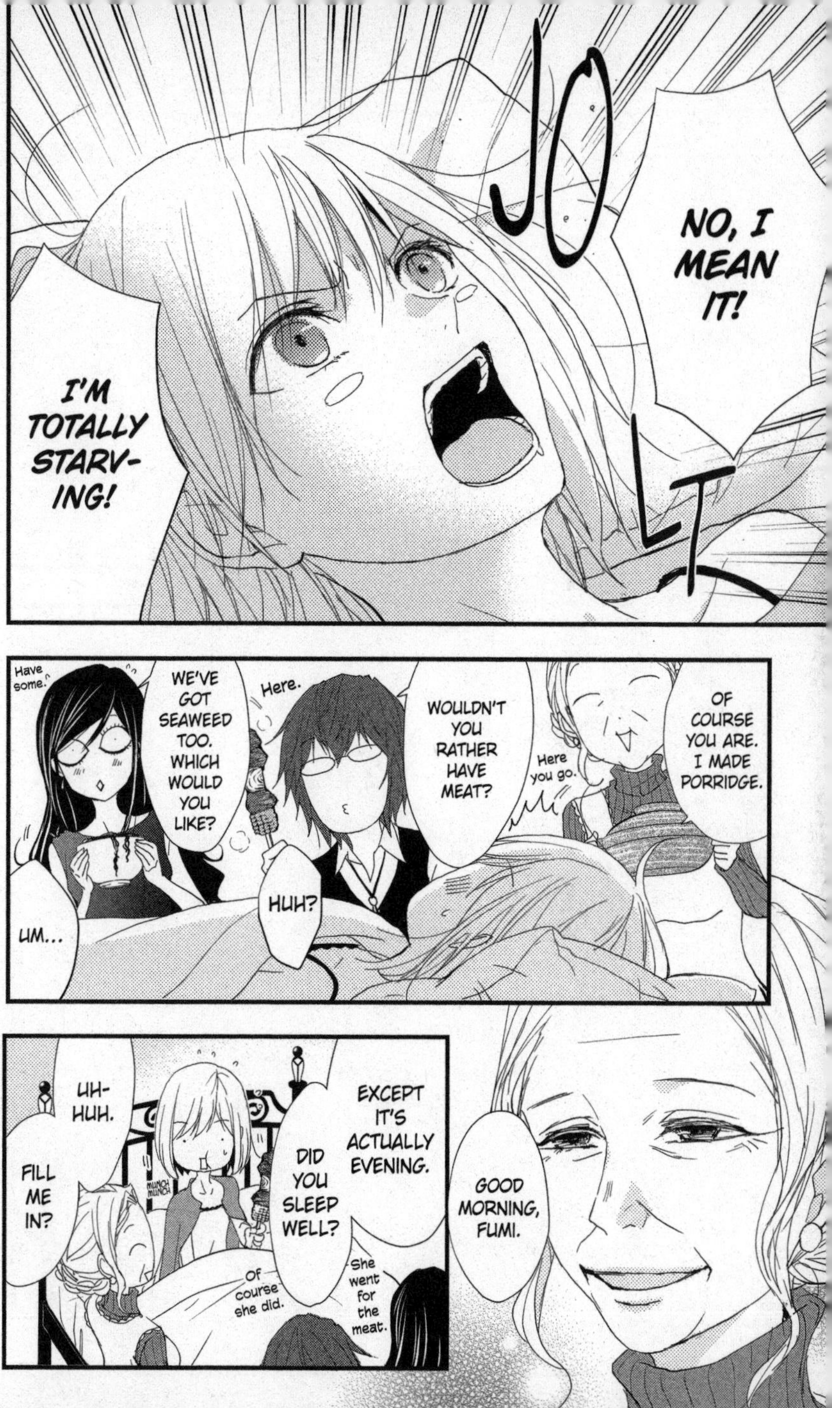
NO, I MEAN IT!
JOLT
I'M TOTALLY STARV-ING!
OF COURSE YOU ARE. I MADE PORRIDGE.
Here you go.
WOULDN'T YOU RATHER HAVE MEAT?
Here.
HUH?
WE'VE GOT SEAWEED TOO. WHICH WOULD YOU LIKE?
Have some.
UM...
GOOD MORNING, FUMI.
EXCEPT IT'S ACTUALLY EVENING.
DID YOU SLEEP WELL?
She went for the meat.
Of course she did.
MUNCH MUNCH
UH-HUH.
FILL ME IN?

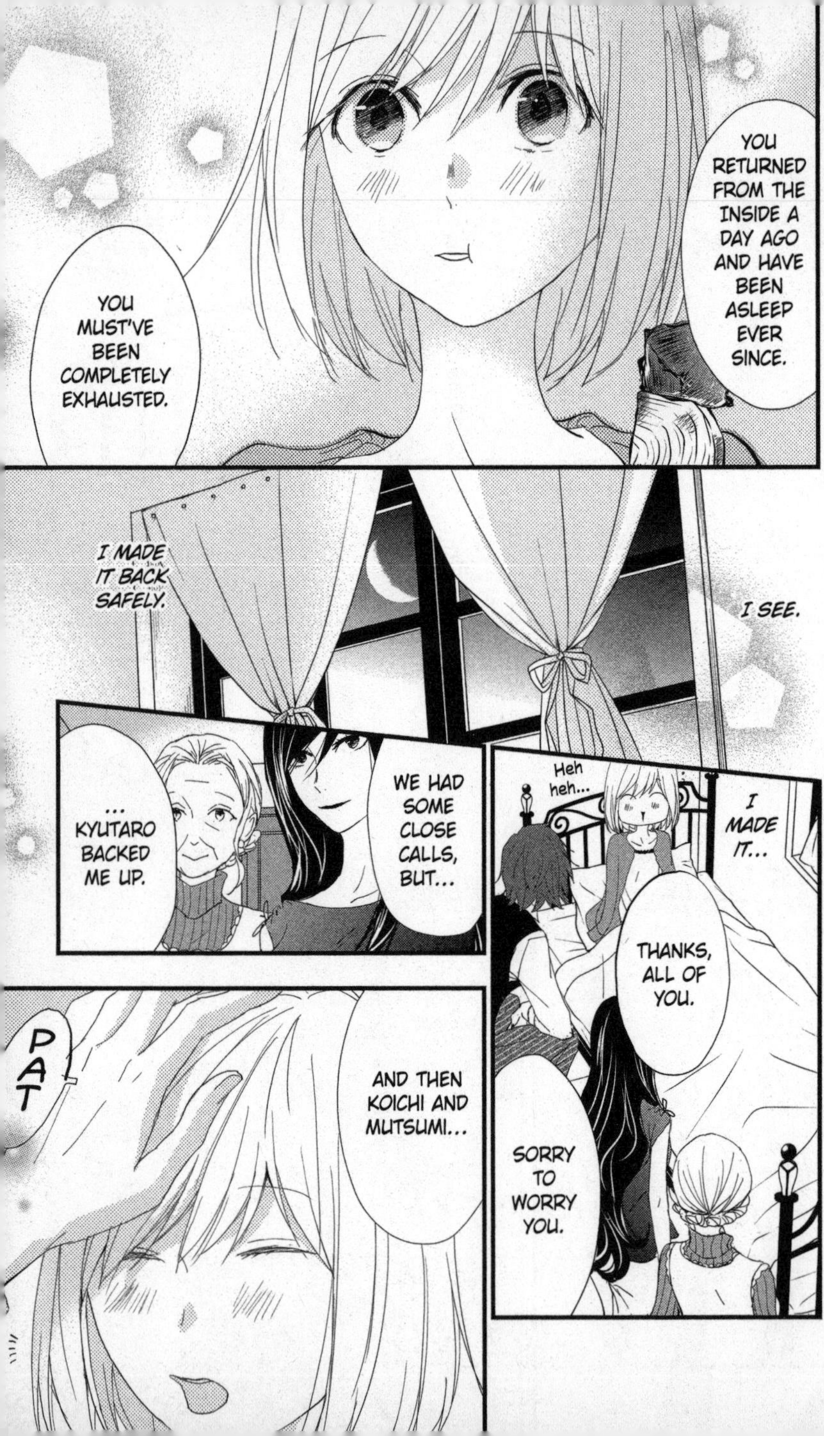
YOU RETURNED FROM THE INSIDE A DAY AGO AND HAVE BEEN ASLEEP EVER SINCE.
YOU MUST'VE BEEN COMPLETELY EXHAUSTED.
I SEE.
I MADE IT BACK SAFELY.
I MADE IT...
Heh heh...
THANKS, ALL OF YOU.
SORRY TO WORRY YOU.
WE HAD SOME CLOSE CALLS, BUT...
...KYUTARO BACKED ME UP.
AND THEN KOICHI AND MUTSUMI...
PAT

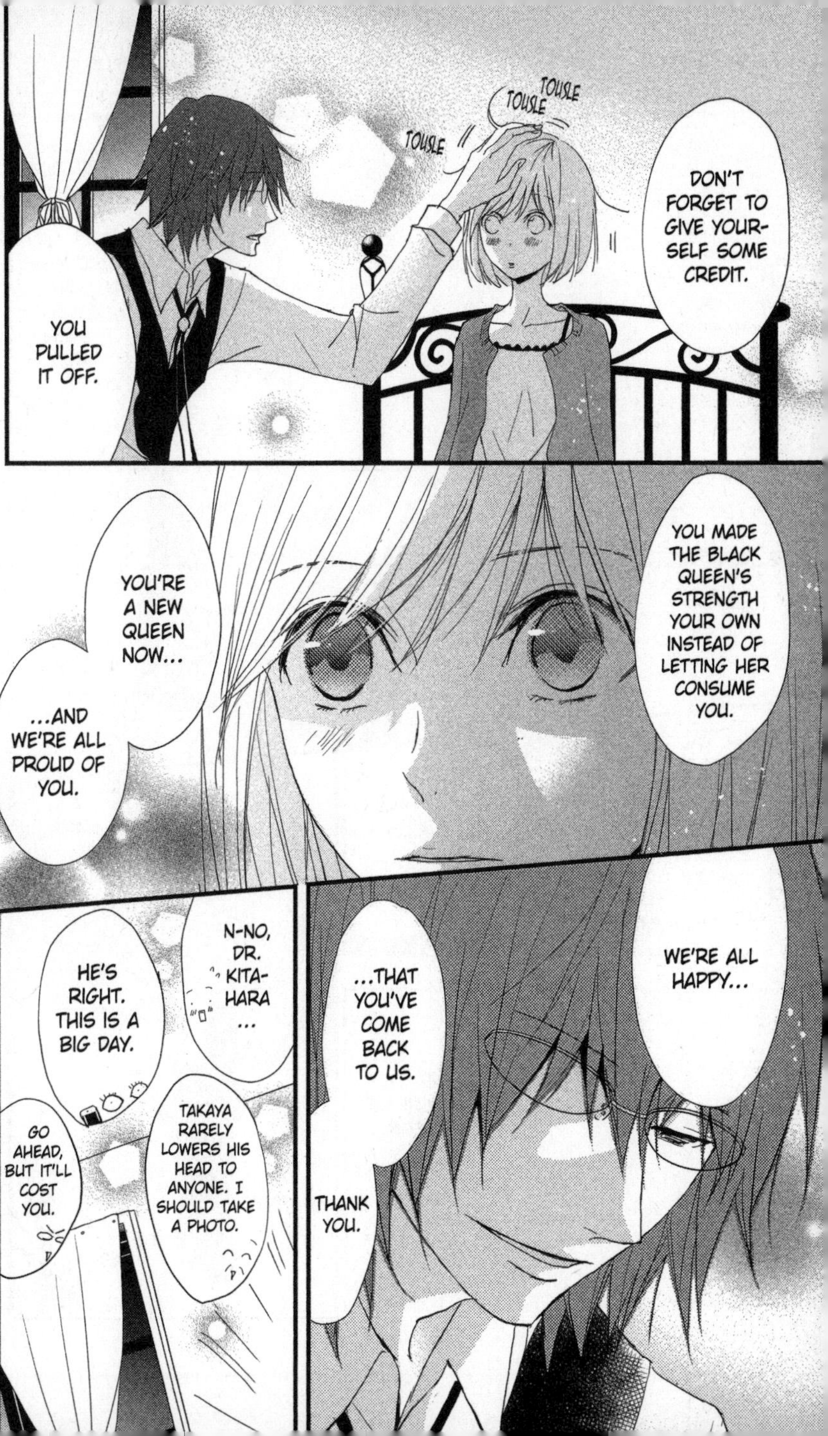
DON'T FORGET TO GIVE YOURSELF SOME CREDIT.
TOUSLE TOUSLE
TOUSLE
YOU PULLED IT OFF.
YOU MADE THE BLACK QUEEN'S STRENGTH YOUR OWN INSTEAD OF LETTING HER CONSUME YOU.
YOU'RE A NEW QUEEN NOW...
...AND WE'RE ALL PROUD OF YOU.
WE'RE ALL HAPPY...
...THAT YOU'VE COME BACK TO US.
THANK YOU.
N-NO, DR. KITAHARA...
HE'S RIGHT. THIS IS A BIG DAY.
TAKAYA RARELY LOWERS HIS HEAD TO ANYONE. I SHOULD TAKE A PHOTO.
GO AHEAD, BUT IT'LL COST YOU.

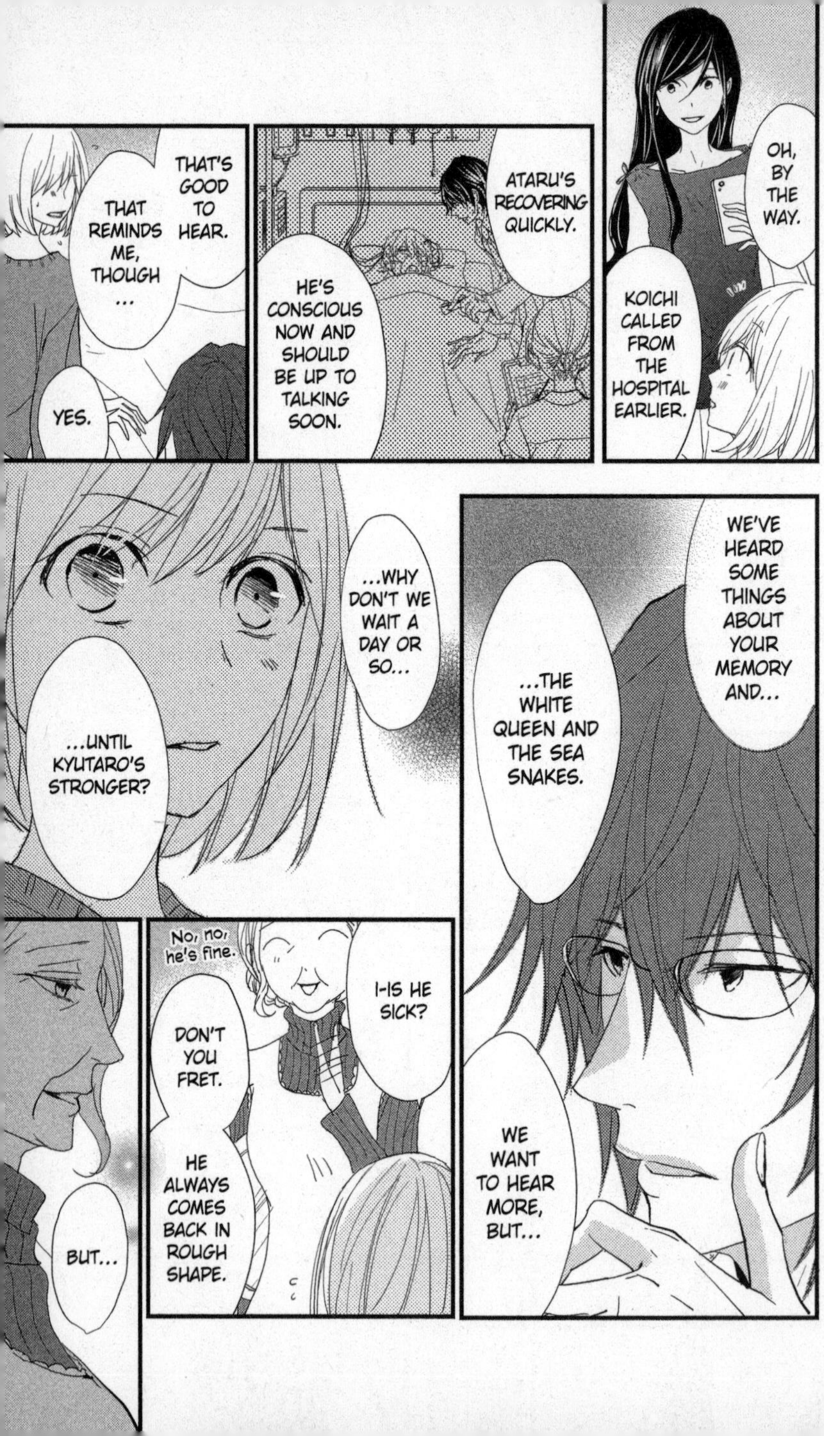
OH, BY THE WAY.
KOICHI CALLED FROM THE HOSPITAL EARLIER.
ATARU'S RECOVERING QUICKLY.
HE'S CONSCIOUS NOW AND SHOULD BE UP TO TALKING SOON.
THAT'S GOOD TO HEAR.
THAT REMINDS ME, THOUGH...
YES.
WE'VE HEARD SOME THINGS ABOUT YOUR MEMORY AND...
...THE WHITE QUEEN AND THE SEA SNAKES.
WE WANT TO HEAR MORE, BUT...
...WHY DON'T WE WAIT A DAY OR SO...
...UNTIL KYUTARO'S STRONGER?
I-IS HE SICK?
No, no, he's fine.
DON'T YOU FRET.
HE ALWAYS COMES BACK IN ROUGH SHAPE.
BUT...

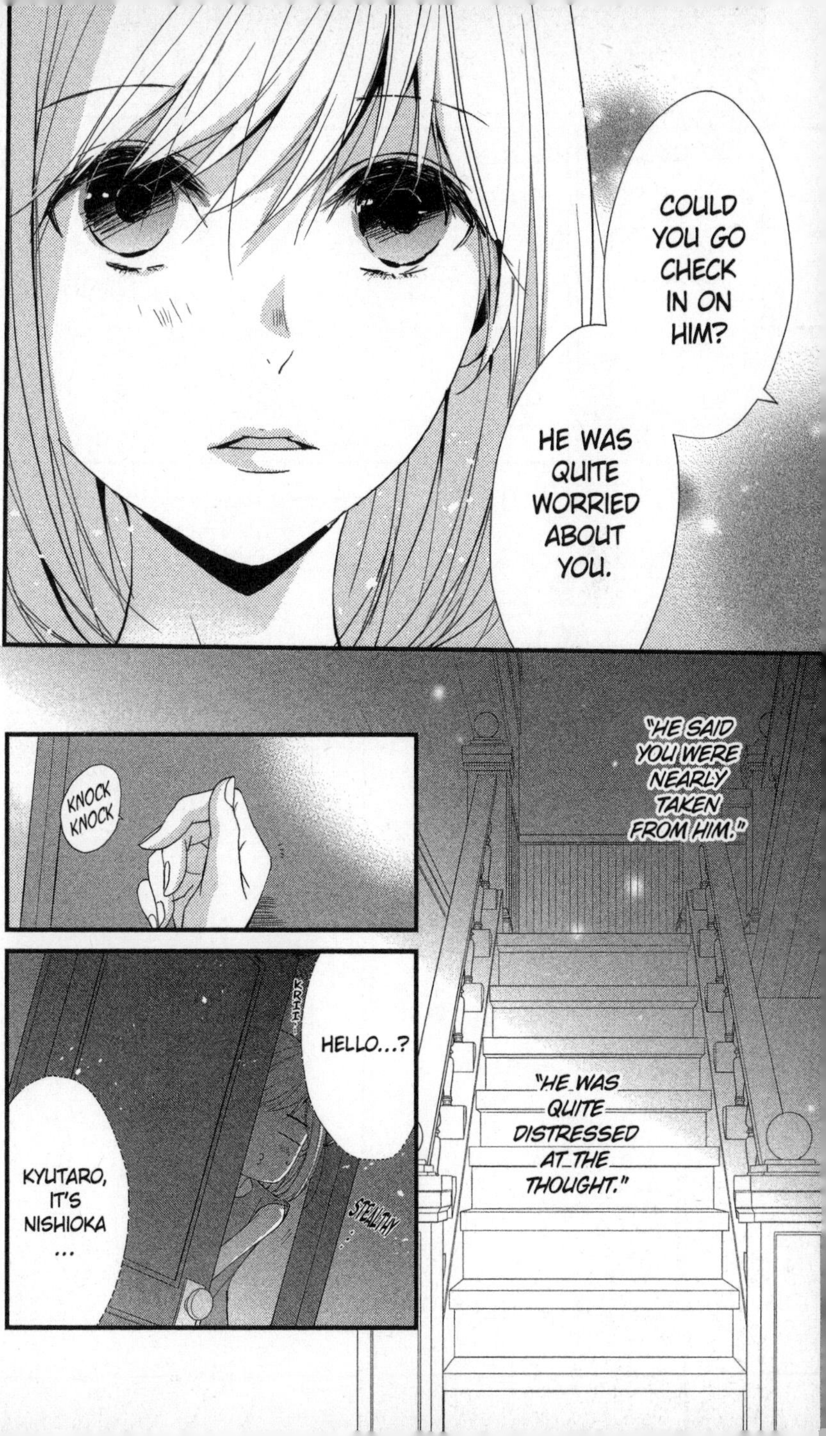
COULD YOU GO CHECK IN ON HIM?
HE WAS QUITE WORRIED ABOUT YOU.
"HE SAID YOU WERE NEARLY TAKEN FROM HIM."
"HE WAS QUITE DISTRESSED AT THE THOUGHT."
KNOCK KNOCK
KRIII
HELLO...?
KYUTARO, IT'S NISHIOKA ...
STEALTHY

NO ...
IT'S COLD ...
IT'S COLD. DON'T GO...
WHY? NO...
WHEN SOMEONE GETS INJURED IN THE INSIDE, IT HURTS THEIR PSYCHE.
DON'T GO...
IT'S STIRRING UP THINGS FROM HIS PAST THAT HURT HIM.
NO.
DON'T GO...
IT'S LIKE LAST TIME...
...WHEN I LOOKED INTO HIS ROOM BY MISTAKE.
... don't go.
Not that way...
THAT NIGHT, YOU SAID ...
"THERE YOU ARE..."
"THANK GOOD-NESS..."

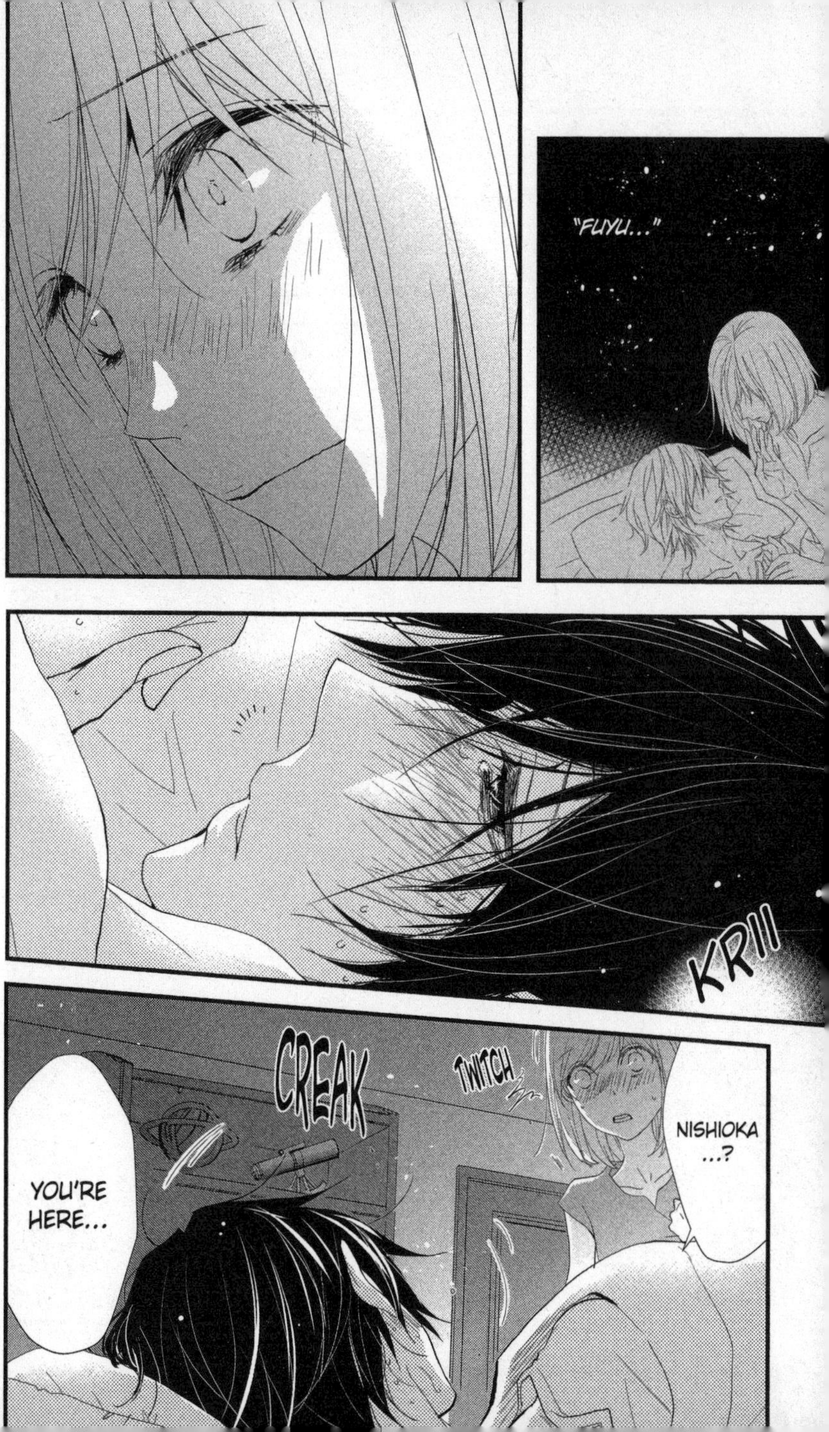
"FUYU..."
KRII
NISHIOKA ...?
TWITCH
CREAK
YOU'RE HERE...

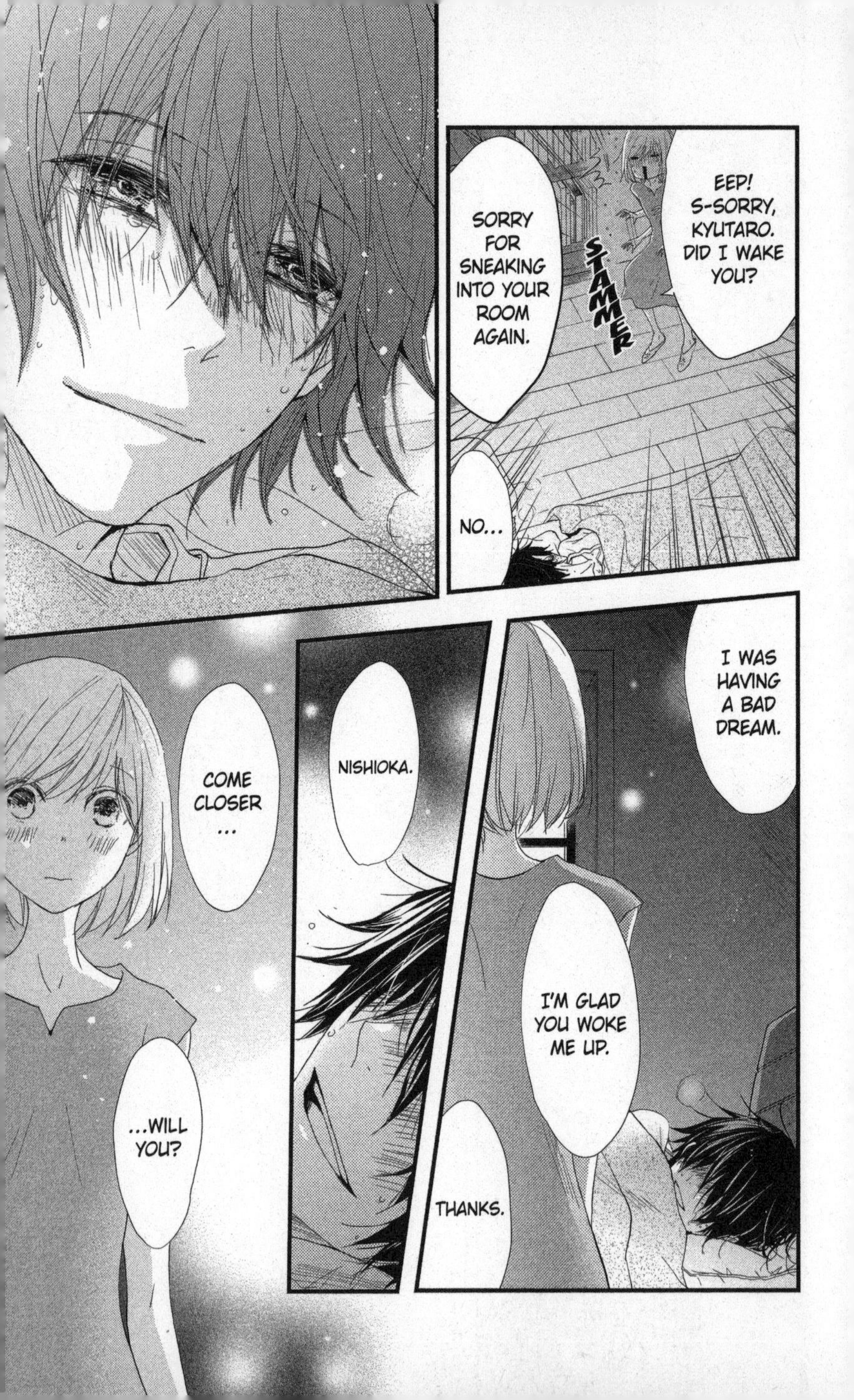
EEP! S-SORRY, KYUTARO. DID I WAKE YOU?
STAMMER
SORRY FOR SNEAKING INTO YOUR ROOM AGAIN.
NO...
I WAS HAVING A BAD DREAM.
I'M GLAD YOU WOKE ME UP.
THANKS.
NISHIOKA.
COME CLOSER...
...WILL YOU?

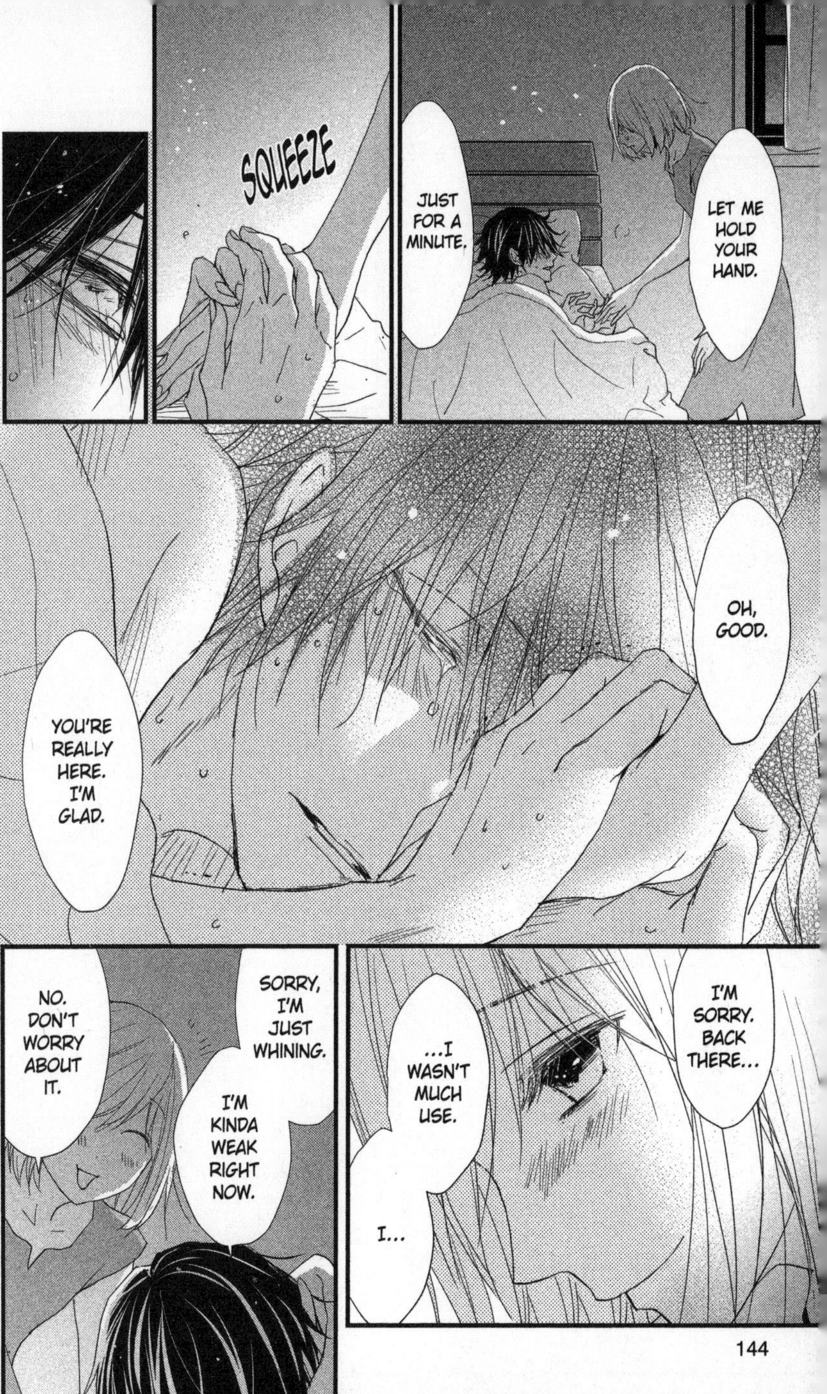
LET ME HOLD YOUR HAND.
JUST FOR A MINUTE.
SQUEEZE
OH, GOOD.
YOU'RE REALLY HERE. I'M GLAD.
I'M SORRY. BACK THERE...
...I WASN'T MUCH USE.
I...
SORRY, I'M JUST WHINING.
I'M KINDA WEAK RIGHT NOW.
NO. DON'T WORRY ABOUT IT.

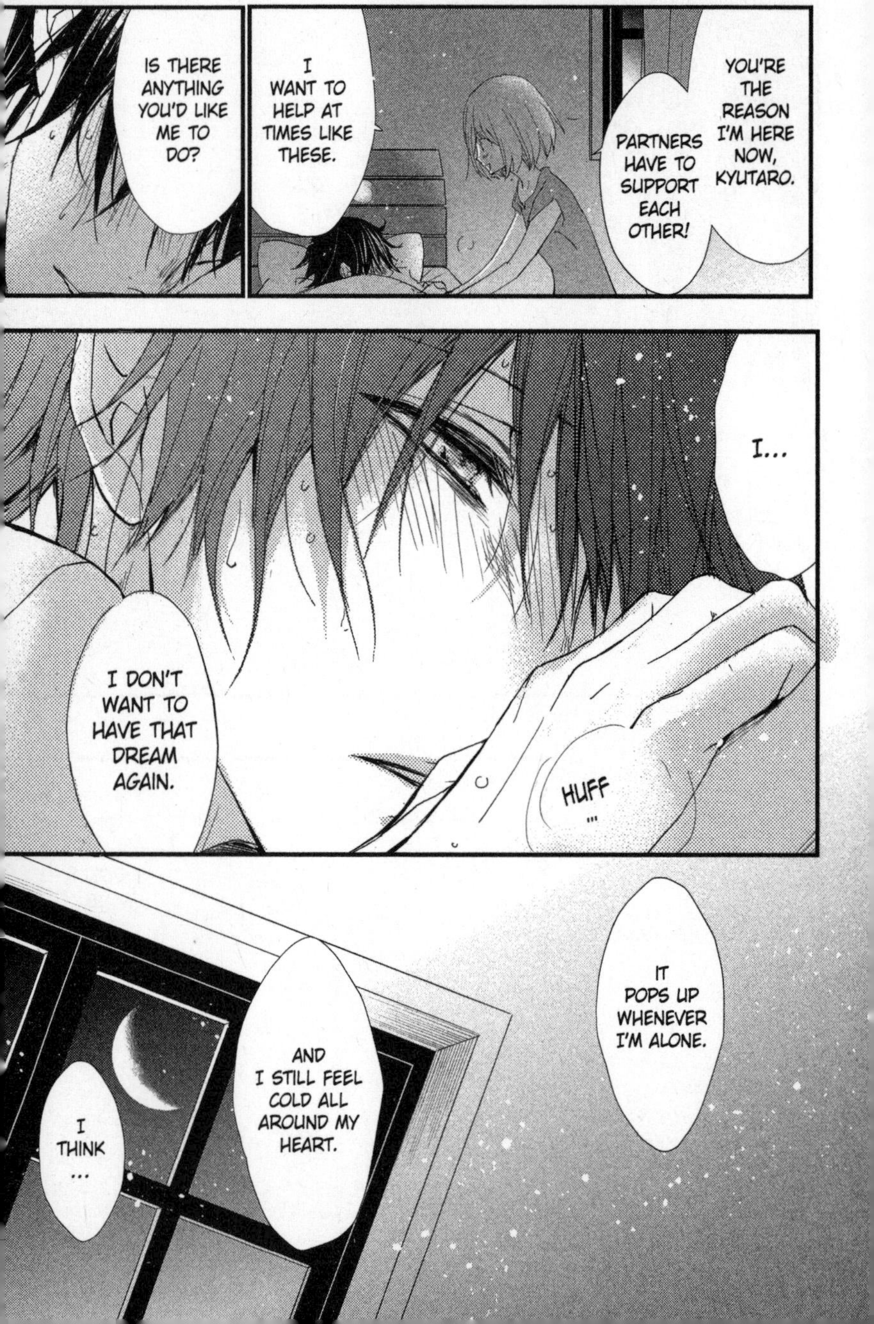
YOU'RE THE REASON I'M HERE NOW, KYUTARO.
PARTNERS HAVE TO SUPPORT EACH OTHER!
I WANT TO HELP AT TIMES LIKE THESE.
IS THERE ANYTHING YOU'D LIKE ME TO DO?
I...
HUFF ...
I DON'T WANT TO HAVE THAT DREAM AGAIN.
IT POPS UP WHENEVER I'M ALONE.
AND I STILL FEEL COLD ALL AROUND MY HEART.
I THINK ...

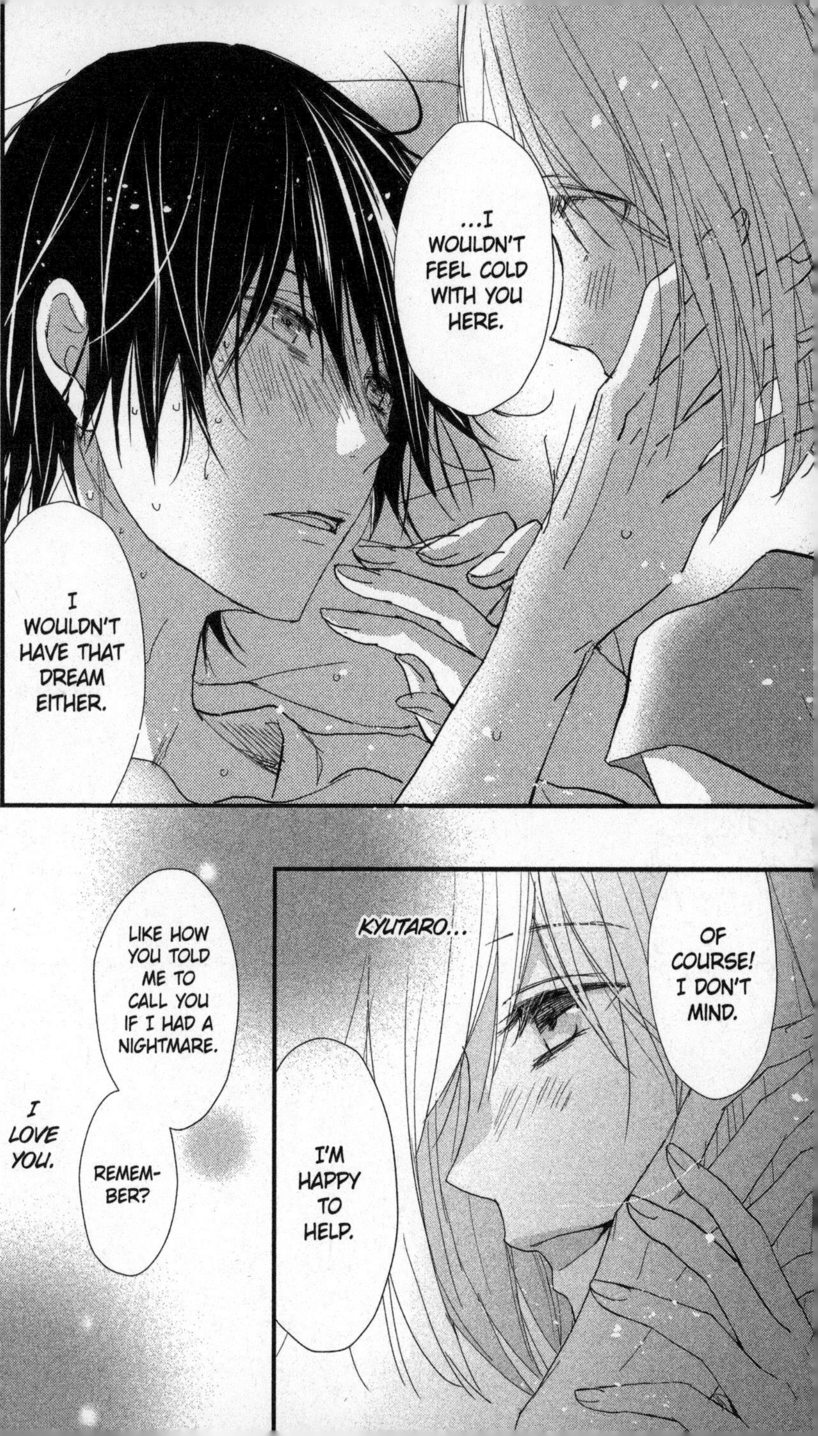
...I WOULDN'T FEEL COLD WITH YOU HERE.
I WOULDN'T HAVE THAT DREAM EITHER.
OF COURSE! I DON'T MIND.
KYUTARO...
I'M HAPPY TO HELP.
LIKE HOW YOU TOLD ME TO CALL YOU IF I HAD A NIGHTMARE.
REMEMBER?
I LOVE YOU.

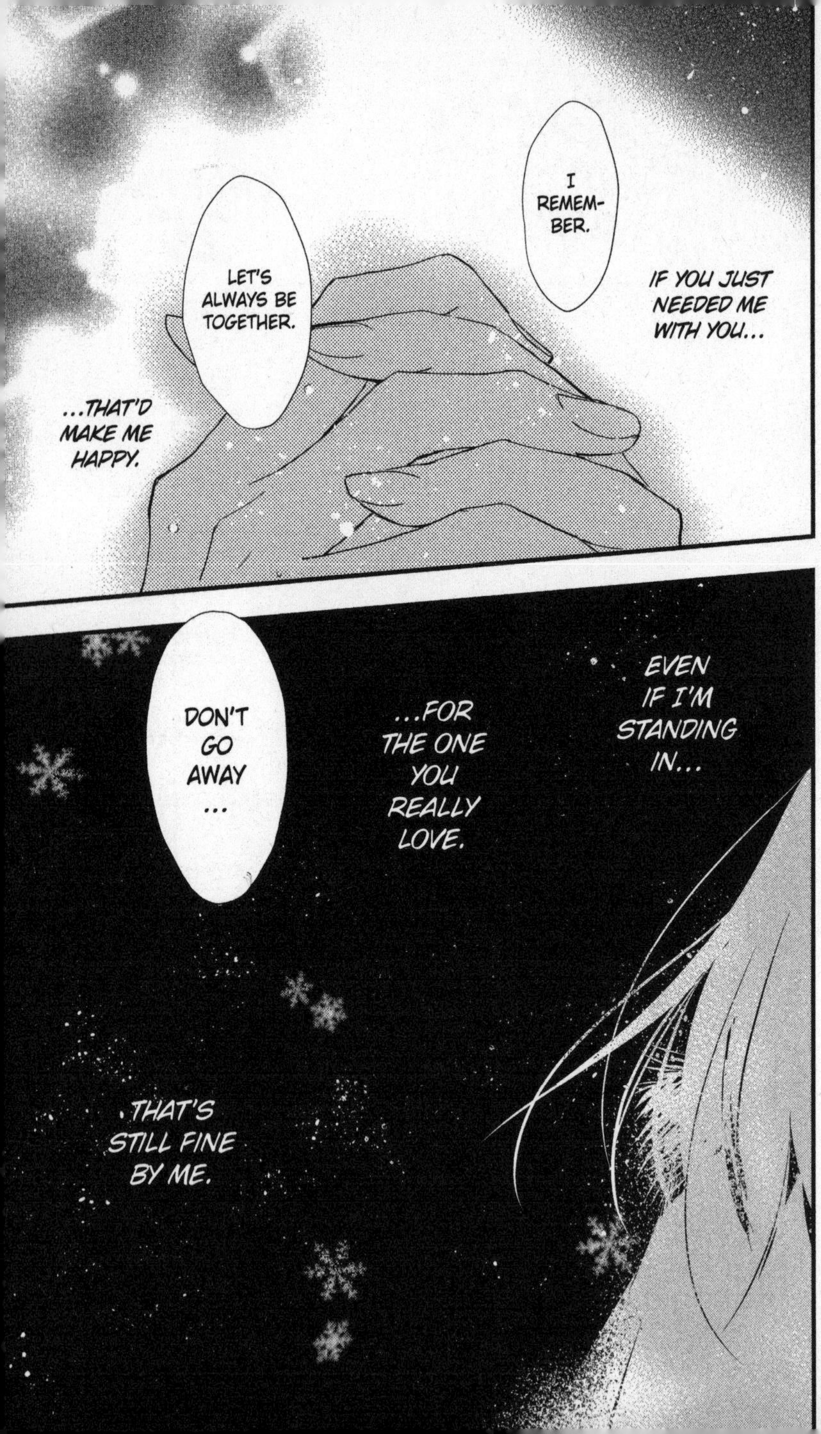
I REMEMBER.
IF YOU JUST NEEDED ME WITH YOU...
LET'S ALWAYS BE TOGETHER.
...THAT'D MAKE ME HAPPY.
EVEN IF I'M STANDING IN...
...FOR THE ONE YOU REALLY LOVE.
DON'T GO AWAY...
THAT'S STILL FINE BY ME.

MONTHLY BETSUCOMI SALE DATE NOTICE ON TWITTER

CHAPTER 25

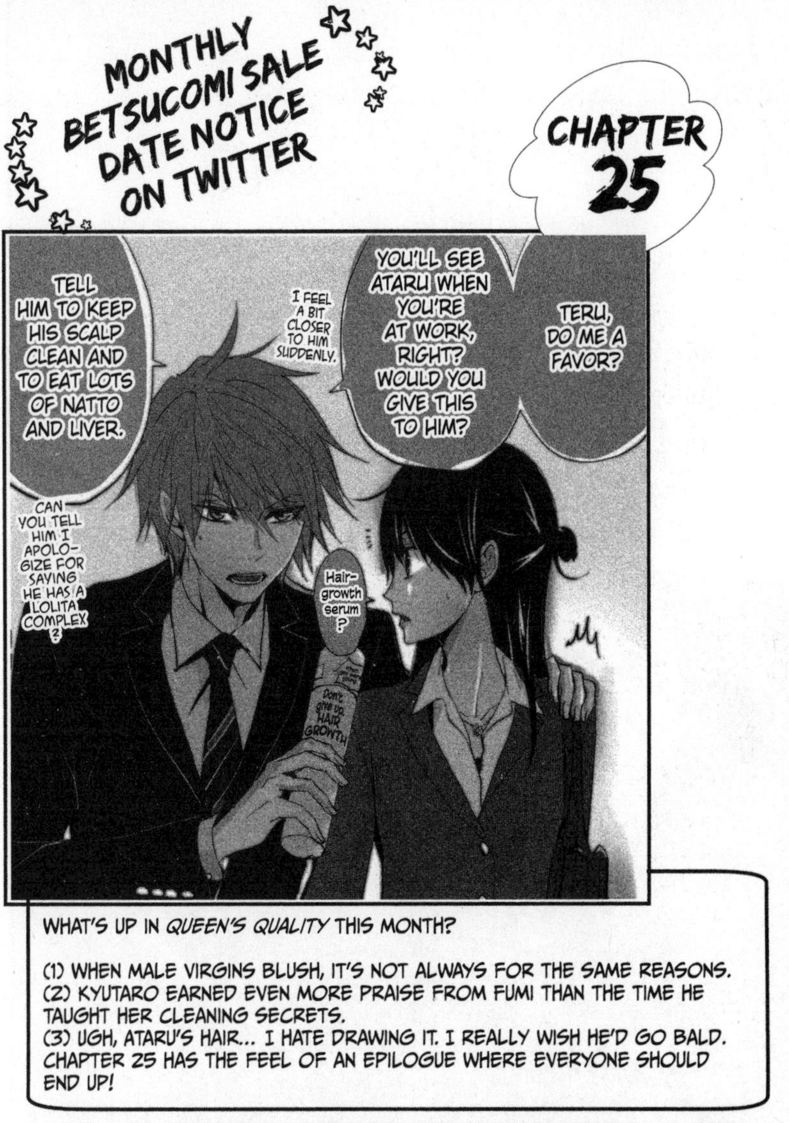
TERU, DO ME A FAVOR?
YOU'LL SEE ATARU WHEN YOU'RE AT WORK, RIGHT? WOULD YOU GIVE THIS TO HIM?
I FEEL A BIT CLOSER TO HIM SUDDENLY.
TELL HIM TO KEEP HIS SCALP CLEAN AND TO EAT LOTS OF NATTO AND LIVER.
Hair-growth serum?
CAN YOU TELL HIM I APOLOGIZE FOR SAYING HE HAS A LOLITA COMPLEX?
Don't give up, HAIR GROWTH

WHAT'S UP IN *QUEEN'S QUALITY* THIS MONTH?

(1) WHEN MALE VIRGINS BLUSH, IT'S NOT ALWAYS FOR THE SAME REASONS.
(2) KYUTARO EARNED EVEN MORE PRAISE FROM FUMI THAN THE TIME HE TAUGHT HER CLEANING SECRETS.
(3) UGH, ATARU'S HAIR... I HATE DRAWING IT. I REALLY WISH HE'D GO BALD.
CHAPTER 25 HAS THE FEEL OF AN EPILOGUE WHERE EVERYONE SHOULD END UP!

THESE TWO ARE KUROSAKI AND TERU, TWO CHARACTERS FROM *DENGEKI DAISY*, A PREVIOUS SERIES OF MINE. KUROSAKI WAS MY ORIGINAL CHARACTER WITH HAIR THAT WAS SO HARD TO DRAW THAT I'D WISH BALDNESS ON HIM.

EVERY ONCE IN A WHILE, I USE CHARACTERS FROM THIS SERIES IN MY TWEETS OR DO BONUS DRAWINGS OF THEM. I EVEN HAD LINE STICKERS MADE OF MY *QUEEQUA* AND *DENGEKI DAISY* CHARACTERS (SEE "KYOUSUKE'S FRIENDS WITH EYES ROLLED BACK" AT THE LINE STORE). I HOPE YOU'LL CHECK THEM OUT!

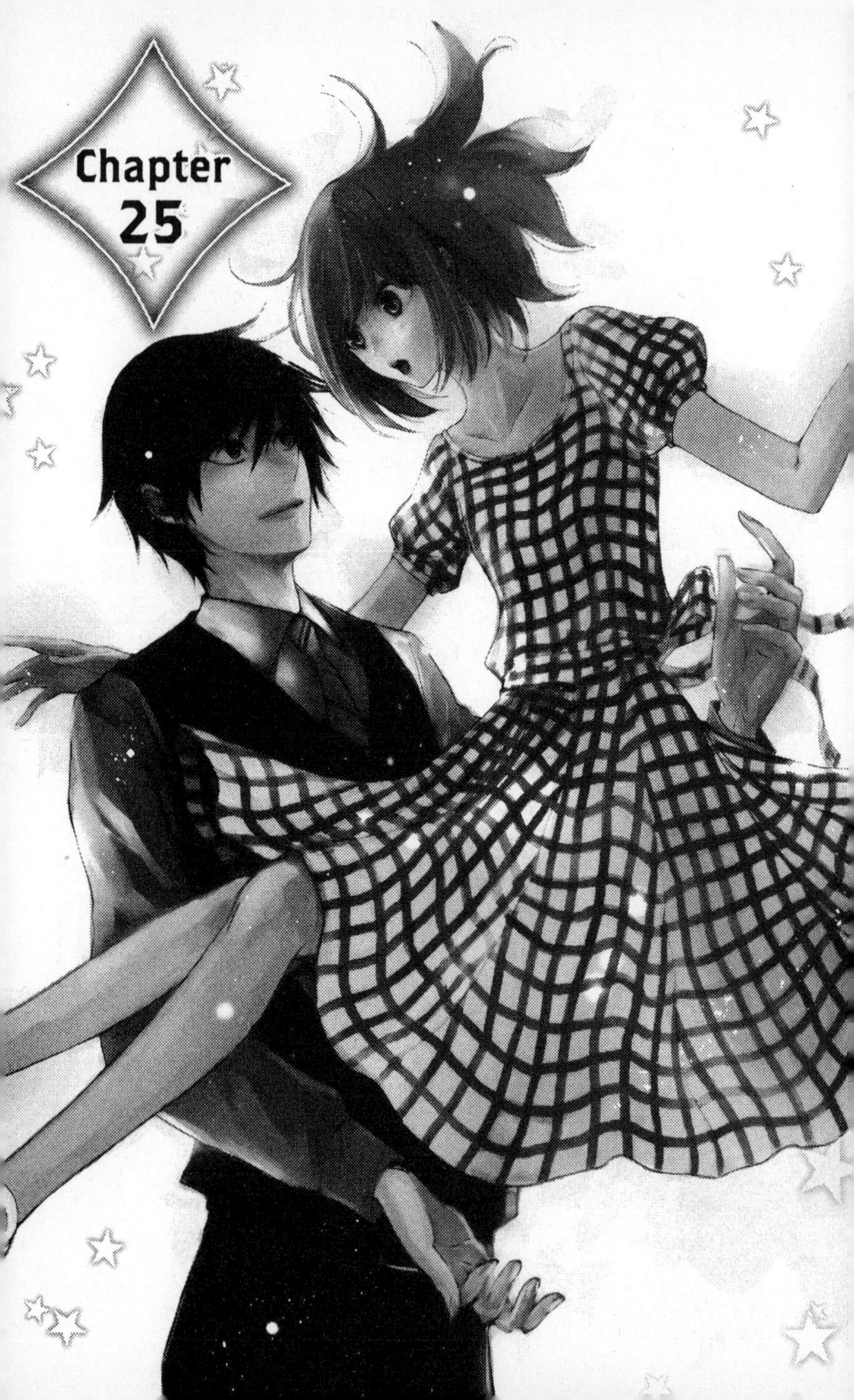
Chapter
25

I know we're right in the middle of everything, but indulge me while I make some greetings here.

There's only one chapter left in volume 5. I've gotten awfully attached to both the Black Queen and Ataru. Thank you for taking this journey with them.

A new story arc begins in the next volume. Fumi and Kyutaro have plenty of difficulties ahead of them, so I hope you'll stick around for the ride. I look forward to seeing you all again!

Kyousuke Motomi

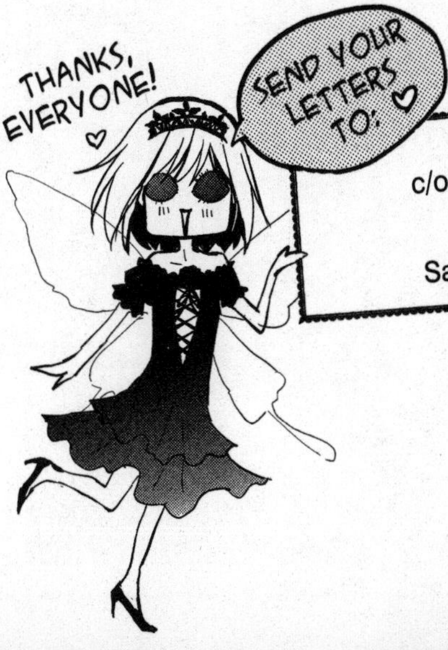
THANKS, EVERYONE!
SEND YOUR LETTERS TO:

Kyousuke Motomi
c/o Queen's Quality Editor
Viz Media
P.O. Box 77010
San Francisco, CA 94107

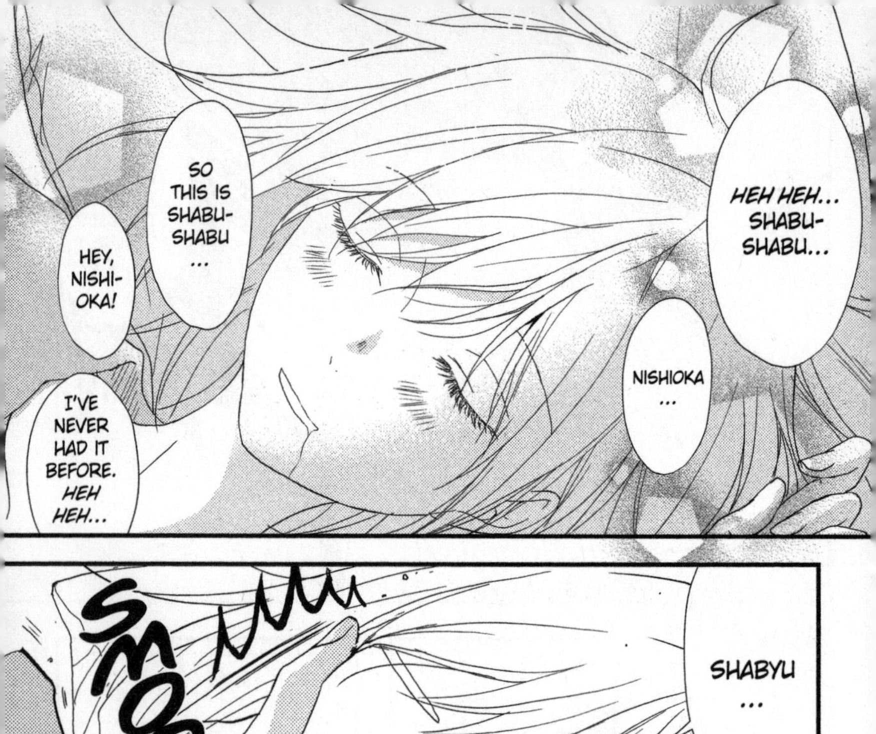
HEH HEH... SHABU-SHABU...
NISHIOKA ...
SO THIS IS SHABU-SHABU ...
HEY, NISHI-OKA!
I'VE NEVER HAD IT BEFORE. HEH HEH...
SHABYU ...
SMOOSH

I'm glad I was finally able to reveal Koichi (the dog). Yes, he is actually a wolf.

My mom called and said, "I enjoyed it because there was a dog in the story!" That was rare praise. (She still buys a *Betsucomi* every month and sends in the questionnaire.) My dog-loving friends all said they enjoyed this chapter. I feel like drawing a dog was definitely the right decision. Dogs save both the world and graphic novels. I love them.

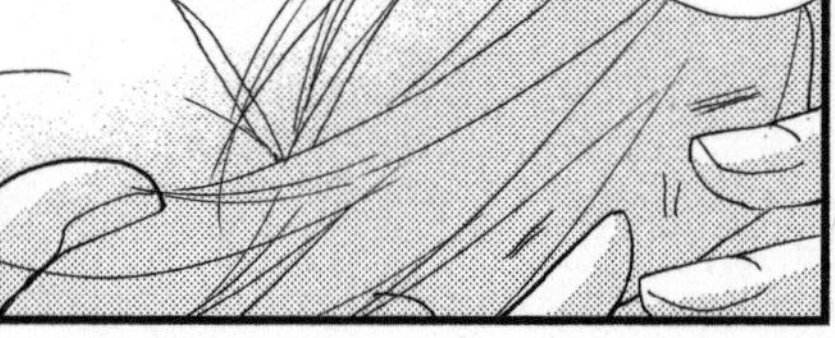
Mutsumi ... ♡
I think the difference between a wolf and a dog is the lushness of the fur here.

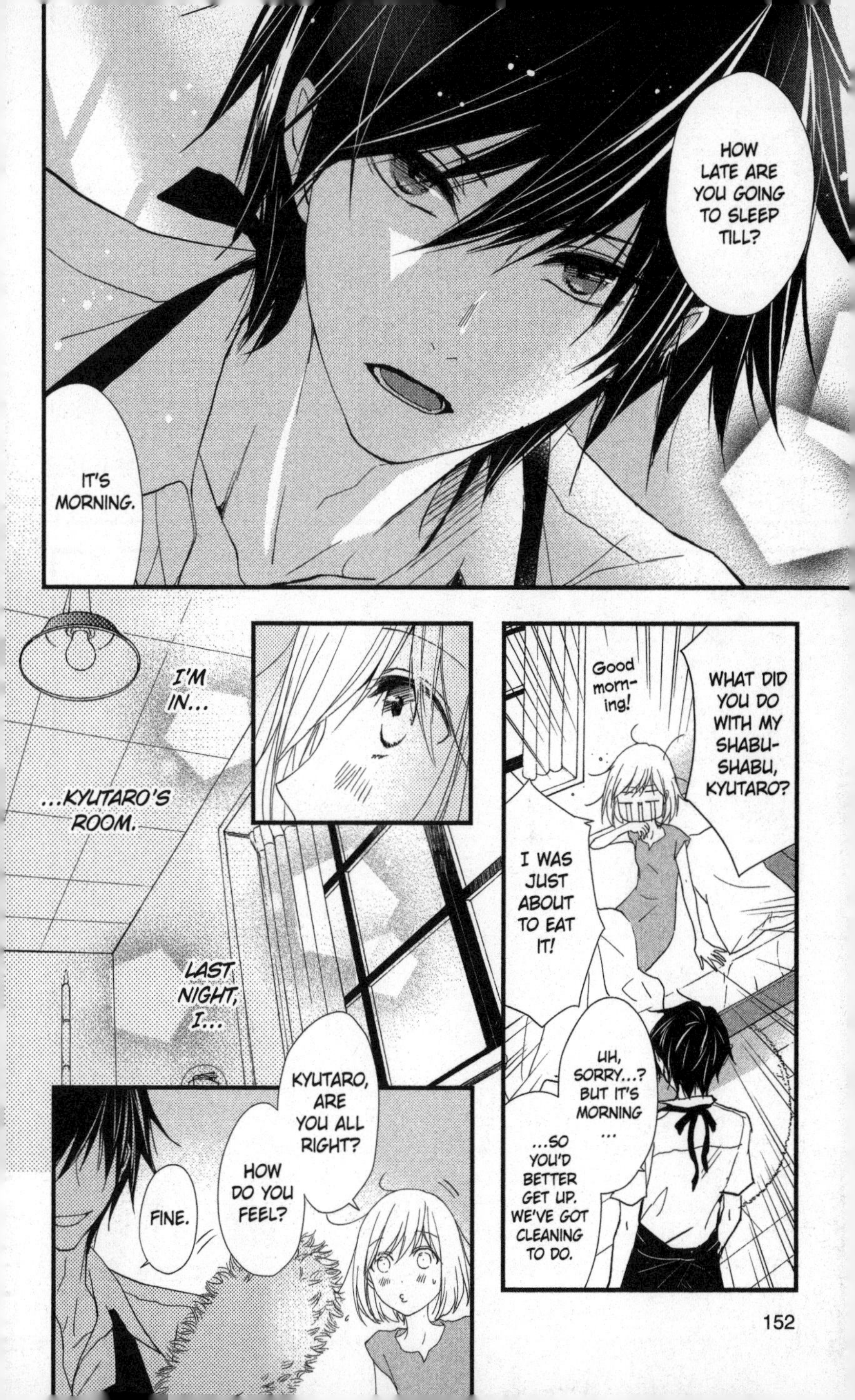
HOW LATE ARE YOU GOING TO SLEEP TILL?
IT'S MORNING.
WHAT DID YOU DO WITH MY SHABU-SHABU, KYUTARO?
Good morning!
I WAS JUST ABOUT TO EAT IT!
UH, SORRY...? BUT IT'S MORNING...
...SO YOU'D BETTER GET UP. WE'VE GOT CLEANING TO DO.
I'M IN...
...KYUTARO'S ROOM.
LAST NIGHT, I...
KYUTARO, ARE YOU ALL RIGHT?
HOW DO YOU FEEL?
FINE.

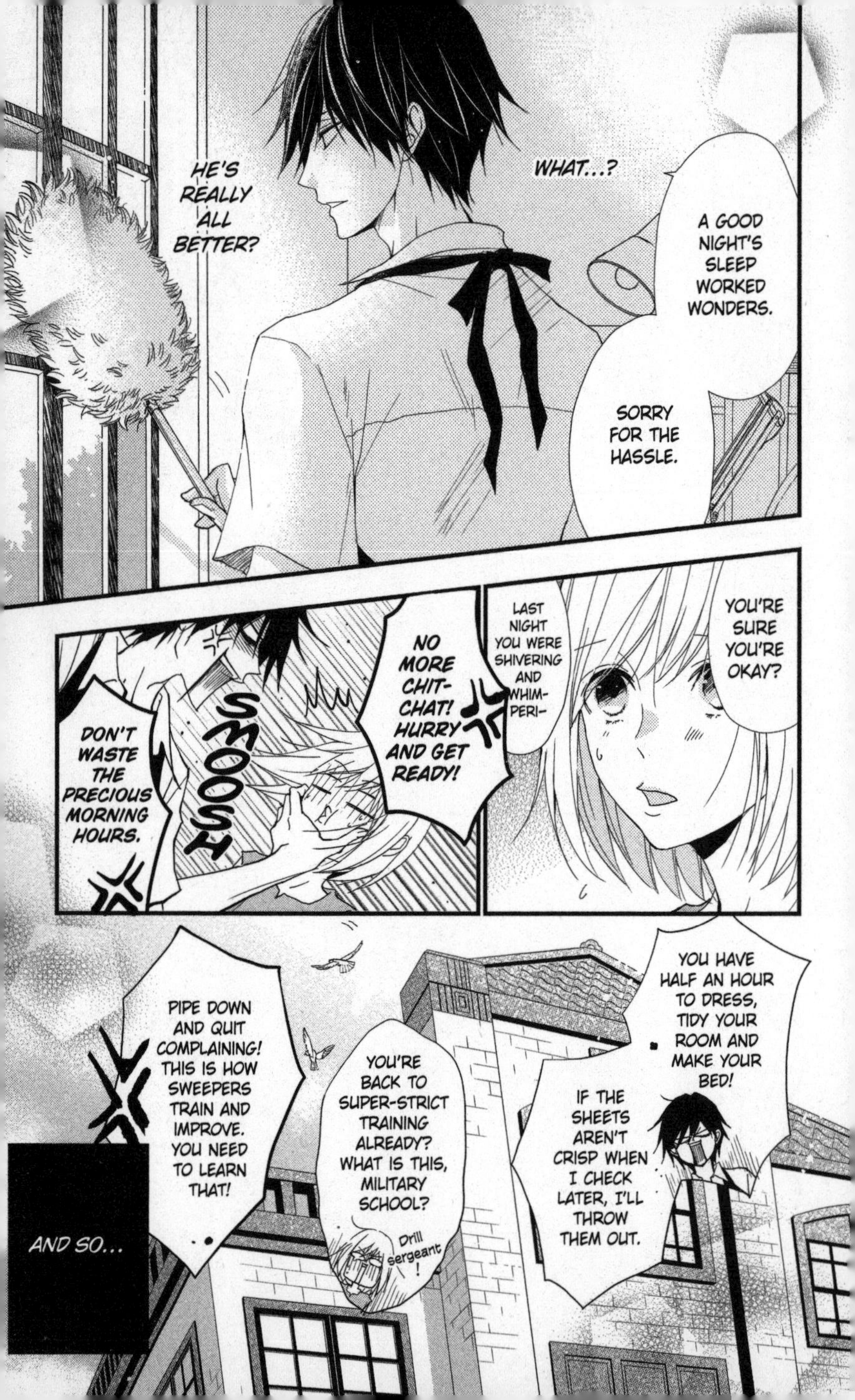
A GOOD NIGHT'S SLEEP WORKED WONDERS.
SORRY FOR THE HASSLE.
WHAT...?
HE'S REALLY ALL BETTER?
YOU'RE SURE YOU'RE OKAY?
LAST NIGHT YOU WERE SHIVERING AND WHIMPERI-
NO MORE CHIT-CHAT! HURRY AND GET READY!
SMOOSH
DON'T WASTE THE PRECIOUS MORNING HOURS.
YOU HAVE HALF AN HOUR TO DRESS, TIDY YOUR ROOM AND MAKE YOUR BED!
IF THE SHEETS AREN'T CRISP WHEN I CHECK LATER, I'LL THROW THEM OUT.
YOU'RE BACK TO SUPER-STRICT TRAINING ALREADY? WHAT IS THIS, MILITARY SCHOOL?
Drill sergeant!
PIPE DOWN AND QUIT COMPLAINING! THIS IS HOW SWEEPERS TRAIN AND IMPROVE. YOU NEED TO LEARN THAT!
AND SO...

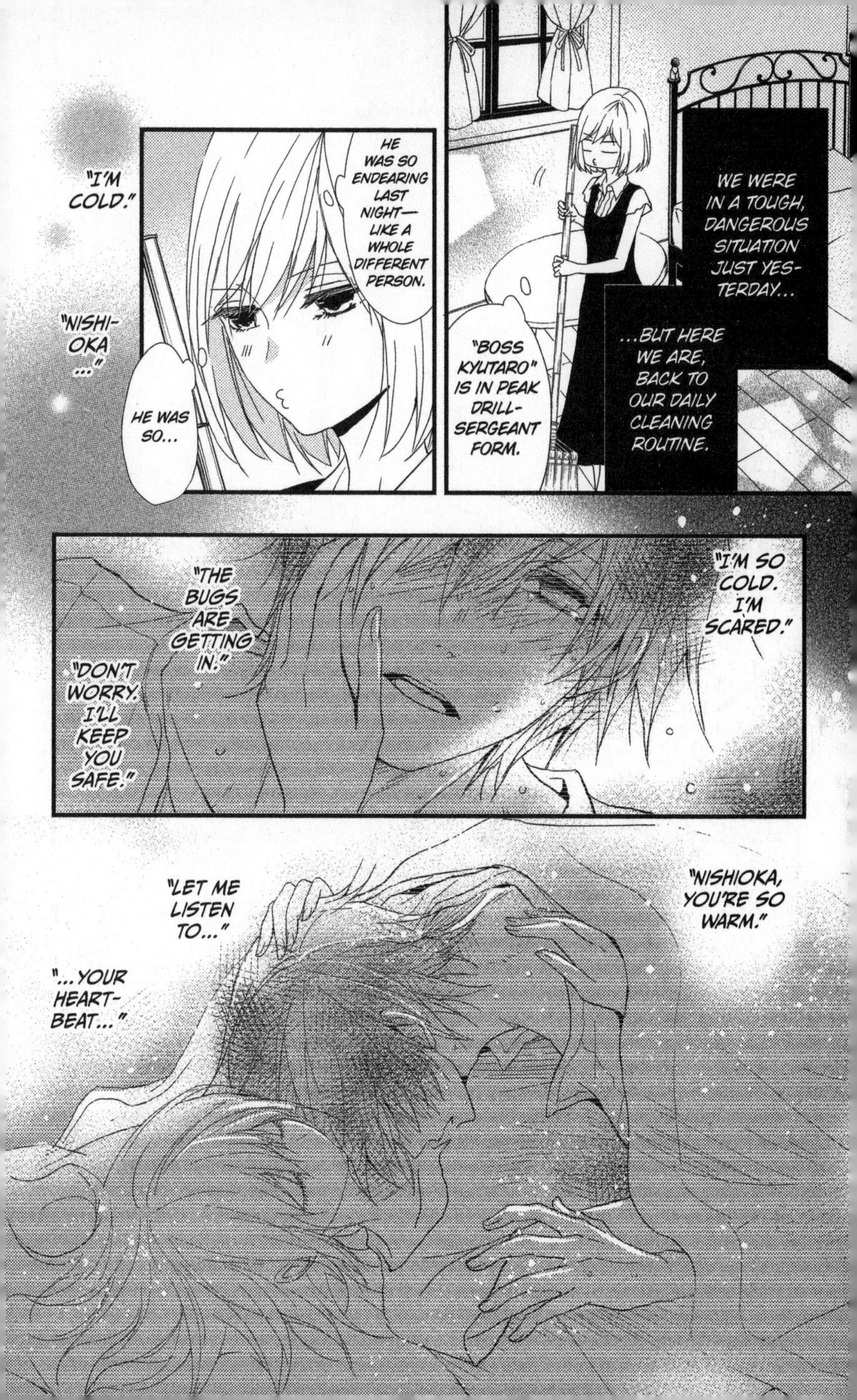
WE WERE IN A TOUGH, DANGEROUS SITUATION JUST YESTERDAY...
...BUT HERE WE ARE, BACK TO OUR DAILY CLEANING ROUTINE.
"BOSS KYUTARO" IS IN PEAK DRILL-SERGEANT FORM.
HE WAS SO ENDEARING LAST NIGHT—LIKE A WHOLE DIFFERENT PERSON.
HE WAS SO...
"I'M COLD."
"NISHIOKA..."
"I'M SO COLD. I'M SCARED."
"THE BUGS ARE GETTING IN."
"DON'T WORRY. I'LL KEEP YOU SAFE."
"NISHIOKA, YOU'RE SO WARM."
"LET ME LISTEN TO..."
"...YOUR HEARTBEAT..."

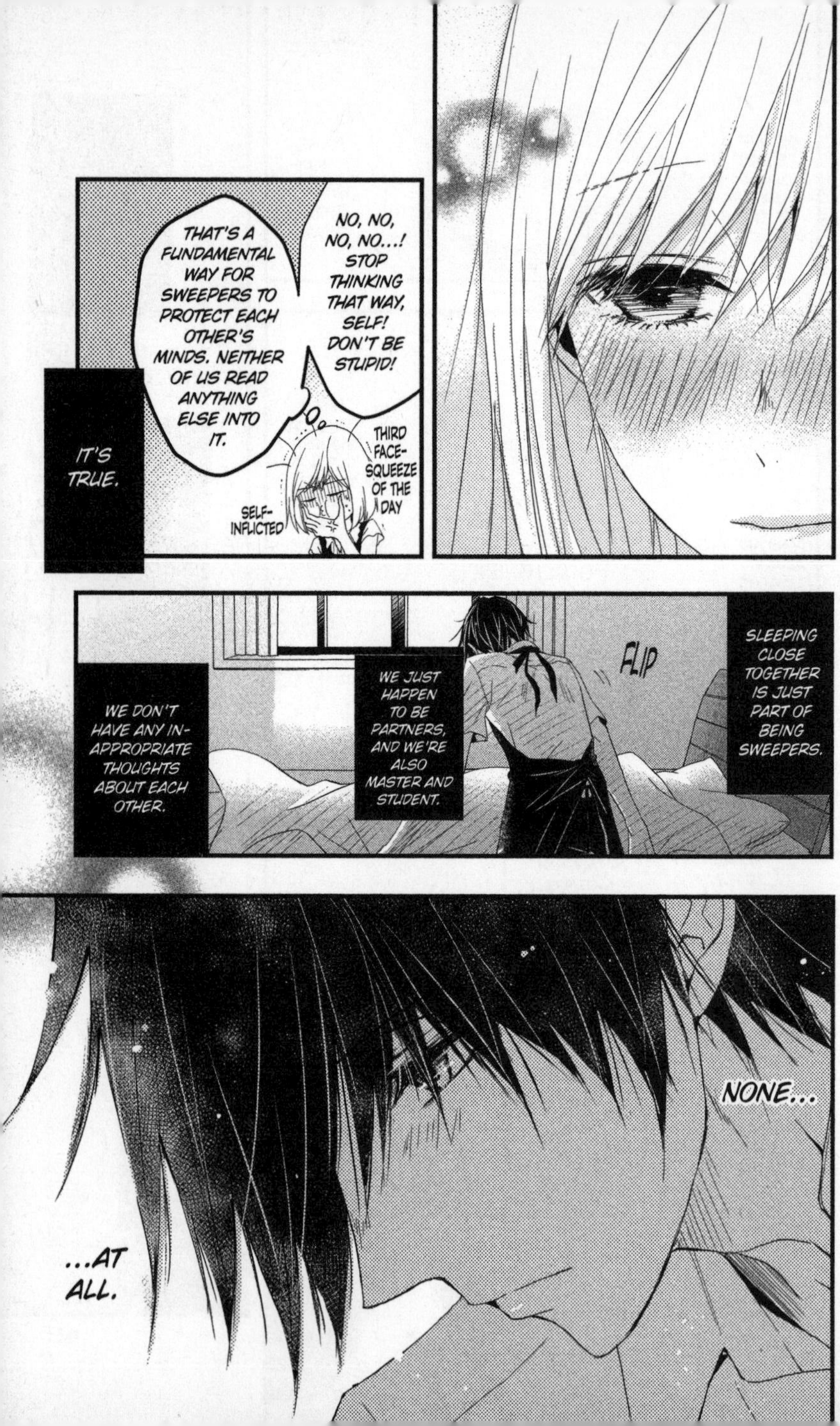
NO, NO, NO, NO...! STOP THINKING THAT WAY, SELF! DON'T BE STUPID!
THAT'S A FUNDAMENTAL WAY FOR SWEEPERS TO PROTECT EACH OTHER'S MINDS. NEITHER OF US READ ANYTHING ELSE INTO IT.
THIRD FACE-SQUEEZE OF THE DAY
SELF-INFLICTED
IT'S TRUE.
SLEEPING CLOSE TOGETHER IS JUST PART OF BEING SWEEPERS.
FLIP
WE JUST HAPPEN TO BE PARTNERS, AND WE'RE ALSO MASTER AND STUDENT.
WE DON'T HAVE ANY IN-APPROPRIATE THOUGHTS ABOUT EACH OTHER.
NONE...
...AT ALL.

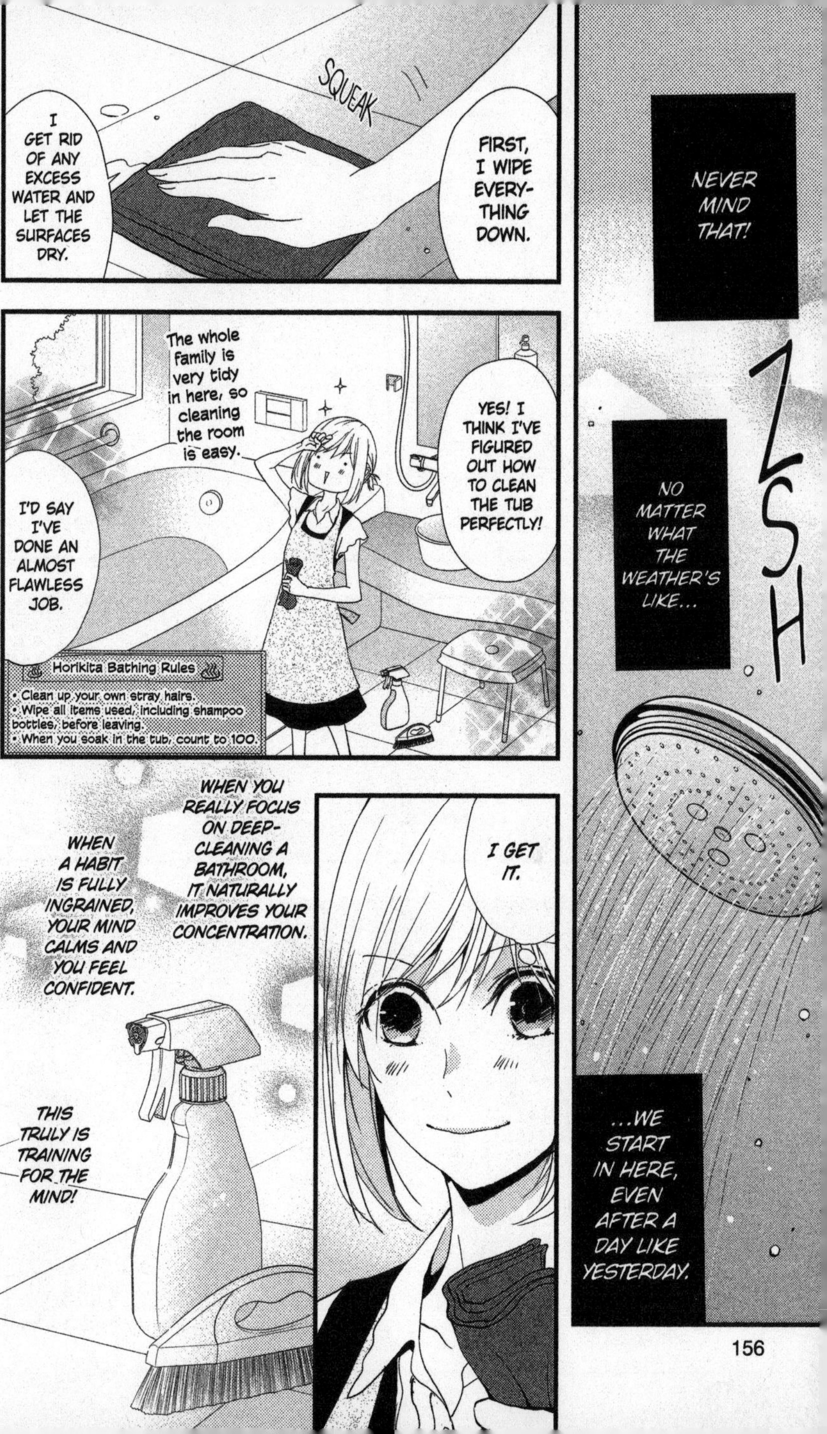
NEVER MIND THAT!
ZSH
NO MATTER WHAT THE WEATHER'S LIKE...
...WE START IN HERE, EVEN AFTER A DAY LIKE YESTERDAY.
SQUEAK
FIRST, I WIPE EVERYTHING DOWN.
I GET RID OF ANY EXCESS WATER AND LET THE SURFACES DRY.
YES! I THINK I'VE FIGURED OUT HOW TO CLEAN THE TUB PERFECTLY!
The whole family is very tidy in here, so cleaning the room is easy.
I'D SAY I'VE DONE AN ALMOST FLAWLESS JOB.
Horikita Bathing Rules
• Clean up your own stray hairs.
• Wipe all items used, including shampoo bottles, before leaving.
• When you soak in the tub, count to 100.
I GET IT.
WHEN YOU REALLY FOCUS ON DEEP-CLEANING A BATHROOM, IT NATURALLY IMPROVES YOUR CONCENTRATION.
WHEN A HABIT IS FULLY INGRAINED, YOUR MIND CALMS AND YOU FEEL CONFIDENT.
THIS TRULY IS TRAINING FOR THE MIND!

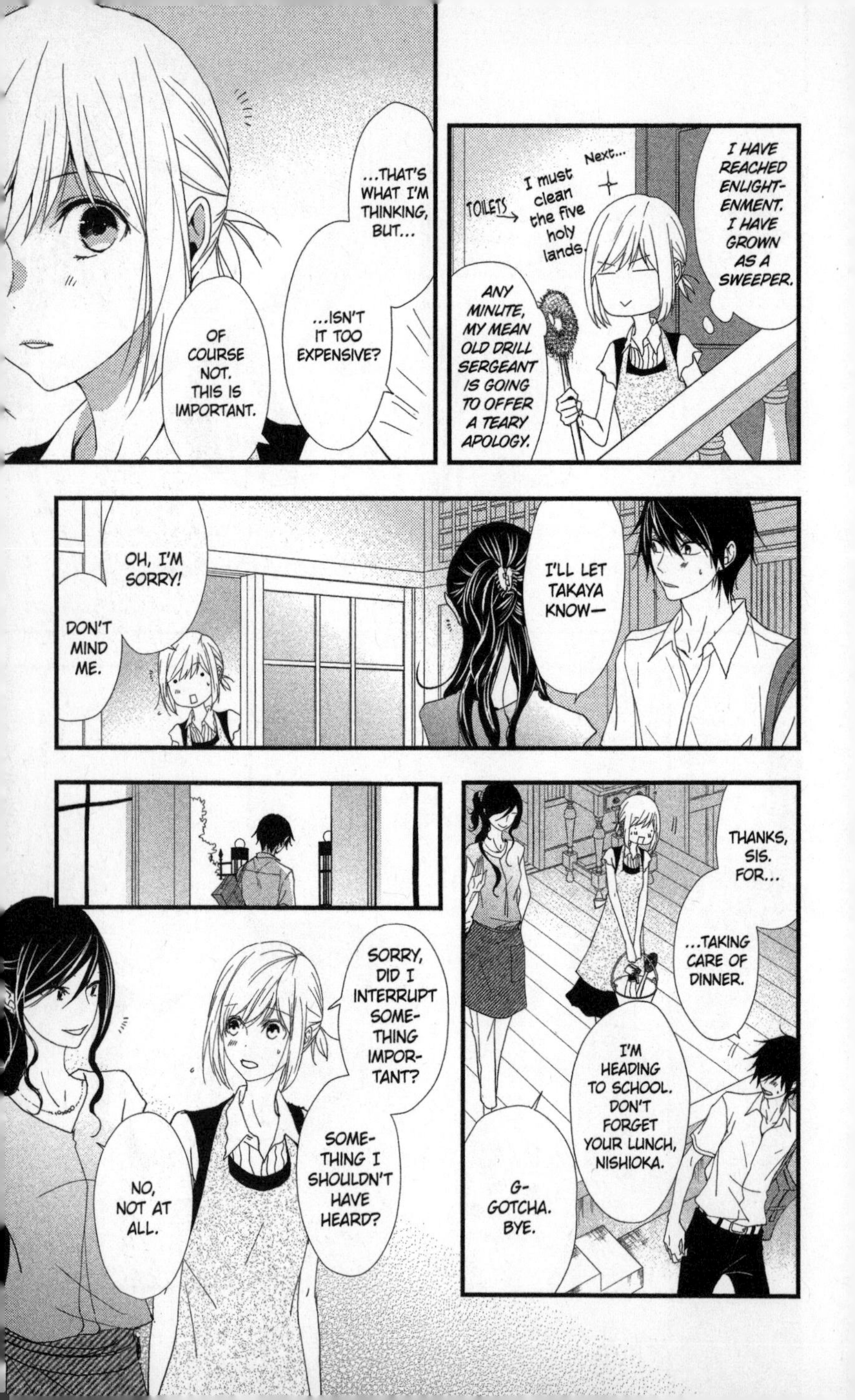
I HAVE REACHED ENLIGHT-ENMENT. I HAVE GROWN AS A SWEEPER.
Next... I must clean the five holy lands.
TOILETS
ANY MINUTE, MY MEAN OLD DRILL SERGEANT IS GOING TO OFFER A TEARY APOLOGY.
...THAT'S WHAT I'M THINKING, BUT...
...ISN'T IT TOO EXPENSIVE?
OF COURSE NOT. THIS IS IMPORTANT.
I'LL LET TAKAYA KNOW—
OH, I'M SORRY!
DON'T MIND ME.
THANKS, SIS. FOR...
...TAKING CARE OF DINNER.
I'M HEADING TO SCHOOL. DON'T FORGET YOUR LUNCH, NISHIOKA.
G-GOTCHA. BYE.
SORRY, DID I INTERRUPT SOME-THING IMPOR-TANT?
SOME-THING I SHOULDN'T HAVE HEARD?
NO, NOT AT ALL.

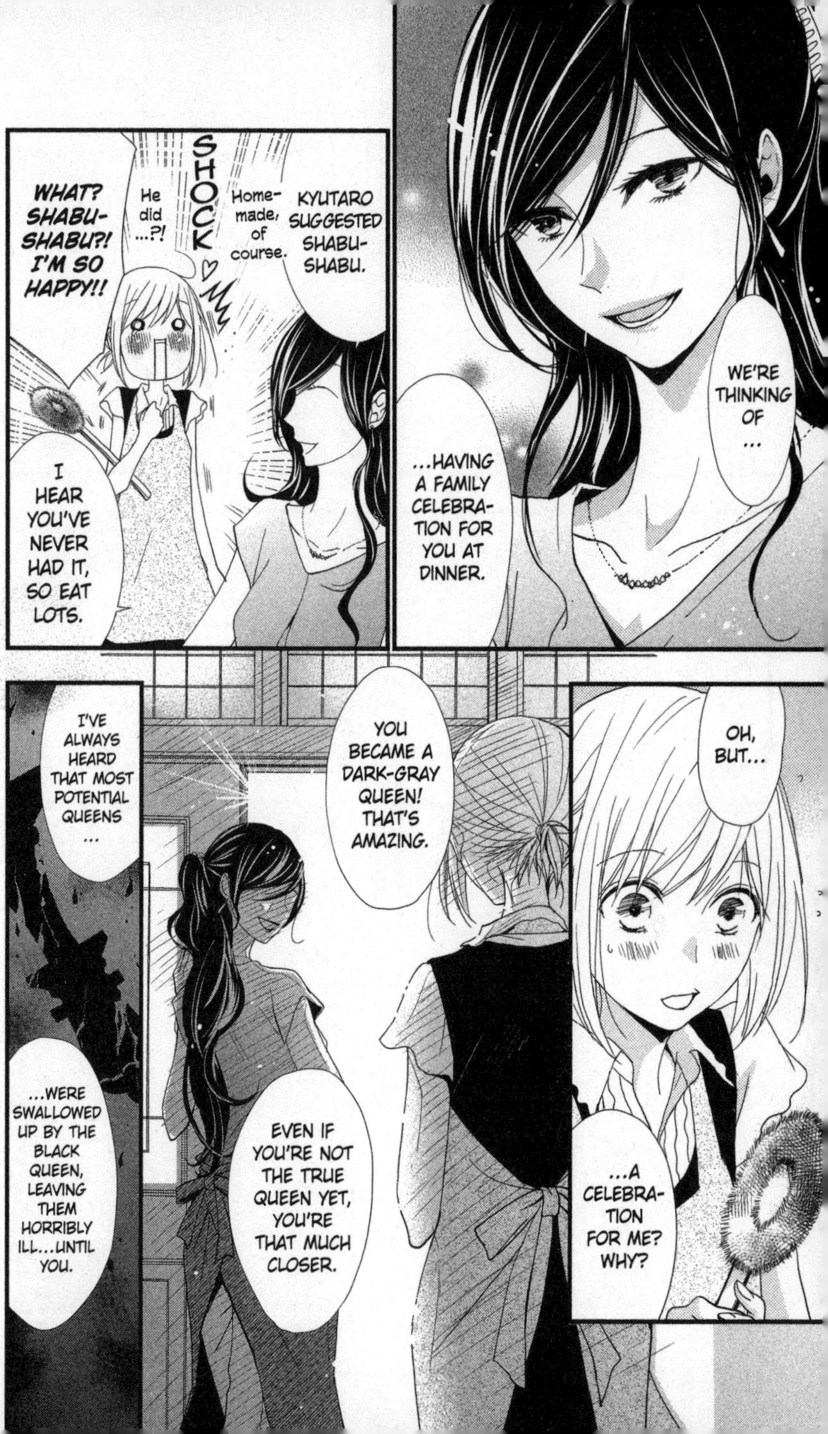
WE'RE THINKING OF ...
...HAVING A FAMILY CELEBRATION FOR YOU AT DINNER.
KYUTARO SUGGESTED SHABU-SHABU.
Home-made, of course.
SHOCK
He did ...?!
WHAT? SHABU-SHABU?! I'M SO HAPPY!!
I HEAR YOU'VE NEVER HAD IT, SO EAT LOTS.
OH, BUT...
...A CELEBRATION FOR ME? WHY?
YOU BECAME A DARK-GRAY QUEEN! THAT'S AMAZING.
EVEN IF YOU'RE NOT THE TRUE QUEEN YET, YOU'RE THAT MUCH CLOSER.
I'VE ALWAYS HEARD THAT MOST POTENTIAL QUEENS ...
...WERE SWALLOWED UP BY THE BLACK QUEEN, LEAVING THEM HORRIBLY ILL...UNTIL YOU.

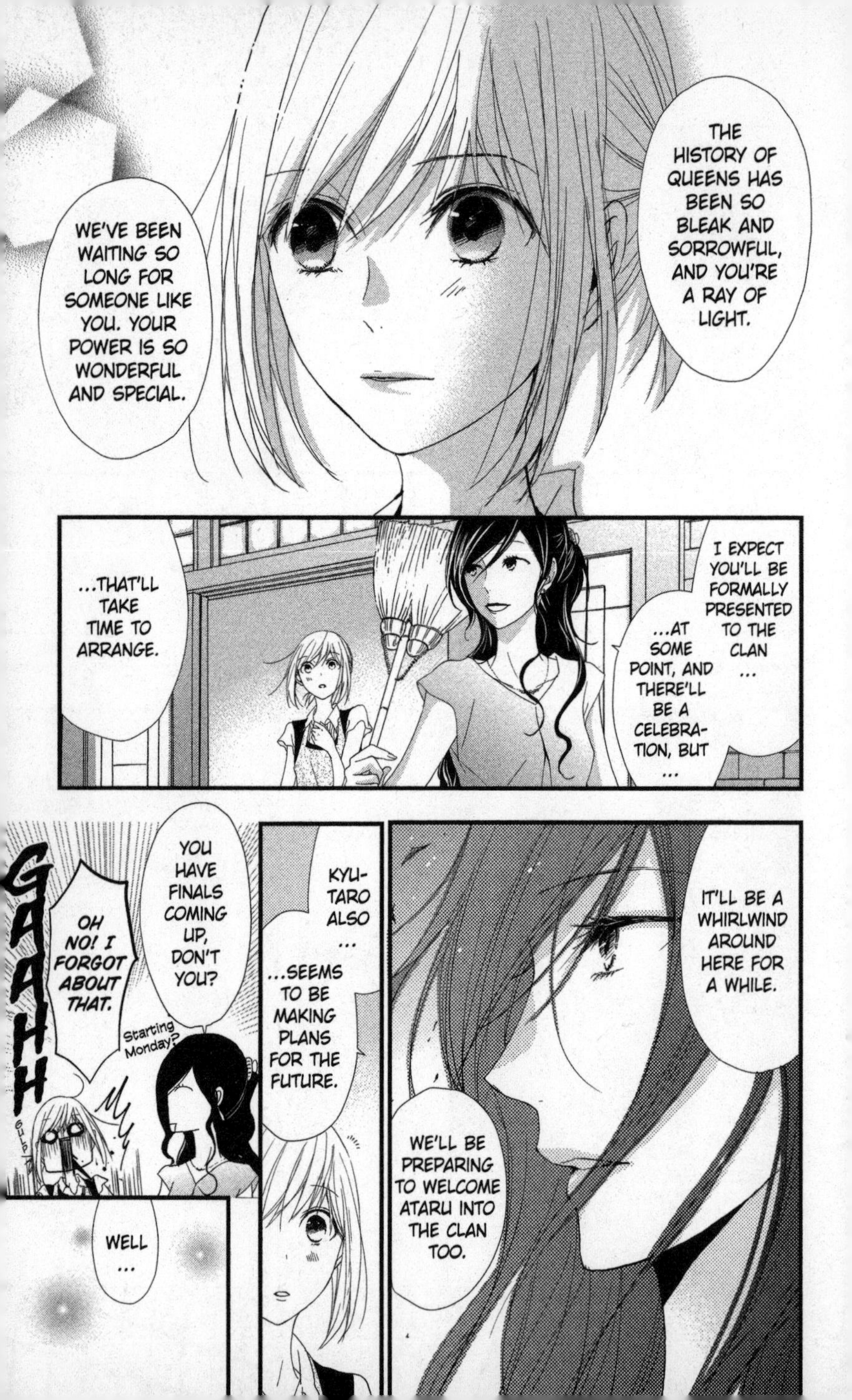
THE HISTORY OF QUEENS HAS BEEN SO BLEAK AND SORROWFUL, AND YOU'RE A RAY OF LIGHT.
WE'VE BEEN WAITING SO LONG FOR SOMEONE LIKE YOU. YOUR POWER IS SO WONDERFUL AND SPECIAL.
I EXPECT YOU'LL BE FORMALLY PRESENTED TO THE CLAN ...
...AT SOME POINT, AND THERE'LL BE A CELEBRATION, BUT ...
...THAT'LL TAKE TIME TO ARRANGE.
IT'LL BE A WHIRLWIND AROUND HERE FOR A WHILE.
WE'LL BE PREPARING TO WELCOME ATARU INTO THE CLAN TOO.
KYU-TARO ALSO ...
...SEEMS TO BE MAKING PLANS FOR THE FUTURE.
YOU HAVE FINALS COMING UP, DON'T YOU?
Starting Monday?
OH NO! I FORGOT ABOUT THAT.
GAAHH
GULP
WELL ...

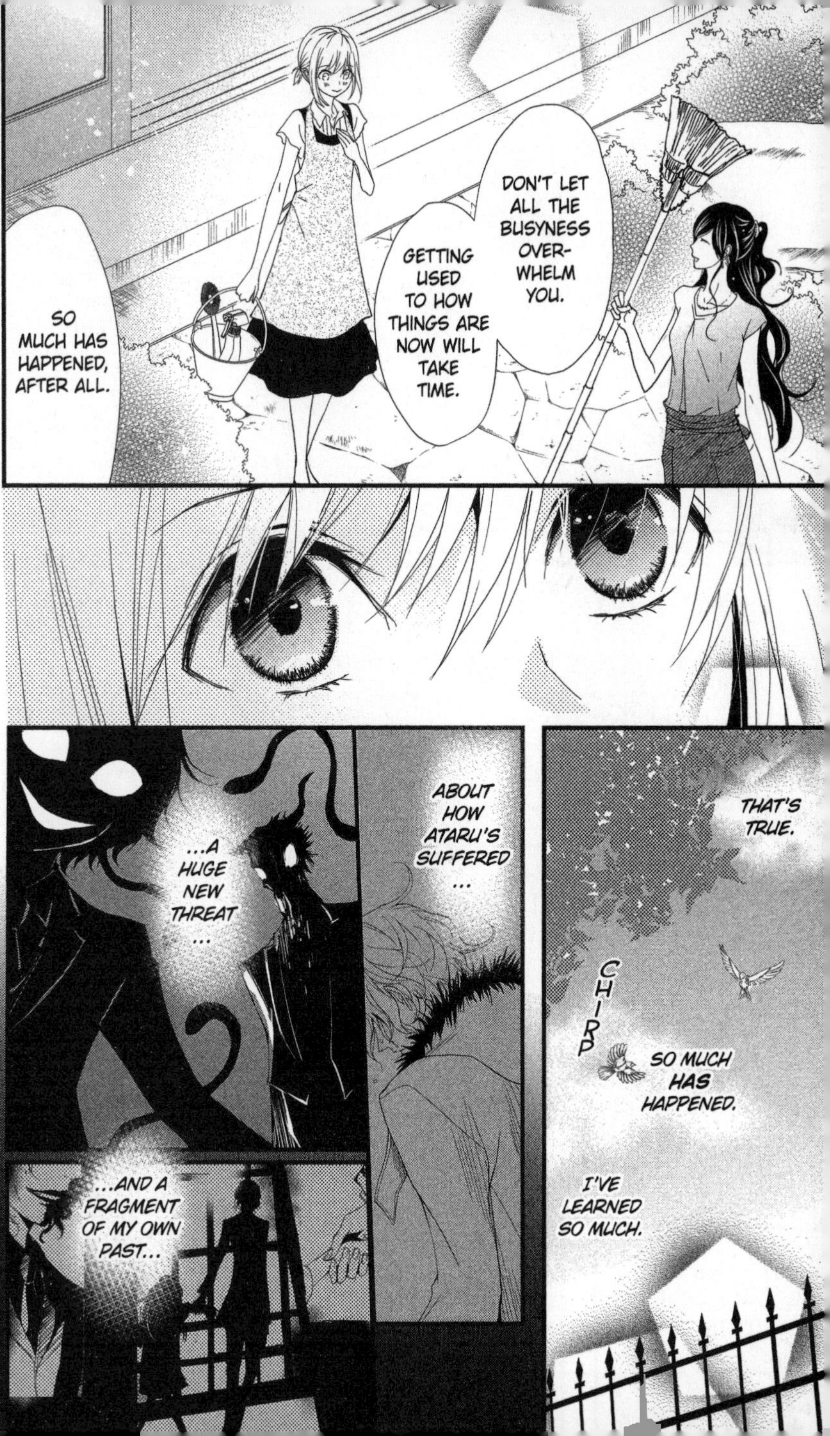
DON'T LET ALL THE BUSYNESS OVER-WHELM YOU.
GETTING USED TO HOW THINGS ARE NOW WILL TAKE TIME.
SO MUCH HAS HAPPENED, AFTER ALL.
THAT'S TRUE.
CHIRP
SO MUCH HAS HAPPENED.
I'VE LEARNED SO MUCH.
ABOUT HOW ATARU'S SUFFERED...
...A HUGE NEW THREAT...
...AND A FRAGMENT OF MY OWN PAST...

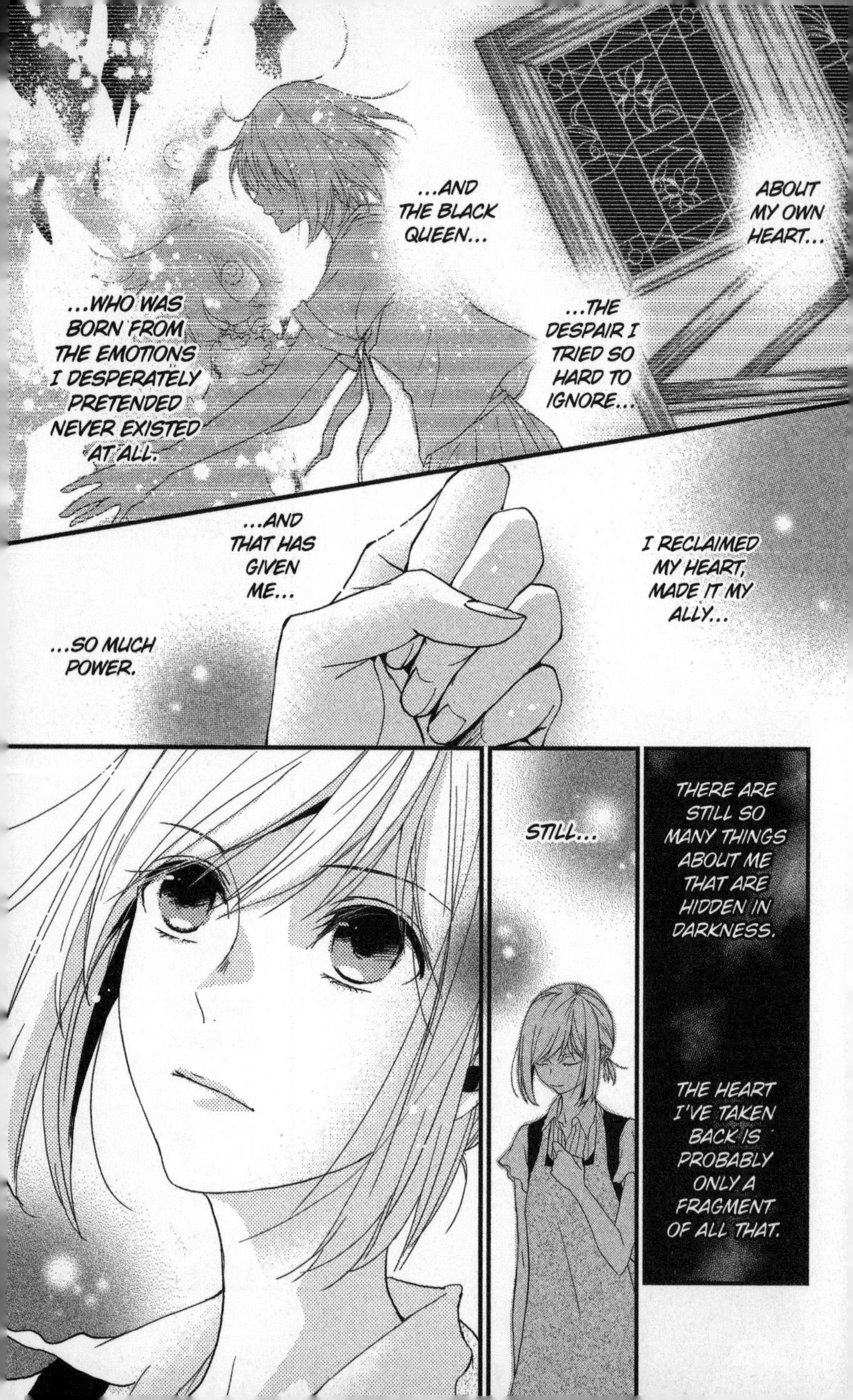
ABOUT MY OWN HEART...
...THE DESPAIR I TRIED SO HARD TO IGNORE...
...AND THE BLACK QUEEN...
...WHO WAS BORN FROM THE EMOTIONS I DESPERATELY PRETENDED NEVER EXISTED AT ALL.
I RECLAIMED MY HEART, MADE IT MY ALLY...
...AND THAT HAS GIVEN ME...
...SO MUCH POWER.
STILL...
THERE ARE STILL SO MANY THINGS ABOUT ME THAT ARE HIDDEN IN DARKNESS.
THE HEART I'VE TAKEN BACK IS PROBABLY ONLY A FRAGMENT OF ALL THAT.

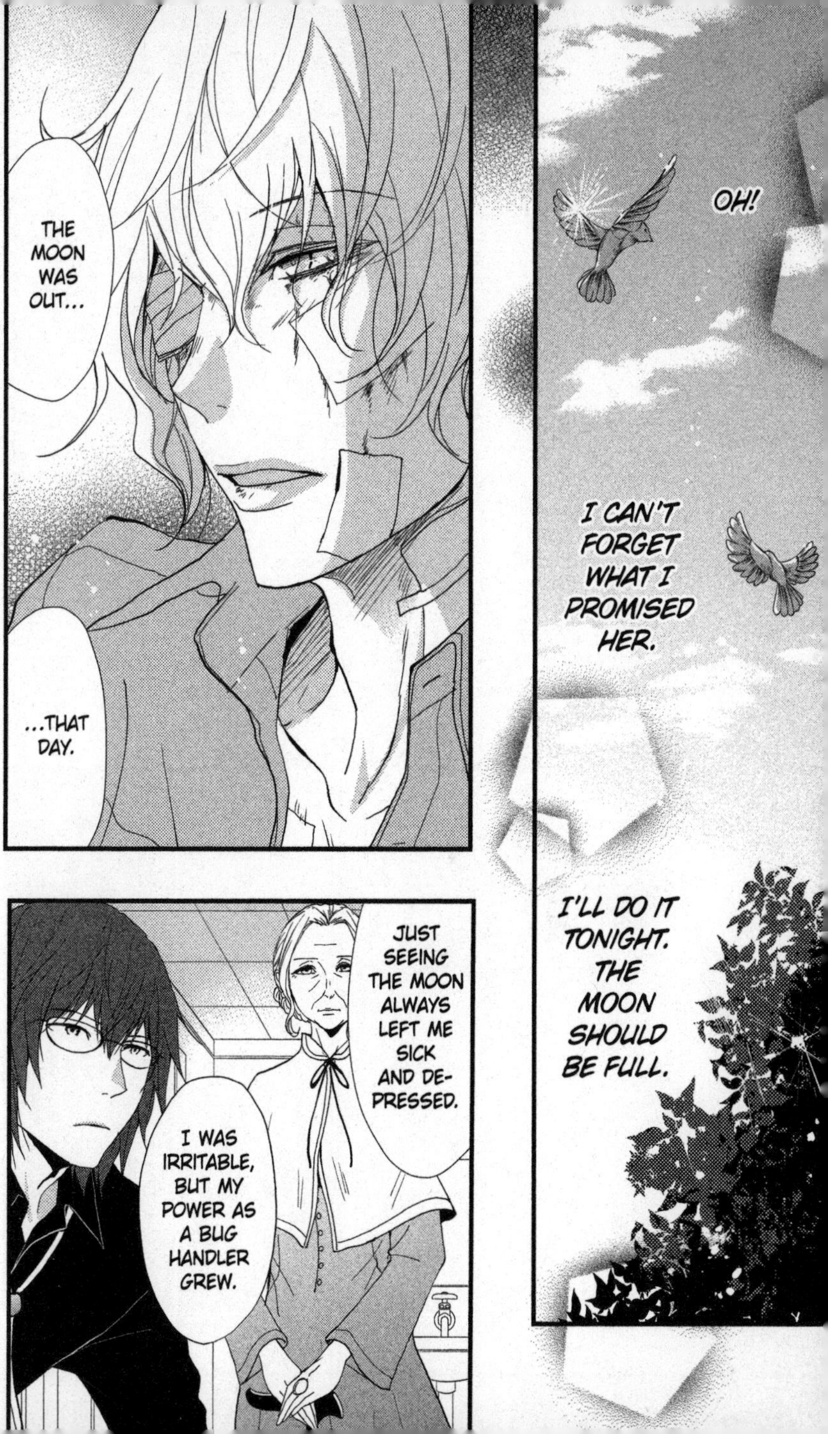
OH!
I CAN'T FORGET WHAT I PROMISED HER.
I'LL DO IT TONIGHT. THE MOON SHOULD BE FULL.
THE MOON WAS OUT...
...THAT DAY.
JUST SEEING THE MOON ALWAYS LEFT ME SICK AND DE-PRESSED.
I WAS IRRITABLE, BUT MY POWER AS A BUG HANDLER GREW.

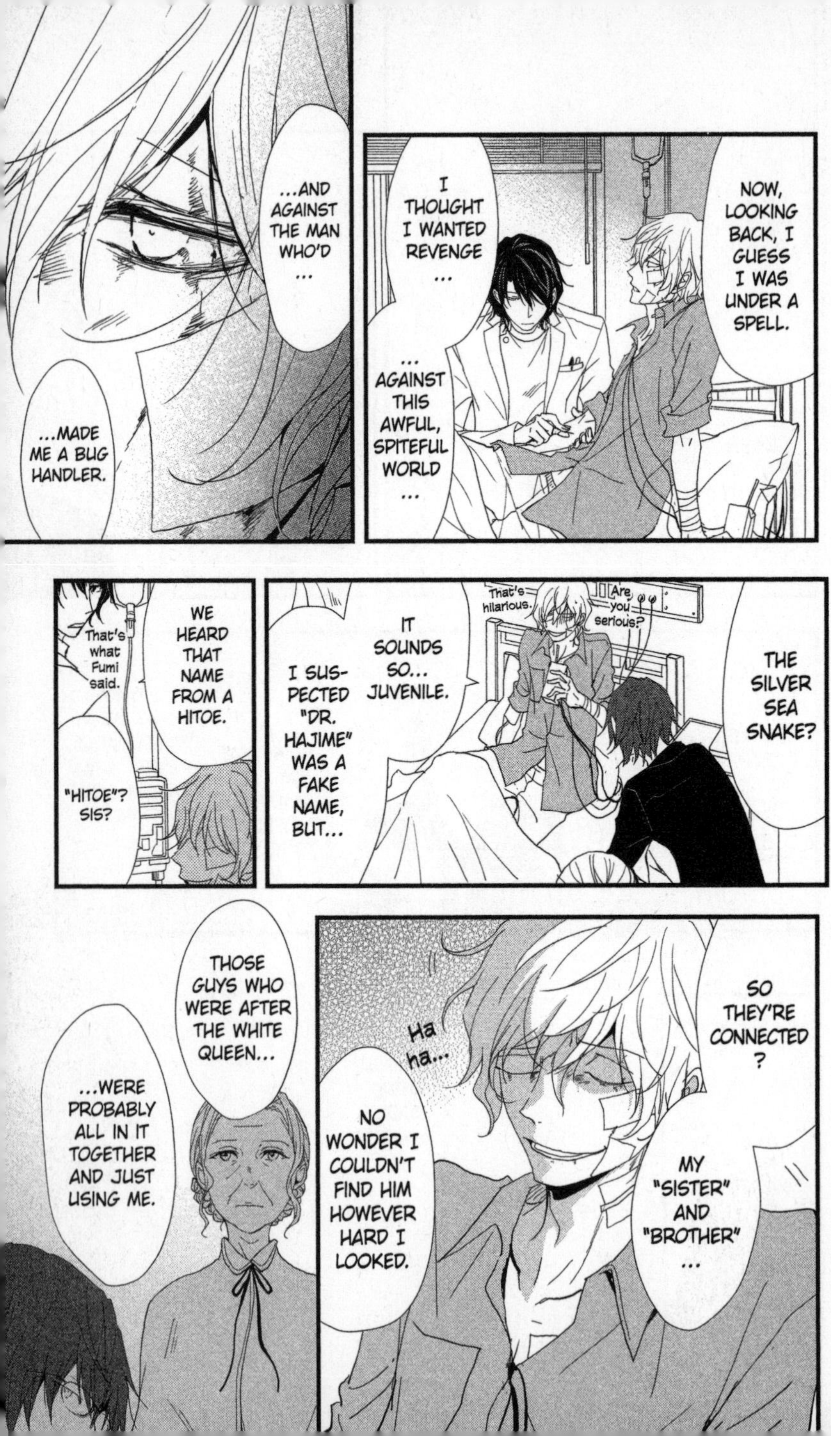
NOW, LOOKING BACK, I GUESS I WAS UNDER A SPELL.
I THOUGHT I WANTED REVENGE ...
... AGAINST THIS AWFUL, SPITEFUL WORLD ...
...AND AGAINST THE MAN WHO'D ...
...MADE ME A BUG HANDLER.
THE SILVER SEA SNAKE?
That's hilarious.
Are you serious?
IT SOUNDS SO... JUVENILE.
I SUSPECTED "DR. HAJIME" WAS A FAKE NAME, BUT...
WE HEARD THAT NAME FROM A HITOE.
That's what Fumi said.
"HITOE"? SIS?
SO THEY'RE CONNECTED?
MY "SISTER" AND "BROTHER" ...
Ha ha...
NO WONDER I COULDN'T FIND HIM HOWEVER HARD I LOOKED.
THOSE GUYS WHO WERE AFTER THE WHITE QUEEN...
...WERE PROBABLY ALL IN IT TOGETHER AND JUST USING ME.

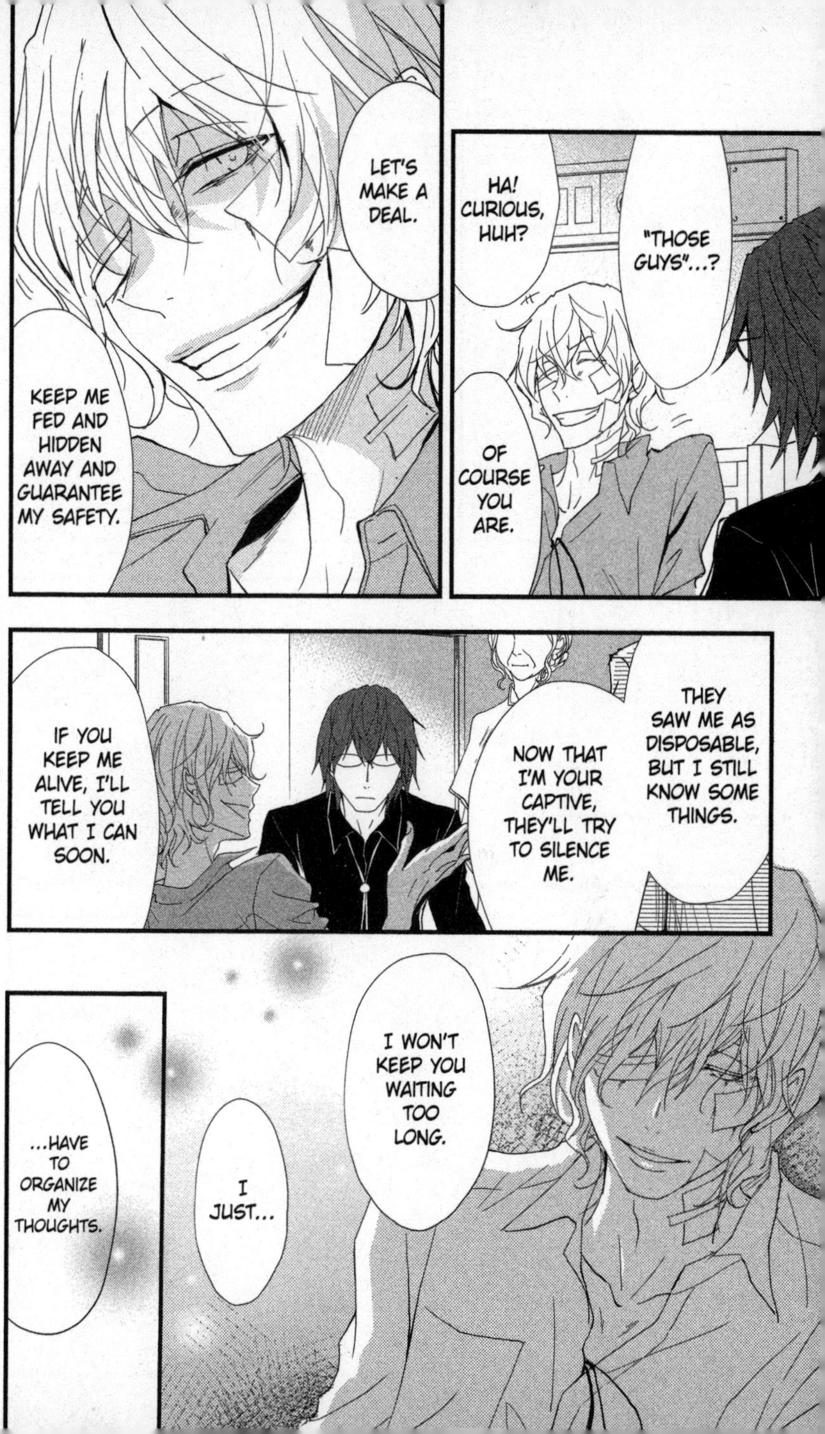
"THOSE GUYS"...?
HA! CURIOUS, HUH?
OF COURSE YOU ARE.
LET'S MAKE A DEAL.
KEEP ME FED AND HIDDEN AWAY AND GUARANTEE MY SAFETY.
THEY SAW ME AS DISPOSABLE, BUT I STILL KNOW SOME THINGS.
NOW THAT I'M YOUR CAPTIVE, THEY'LL TRY TO SILENCE ME.
IF YOU KEEP ME ALIVE, I'LL TELL YOU WHAT I CAN SOON.
I WON'T KEEP YOU WAITING TOO LONG.
I JUST...
...HAVE TO ORGANIZE MY THOUGHTS.

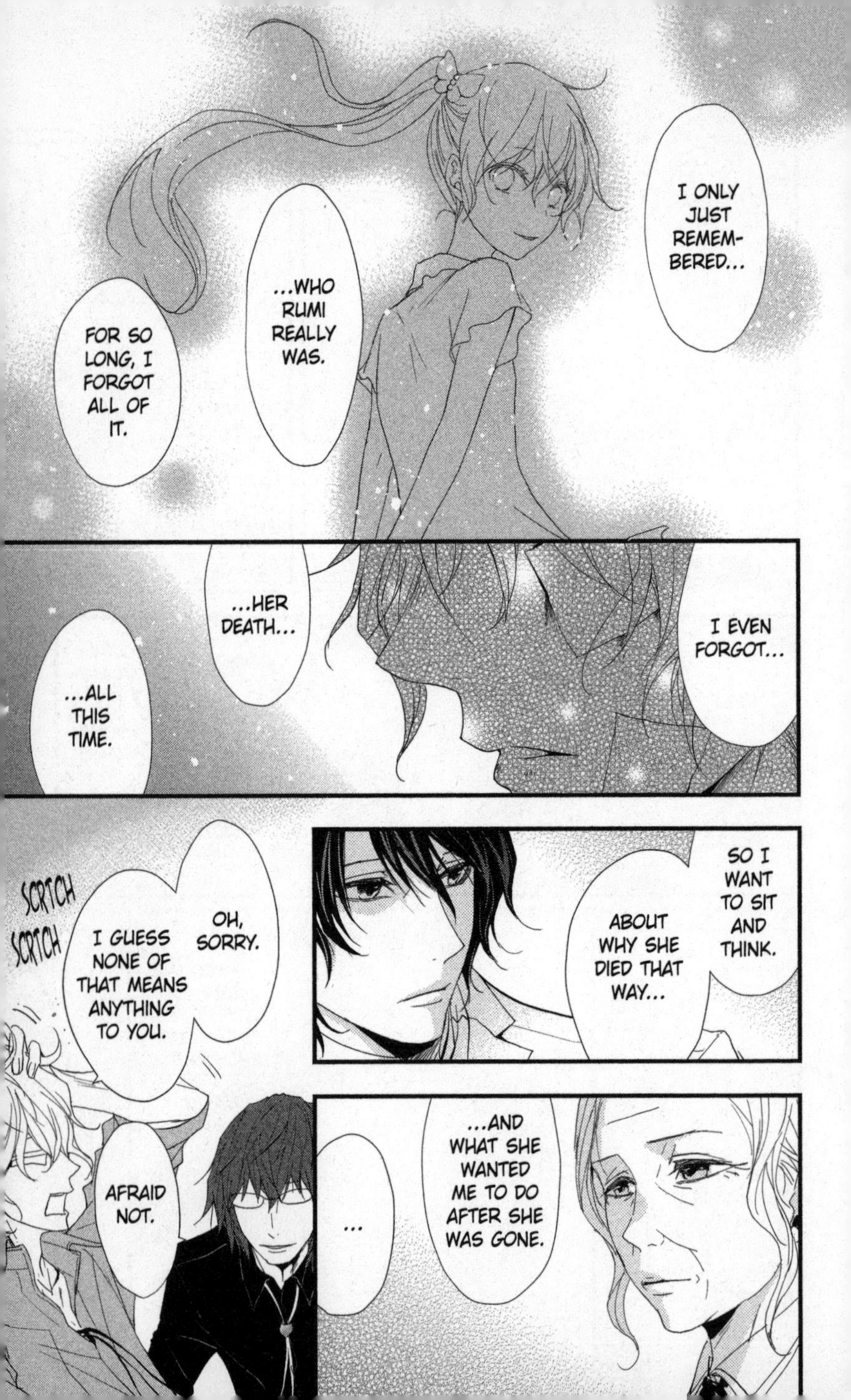
I ONLY JUST REMEM-BERED...
...WHO RUMI REALLY WAS.
FOR SO LONG, I FORGOT ALL OF IT.
I EVEN FORGOT...
...HER DEATH...
...ALL THIS TIME.
SO I WANT TO SIT AND THINK.
ABOUT WHY SHE DIED THAT WAY...
...AND WHAT SHE WANTED ME TO DO AFTER SHE WAS GONE.
...
OH, SORRY.
I GUESS NONE OF THAT MEANS ANYTHING TO YOU.
SCRTCH SCRTCH
AFRAID NOT.

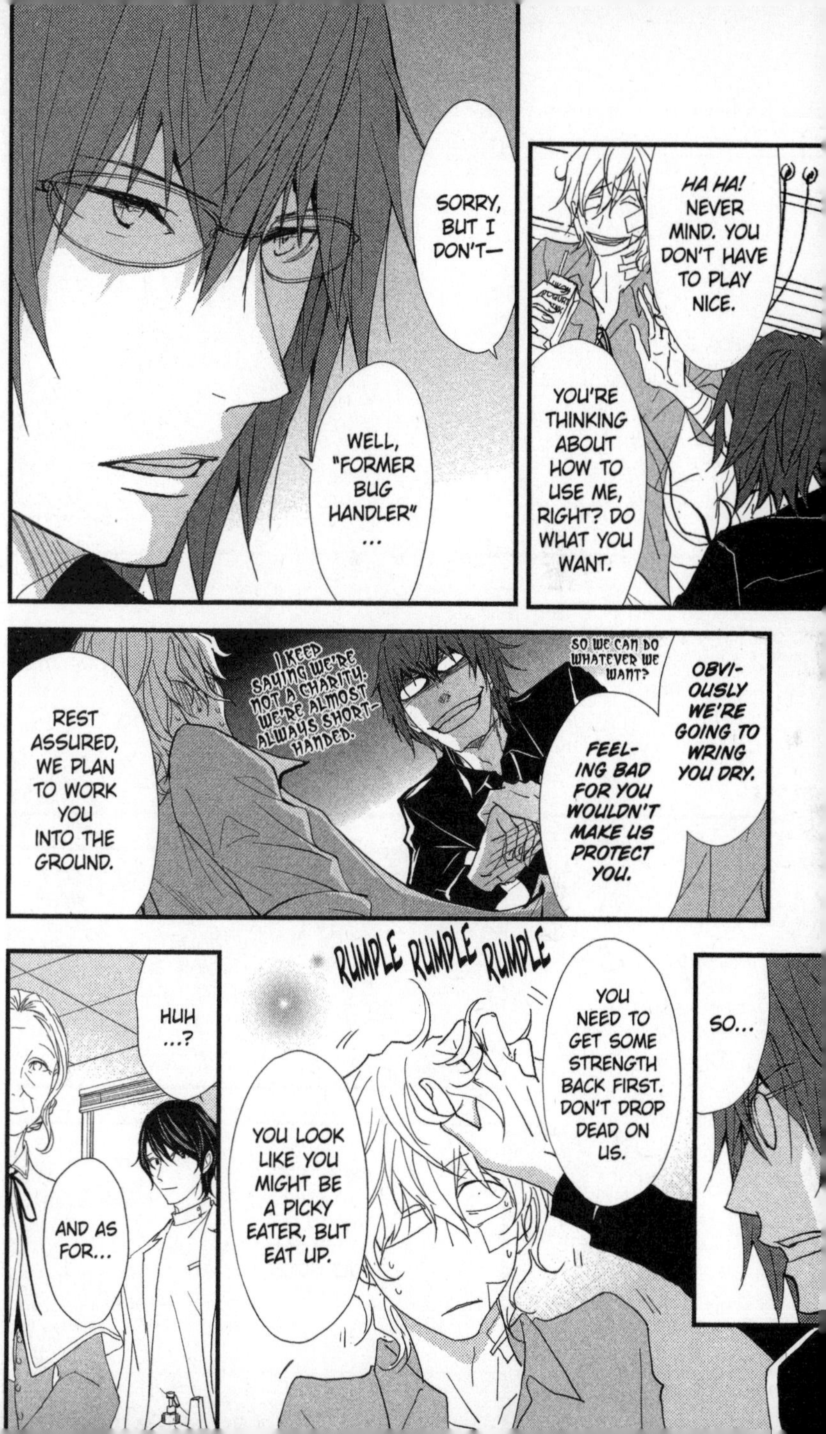
HA HA! NEVER MIND. YOU DON'T HAVE TO PLAY NICE.
YOU'RE THINKING ABOUT HOW TO USE ME, RIGHT? DO WHAT YOU WANT.
SORRY, BUT I DON'T—
WELL, "FORMER BUG HANDLER"...
OBVI-OUSLY WE'RE GOING TO WRING YOU DRY.
SO WE CAN DO WHATEVER WE WANT?
FEEL-ING BAD FOR YOU WOULDN'T MAKE US PROTECT YOU.
I KEEP SAYING WE'RE NOT A CHARITY. WE'RE ALMOST ALWAYS SHORT-HANDED.
REST ASSURED, WE PLAN TO WORK YOU INTO THE GROUND.
SO...
YOU NEED TO GET SOME STRENGTH BACK FIRST. DON'T DROP DEAD ON US.
RUMPLE RUMPLE RUMPLE
YOU LOOK LIKE YOU MIGHT BE A PICKY EATER, BUT EAT UP.
HUH ...?
AND AS FOR...

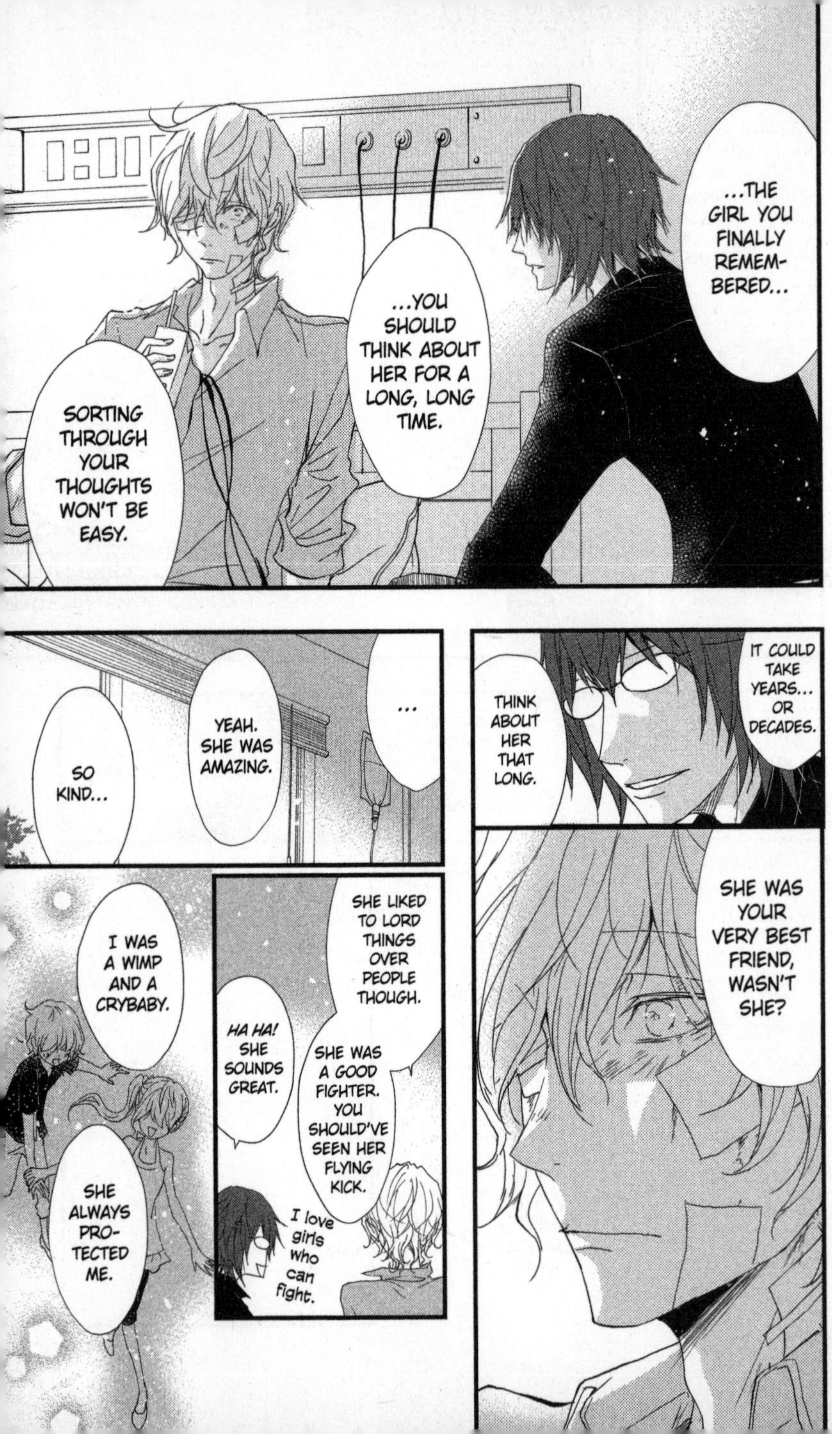
...THE GIRL YOU FINALLY REMEMBERED...
...YOU SHOULD THINK ABOUT HER FOR A LONG, LONG TIME.
SORTING THROUGH YOUR THOUGHTS WON'T BE EASY.
IT COULD TAKE YEARS... OR DECADES.
THINK ABOUT HER THAT LONG.
...
YEAH. SHE WAS AMAZING.
SO KIND...
SHE WAS YOUR VERY BEST FRIEND, WASN'T SHE?
SHE LIKED TO LORD THINGS OVER PEOPLE THOUGH.
SHE WAS A GOOD FIGHTER. YOU SHOULD'VE SEEN HER FLYING KICK.
HA HA! SHE SOUNDS GREAT.
I love girls who can fight.
I WAS A WIMP AND A CRYBABY.
SHE ALWAYS PROTECTED ME.

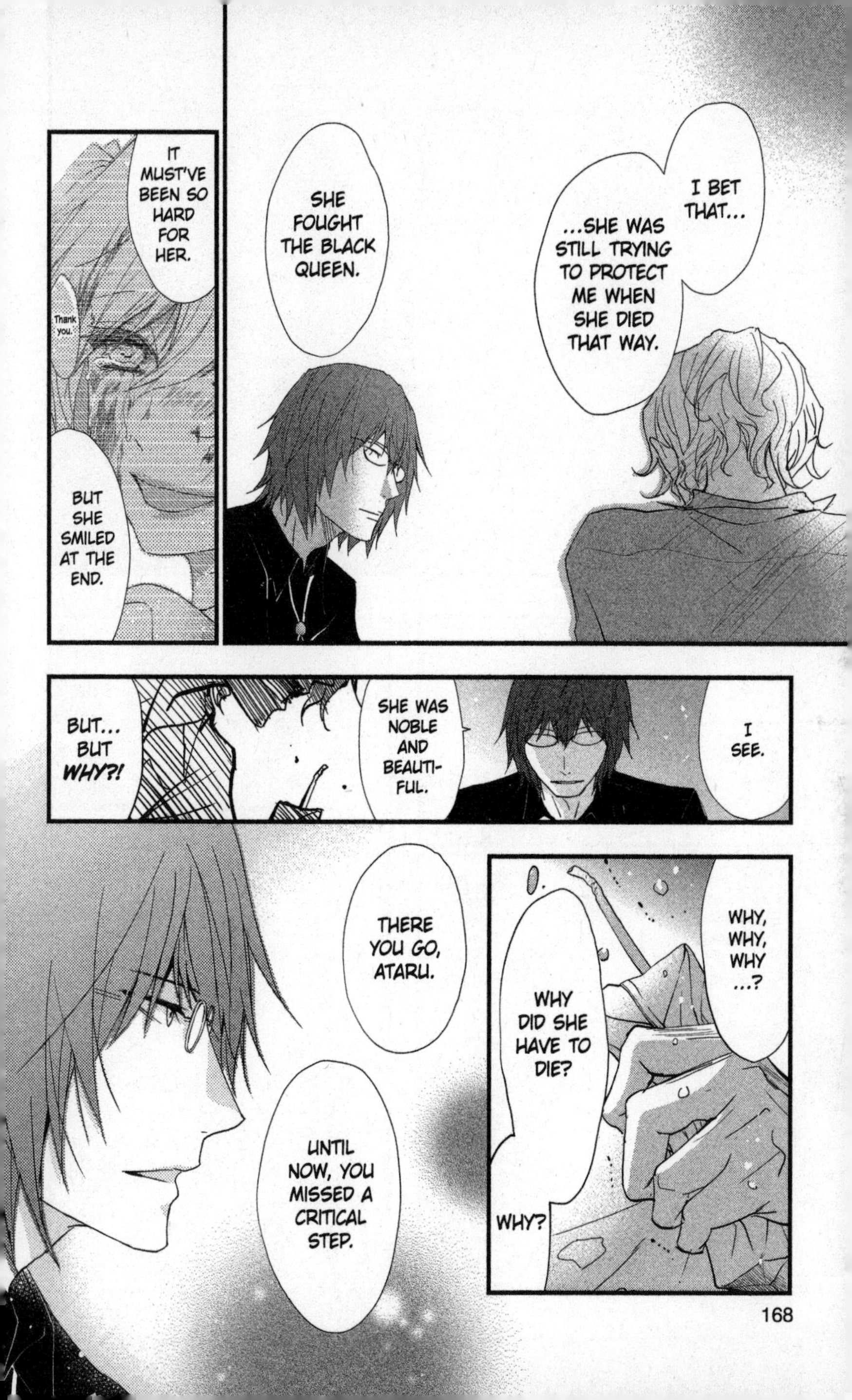
I BET THAT...
...SHE WAS STILL TRYING TO PROTECT ME WHEN SHE DIED THAT WAY.
SHE FOUGHT THE BLACK QUEEN.
IT MUST'VE BEEN SO HARD FOR HER.
Thank you.
BUT SHE SMILED AT THE END.
I SEE.
SHE WAS NOBLE AND BEAUTI-FUL.
BUT... BUT *WHY?!*
WHY, WHY, WHY ...?
WHY DID SHE HAVE TO DIE?
WHY?
THERE YOU GO, ATARU.
UNTIL NOW, YOU MISSED A CRITICAL STEP.

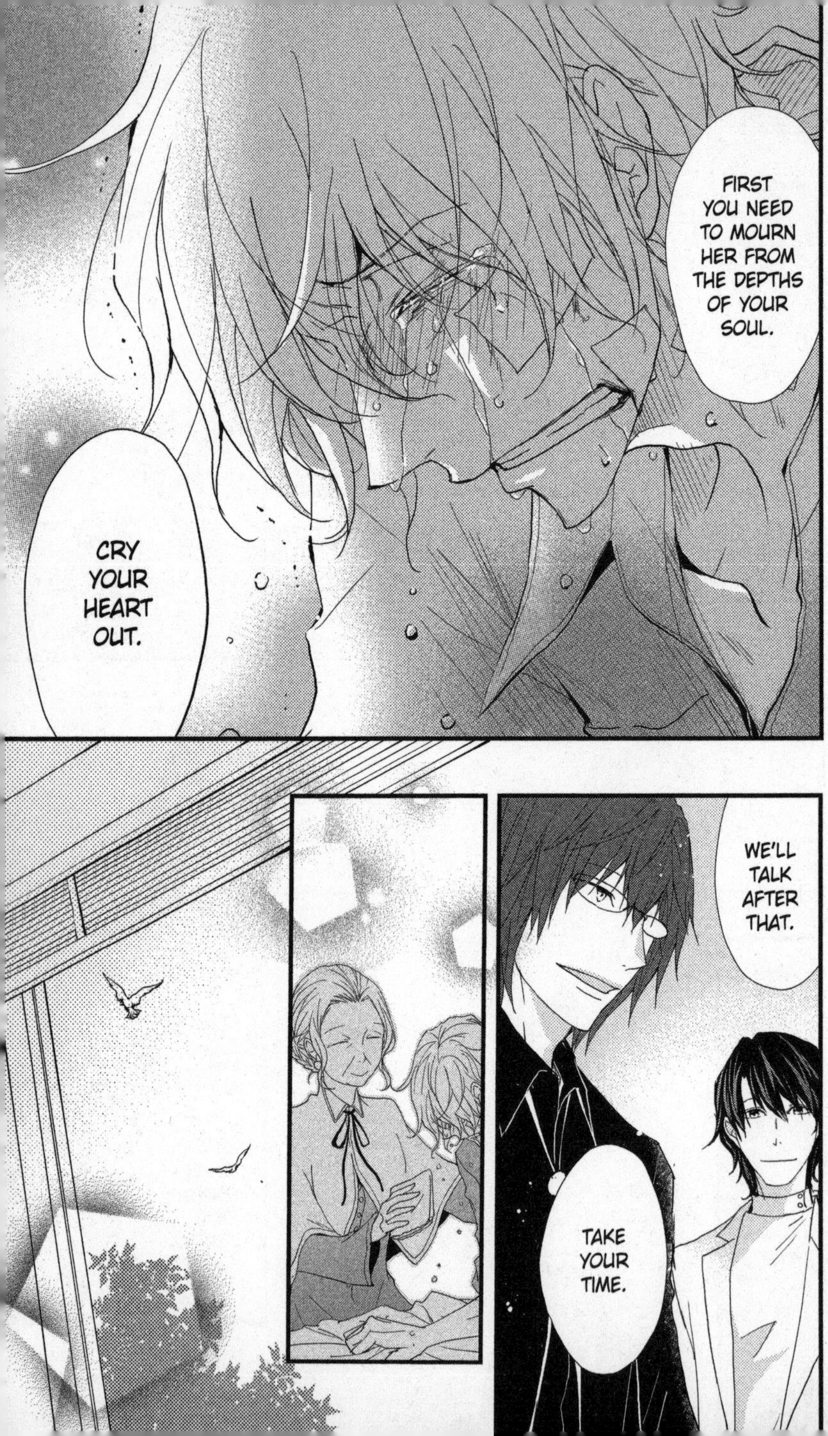
FIRST YOU NEED TO MOURN HER FROM THE DEPTHS OF YOUR SOUL.
CRY YOUR HEART OUT.
WE'LL TALK AFTER THAT.
TAKE YOUR TIME.

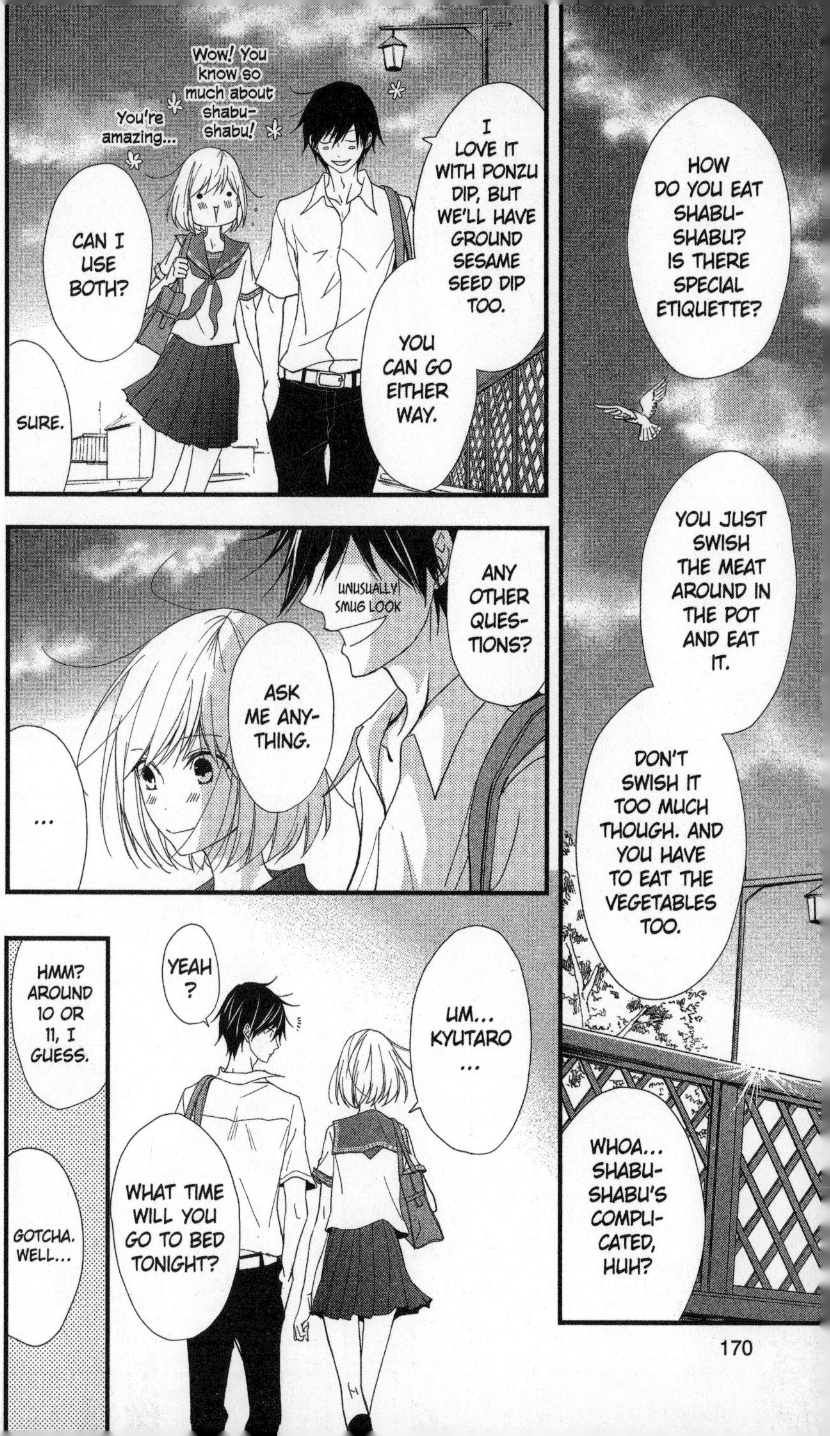
HOW DO YOU EAT SHABU-SHABU? IS THERE SPECIAL ETIQUETTE?
YOU JUST SWISH THE MEAT AROUND IN THE POT AND EAT IT.
DON'T SWISH IT TOO MUCH THOUGH. AND YOU HAVE TO EAT THE VEGETABLES TOO.
WHOA... SHABU-SHABU'S COMPLICATED, HUH?
I LOVE IT WITH PONZU DIP, BUT WE'LL HAVE GROUND SESAME SEED DIP TOO.
Wow! You know so much about shabu-shabu!
You're amazing...
CAN I USE BOTH?
YOU CAN GO EITHER WAY.
SURE.
ANY OTHER QUESTIONS?
UNUSUALLY SMUG LOOK
ASK ME ANY-THING.
...
UM... KYUTARO...
YEAH?
WHAT TIME WILL YOU GO TO BED TONIGHT?
HMM? AROUND 10 OR 11, I GUESS.
GOTCHA. WELL...

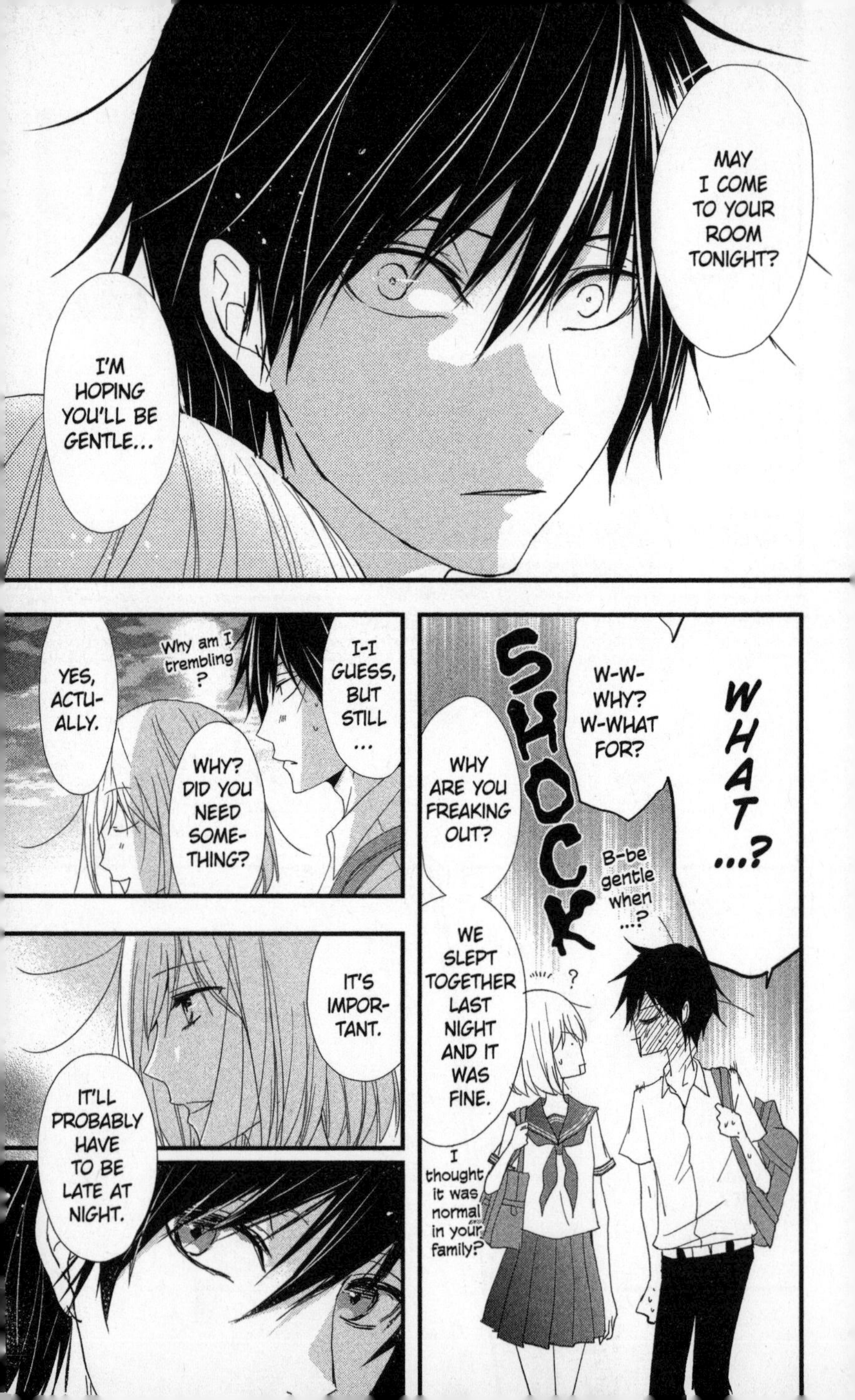
MAY I COME TO YOUR ROOM TONIGHT?
I'M HOPING YOU'LL BE GENTLE...
WHAT...?
W-W-WHY? W-WHAT FOR?
SHOCK
B-be gentle when...?
WHY ARE YOU FREAKING OUT?
WE SLEPT TOGETHER LAST NIGHT AND IT WAS FINE.
?
I thought it was normal in your family?
I-I GUESS, BUT STILL...
Why am I trembling?
YES, ACTUALLY.
WHY? DID YOU NEED SOMETHING?
IT'S IMPORTANT.
IT'LL PROBABLY HAVE TO BE LATE AT NIGHT.

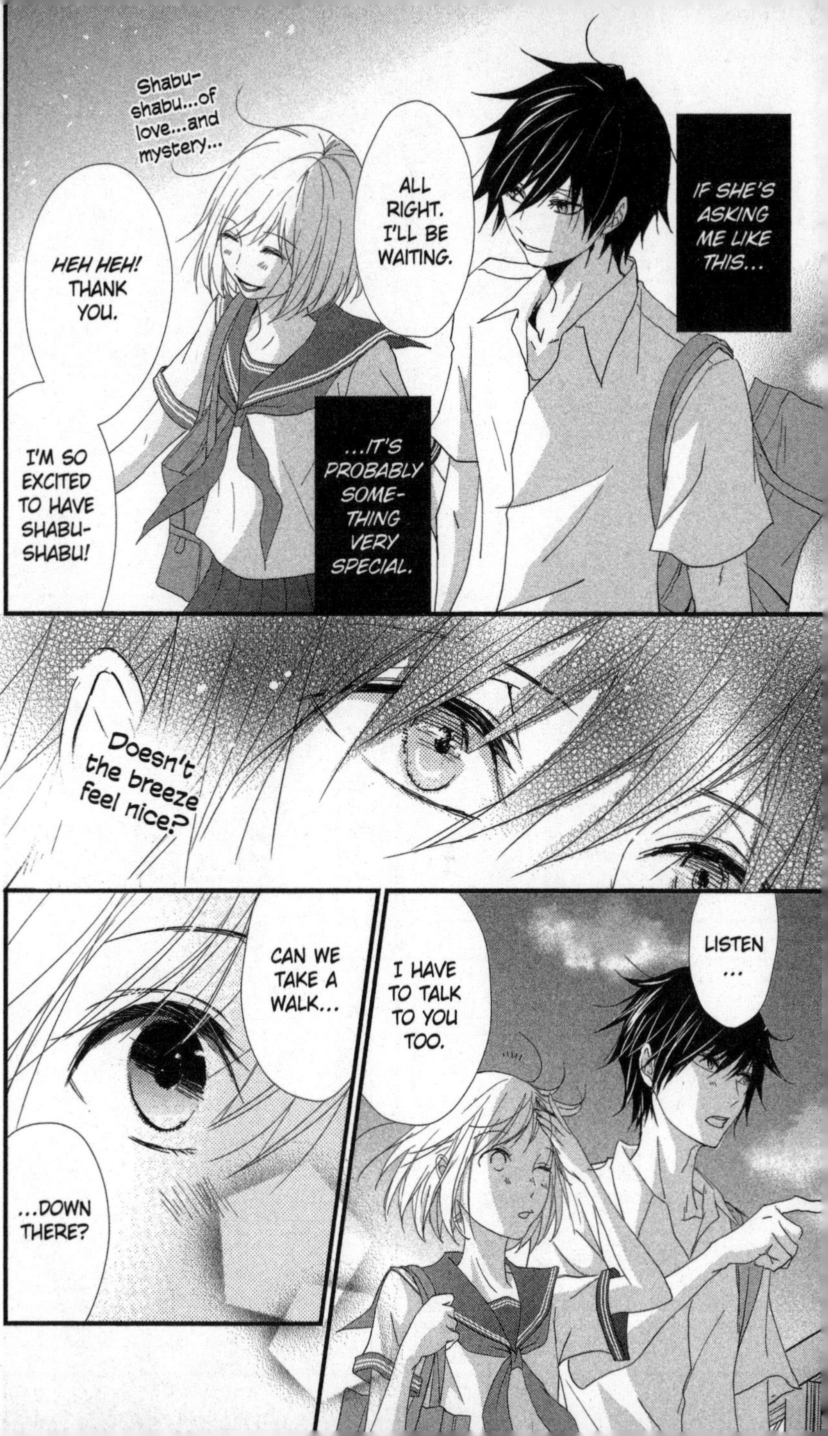
IF SHE'S ASKING ME LIKE THIS...
ALL RIGHT. I'LL BE WAITING.
Shabu-shabu...of love...and mystery...
HEH HEH! THANK YOU.
...IT'S PROBABLY SOMETHING VERY SPECIAL.
I'M SO EXCITED TO HAVE SHABU-SHABU!
Doesn't the breeze feel nice?
LISTEN...
I HAVE TO TALK TO YOU TOO.
CAN WE TAKE A WALK...
...DOWN THERE?

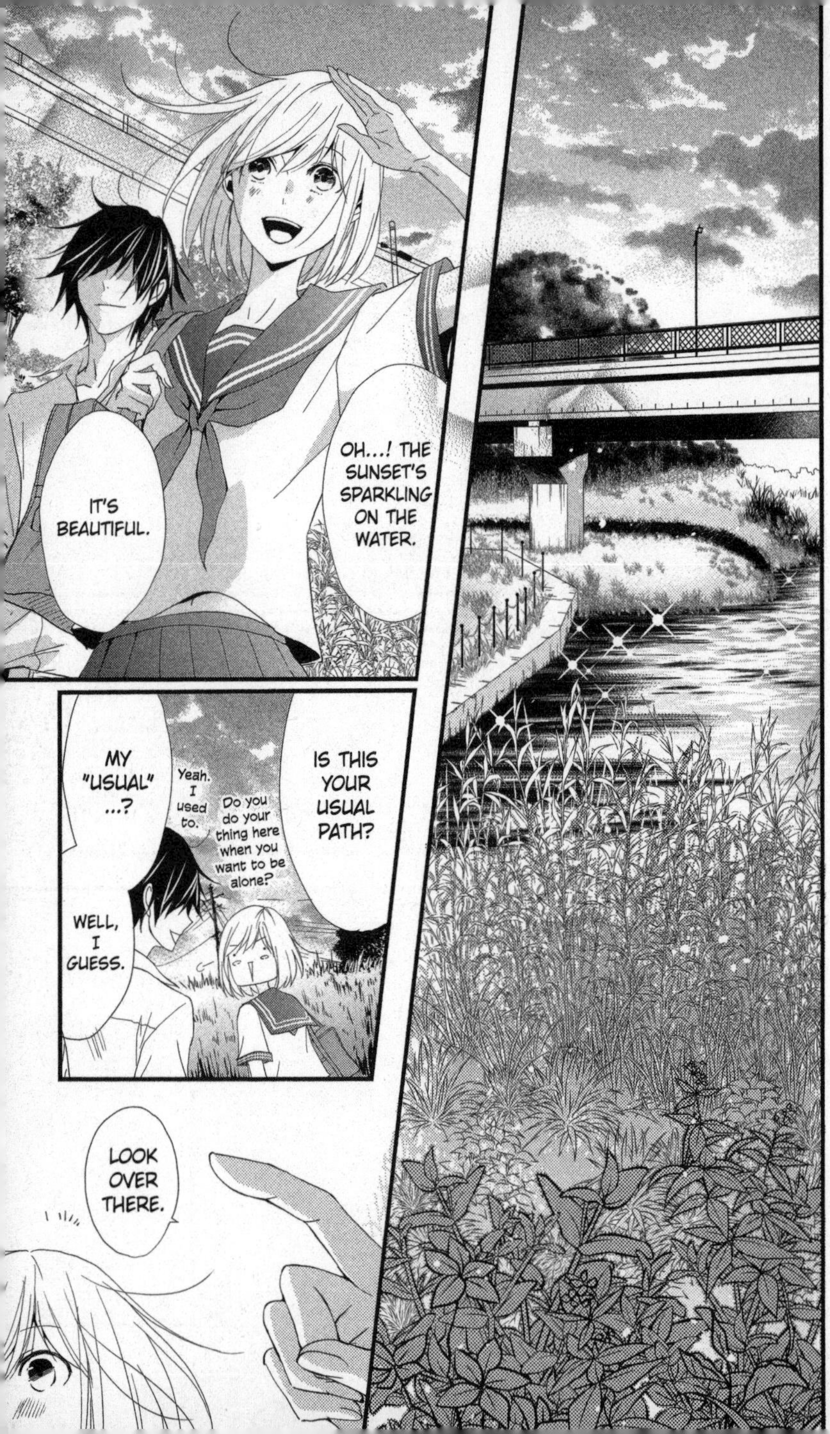
OH...! THE SUNSET'S SPARKLING ON THE WATER.
IT'S BEAUTIFUL.
IS THIS YOUR USUAL PATH?
Do you do your thing here when you want to be alone?
Yeah. I used to.
MY "USUAL" ...?
WELL, I GUESS.
LOOK OVER THERE.

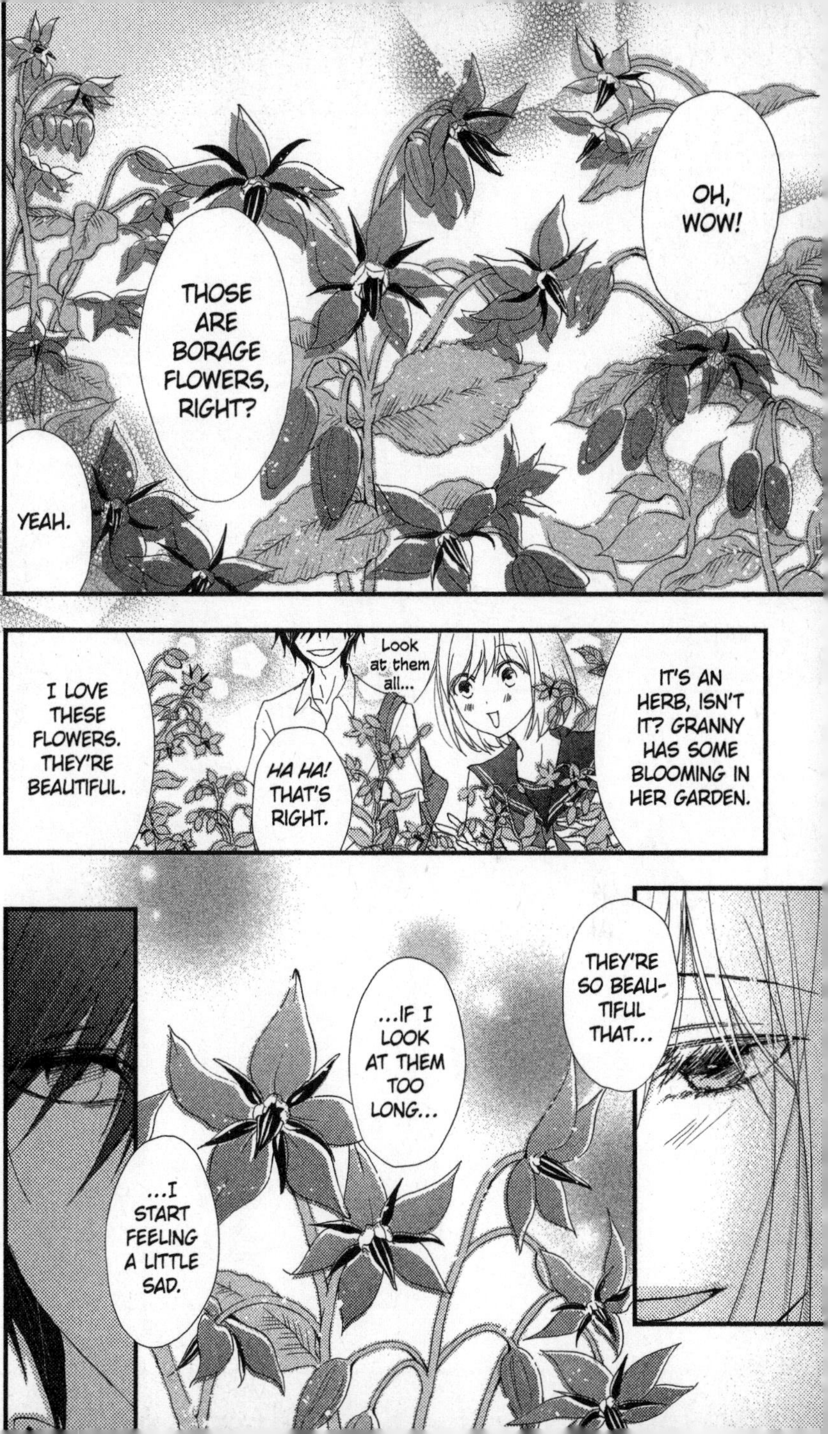
OH, WOW!
THOSE ARE BORAGE FLOWERS, RIGHT?
YEAH.
IT'S AN HERB, ISN'T IT? GRANNY HAS SOME BLOOMING IN HER GARDEN.
Look at them all...
HA HA! THAT'S RIGHT.
I LOVE THESE FLOWERS. THEY'RE BEAUTIFUL.
THEY'RE SO BEAU-TIFUL THAT...
...IF I LOOK AT THEM TOO LONG...
...I START FEELING A LITTLE SAD.

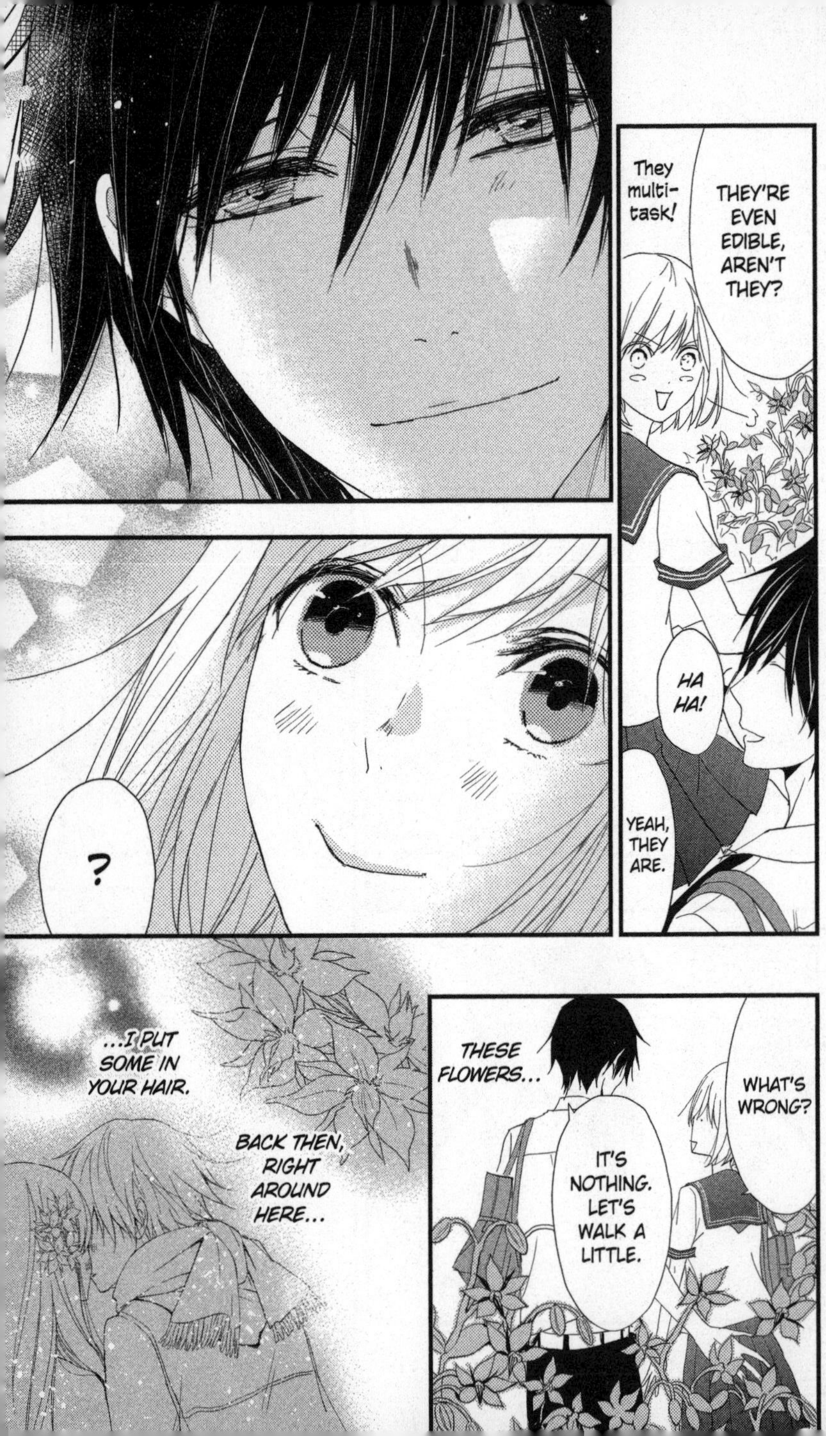
THEY'RE EVEN EDIBLE, AREN'T THEY?
They multi-task!
HA HA!
YEAH, THEY ARE.
?
THESE FLOWERS...
WHAT'S WRONG?
IT'S NOTHING. LET'S WALK A LITTLE.
BACK THEN, RIGHT AROUND HERE...
...I PUT SOME IN YOUR HAIR.

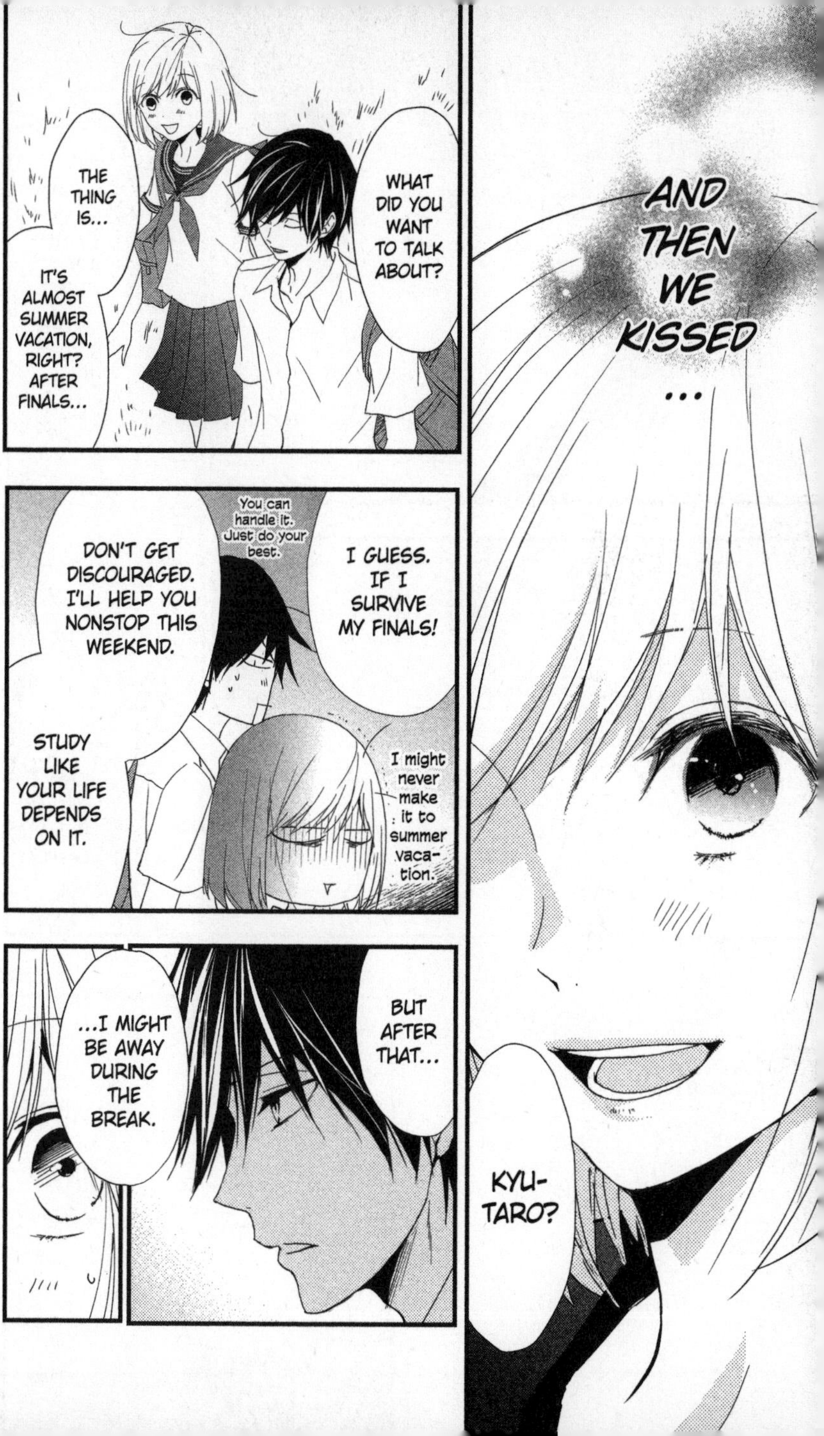
AND THEN WE KISSED ...
KYU-TARO?
WHAT DID YOU WANT TO TALK ABOUT?
THE THING IS...
IT'S ALMOST SUMMER VACATION, RIGHT? AFTER FINALS...
I GUESS. IF I SURVIVE MY FINALS!
You can handle it. Just do your best.
DON'T GET DISCOURAGED. I'LL HELP YOU NONSTOP THIS WEEKEND.
I might never make it to summer vaca-tion.
STUDY LIKE YOUR LIFE DEPENDS ON IT.
BUT AFTER THAT...
...I MIGHT BE AWAY DURING THE BREAK.

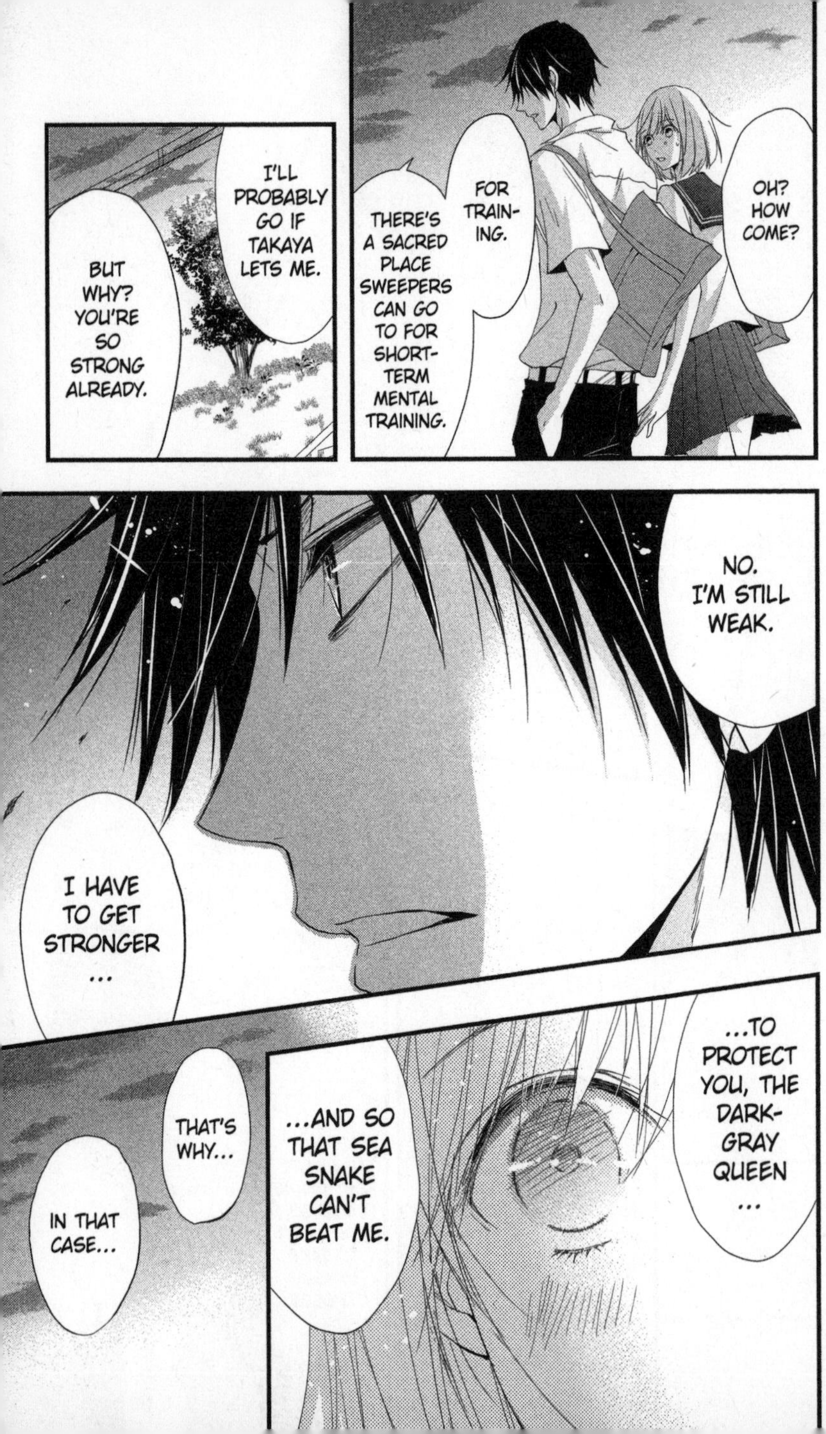
OH? HOW COME?
FOR TRAIN-ING.
THERE'S A SACRED PLACE SWEEPERS CAN GO TO FOR SHORT-TERM MENTAL TRAINING.
I'LL PROBABLY GO IF TAKAYA LETS ME.
BUT WHY? YOU'RE SO STRONG ALREADY.
NO. I'M STILL WEAK.
I HAVE TO GET STRONGER...
...TO PROTECT YOU, THE DARK-GRAY QUEEN...
...AND SO THAT SEA SNAKE CAN'T BEAT ME.
THAT'S WHY...
IN THAT CASE...

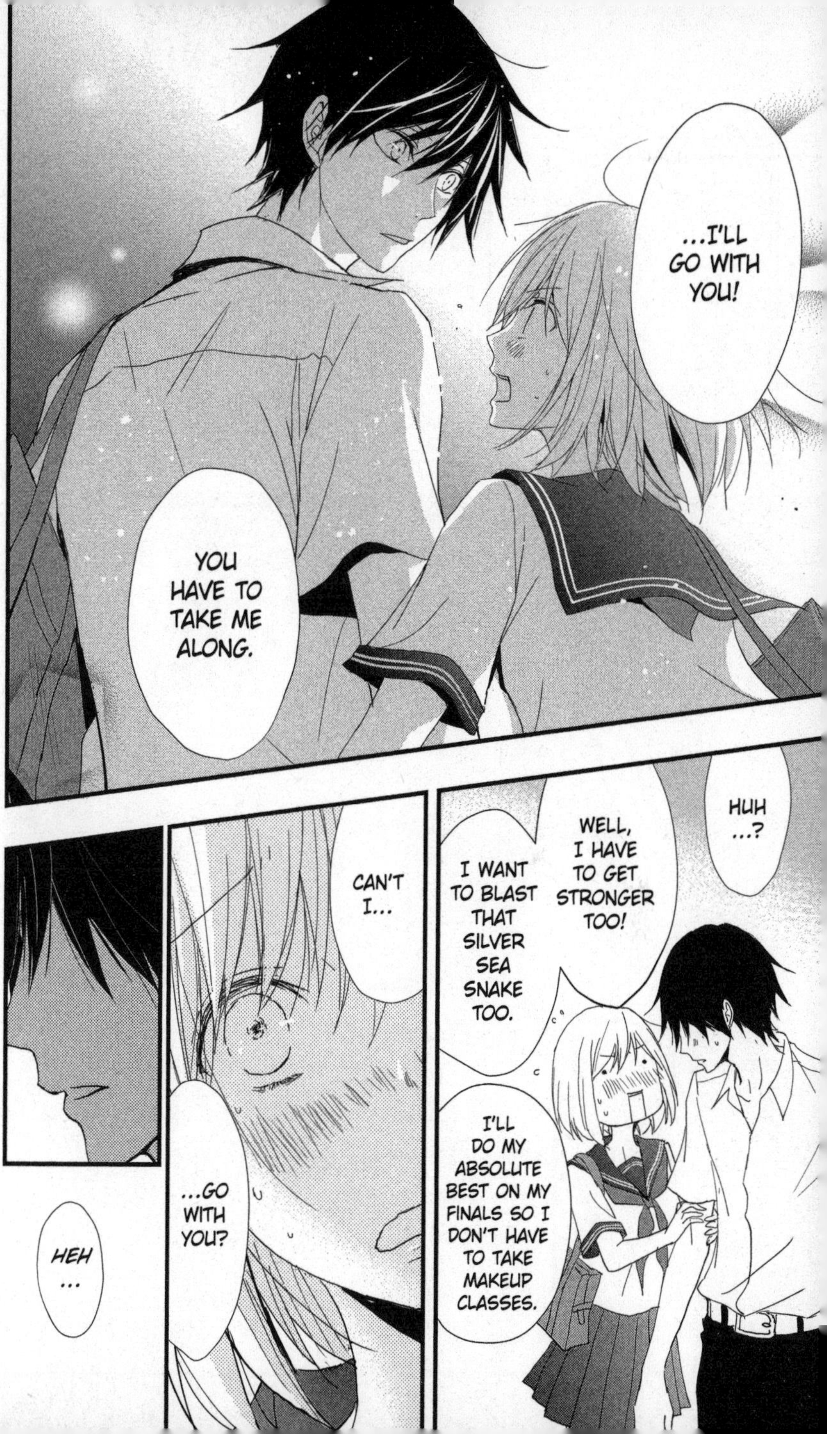
...I'LL GO WITH YOU!
YOU HAVE TO TAKE ME ALONG.
HUH ...?
WELL, I HAVE TO GET STRONGER TOO!
I WANT TO BLAST THAT SILVER SEA SNAKE TOO.
I'LL DO MY ABSOLUTE BEST ON MY FINALS SO I DON'T HAVE TO TAKE MAKEUP CLASSES.
CAN'T I...
...GO WITH YOU?
HEH ...

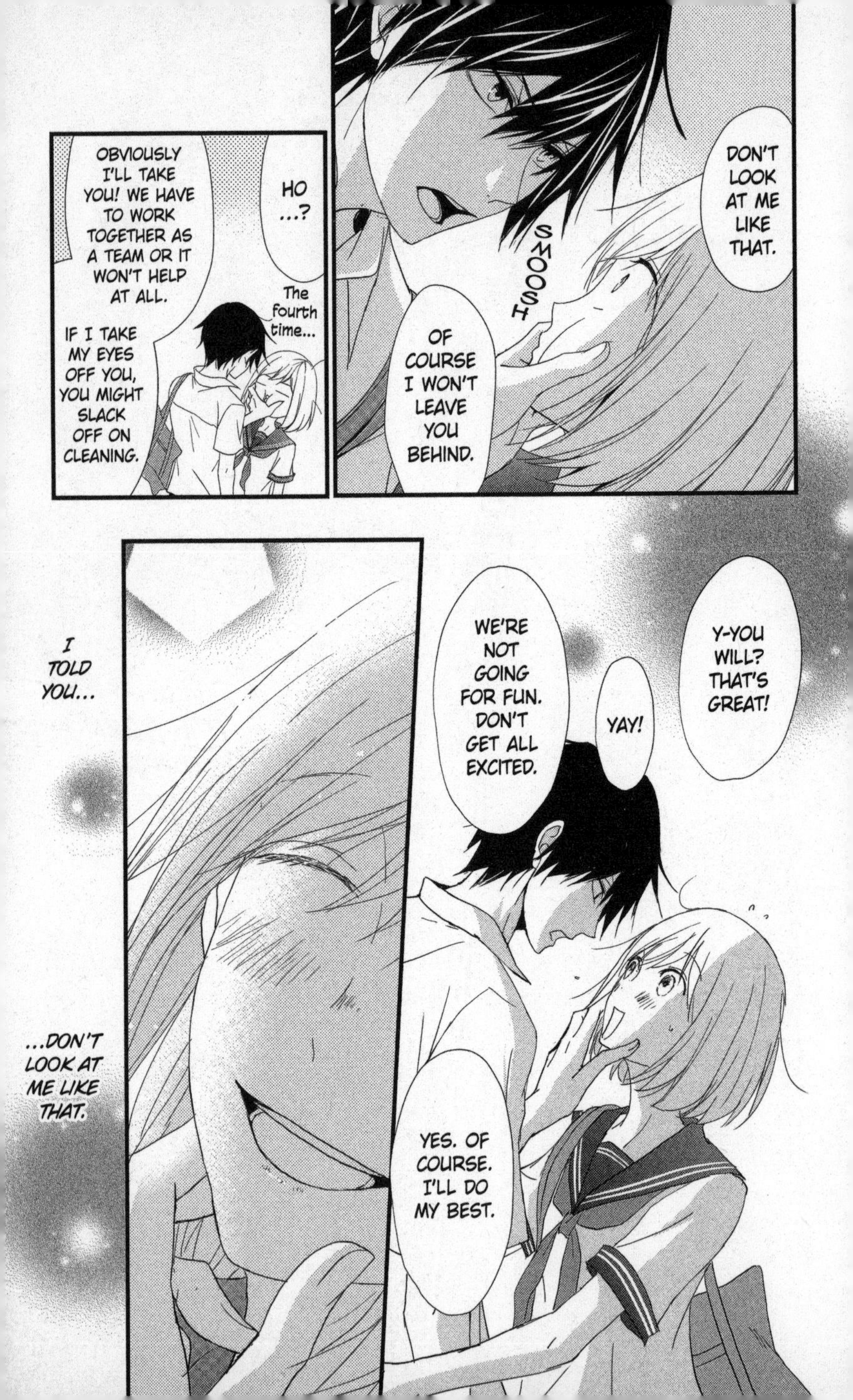
DON'T LOOK AT ME LIKE THAT.
SMOOSH
OF COURSE I WON'T LEAVE YOU BEHIND.
HO ...?
OBVIOUSLY I'LL TAKE YOU! WE HAVE TO WORK TOGETHER AS A TEAM OR IT WON'T HELP AT ALL.
The fourth time...
IF I TAKE MY EYES OFF YOU, YOU MIGHT SLACK OFF ON CLEANING.
Y-YOU WILL? THAT'S GREAT!
YAY!
WE'RE NOT GOING FOR FUN. DON'T GET ALL EXCITED.
YES. OF COURSE. I'LL DO MY BEST.
I TOLD YOU...
...DON'T LOOK AT ME LIKE THAT.

YOUR LIPS LOOK DRY.
IT'S BEEN BOTHERING ME.
I WANT TO MOISTEN THEM WITH MINE.
CAN'T I TELL YOU YET...
...THAT...
...I LOVE YOU SO MUCH I'M LOSING MY MIND?

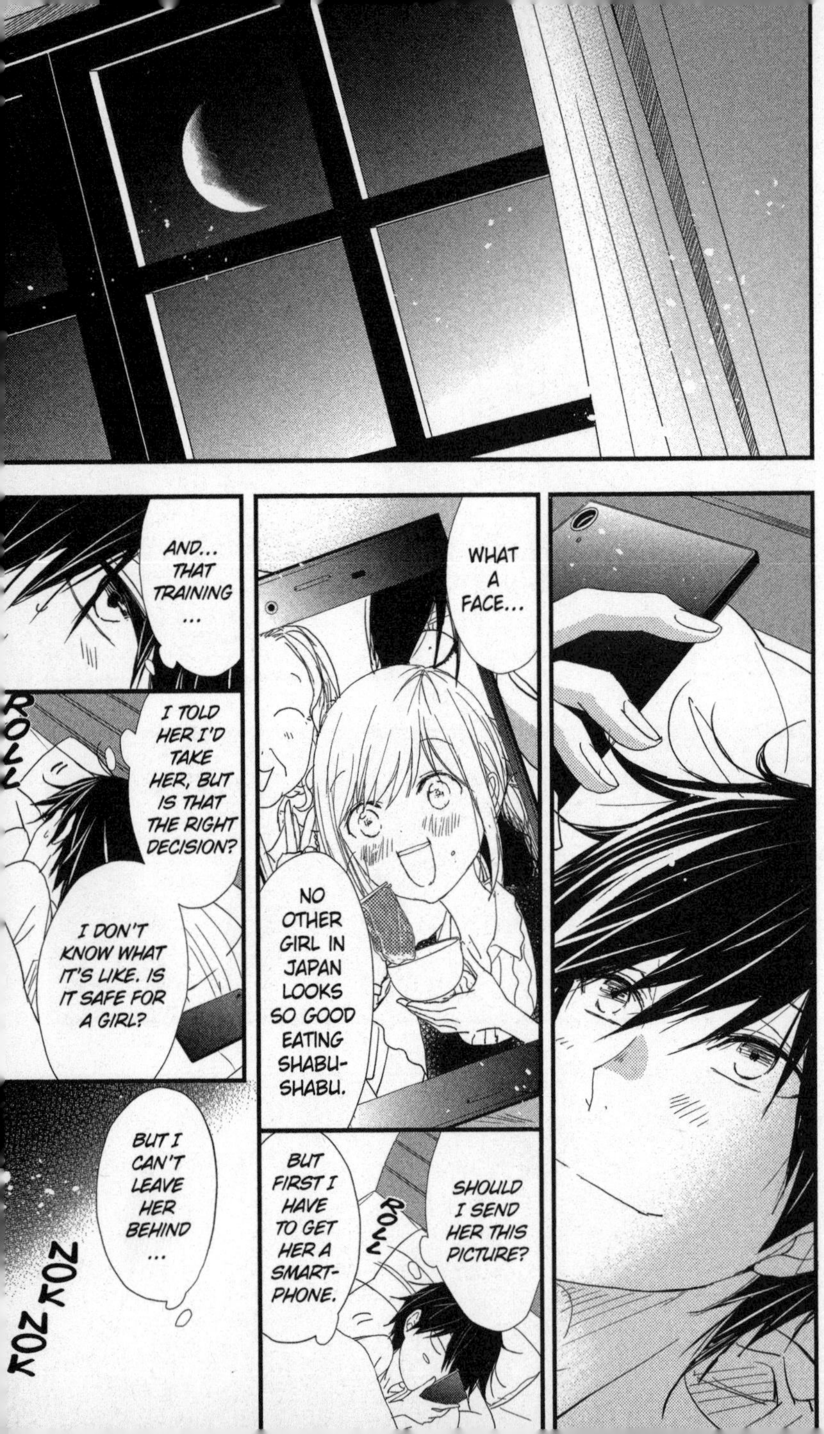
WHAT A FACE...
NO OTHER GIRL IN JAPAN LOOKS SO GOOD EATING SHABU-SHABU.
SHOULD I SEND HER THIS PICTURE?
ROLL
BUT FIRST I HAVE TO GET HER A SMARTPHONE.
AND... THAT TRAINING...
ROLL
I TOLD HER I'D TAKE HER, BUT IS THAT THE RIGHT DECISION?
I DON'T KNOW WHAT IT'S LIKE. IS IT SAFE FOR A GIRL?
BUT I CAN'T LEAVE HER BEHIND...
KON KON

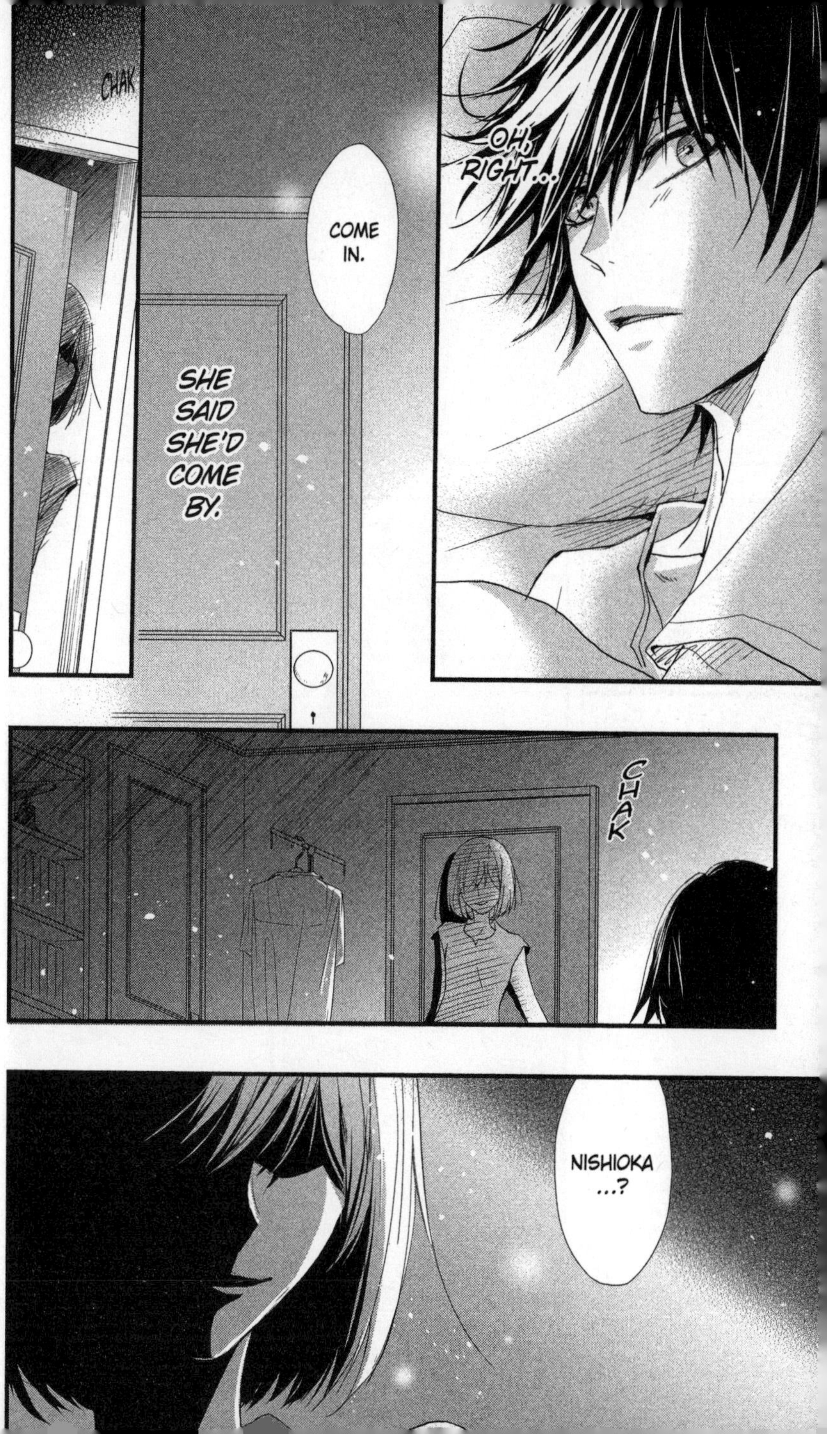
OH, RIGHT...
COME IN.
SHE SAID SHE'D COME BY.
CHAK
CHAK
NISHIOKA ...?

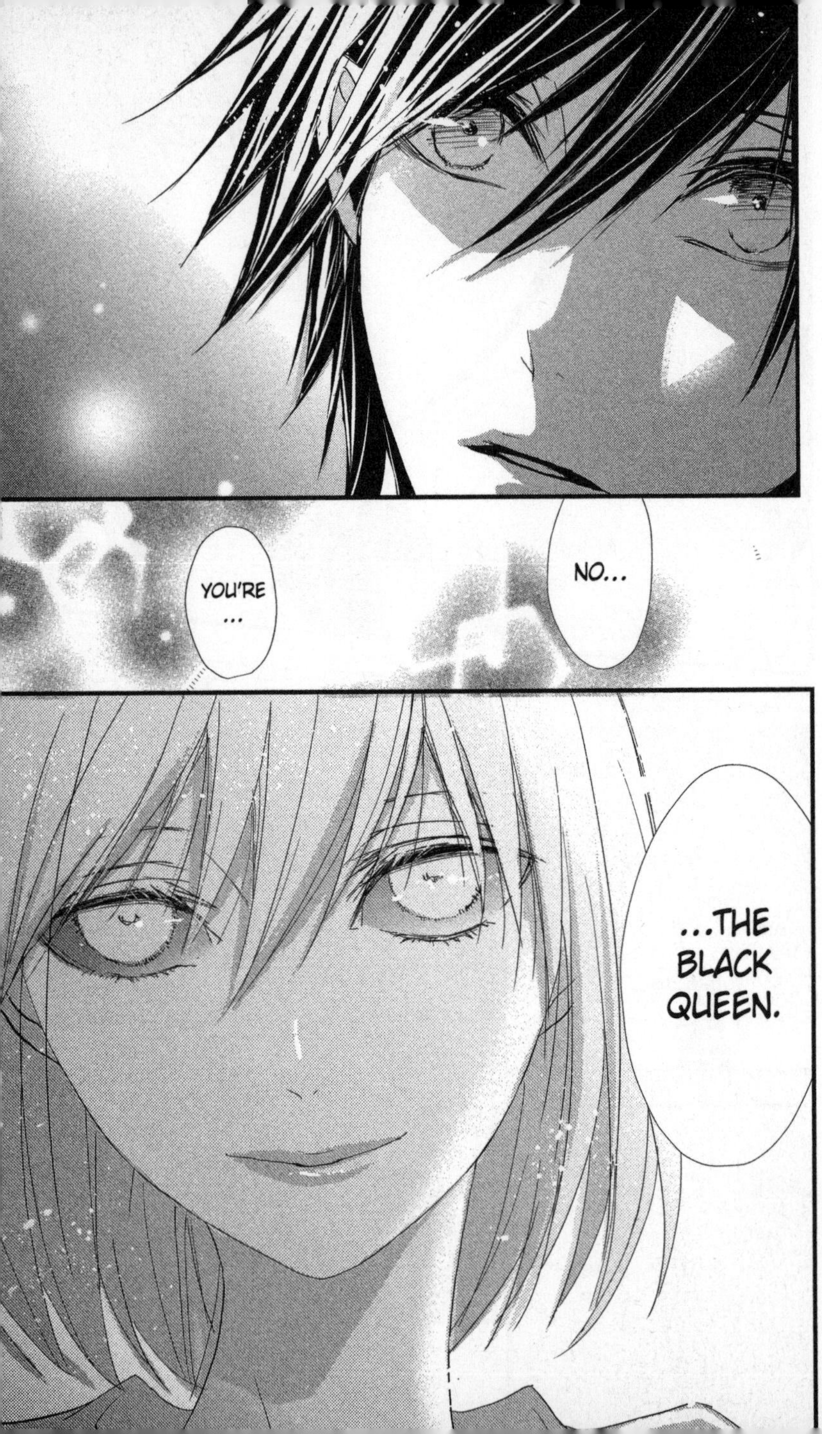
NO...
YOU'RE ...
...THE BLACK QUEEN.

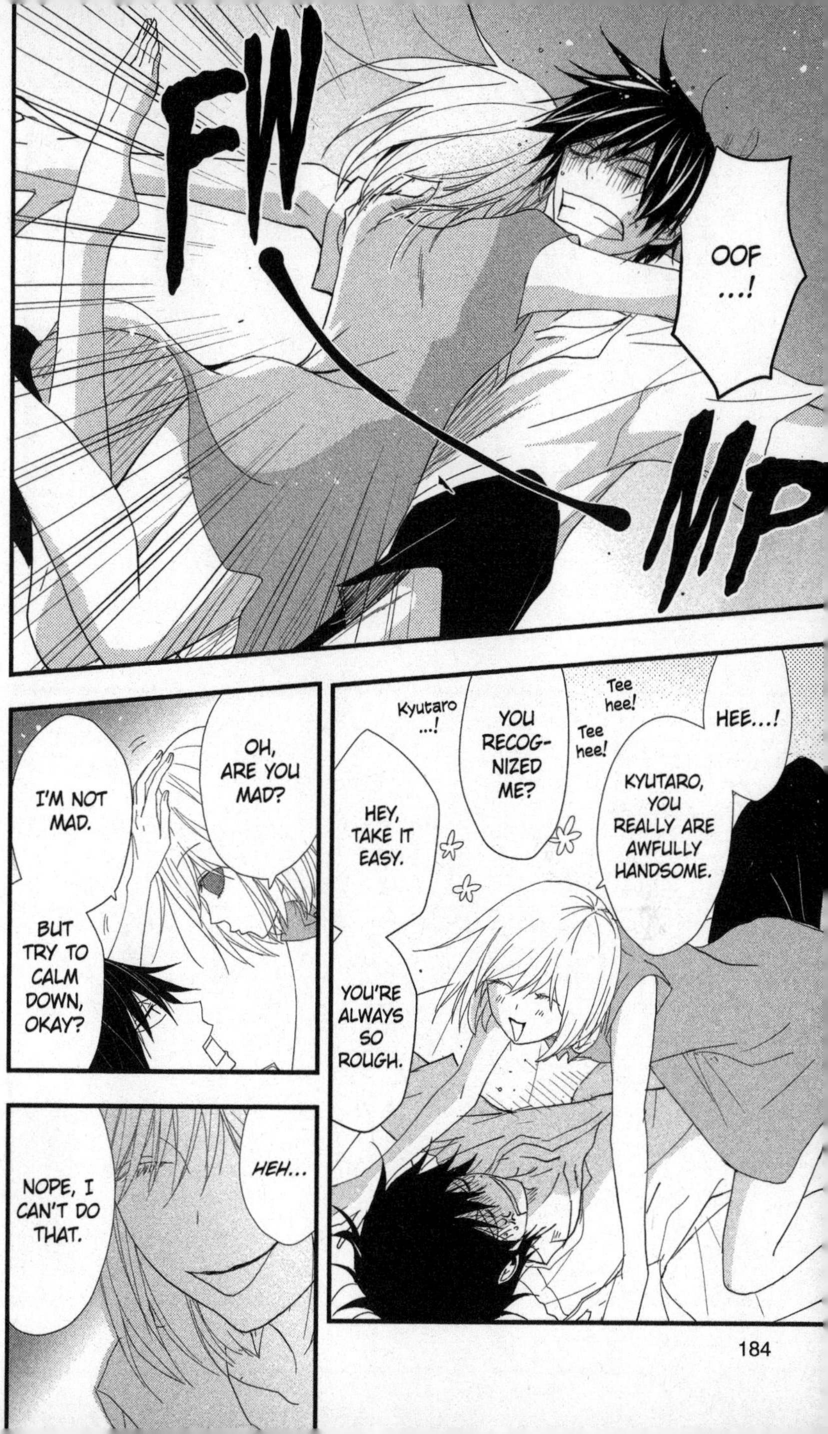
FWMP
OOF ...!
HEE...!
Tee hee!
Tee hee!
KYUTARO, YOU REALLY ARE AWFULLY HANDSOME.
YOU RECOG-NIZED ME?
Kyutaro ...!
HEY, TAKE IT EASY.
YOU'RE ALWAYS SO ROUGH.
OH, ARE YOU MAD?
I'M NOT MAD.
BUT TRY TO CALM DOWN, OKAY?
HEH...
NOPE, I CAN'T DO THAT.

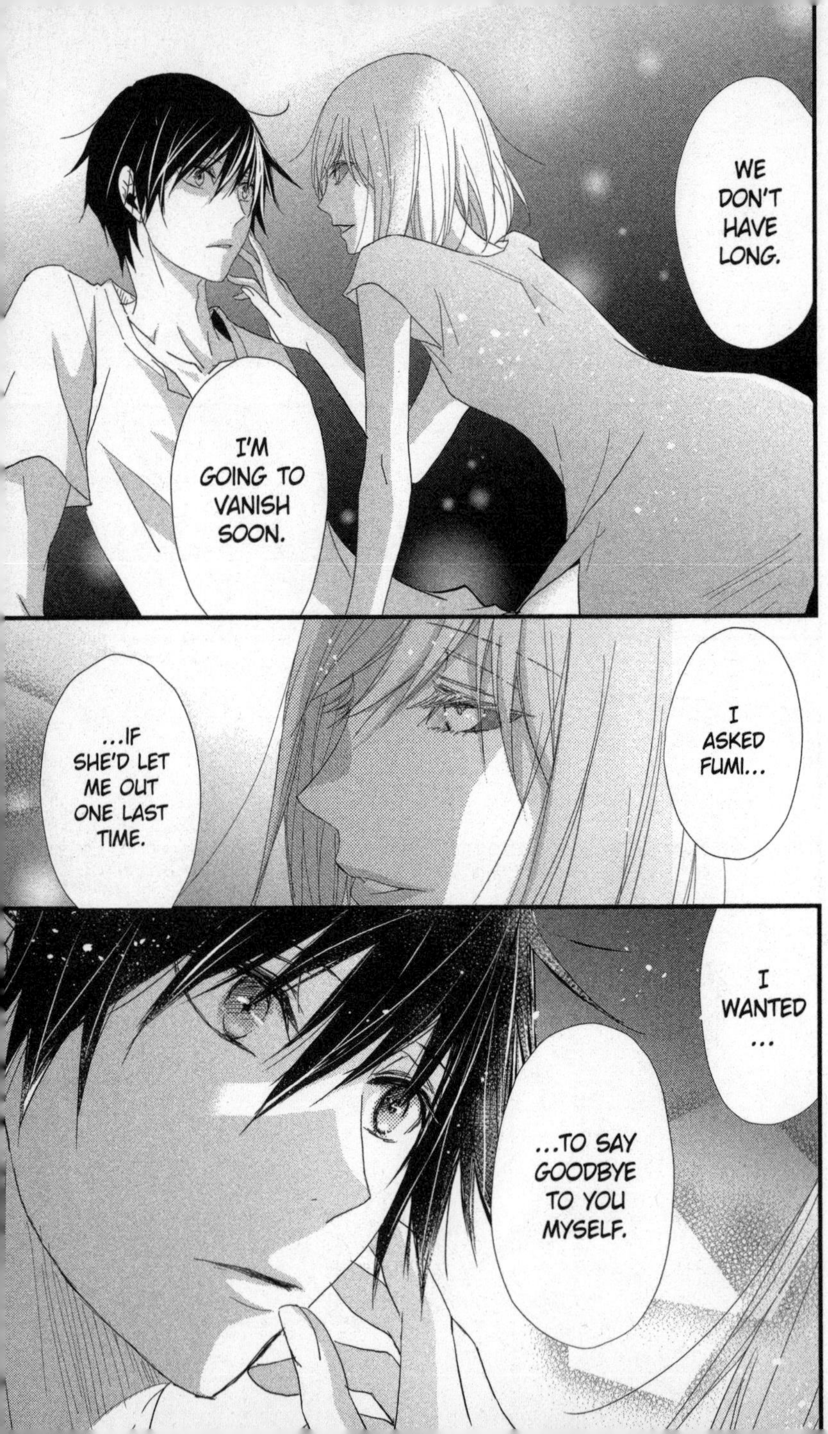
WE DON'T HAVE LONG.
I'M GOING TO VANISH SOON.
I ASKED FUMI...
...IF SHE'D LET ME OUT ONE LAST TIME.
I WANTED ...
...TO SAY GOODBYE TO YOU MYSELF.

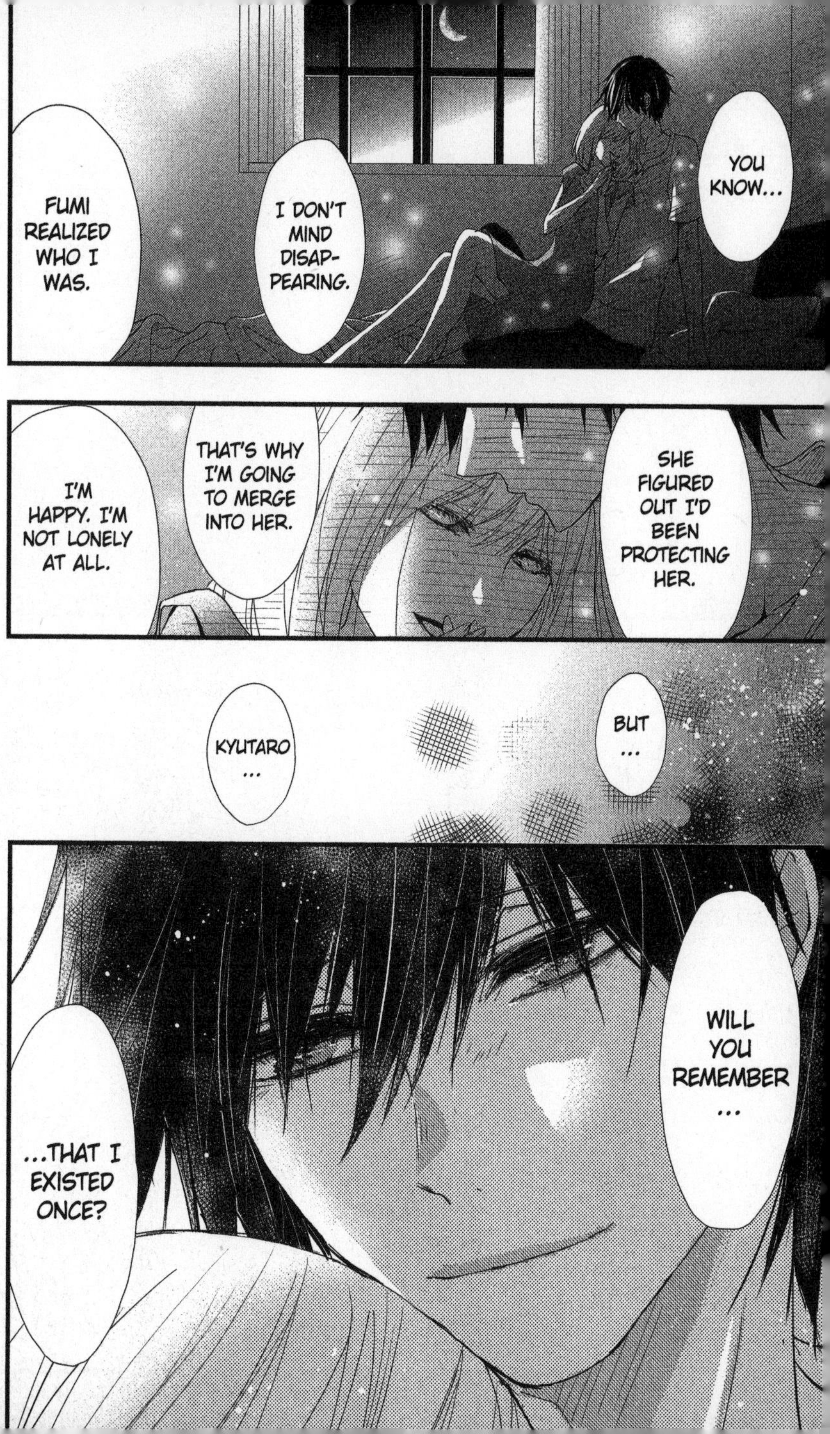
YOU KNOW...
I DON'T MIND DISAP-PEARING.
FUMI REALIZED WHO I WAS.
SHE FIGURED OUT I'D BEEN PROTECTING HER.
THAT'S WHY I'M GOING TO MERGE INTO HER.
I'M HAPPY. I'M NOT LONELY AT ALL.
BUT...
KYUTARO...
WILL YOU REMEMBER...
...THAT I EXISTED ONCE?

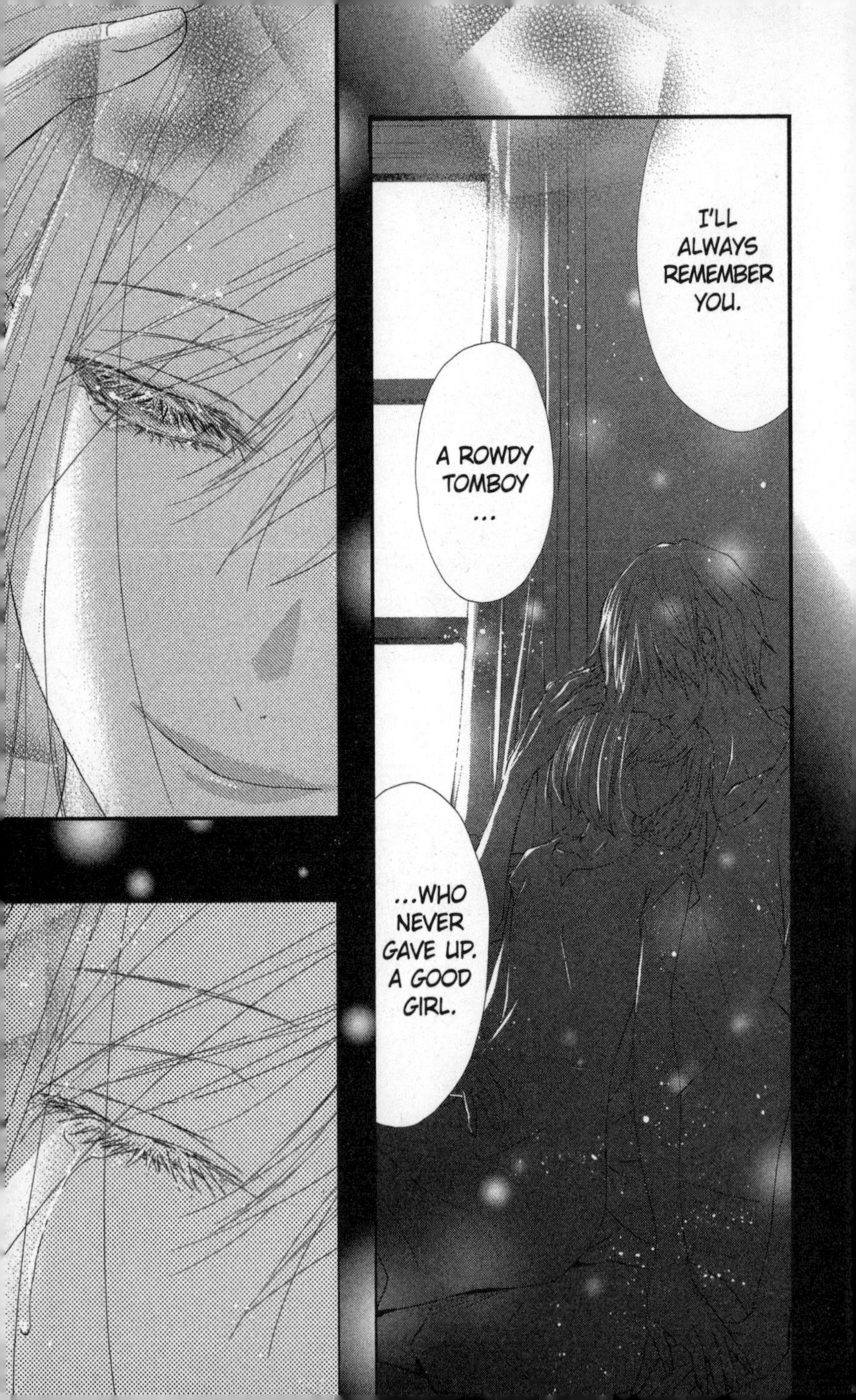
I'LL ALWAYS REMEMBER YOU.
A ROWDY TOMBOY ...
...WHO NEVER GAVE UP. A GOOD GIRL.

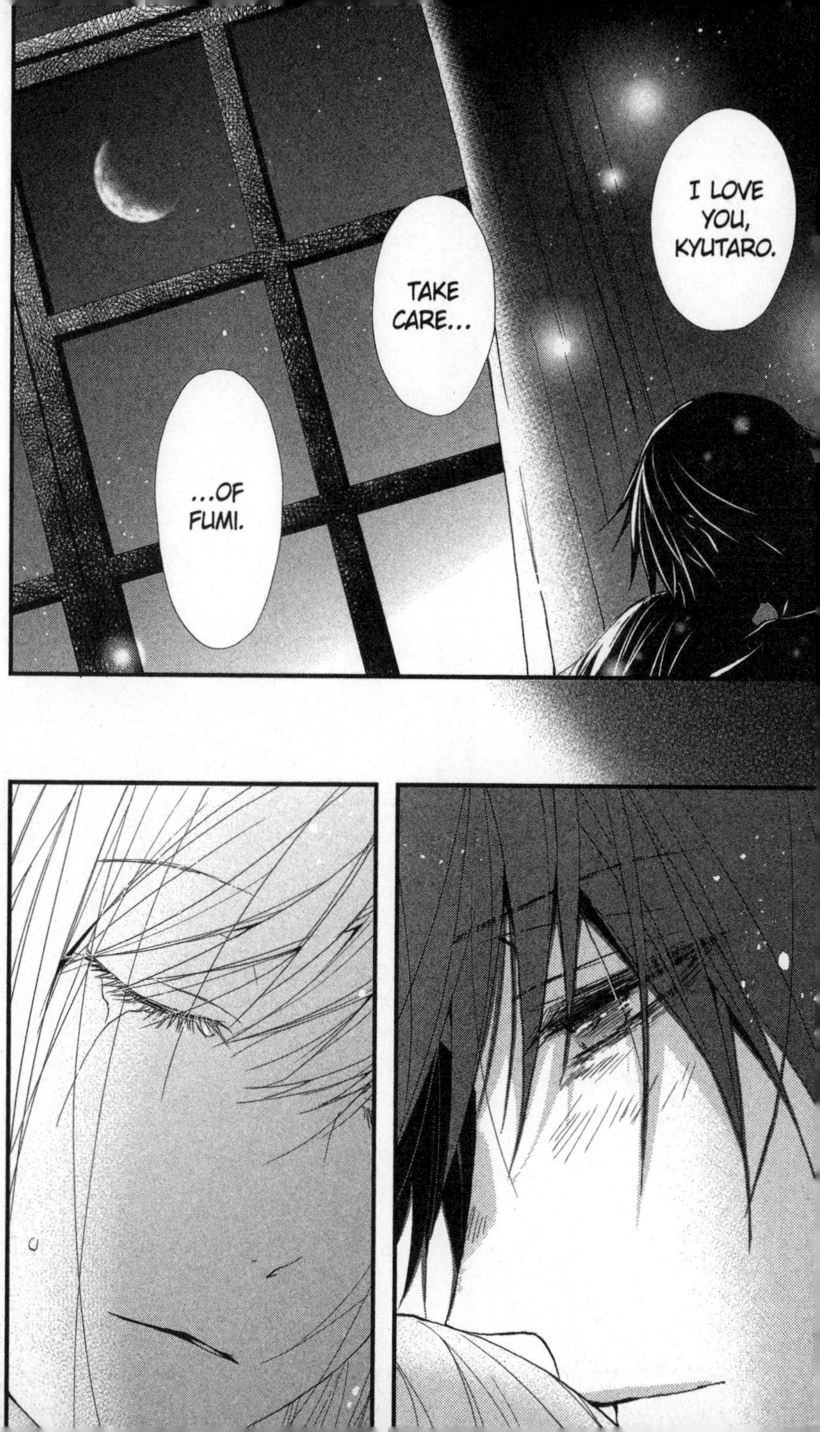
I LOVE YOU, KYUTARO.
TAKE CARE...
...OF FUMI.

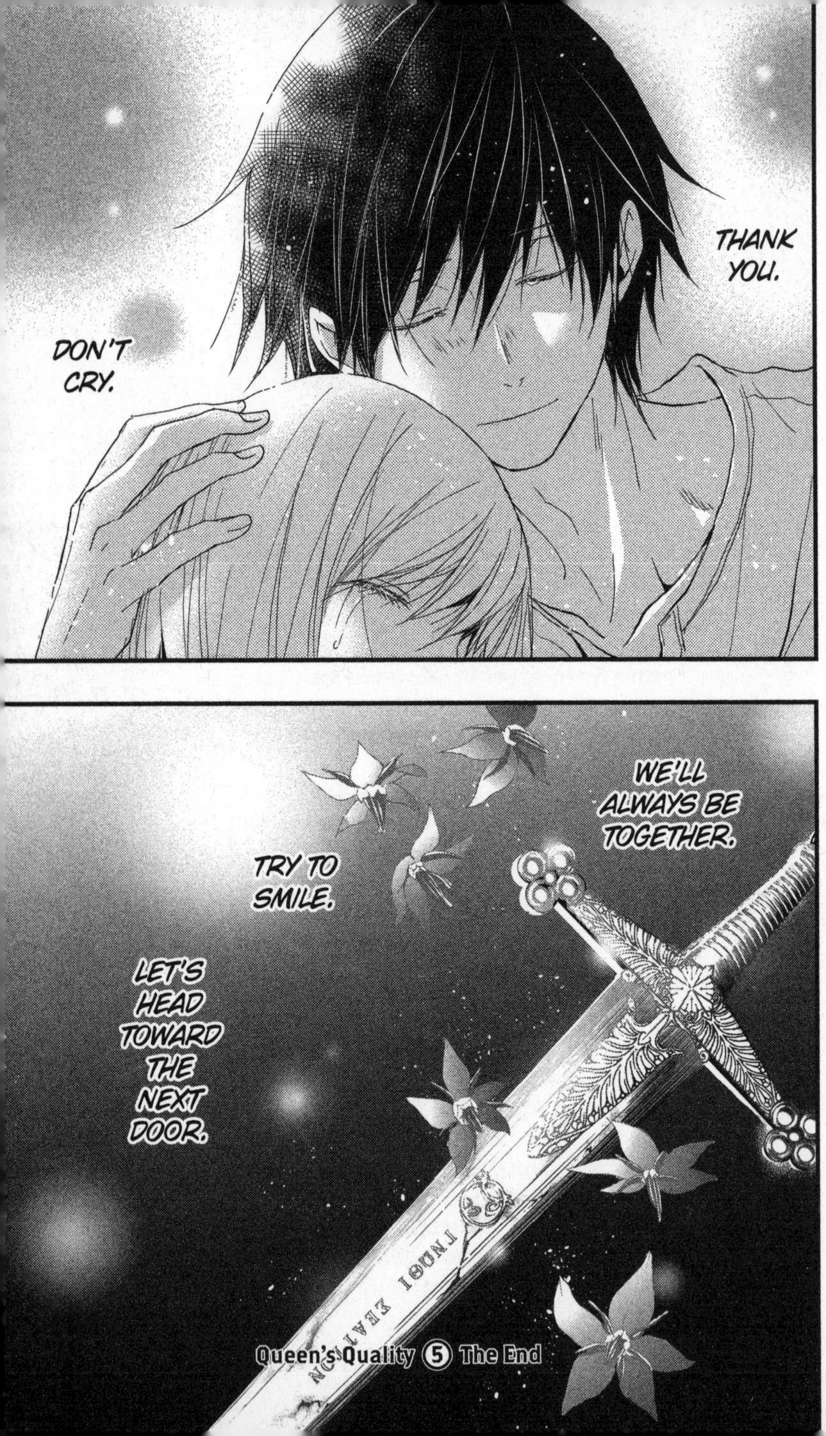
THANK YOU.
DON'T CRY.
WE'LL ALWAYS BE TOGETHER.
TRY TO SMILE.
LET'S HEAD TOWARD THE NEXT DOOR.
Queen's Quality 5 The End

More on coffee… A friend of mine gave me a coffee mill for my birthday, and I'm in seventh heaven. Freshly ground coffee is so delicious, and the caffeine packs such a punch that I can get a lot of work done.

—Kyousuke Motomi

Author Bio

Born on August 1, **Kyousuke Motomi** debuted in *Deluxe Betsucomi* with *Hetakuso Kyupiddo* (No Good Cupid) in 2002. She is the creator of *Dengeki Daisy*, *Beast Master* and *QQ Sweeper*, all available in North America from VIZ Media. Motomi enjoys sleeping, tea ceremonies and reading Haruki Murakami.